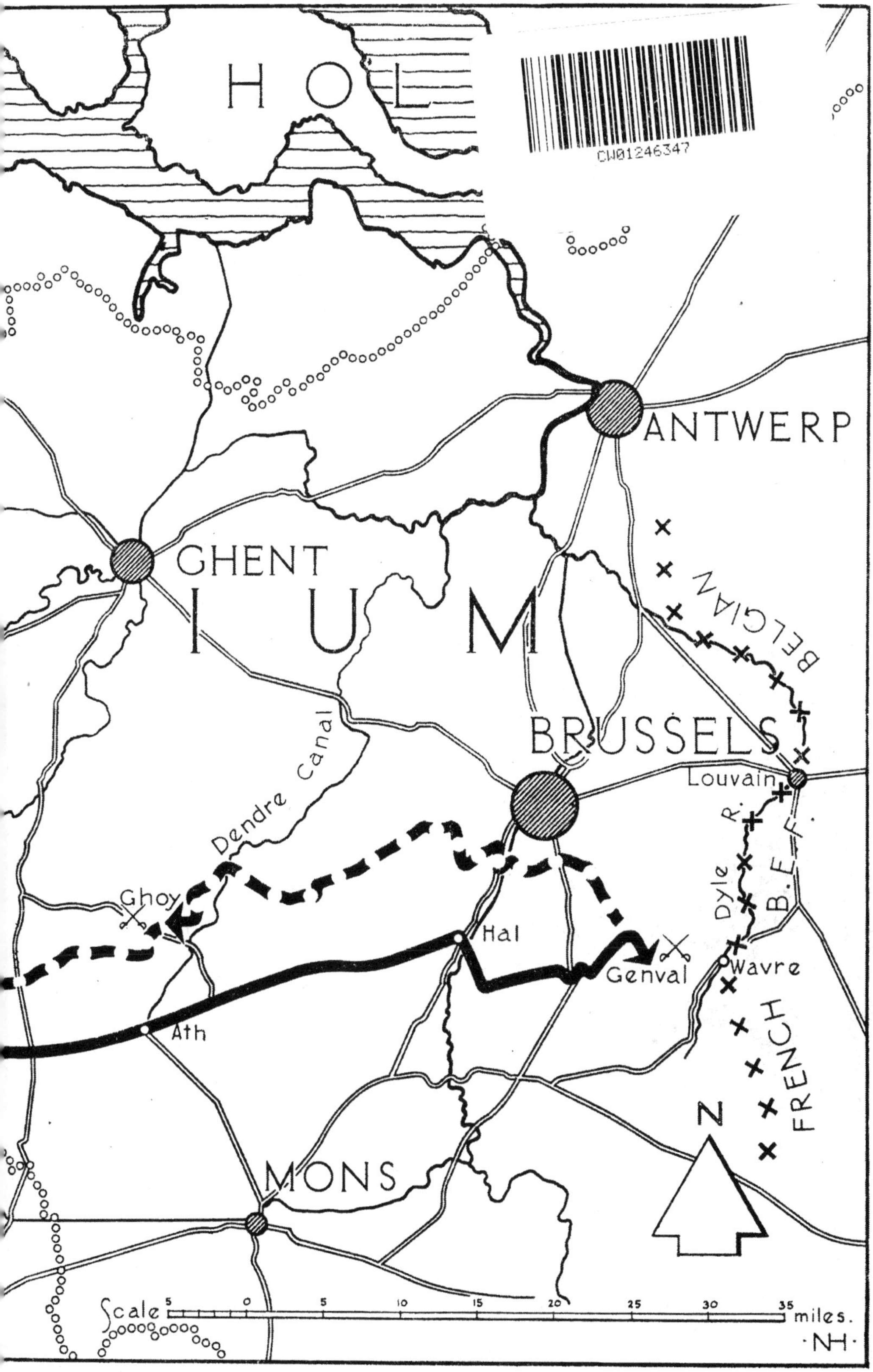
HOL
ANTWERP
GHENT
IUM
BRUSSELS
Louvain
BELGIAN
Dendre Canal
Ghoy
Hal
Genval
Dyle R.
B.E.F.
Wavre
Ath
FRENCH
N
MONS
Scale 5 0 5 10 15 20 25 30 35 miles.
·NH·

STRAIGHT ON FOR TOKYO

The War History of

THE SECOND BATTALION
THE DORSETSHIRE REGIMENT
(54th Foot)

1939   1948

Lieutenant-Colonel O. G. W. WHITE, D.S.O., O.B.E.

Copyright © 2016 Jenny Jeapes

Second Edition
Published by Semper Fidelis Publications, September 2016

ISBN 978-0-9929033-3-6

A CIP Catalogue Record for this book is available from the British Library.

All rights reserved. No part of this book may be reproduced in any form or by any means, electronic or mechanical including photo-copying, recording or by any information storage and retrieval system, without permission from the authors in writing.

First published in December 1948, Gale & Polden Ltd

Typeset in Freight Text Pro / 11pt

Produced in the United Kingdom by Bluemoon Print and Promotions

1755 **LIV** 1948

DEDICATION

This Story is dedicated to those Officers and Men of

His Majesty's Fifty-Fourth Regiment of Foot,

2nd Battalion The Dorsetshire Regiment,

who

for one hundred and ninety-three years,

have engaged the King's Enemies

and

maintained the King's Peace

throughout the world

and

especially to my Comrades in Arms

who,

between 1939 and 1946, followed

the long and arduous road from Flanders to

TOKYO

XIV Army Sign

*"Now this is the road that the White Men tread
When they go to clean a land—
Iron underfoot and levin overhead
And the deep on either hand.
We have trod that road—and a wet and windy road—
Our chosen star for a guide.
Oh, well for the world when the White Men tread
Their highway side by side."*

                                                KIPLING

*"Man cannot tell, but Allah knows
How much the other side was hurt!"*

KIPLING

CONTENTS

		PAGE
	A Family Foreword by Jenny Jeapes (née White)	xiii
	Introduction to this new Edition by Christopher Jary	xv
	Foreword by General Sir Montagu Stopford	xxi
	Author's Preface	xxv
1.	To France	1
2.	Into Battle	14
3.	The Battle of Britain, 1940-41	42
4.	In the Wake of the *Sarah Sands*	47
5.	The Advance to Kohima	73
6.	The Key to Kohima	95
7.	The Break-out from Kohima	132
8.	The Pursuit down the Manipur Road	145
9.	Forward into Burma	163
10.	Milestone 82 Again	178
11.	*The Duke Desires the Infantry will Step Out*	185
12.	How Bare Was Our Buff	217
13.	*Where The Flying Fishes Play*	235
14.	*Come you back, you British soldier, Come you back to Mandalay*	250
15.	Popalong to Popa	273
16.	*The King is Dead, Long Live the King!*	296
17.	Time means nothing in the Orient	304
18.	Arrival among the Nips	315
19.	Operation Primus	330
20.	*Over the Hills and Far Away*	342
	Epilogue	364
	Appendices	
A	Roll of Honour	368
B	Honours and Awards	374
C	*The Dorsets certainly get around*	378
D	Memorials	385
E	Clothing, Equipment, Arms and Accoutrements	388
F	B.B.C. Broadcast, 17th May 1944	395
	Glossary	397
	Index	403

ILLUSTRATIONS

	PAGE
The Bungalow, Kohima, 27th April 1944	*Front cover*
Colonel Steve	40
Exercise, Louvencourt	40
Rumegies, February 1940	40
Farewell Visit of HM The King, April 1942	41
2nd Dorset Officers, April 1942	67
India 1942-44	68
Norsets, Belgaum, November 1942	69
Major-General George Wood	70
Brigadier Jock McNaught	70
Major-General John Grover	89
Major-General Cameron Nicholson	89
Brigadier V F S Hawkins	90
Brigadier M M A R West	90
General Sir Monty Stopford	91
Dorset Graves, Kohima, 1944	92
Sorties from Garrison Hill, Kohima, 1944	93
Bungalow Spur After the Battle, Kohima, 1944	94
Lieutenant-Colonel Knocker White	123
Burma 1944-45	124
Two Rivers – Two Bridges	125
Sure by Tamu and Kalewa and through Ye-u we must go…	126
Crossing the Irrawaddy, 25th February 1945	127-8
Mountbatten visits 2 Div	129
The Race to Mandalay	130
The Advance to Popa	271
The Final Advance	272
Major-General Punch Cowan	313
5th Infantry Brigade, October 1945	313
Generals Cowans and Grover	313
The Return of the Colours, January 1946	314
Captain Hugh Wetherbee receives his MC	314
Kohima Day, Japan, 1946	358
Tokyo, June 1946	359
Plassey Day, 1946	360-1
Shikoku	362
Farewell Parade of the 54th, Dorchester, 6th January 1948	363

MAPS

	PAGE
France and Belgium, 10th – 31st May 1940	*Front endpapers*
The Stand at Festubert	35
The Burma Campaign	79
Zubza to Kigwema	88
Kohima: The DC's Bungalow and Garrison Hill	122
The Manipur Road	162
The Tamu Road	176
Chindwin to Shwebo	191
The Battle of Ye-U and Crossing of the Mu River	214
The Advance to Mandalay, 1945	234
The Irrawaddy Crossing	248
Dirty Pagoda Hill	260
North Central Burma	260
Japan, 1946	*Back endpapers*

A FAMILY FOREWORD

BY

JENNY JEAPES (NÉE WHITE)

I have no pre-war memories of my father, so my first memories are of his return at the end of 1946 and the rattle of his Olympia typewriter from his study as he obeyed the injunction to get it all down on paper. On first reading the book I found it just a catalogue of names and places that meant nothing to me. However, over sixty years later, having learnt some regimental history and lived on the sub-continent, reading it before our departure for Kohima with the Royal British Legion in 2014 I found it a gripping tale.

The book was never far away during our time there; visiting the area brought my father back to me, and I felt I knew him better than I ever had before. Standing beside the Dorset Memorial as my husband adjusted his camera, I looked up at the surrounding hills and realised for the first time how much he must have loved the country.

A major disappointment was that travelling with the RBL we had to follow Foreign Office guidelines and not include Imphal in our itinerary. I was lucky enough however to be included in a group that travelled a few miles down the Imphal road; reading the account of his learning that he was to take command of the battalion I looked up to find we were entering Kigwema, the exact village where this happened.

It gives me the greatest pleasure that this book has been re-published after so many years, thus enabling several generations to learn more of what the Duke of Edinburgh rightly described as the forgotten campaign.

September 2016

INTRODUCTION TO THIS EDITION

BY

CHRISTOPHER JARY

In 2012 I was asked to write the final volume of the Dorset Regiment's history, covering the period 1939-1967. I already knew a little about the 1st Battalion's experiences in the siege of Malta and in the campaign in North West Europe. I knew rather more about the advance of the 4th and 5th Battalions from Hill 112 to Bremen because my father had been beside them most of the way. But of the 2nd Battalion, who fought first with Gort's British Expeditionary Force in France in 1940 and then in Slim's Fourteenth Army in Assam and Burma in 1944-45, I knew practically nothing. Reading of their brave rearguard action near Festubert in May 1940 and of how they defeated the Japanese at Kohima four years later, I became lost in admiration for all they had achieved. Those achievements remain a deep source of pride for the Dorset Regiment and the County, and this was demonstrated in May last year by the large turn-out in Dorchester for the unveiling of the Kohima Stone. But I believe the part they played merits more than regimental and local interest because the 2nd Dorsets' successes were central to the campaign in France and the campaign in Assam and Burma.

It is seven decades since this remarkable book was written, and the publication of this new edition is long overdue. It is remarkable in three ways – for the story it tells, for the characters it portrays and for the quality of its telling – which together produce an outstanding account of an infantry battalion at war. The Battalion in question is the 2nd Battalion of The Dorset Regiment. Written shortly after the war by Geoffrey White, one of the Battalion's commanding officers, it paints a vivid picture of both the campaigns in which the Dorsets excelled.

Let us first consider the quality of the story, which is really two very different stories. The first begins in late May 1940, when the British Expeditionary Force was in retreat towards the Channel coast. On 25th May the 2nd Dorsets, part of the 2nd Division, were ordered to make a stand on the La Bassée Canal below Festubert to allow the greater part of the Division to withdraw. Here, through three long days, their widely dispersed companies defended a broad front against repeated attacks by a much larger force. The Battalion held on until, outflanked by German soldiers who had crossed the Canal to the west, they were given permission to withdraw fighting. Two company commanders, Bob Goff and Sam Symes, then pulled off the difficult task of withdrawing their companies while in close contact with the enemy, and the Battalion withdrew into Festubert. The German attacks continued to press hard but, time after time, their tanks and infantry were repelled. Now, with the enemy line of advance crossing behind him, their Commanding Officer, Lieutenant-Colonel Eric Stephenson, assembled his 245 survivors and 40 men from other units, and personally led them to safety. Compass in hand, his Second-in-Command at his side with a map, Colonel Steve navigated them in the dark through pouring rain across fields, fences, roads and canals – even across the path of an advancing German column – until they reached Estaires in the early morning of 28th May. Their arrival was unexpected. Their commanders had expected the entire Battalion to have been killed or captured. It was here that they first heard of the plan to evacuate the BEF. The 2nd Dorsets' stand at Festubert had bought time for others to escape but, thanks to their Colonel's leadership, they brought more of their soldiers home than any other battalion in the Division. Colonel Steve did not spare himself until 0830 on 31st May, when he led his men ashore at Margate.

The second story starts on 26th April 1944, when the 2nd Dorsets (still with several Festubert survivors among their number) filed up Garrison Hill, Kohima, to relieve the Royal Berkshires. Here, in the incongruous surroundings of a British diplomat's bungalow, amid terraced gardens and tennis court, they withstood savage, relentless attacks by the Japanese who were desperate to capture the position. On their first night at Kohima a veteran of Festubert, Major John Bowles, got his Company beyond the Japanese positions and established them behind the bungalow, overlooking the Dimapur road, where they remained for five days until relieved by B Company. For seventeen days, amid the cacophony of mortaring, shelling and machine gun fire and the stench of rotting bodies, in a series of vicious little battles and skirmishes the 2nd Dorsets held their own against a fierce and unforgiving enemy. Finally, on 13th May, supported by Sergeant Gerry Waterhouse's tank which had been manhandled up the precipitous slope, Clive Chettle's D Company led the attack on the Japanese positions around the tennis court and broke the back of the Japanese defences. *Suddenly*, Private Tom Cattle later remembered, *some of the Japs started running. And we knew we had done it. We mowed them down as they ran. There were bodies that had been there weeks, covered in flies and maggots; the stench was terrific.* The 2nd Dorsets' hard-won, spectacular victory in this battle was the turning point in the battle of Kohima, which was itself the turning point in the entire campaign in Burma.

Alone, either the story of Festubert or the story of Kohima would justify a book. This book includes both. And it covers still more because the 2nd Dorsets, now commanded by White himself, helped lead the advance south-east, past Imphal across the Chindwin, the Mu and the Irrawaddy, and down beyond Mandalay. Depleted in numbers and exhausted in energy, they were finally withdrawn from battle in April 1945 after capturing Mount Popa. The book then tells the story of how, chosen by Bill Slim to be one of three British battalions to join the largely American force occupying Japan, they finally encountered their once implacable, now defeated enemy in his homeland.

That, very briefly, is an outline of the unique story that this book tells. But a story is of little interest without characters. What of those who together formed the 2nd Battalion? Two quite different but equally distinguished commanding officers stand out: Stephenson and White himself. Colonel Steve was not far short of fifty when, after their heroic defence of Festubert, he led the remnants of his Battalion to safety. As CO of the first Dorset battalion to fight in the Second World War he set a dazzling standard of courage, endurance and care for his men that others would struggle to match. Knocker White was eighteen years younger and a distinguished sportsman, whose energy and devotion to the Regiment became legendary. Second-in-Command of the Battalion at Kohima, he took command on 8th June 1944 and made the 2nd Battalion very much his own: his proprietorial affection for his officers and men shines through his book. A third distinguished CO who was denied the chance to command them in battle was George Wood, whose humanity and high standards of professionalism permeated the entire Battalion. George Wood's reputation as a commander would be won later, when he commanded not a battalion of Dorsets but an entire division.

Some 2nd Battalion characters served with them only in France. By 1940 Major Bob Goff, who had won an MC as a platoon commander in 1917, and Major Dayrell Stayner were both, like their distinguished Colonel, a bit long in the tooth for front line service. Goff later commanded an OCTU and then took command of the 9th Dorsets in

England. Captured at Dunkirk, Stayner became Senior British Officer at Colditz Castle before returning to Dorchester to establish the Keep Military Museum. Major Sam Symes later commanded the 2nd Worcesters in Burma and won the DSO. Sergeant Jimmy James, who won the Military Medal near Festubert, left the Battalion to join the Commandos but returned and later became RSM of the 1st Battalion. Oner Bray, Chips Heron and John Peebles, who all earned Military Crosses in the retreat in France, also volunteered for the Commandos. Peebles was killed in a training accident but the others returned to the Dorsets to play leading roles in the Dorset Territorials.

Many 2nd Battalion men stayed in France as prisoners of war. Among them was Private Thomas Tabb MM, who swam the canal with Sergeant Jimmy James and Private James Sinnott. Sadly, Sinnott was killed next day at Festubert while Thomas Tabb spent the rest of the war in prison camp. Another was Private Leonard Tyrrell, who finally returned from prison camp in 1945 only to be recalled to fight in Korea. Fighting with the 1st Glosters on the Imjin River in April 1951, he was captured and spent another two and a half years as a prisoner of the Chinese. Three more – Sergeant Austin Hopkins and Privates Graham and Knight – were later decorated for escaping from capture.

Some served in both France and Burma. Sergeant Walter Cooper – known to all as Gary – won a DCM at Festubert, leading his Bren gun carriers in a counter-attack on the Germans, but he survived to serve throughout the campaign in Assam and Burma and eventually to become RSM. Another veteran was the Padre, Captain Gus Claxton. Perhaps uniquely for a chaplain, he served with the same Battalion in France, England, India and Burma throughout the war. In Burma he was often seen in the company of the 2nd Dorsets' gallant Medical Officer, Captain Joe Chamberlin. Chamberlin encountered the 2nd Dorsets in France before Dunkirk, liked them, and swapped places with a brother MO to join them in England. In Burma he and Gus became part of the Battalion furniture, earning a reputation for gallantry and self-sacrifice that was second to no one. Among C Company's stretcher-bearers was another hero, Private Henry Jesty from Yetminster. Oblivious to enemy fire, he was always to be found tending the wounded in the most dangerous places. Seemingly indestructible, he survived to receive an MM and a mention in Despatches, and to become the Battalion's Medical Sergeant.

Sadly, some characters did not survive, among them Corporal Harry Softley, who had boxed for the 1st Battalion before the war and who was killed trying to rescue some of his comrades under fire.

Lieutenant Robin Cuthbertson, commanding 13 Platoon, was killed by machine gun fire while checking that no wounded men had been left behind in his Platoon's position. Commanding A Company was John Bowles, who had been mentioned in Despatches as a Warrant Officer at Festubert. In Burma he would be mentioned again before being killed at Thayetpinzuon. The Dorsets' Gunner Forward Observation Officer, Jimmy Thom, then took command of Bowles's company of Dorsets while continuing to direct the fire of his own Battery. Leading another part of that same attack were Major Tommy Tucker, a Hampshire officer but also a proud 2nd Dorset, and Lieutenant Jock Given. Six months earlier as a Sergeant, Given had won the Military Medal and a commission in the field for his spectacular part in defeating the Japanese on the tennis court. His figure is prominent in Jock Murrills's oil painting which depicts Sergeant Waterhouse's tank and some of the men of Clive Chettle's D Company.

The Battalion's Guerrilla Platoon, used for fighting patrols, was commanded successively by four energetic young officers, John O'Driscoll, Dick Purser, Andrew Mackenzie and Snagger Highett, all of whom distinguished themselves for their daring and leadership. Such was the parsimony with which gallantry awards were made in Burma, only one of these – Highett – was decorated late in the campaign. Another legendary fighting soldier and patrol leader was Sergeant Yorky Seale DCM, a miner's son from Heckmondwike, of whom Joe Chamberlin wrote: *those like the indestructible Sergeant Seale who picked bits of mortar bombs out of themselves and soldiered on*. On 15th March 1945 near Kadozeik Seale took a burst of shrapnel in his foot and finally had to be evacuated. By that time, as well as his DCM, he had earned a mention in Despatches and a Commander in Chief's Certificate for Gallantry.

The 2nd Dorsets were a creative Battalion. In Headquarters was Tiger Havers, the Battalion's devoted Intelligence Officer, who became an architect and later wrote his own book – *March On!* – about the campaign in Burma. Second-in-Command of A Company was Jock Murrills, whose paintings and pen and ink sketches illustrate this book. In D Company Tom Cattle from Corfe Castle, who became a very youthful Sergeant and in civilian life a police officer, later wrote his own touching memoirs. But the Battalion's creative talent started at the top. Knocker White was himself a gifted writer, and this is the third factor that makes this book stand out. In it White describes with a writer's eye – tinged with the eye of love with which any good Colonel sees his battalion – the humour, the horror, the exhaustion, the bravery, the stoicism, the fear, the triumph and the tragedy that were the experience of the Second World War infantryman.

A minor complication with republishing a book written nearly seventy years ago is the change in perspective. A modern writer, for example, would be more sensitive to the feelings of any Japanese readers. But the modern writer has not spent more than a year of his life fighting Japanese soldiers in the jungles and plains of Burma; he has not seen his enemy straining every nerve to break into the hospital at Kohima to bayonet the wounded; and he has not seen many of his friends killed around him by an aggressive and relentless enemy who took no prisoners. Knocker White's 1948 view of his recent enemy does not sit happily with 21st Century attitudes, but neither do the events he is describing. It is not for a modern editor to act as some sort of moral censor. Colonel White described how he felt and most reading his book today can understand his feelings.

Thanks are due to Nick Speakman, who worked alongside me through every phase of the production of this new edition, to Charles and Jackie Cooper, who produced the one feature the original lacked – a good index – and to Ben Clark of BlueMoon, whose professionalism and attention to detail have once again created a handsome book. Finally, our thanks to the Jeapes family for encouraging us to reprint this book. As the grand-daughter of one distinguished Dorset, the daughter of another and the wife of a third, it is fitting that Jenny should have provided a family foreword to this edition. All of us at the Keep Military Museum are very grateful to Jenny and her brother Owen White for allowing us to reprint their father's book. It will make you laugh, cry and marvel at the achievements of the young men of the 2nd Dorsets, who met their enemy – German and Japanese – head-on in battle, winning high honours for their Regiment and for themselves a place in history.

September 2016

FOREWORD

BY

GENERAL SIR MONTAGU STOPFORD
G.C.B., K.B.E., D.S.O., M.C., A.D.C.

I FIRST BECAME ACQUAINTED WITH the 2nd Battalion The Dorsetshire Regiment, in the 2nd Division, when I arrived in India at the end of 1943 to take command of the XXXIII Indian Corps, which was then forming. At that time I had the good fortune to fall into the hands of George ("Sam" to all of us at Corps Headquarters) Wood, who was already installed as B.G.S. and who appears at frequent intervals in this story as an ex-Commanding Officer of the Battalion. Sam guided me through the many momentous events which lay ahead during the ensuing months and, amongst other things, he made it abundantly clear that the Fifty-Fourth would take on any task which came its way. That he was right is borne out in Lieutenant-Colonel White's story, which gives a vivid description of the Battalion's Odyssey from England, through the operations which culminated in the evacuation from Dunkirk, out to India, through the Burma campaign of 1944-45, on to Tokyo and so home via Malaya.

One aspect of military tradition which the story brings out is the tremendous esprit de corps which permeated the Battalion: that spirit which throughout the history of the British Army has enabled its Infantry to overcome almost insuperable difficulties when outnumbered, short of rations, and facing hitherto unknown geographical and climatic conditions.

The Fifty-Fourth had its full share of experience of all these adversities as is described most graphically and accurately in this book.

In Burma, British, Indian and African troops were fighting for the first time an enemy whose physical courage in battle has probably never been surpassed. It is literally true that until the end of the campaign, when they were in the last stages of debility owing to disease and starvation, the Japanese would fight until every man was killed. Those who found themselves in situations in which capture was inevitable would commit suicide with their own grenades; they would destroy their wounded and sick rather than that they should fall into our hands alive, and cases were even known when they would convert themselves into anti-tank mines by sitting in holes in the ground with a shell or aeroplane bomb between their knees and detonate the fuse with a tap from a stone when our tanks were on top of them. As may be imagined, and is brought out in the description of the Battle of Kohima, these characteristics resulted in the most bitter fighting.

In addition to the Japanese, the enemies of disease and climate had to be overcome: a most difficult task where the British soldier was concerned, as it was only by the enforcement of the very strictest hygiene discipline that he could be induced to take the precautions and preventive medicines which science had provided.

When once he had acquired the habit, he realized its value and the rate of sickness from preventable disease dropped astonishingly, with a consequent increase in fighting efficiency.

There are many outside the Services who misunderstand the necessity for, and true meaning of, discipline, but without it the Japanese would not have been beaten and the Fourteenth Army would have rotted from disease.

Good discipline is born of high morale and no unit in my experience in Burma exemplified this better than the 2nd Battalion The Dorsetshire Regiment. Their tails were always up, no matter what they were called upon to undertake or what hardships they had to endure.

Lieutenant-Colonel White has written of many things which should be of interest to a wide field of readers, both in and outside the Army, as, not only has he described the life of the Battalion over a period of nearly eight and a half years, but he has explained how the technique of defeating the Japanese, the climate and disease in Burma was built up.

He also pays well-deserved tributes to the "other Arms and Services", to the R.A.F. and the U.S.A.A.F., all of whom at one time or another played their part in helping the Battalion to achieve its numerous successes.

I would like to take this opportunity of sending my good wishes to many old friends of all ranks in the Battalion, a number of whom at one time or another served on my staff in the Burma campaign and after. Wherever they may be I know that they will keep alive the great spirit of the 2nd Battalion The Dorsetshire Regiment which played such a fine part in South-East Asia. Although the story ends with the disbandment of the Battalion, a day may come when it will enter the lists again, and if this happens I doubt not that it will be "Primus in Somewhere".

[signature: Li. Ph. Stopford]

HEADQUARTERS, NORTHERN COMMAND
YORK
JANUARY 1948

XXXIII Indian Corps Sign

AUTHOR'S PREFACE

I have made for you a song
And it may be right or wrong,
But only you can tell me if it's true.

[RUDYARD KIPLING:
Prelude to Barrack Room Ballads]

I SUPPOSE THAT the intention to write the story of our adventures has been in my mind ever since those soaking-wet days on the way to Tamu in 1944 when I tried to get the censor to pass an "up to the fall of the last wicket" account of our campaign in Burma for the information of those at home. So full, however, and varied has been our existence since those days that it was not for three years that I found the opportunity to sit down to this task.

It was Oscar Wilde, I understand, who once said: "Anyone can make history. Only a great man can write it", so I must ask the reader to bear with me, especially when he realizes that this story has been written during the Staff College course. One's "masters", controlled by a strict curriculum, were apt to make grave demands on what elsewhere would be considered "spare time", and as a student one lacked the assistance of one's never-failing and always cheerful battalion orderly-room staff.

I have recorded the adventures of "a Battalion of a famous West Country regiment" primarily for my comrades-in-arms, those officers and men of the 2nd Battalion The Dorsetshire Regiment who, between September, 1939, and June, 1946, made the great march to Tokyo by way of France, Flanders, Assam and Burma. We were, I like to think, essentially a happy battalion, fortunate enough to serve throughout the war in a brigade renowned for its mutual good spirit and in a division of which we were immensely proud.

I hope that these chronicles will not only interest past and present members of the Regiment but also that host of friends we made in the 2nd Division and the XXXIII Corps and subsequently in Brindiv and B.C.O.F., as well as those many hundreds of others, civilian and soldier alike, whom we encountered in a variety of circumstances during those exciting years. I would like to think that those countless officers who supported us, fought with us and provided for us will find many a happy memory and stirring recollection in this tale, which in its way provides some account of how we all, in the 2nd Division, lived and fought, and what, finally, we of the 5th Infantry Brigade found in far-off Japan.

I make no apology for the personal touch which flavours these records. The Fifty-Fourth has been my virtual home, even from before my first Christmas Day, when the men of my father's company, decorating their dining-room, fashioned laboriously with dabs of cottonwool stuck on to a G.S. blanket a seasonal greeting to "Captain and Mrs. O. W. White and Master Geoffrey White". During the war I was not only fortunate enough to serve five whole years with the Battalion but privileged to command for nigh on three. I am therefore in the happy position of having been an actor in a leading role and now a would-be chronicler of some of the most adventurous days the Battalion has ever seen.

I have two chief collaborators to whom I am most deeply indebted. Captain Norman ("Tiger") Havers, M.B.E., who was Intelligence Officer throughout the conflict, has undertaken once again his old task of producing the necessary map cover. To Major H. C. ("Jock") Murrills, a former Mortar Officer, we owe the magnificent coloured Frontispiece and the design for the jacket. Both these were painted from his notes made actually on the spot. The notes for the Frontispiece were made even whilst Jock, as second-in-command of "A" Company, was hanging on like grim death to the isolated position below the Bungalow, and he found time on the rush through to the Mu to make the notes of the ruined pagoda during our short halt on Christmas Day, 1944.

Without the co-operation of Colonel E. L. Stephenson, D.S.O., M.C., Colonel R. E. C. Goff, O.B.E., M.C., Lieutenant-Colonel B. G. Symes, D.S.O., O.B.E., and Major H. V. Thomas the account of the 1940 campaign in France and Flanders would have been but a very meagre narrative. Major-General G. N. Wood, C.B., C.B.E., D.S.O., M.C., Brigadier M. M. A. R. West, D.S.O., and Brigadier R. S. McNaught, D.S.O., gave up much of their valuable time to read my original manuscripts, and I am most grateful to them for their advice and encouragement. I would like to thank all these officers.

My thanks are also due to Lieutenant-Colonel H. N. Cole, O.B.E., T.D., and the staff of Gale & Polden Ltd. for their unfailing assistance in producing the book under these most difficult present-day conditions, and not forgetting O.R.Q.M.S. Vaughan and his team of clerks in the

Battalion Office who not only deciphered my handwriting but helped to maintain my original records under certainly none-too-easy office conditions in the field. Finally, I would like to thank Miss P. Craig McGlinchy, well known to generations of Staff College students, who undertook to type the manuscript.

Acknowledgment is made to the Imperial War Museum for permission to reproduce the bulk of the photographs used in this book. In selecting them I received great assistance and co-operation from the Manager of the Photographic Department and his staff, for which I am most grateful.

I cannot close this Preface without expressing my appreciation to General Sir Montagu Stopford, G.C.B., K.B.E., D.S.O., M.C., A.D.C. Gen., for his continued support and interest in the production of this book. Seldom has a distinguished commander been better known or held in more affection by the infantryman than was General Sir "Monty" as Commander of the XXXIII Corps. Then men came to look forward to the arrival, hot on their heels, after even the longest advance, of the General's familiar bush-hatted figure approaching at rifleman's pace, with his presentation pointer staff tucked underneath his arm. They knew that when he talked to them he was genuinely interested in their activities, and many a grouse or worry was soon put to rights after one of these roadside conversations. That General Stopford has agreed to write the Foreword to this story is not only a signal honour but sets the seal to the final and certainly one of the most thrilling decades in the history of the Fifty-Fourth Regiment of Foot.   O. G. W. W.

FARNBOROUGH, HANTS
JANUARY, 1948

CHAPTER ONE

TO FRANCE

"Dépêchez mon Colonel, le dirigeable s'attend"

[Conversational phrase from an English-French vocabulary issued 1939.]

To the eager student of the French language in the B.E.F. in 1939 the above phrase must have made a delightful variation to the usual "pen of my aunt" theme, but how much more appropriate is it when read as a sign of the times? In the year of the outbreak of the Second World War the British public, in accordance with their immemorial peacetime custom, had allowed their land forces, both in man power and equipment, to fall seriously below the safety margin. Now, at the first sound of the bugle, they calmly expected their Army to set out for war without adequate preparation and with old-fashioned equipment. "Get a move on, Colonel, your balloon is waiting!"

Little did the 2nd Battalion The Dorsetshire Regiment, whose achievements and experiences will be unfolded in this book, think, as they mobilized for this latest conflict, just how long a trek lay before them. A journey which would take them on to battlegrounds familiar to their forebears, in the "Cockpit of Europe", into hitherto untrodden domains beyond the mighty Brahmaputra River, to end on the very threshold of the Mikado's Palace in Tokyo.

The hero of these chronicles, His Majesty's one-time Fifty-Fourth Regiment of the Line, was quartered at Aldershot in 1939 after having spent a busy twenty years between the wars. The Battalion had played a prominent part in quelling an ugly revolt in South India in the early twenties, and, moving via Egypt and Aldershot, had been one of the last of the British battalions to quit the Rhine when, in 1929, it suddenly became fashionable to leave the Germans to their own devices. The next decade was taken up with the periodic peregrinations customary to those who serve their country in the land forces, and during this time they had played their part in maintaining order in Palestine, assisting to settle a problem which remains unsolved to this day. They now found themselves, on the eve of mobilization, in the 5th Infantry Brigade, in the 2nd Infantry Division, with both of which formations they were to serve continually for the next seven and a half years.

In company with the remainder of the Infantry of the Line, they were to need every scrap of experience gained from this good schooling between the wars, because on their first arrival at Aldershot in the spring of 1938, they found that they had to train under the greatest difficulties of shortage of man power and out-of-date equipment. During the higher training of 1938 they had had to function without "D" Company, that company which but a couple of years earlier had been the pride of the Battalion, and before their machine guns had been removed had made a great name for themselves among the machine gunners of the Army at home. It was not until the Munich crisis of 1938 that the Dorsets even received their Bren guns, anti-tank rifles and proportion of modern vehicles.

Throughout the summer of 1939 the normal life of England's "No. 1" garrison continued—training, competitions of all kinds, and the Aldershot Tattoo. Apart from periodic P.A.D. exercises and trial blackouts, one thing more than anything else brought home the imminence of war. For the first time reservists were called up for training in the new weapons, which were by now slowly becoming more plentiful, and during August a partial mobilization was held. So when, on that Sunday morning of the 3rd of September, 1939, the Prime Minister finally removed all doubts as to the urgency of the situation, things were well in hand and preparations for the move of the British Expeditionary Force to France proceeded with increased energy.

In June, 1939, the 1st Battalion of the Regiment had been moved from India to Malta and a number of officers and other ranks were at home on leave and courses. The Thirty-Ninth's (1st Battalion) loss was the Fifty-Fourth's gain, and by the simple procedure of all 1st Battalion officers then in the United Kingdom being directed to the 2nd Battalion, Lieutenant-Colonel E. L. Stephenson, M.C., soon gathered to himself a very powerful team of officers to take to the wars. It might be well at this juncture for the reader to take a look with me into the officers' mess at Oudenarde Barracks, and meet over a Sunday morning glass of gin those leaders of the Battalion who were assembling from all over the country.

There is Colonel "Steve" himself, the only pre-1914 officer still serving in the Battalion. A campaigner with a first-class record in Mesopotamia in the Kaiser's War, he had spent a decade between the wars in that nursery for officers, the Sudan Defence Force. He took over command in the spring of 1939 and is now to lead the Fifty-Fourth in this their latest campaign. That tall officer over by the fireplace is Major Dayrell Stayner, the Second-in-Command, who had received his first commission in October, 1914, and has twenty-five years' regimental and staff experience behind him. He is talking to the two senior company commanders, Tom Molloy, recently returned from a long tour on the West Coast of Africa, and Bob Goff, the late Adjutant of the 1st Battalion. Both these are old campaigners of the First World War. Sam Symes, who is so kindly pressing the bell to give us a drink, is to command "B" Company after only recently rejoining the Battalion from a long tour abroad. He was talking, as we came up, to Patterson, an old Regular officer who had been for some years on the reserve. The Adjutant is Howard Cowie, who for two years running has won his place in the Army Revolver XXX at Bisley. Jan Bradford, another officer corralled at home from the 1st Battalion, is to command the Brigade Anti-Tank Company; he is talking to "The Link", Captain Linklater, the only company commander we have not yet met, who is commanding "A" Company.

A number of old friends have turned up—officers who during the long years of peace decided to engage themselves in the service of their country at just such a time as this, and who year after year had spent a few weeks or days polishing up their technique by doing short attachments with the home battalion. "Gragger" Green, a schoolmaster from Sherborne, Hickling, another schoolmaster, and Donald Baynes, all of whom had appeared at Portland, Dover and Aldershot from time to time. There were younger officers, such as Brewster and Bell-Syer, from the Supplementary Reserve, and Cotton from the Regular Army Reserve of Officers. Amidst all this gathering of khaki I suddenly descried an old and familiar figure with the inevitable cigarette drooping from his lips; it was Griffin, an old Supplementary Reserve officer who a year later was to con- trive such a successful escape from the hands of the Boche.

A stranger to this gathering of the clan was Sam Loxton, the doctor posted to the Fifty-Fourth. A gynaecologist by trade, he had already taken up the needles of the Regimental Medical Officer and had started inoculating the Battalion against the many and varied ills that they were likely to encounter. But these early passes with a blunt needle were nothing to the miscellany of germs with which they were all to be impregnated in the five and a half years before the familiar figure of the one-time Medical Officer was once more encountered in the jungles of Burma.

Outside, in the men's lines, the reservists were not too happy. A number of them had been doing their course with the Battalion when war was declared. These men were allowed a bare forty-eight- hour pass to return to their homes, square up their domestic problems, fix up their families and do the hundred and one chores which fall to the lot of the citizen whose services for some considerable time would be required by the Army. The authorities must have realized at this stage that it was impossible to ship the B.E.F. overseas in under three weeks and should have approved of a longer leave for reservists and indeed any officer or soldier who required to straighten out his domestic affairs. This was just one of those points of staff duties well beyond the power of the battalion commander to control, but for which he, as the commander on the spot, was expected to answer.

It was another three weeks before the Brigade were able to sail - they had long been prepared, and in point of fact were living under most uncomfortable conditions and "raring to go". Owing to Oudenarde Barracks being used as a mobilization centre for a large number of G.H.Q. "back-room boys", and in the interests of dispersion against bombing, the infantry had to move out, and during the whole of this time two of the Dorset companies were billeted in rotation at Blackwater.

Before the Battalion sailed they received two shocks. The first was when "Bolly" was medically down-graded and his job as Quartermaster had to be rapidly refilled. Major J. R. H. Bolingbroke, D.C.M., had been Quartermaster of the 2nd Battalion for eighteen years, before which he had been the Regimental Sergeant-Major. He was a tradition in the Regiment, and countless subalterns had passed through his wise old hands. With the Commanding Officer, he was one of the two surviving "Norsets" who had fought through the operations at Kut al Amara in 1915, when the Norfolks and the Dorsets combined to fight the Turk as the "Norsets". Thirty-five years of regimental soldiering had not impaired his sense of humour or energy. Countless were the stories of the great days at Bangalore when he was Regimental Sergeant-Major and the present Colonel was Adjutant to the fiery Colonel Tommy Radcliffe. In his official capacity he was never an "easy" Quartermaster, and his famous "No authority, young man, no authority; can't let you have it", had in the past turned away from his stores many a supplicant for that "little bit extra".

This great gap in the Battalion order of battle was filled by R.S.M. Edwards. One of the more unfortunate results of the British Army quartermaster system (from the point of view of the rising generation) is that quartermasters once in the saddle take an unconscionable time a-dying, and "Chippy" Edwards had been a warrant officer since 1916 and Regimental Sergeant-Major for ten years before his chance of promotion came round. The reader will hear more of Edwards and his great work as Quartermaster throughout these records. It is enough to say that at this time, with the regrouping consequent on "Bolly's" departure, there was formed that great "Q" team which was to give the Battalion such first-class service throughout their wanderings and campaigns. R.Q.M.S. Dutot, the one-time Provost Sergeant of the 1st Battalion, having stepped into Edwards's shoes as Regimental Sergeant-Major, his place was filled by C.S.M. Arthur Bell. Right from the word "Go", when the new "Q" team assumed the mantle of the old, they made it a point of honour that if anyone was to go short of equipment that could possibly be provided or lack a hot meal in the evening, it was not to be the Fifty-Fourth—a tradition which, in his turn, Edwards was to hand on to his successor in the maelstrom of Kohima.

The second blow to the Battalion was the sudden illness of the Commanding Officer. Luckily Steve's incapacity was comparatively short-lived, and, although Tom Molloy in point of fact took the Battalion overseas (Dayrell Stayner having departed with the advance party), Steve rejoined them a short time later and was able to lead them through the first winter of the war, and, more important still, fight the Battalion through the campaign of 1940.

During mobilization all units of the 2nd Infantry Division were ordered to put up their new divisional sign on their vehicles. This was not to be the three stars worn by their predecessors in the Kaiser's War but a new badge designed by the lately arrived Divisional Commander, General Lloyd. The General's last command had been a Guards brigade, whose sign was a key; on coming to the 2nd Division he decided to double this emblem and hence was developed the badge that the 5th Infantry Brigade were eventually to carry to Tokyo.[1]

On Saturday, the 23rd of September, the Battalion marched down

---

[1] The crossed keys badge of the 2nd Infantry Division was, throughout the war, the subject of much conjecture. In view of the century or so of continuous service of this Regular division, since the days of "Daddy" Hill in the wars against Napoleon, a great story of the antiquity of the badge had sprung up. Much in favour as I am to give every possible credence to a tradition connecting the present badge through the arms of the Archbishop of York to the old Saxon "fyrds" of the pre-Norman days, I must say that I reproduce the above story of the origins of the sign on the authority of General Sir Charles Lloyd himself.

Queen's Avenue en route to the station.[2] Compared with the variety of kit and equipment they were to gather in the course of the war, they were in skeleton order with their one battledress, one pair of boots and one blanket and greatcoat. They must, however, have been carrying everything, as they appeared to the spectator seeing them oif to be grossly overburdened. Showing in Aldershot at that time was the film of A. E. W. Mason's "Four Feathers" in glorious technicolour. Nothing could have been farther removed from the traditional departure of troops for overseas, so admirably depicted in this film, than the furtive slinking away to war of one of the most famous of His Majesty's infantry divisions as this element of the 5th Infantry Brigade cast off and slid into the Channel from Southampton. Not a cheer or a wave from the vast concourse of two officers (one naval and one military), a corporal of the Military Police and a couple of dockyard hands who witnessed the departure of the *Ulster Monarch* (or was it *Queen*?) with on board the Headquarters, 5th Infantry Brigade, 10th Field Regiment, Royal Artillery, and the Fifty-Fourth. It was fully realized that security at such a time must be the overriding factor, but surely cannot something

---

2 The distribution of officers within the Battalion on "marching out" of Aldershot was as follows:

Commanding Officer	Major D. J. P. P. Stayner (vice Lieutenant-Colonel E. L. Stephenson, M.C., sick).
Second-in-Command	Major T. P. L. Molloy.
Adjutant	Captain H. E. Cowie.
Intelligence Officer	Acting Captain R. H. Wheatley.
O.C. H.Q. Company	Captain D. A. Affleck-Graves.
Signal Officer	Lieutenant H. V. Thomas.
Carrier Platoon	Lieutenant H. A. A. Bray.
Quartermaster	R.S.M. F. J. Edwards.
Mechanical Transport Officer	Lieutenant A. V. N. Bridge.
Medical Officer	Captain S. D. Loxton, R.A.M.C.
O.C. "A" Company	Captain R. H. Linklater.
Second-in-Command, "A" Company	Acting Captain P. W. H. Brind. Lieutenant D. M. Baynes.
O.C. "B" Company	Major B. G. Symes.
Second-in-Command, "B" Company	Acting Captain H. J. Hickling. Lieutenant R. W. D. Griffin.
O.C. "C" Company	Acting Captain N. Patterson.
Second-in-Command, "C" Company	Lieutenant I. F. R. Ramsay. Second-Lieutenant A. G. Watts.
O.C. "D" Company	Major R. E. C. Goff, M.C.
Second-in-Command, "D" Company	Acting Captain W. L. Smith. Lieutenant C. V. H. Brewster.
First Reinforcements	Captain J. T. Cotton. Captain G. G. Green. Second-Lieutenant C. H. S. Saunders. Second-Lieutenant R. L. Bell-Syer.

better than this be achieved in these days of total warfare in the way of a send-off for the armies of Britain dispatched to fight their country's cause?

After a slow journey across France, pausing on the way to allow the mechanical transport, which had gone by another route, to catch up, the Battalion found themselves early in October in the little village of Rumegies on the Franco-Belgian frontier. Here they were ordered to take up a defensive position behind the international boundary, which at this point was merely an eight-footwide anti-tank ditch, about as many feet deep, with two feet of water in the bottom.

Rumegies itself was a long, straggling village, and the Battalion occupied the northern end with three rifle companies out. "C" Company (Patterson) were the right forward company, with "A" (Linklater) on the left, both covering the anti-tank ditch. "B" Company (Symes) supported these two from the hamlet of Bezanois, which lay on a slight rise in the ground, whilst "D" Company (Goff) wired itself in on another slight ridge about four hundred yards to the west of the village, the troops, however, living in billets in the village.

The 2nd Royal Warwickshire Regiment occupied the southern half of the village, whilst the 1st Queen's Own Cameron Highlanders, the third infantry battalion in the Brigade, were to the north of Mouchin, and the Brigade Headquarters was at Landas.

"B" Echelon, with the transport, were quartered at Marchiennes, a village on the Scarpe River about twelve kilometres to the southwest, where they were joined by the first reinforcements and the Carrier Platoon.

Once the Battalion had settled down work began in earnest. Work at this stage implied digging and erecting a strong defensive position to thicken up the French pre-war defences on this line. As they found them, these defences consisted of a series of pretty solid concrete blockhouses at about a kilometre interval, sited to cover the anti-tank ditch. There was little enough in these parts to encourage faith in the Maginot Line slogan of *"On n'y passe"*[3]; much rather did the French appear to rely on their other and even more fatal cry of those days, *"Nous gagnerons parceque nous sommes les plus forts."*[4] These concrete posts were wired in and manned by the equivalent of a British rifle section and their armament consisted of a 25-mm. anti-tank gun and a light automatic: a periscope completed the equipment. There were no other defences on this boundary over which the Germans had once

---

3 They shall not pass here.
4 We will win because we are the strongest.

poured, and as far as could be seen, there was no reason why the Hun should not make a second attempt. The nearest fort was at Maulde, in the French zone about six kilometres to the south-east, and this contained only one artillery piece of any calibre.

Each of the forward rifle companies had one of these blockhouse section posts in its area and as soon as the engineer stores arrived the Battalion set to to erect a fine triple double-apron fence along the whole Battalion front linking up with the Royal Warwicks on the right and the Camerons to the left. To cover this wire we began to build an elaborate system of small concrete posts of our own.

Digging section posts in the forward company areas was fraught with constant difficulties. Water was reached within a very few feet of the top and the posts were flooded, and very soon these companies had perforce to resort to the construction of breastworks.

If digging had been tough enough, the construction of these breastworks was a herculean task. The local soil, soaked as it was, seemed to weigh far heavier per shovelful than any soil anywhere else, and everything had to be man-handled to the positions. "C" Company managed to obtain a light railway to assist them in running cement and other stores to the forward positions. The track arrived in sections and very soon "C" Company were to be heard chanting the following words to a well-known topical melody:

Heigh-ho, heigh-ho, and off to work we go,
With a railway track upon our back,
Heigh-ho, heigh-ho, heigh-ho.

Perhaps it was a good thing that the Battalion were never called upon to defend these positions against the Hun, because, despite all their efforts, these wee concrete posts, in the words of the Signal Officer of the time, "stood up all over the landscape like sore thumbs".

Higher authority took great interest in these fortifications, and every visiting commander had his own ideas on the siting of slit trenches—ideas which were invariably in complete disagreement with the views of the unit holding that particular sector and the next higher commander.

Added complications arose with the arrival of the first frosts, when every sort of artifice was resorted to to keep the concrete at the required temperature during the time it was setting.

It was probably a very good thing that the Battalion were kept so busily employed during these long, dreary months, because there was little else to do. There was a shortage of everything in the forward divisions—clothing, equipment and amenities. When the day's digging was finished at about 4.30 in the evening the troops, soaked through, marched back to their billets and sat down to the evening meal. The billets were crude in the extreme, consisting in the main in barns and lofts. For example, a platoon of "B" Company lived in a loft, the only approach to which was by way of a very insecure outside ladder. Facilities for drying clothes were practically non-existent, but the health of the Battalion remained remarkably good. The village itself, apart from a couple of cafés, could provide no source of entertainment for the men, and the nearest towns were Orchies, where the 2nd Division Headquarters was situated, and St. Amand, in the French zone, both about eight kilometres away. The best "hunting grounds" for those fortunate enough to secure a pass were Douai, about sixteen kilometres away, and Lille. For some reason the larger towns were placed out of bounds for some time, a restriction felt bitterly by the men, who had no other outlet for their energies in the rural areas of the "front line". However, as work progressed so the tempo eased, and by mid-November it was found possible to organize trips to the towns on Sunday afternoons.

Units made their own entertainments, and the "Flamers" concert party got away to a quick start when Captain Tom Affleck-Graves, assisted to a large extent by Private Peatey of the Intelligence Section, opened up in H.Q. Company billets at the end of October.

On the amenity side, the smokes situation improved rapidly, and before long the N.A.A.F.I./E.F.I. opened up a good supply depot in Orchies. Bathing presented difficulties, but these were not insuperable and very soon the basement of the Rumegies Brewery was converted, with the help of the Pioneers and the Sappers and a most Heath-Robinson water-heating machine, into a serviceable bath-house.

Undoubtedly the most popular form of evening amusement for the men was letter writing—an enthusiasm not shared by the company officers who had to divide the censoring between them.

At the end of October a great stir went round the Battalion when it was announced that leave, that magic word "leave", to the United Kingdom would open on the 17th of December.

On the last day of the month the Commanding Officer, Lieutenant-Colonel Stephenson, rejoined the Battalion from the United Kingdom, and the next day the Padre left. I don't think that these events were in any way connected, but the departure of the Padre left a vacancy for a new chaplain, who was to serve with us throughout the entire war and remain longer than any officer, except Paget Fretts, and all but a handful of men who were serving with the Battalion in 1939. Padre Claxton's arrival in the Battalion itself caused a bit of a stir. The story goes that he was overdue (we later came to observe and respect Gus's lack of appreciation of such a minor matter as a question of time), and it was not until "C" Company rang up to say that they had caught a spy prowling around their blockhouse that it was realized that the new chaplain was in their midst. Thus very early on Gus Claxton displayed that great interest in martial matters which always marked him.

November passed quietly enough. The Duke of Gloucester passed through Rumegies on his tour of inspection; we were not to see him again for three years, when he came to stay at Ganesh Kind with the Governor of Bombay on his tour through India and the East in 1942.

At the beginning of December there was a pleasant break, as the Battalion were pulled out of the line for a period of rest in a back area at Agny, about three kilometres south of Arras on the main railway line to Paris.

Just before the Battalion left this rest area they received orders to send one company to join the 4th Infantry Brigade on a short tour on the active part of the front in the Maginot Line area. Bob Goff's "D" Company, with Brewster and our "lend-lease", "Rhodesia" Smith, were selected for this duty. This company held their Christmas prematurely and had a riotous send-off on the 23rd of December.

After a very cold railway journey the company arrived at Metz, from where they had to slide and slither along the frost-bound roads to the front line. At the special request of the 2nd Norfolks, "D" Company were attached to this battalion. Thus started the second series of active association between these two battalions which had been begun in Mesopotamia in 1915 and was to be continued throughout this war.

The new "Norsets" took over a position well in front of the Maginot Line from the Black Watch. This was the first occasion of the war that elements of the Battalion found themselves up against the enemy. "D" Company were allotted the centre company area on a battalion front of three miles, of which Bob Goff's frontage was two thousand yards covering a railway line and embankment, which ran straight into the enemy lines, a thickly wooded ridge and a large but uninhabited village. "Rhodesia" Smith had the thankless task of clearing this village every morning. Despite the snow on the ground, both sides showed an amazing amount of patrolling activity. During this time the Norfolks had one officer killed whilst on patrol and Captain (now Lieutenant-Colonel) Peter Barclay earned the Military Cross.

Most of the time was taken up with digging and erecting defences in the Battalion sector, and the company earned special praise from the commander of the 4th Infantry Brigade for the headway they made in the bitterly cold weather and in the frozen ground.

After a spell in the front line the "Norsets" were relieved by a battalion of the Border Regiment and withdrew to a position just in front of the Maginot Line, where they continued their everlasting work on the construction of defences.

It was an interesting month and physically the company stood up extremely well to the bitter winter conditions, but were all, from contemporary accounts, dismayed at the laissez-faire attitude of the local garrison, a spirit so ill according with the aggressive reputation of our allies.

The Battalion, less "D" Company, returned to the line on Christmas Eve and took over the 4th Infantry Brigade's sector, with one company of the Royal Scots and rear parties of the other battalions of the Brigade to assist fill the gaps. The frontier turned towards north-east in this sector, and most of the Battalion were quartered about Lecelles, with "B" Company on the left about the eastern edge of Rumegies. The right-hand neighbours were a French battalion of Algerian infantry, with a very good lot of white officers. Christmas Eve was not a happy choice of date for the arrival and take-over of a new sector of the line, especially as they were expected to celebrate and settle in at the same time. In addition, the pudding failed to arrive and, despite the free issue of a bottle of stout a head, a present from the firm of Guinness, the Christmas fare and celebrations were certainly not up to the standard usually maintained by the Regiment, even on service.

New Year's Day, 1940, found the weather getting colder and colder. The influx of woollen comforts certainly did not help the sentries to keep awake and alert; they couldn't hear their own officers approaching, let alone a "cat burglar" trained enemy.

On the 14th of January there was a scare—the Germans were thought to be invading Belgium, and the Battalion packed up hurriedly, dumped their heavy kit at Planard and reoccupied their old positions at Rumegies, waiting for the code word to set them off on Plan "D," the advance into Belgium. By the 20th this "flap" had died down and the Battalion were not only "stood down" but leave was reopened. But the activity had the advantage of distracting men's minds from the eternal and everlasting monotony of the old gossip and grouses—for the officers there was the feeling that promotion was bad in the B.E.F. and their contemporaries at home were shooting up the scale on the new war-time acting and temporary ranks; for the men there was the indignation (why so heartfelt was never really understood) over the dismissal of Mr. Hore-Belisha (the War Minister), and, for all, there was the never-ending topic of the cold and constant guesses as to just how many trucks of the M.T. Platoon would be "runners" the next day. In the P.R.I.'s office seventy-five thousand cigarettes were sold in a week, which was over and above the free issue of fifty cigarettes per man, and quite a number of men were on leave and detachment—not bad smoking—but as, later, we found in Burma, there was mighty little else to do.

Despite the efforts of the Press at home to paint a very much worse picture of the conditions than they actually were, a matter which caused dissatisfaction among the soldiers, who like to do their own grumbling in their own way, the Battalion settled down happily enough in their first winter of the war.

Life continued in its same constantly varying strain. It is one of the extraordinary things about soldiering that, however quiet and dull the big picture, the domestic world is one of constant change and minor variation. Officers, non-commissioned officers and key men came and went continually, Tom Molloy into hospital at Agny and back again in January, the Adjutant on leave and then away for good. At Battalion Headquarters the subalterns chartered a room in a farm where they opened the Zig-Zag Club and could retire to drink beer and natter to their hearts' content.

Howard Cowie had sat for well over the three years of his statutory term in the Adjutant's chair, having taken over in September, 1936. He had in his quiet, imperturbable way seen the Battalion through all the changes in establishment during this period and, at the end, had successfully, against the most amazing difficulties, like all adjutants at the time, mobilized the Battalion and seen it come to war. He had not in the meantime neglected to pursue his own particular sport and, as I have recorded, not only gained his place for two years in the Army Revolver XXX but in 1938 had managed to train three other officers to the same standard. He departed now to take over an important job at the newly formed Company Commanders' School in the United Kingdom, where his great experience and coaching abilities would be put to their best value. Later in the war he was to take over the 4th Battalion and train them and take them overseas for the invasion of Normandy.

The new Adjutant was Peter Brind, who was one of the 1st Battalion officers at home in August, 1939, who had been mobilized with the 2nd Battalion.

Some time during the early spring the Medical Officer, Sam Loxton, departed to the 5th Field Ambulance as Adjutant, and his place was taken by one Richards.

At the beginning of April, with the coming of warmer weather, a big "manning" exercise was held which did the Battalion a lot of good after a long period of winter quarters. But more was to come in these efforts to shake off the winter lethargy, and on the next day, the 4th of April, the Battalion departed to Louvencourt, on the Albert—Moullens road in the old Somme battlefield area, for a period of intensive training. After flogging over these old battlefields by day and night the troops (and the officers) were able to get into Amiens of an evening, which by all accounts maintained its last war reputation as a "rehabilitation" centre.

During the course of one night operation, which consisted almost entirely of marching, the Battalion were filmed. The object of the exercise, the "movie" part of it that is, was to produce some shots to be included in the news reel at home in the event of the march into Belgium.

These manoeuvres in the Somme area were brought to a sudden close by a signal received at 0430 hrs. on the 9th of April recalling the Battalion to Rumegies. The Boche had invaded Scandinavia and from then on the B.E.F., or at any rate the forward divisions, were maintained in a constant state of readiness.

Even in this state, departures among the old regular officers continued. Linklater, commander of "A" Company, had already departed for a tour of duty with the Ordnance, and now, right at the beginning of May, when the Battalion was getting all set, Tom Affleck-Graves left for a course at the Staff College.

May must have opened very quietly, as I find on referring to old records that not only the Adjutant of the Fifty-Fourth but also the Commander of the 5th Infantry Brigade, Brigadier G. I. Gartland, D.S.O., M.C., departed on leave in the first few days of the month. This left the Battalion with Dayrell Stayner in the Commanding Officer's chair and Thomas, the Signal Officer, answering for the Adjutant, whilst the Colonel departed to Brigade Headquarters to stand in for the Brigadier.

Some time during the spring the Brigade had undergone some change. In accordance with higher policy, two Territorial battalions were posted to the 2nd Division. The 2nd Battalion The Royal Warwickshire Regiment departed and in their place we welcomed the 7th Battalion The Worcestershire Regiment, who were to fight alongside us in the 5th Infantry Brigade until the cessation of hostilities in South-East Asia five and a half years later.

CHAPTER TWO

INTO BATTLE

"Ascension du dirigeable"

"The Balloon goes up"

AS FAR AS the 2nd Battalion The Dorsetshire Regiment were concerned the Colonel had most certainly "caught his balloon", but what he was able to do, under the circumstances, with his limited equipment against overwhelming numbers on the ground and a complete lack of air superiority, let alone parity, we will now see.

Early in the morning of the 10th of May the Battalion were awakened to the sound of air activity, and this was very soon followed by a signal from Brigade indicating that after all these months of waiting "the battle was on". Major Stayner continued to command the Battalion in the absence of the Commanding Officer, who was still at Brigade Headquarters answering for the Brigadier. During the first few days of May the April "flap" had died down, leave to the United Kingdom had been recommenced and various officers had departed to their extra-regimental employment; such as Tom Molloy to his tactical school and "B" Company were about five miles to the rear digging a Divisional assault course.

However, Plan "D" had long been considered and rehearsed and throughout the 10th of May the bits and pieces reassembled at Rumegies. Perhaps the hardest of the commitments they had to find, with a large party still on United Kingdom leave, was the five officers and twenty other ranks required to furnish the Divisional traffic-control posts to the River Dyle. This party included a valuable company commander in the person of Sam Symes. Another company commander, Donald Baynes, who had taken over "A" Company from Peter Brind, was away on leave, his place being taken by a young officer, John Peebles.

There was considerable air activity during the day and the Battalion saw their first Hun machine shot down in flames over Howarderies, just over the Belgian border.

At 0200 hrs. on the 11th of May the Battalion left their billet area at Rumegies, crossing the frontier by a footbridge, and advanced through the woods towards Tournai. It was a very fine night and the singing of the nightingales in these Belgian woods remains firmly in the memory of those who made the march. At first light they halted in the village of Marais de Wirie, about four miles east of Tournai, on the main road to Brussels. The mechanical transport, which had moved by a more circuitous route, joined the Battalion here.

They remained in Marais for twenty-four hours, presumably to allow the leading brigades to be lifted to the Dyle River, and on the morning of the 12th embussed and moved off at two-hundred-yard intervals between vehicles. There was quite a lot of air activity, but the Battalion were not attacked, though the Anti-Aircraft Platoon, under Lieutenant Fretts, part of the traffic-control personnel organization, which had moved independently on the 10th of May to Rhode St. Gehese, south of the capital, were in action during the day. Their route took them near the battlefield of Waterloo, and at 1715 hrs. the Battalion reached its destination at Genval, about ten miles southeast of Brussels. The refugee problem had not been too acute up to now, the majority of west-bound traffic consisting of cars of well-to-do citizens pulling out with mattresses strapped to the roofs of their expensive-looking cars.

At this juncture the extreme right of the B.E.F. lay at Wavre, a town about four and a half miles due east of the Battalion position. From this town the British front ran north in the Dyle Valley to Louvain, about thirteen miles away. The Royal Scots were on the right of the B.E.F. and the French took on the line to the south. North of Louvain, on the British left, the Belgians took over.

In this position the 5th Infantry Brigade were in Divisional reserve and on arrival the Battalion took up a position, with Battalion Headquarters sharing a soda-water factory in Genval with Headquarters of the 5th Infantry Brigade. "A" Company were on the right, facing east and extending northwards from Genval; "C" Company on the left had their headquarters at Rixensart, about two thousand yards to the north; "B" Company were in reserve in the rear of "A" Company; and "D" Company took up a position in the centre of the Battalion area. "B" Echelon were divorced from the Battalion (presumably brigaded) and found themselves ensconced at Watermael Buitsfort in the reserve line south-east of Brussels, about eight miles to the north-west. There was constant slight regrouping in the Battalion position. The Dorsets were in Divisional reserve and had a frontage of about five thousand yards. On our left we were in touch with the 7th Worcesters and met the 13th Algerian Tirailleurs on our right.

Headquarters, 2nd Infantry Division, occupied La Hulpe, a village about two miles to the north-west, and the Divisional artillery came in on the Battalion's right rear. From the word "Go" the Battalion were going to become acclimatized to having the gunners firing from very near to the Battalion area.

On the 13th of May, whilst a certain amount of regrouping was going on and platoons of H.Q. Company and Battalion Headquarters were engaged in a restless game of general post, the Brigadier returned from leave and Lieutenant-Colonel Stephenson resumed command of the Battalion. At the same time Major Stayner was posted to command the 8th Battalion The Lancashire Fusiliers in another brigade in the Division.

The traffic-control personnel who had been detached for the Divisional concentration on the Dyle returned during this day, and with the exception of No. 2 (Anti-Aircraft) Platoon, who rejoined the next day, the Battalion was complete with its own Commanding Officer; Tom Molloy had taken over Second-in-Command.

The various digging activities in the area attracted the attention of the enemy air force, but no damage was done. One diarist of those days emphasizes that the only British aircraft seen during this time were a few Lysander Army co-operation planes, valiantly trying to carry out their tasks against overwhelming odds.

This was the night when it was announced that the enemy had seized the bridge at Maastricht.

On the 14th there was still more domestic regrouping in the Battalion area, "D" Company being moved forward to cover the Lashe River. This and sundry other movement attracted the attention of the enemy air force again, and "D" Company's move had to be completed after dark. The wooded area was most inflammable and there was some danger of forest fires from incendiary bombing. With so little news, alarms and rumours were apt to be rife. On this day there was a scare of a gas attack, a message coming through that the 10th Field Regiment had been gassed. It turned out that they had indeed been gassed, but the casualties were caused by carbon-monoxide poisoning in some of the gun pits.

A report of enemy parachutists completed the day's alarms, a day which was topped off by a concentration fired by the whole of the Divisional artillery—an impressive performance at this time when so few of the Battalion had ever before witnessed a display of the fire power of the Division.

The 15th of May proved to be the last day that they were to remain in these positions. It was a piping-hot day and, to make matters worse, "C" Company ran out of water very early. When the "F" Echelon truck went up to remedy this situation it was ditched. Eventually succour was brought to them by the "B" Echelon truck, but "C" Company had a bad day with their mechanical transport, and managed also to ditch their company commander's P.U., a vehicle which subsequently had to be abandoned.

The war was getting very close, the enemy having made a determined attack on the French colonial troops on the right. This attack was skilfully carried out; parties of Germans infiltrated ahead armed with sub-machine guns and "wrote off" the white officers, leaving the battalion leaderless, a method of attack which did nothing to enhance the morale of these already confused native troops.

During the day, with the Boche established across the Dyle to our south, unit commanders were given the order to prepare to withdraw, and Tom Molloy set off to reconnoitre the La Hulpe area.

Meanwhile, everyone had been pretty busy. Earlier in the day Battalion headquarters and "B" Company had made another move, this time to a sanatorium in Rixensart, and when the Algerians broke, "D" Company and a section of carriers were moved up to the railway to stop the gap.

Finally, to cap the day, news came through on the wireless that the enemy motorized formations were thirty miles west of Sedan, which put them roughly about fifty miles to our south and getting behind our rear.

From now on the story develops on lines only too familiar to students of military history. Corunna and Mons were to be repeated in this tale of withdrawal of a small and heroic British Army against overwhelming odds—a story enlivened only by the staunch fighting and unexampled bravery of those gallant few holding off the German hordes.

The first step back, starting at 0100 hrs. on the 16th, was an extremely short one to La Hulpe. Owing to some delay in the signals, "A" Company and a platoon of "D" Company did not get away for another couple of hours, and then only, as it proved, just in time. The companies were extremely scattered on this occasion and the Signal Officer records feelingly that he had to run out about four miles of line, about only half of which was subsequently recovered.

Throughout the 16th the Battalion held this position, with the Worcesters on the left and the Camerons in reserve. During the day they witnessed the last of the Lysanders, with their gallant Army pilots, being shot out of the sky by Me.109's, their only consolation being the sight of a Boche observation balloon being shot down in flames somewhere to the east. At about noon confirmation came through to the effect that the French were withdrawing on the right. No confirmation was needed to tell of the fate of the Algerians, who, their leaders having been killed, were found on the roads to the west crying, "Ou est la route pour France?"

During the day Sam Symes was ordered to move "B" Company forward to fill the gap on "C" Company's right. Suddenly a battalion deployed for the attack surprisingly appeared on his right flank. This turned out to be a battalion of the King's Own Yorkshire Light Infantry from the 48th Infantry Division, who were putting in a counter-attack to recover the La Hulpe position, at that time held by "C" Company of the Dorsets! In this case "the fog of war" nearly had the most disastrous consequences, and it was only by hurried and frantic telephoning that the artillery concentration due to be put down on the Dorsets by the 48th Division was prevented, and the counter-attack cancelled with two minutes to spare.

At dusk the rearward movement continued, again for only a short hop to a position behind the lakes lying immediately to the north of La Hulpe. However, this position, which the Battalion began digging on a three-thousand-yard front, soon proved to be untenable, and orders were issued for an immediate withdrawal through the Forêt de Soignes to the Hippodrome Racecourse, about six miles to the north-west, just outside the Brussels suburbs. This time it was "C" Company who had to fight their way out, but by first light the Battalion were assembled at the rendezvous. The Battalion had not yet got its second wind, and everyone was very tired by the morning of the 17th, when orders were received in this racecourse area to start out immediately on a long step back to Ghoy, some twenty-four miles or so due west of Brussels. Leaving a covering force of Brens and anti-tank guns under the command of Major Bob Goff to cover the Loth bridges, the Battalion set out on foot through the south-western suburbs of the Belgian capital, and at about 1330 hrs. reached the area of Lennick St. Martin, from where they were ferried forward in bits and pieces to the area of Ghoy. By now the refugee problem was becoming serious and the traffic problem was by no means helped when the 4th Infantry Brigade were encountered on the way.

During the night of the 17th/18th of May the Battalion concentrated more or less in the Ghoy area. "B" and "D" Companies had overshot the mark and at one time had found themselves in Renaix (the old Corps Headquarters location). Early the next morning the Dorsets occupied a position covering the Dendre Canal, with the Worcesters on the right and the 8th Lancashire Fusiliers on the left.

It was here that the Battalion had their first real encounter with the enemy. In the evening the level of the water in the canal dropped, the canal having been breached by sabotage. The enemy advanced, mainly against "B" Company's sector, and a smart engagement ensued, during which our mortars knocked out a Boche medium machine gun.

Outside news, never very cheerful throughout this time, was more than usually depressing that evening with a report that the enemy were in Cambrai, only twenty miles south of our winter quarters at Rumegies, and no one was particularly surprised when at eight o'clock orders came through for the withdrawal to be continued that evening. Other news that evening told them that G.H.Q. had had to pull out of Arras and were settling down on the coast.

The brigaded carriers of all three platoons, under the command of Lieutenant "Oner" Bray of the Dorsets, were left behind to cover the withdrawal of the Brigade Group from this position. Their orders were to hold the line of the Dendre Canal until 1200 hrs. on the 19th of May. They had to fight hard during the morning, and for some time considerable anxiety was felt for their fate. In this action P.S.M. Giles, commanding the Dorset Platoon in place of Lieutenant Bray, was awarded the Distinguished Conduct Medal. For his gallantry and outstanding leadership on this and subsequent occasions Lieutenant Bray earned the Military Cross.

It was also at Ghoy that Gus Claxton, the Padre, was nearly left behind for the second time. The Signal Officer, returning to the Battalion Headquarters billet, just as everyone was moving off, noticed a tin hat with a chaplain's badge lying about. Looking around further, he discovered the chaplain sound asleep and promptly woke him up.

The weather and the nights were especially fine at this time, and at about half an hour after midnight the Battalion set out on their twelve-mile march to Frasne les Buissenal, where they hoped to pick up transport to carry them the further dozen miles to Tournai. At first light the Battalion passed through Lahamaide, and an observer reports them as looking very tired but going well, whilst in the clear May morning air above them large numbers of Boche aircraft were seen streaming westwards on their morning "hate".

Tournai, when they arrived, was in flames and for the first time the Dorsets saw for themselves the result of indiscriminate bombing and machine-gunning of civilians from the large number of dead and wounded lying among the ruins of the town. The Battalion took up a defensive position centred around the village of Orcq, which lay about a mile and a half to the west of the town, and their forward defensive localities ran in one place through Tournai railway station. The specialist platoons were split up over the country, with "B" Echelon at Taintignies, two or three miles to the south, the mortars were sent to St. Maur, two miles away to the south-east of Battalion Headquarters, and the carriers took up a position in rear of the canal.

Battalion Headquarters received some unwelcome attention from the air and three bombs landed in the courtyard of the monastery where they were set up, doing little damage except to write off two motor-cycles and further to deplete their rapidly diminishing stock of signal cable.

Whilst the defended localities were engaged from time to time throughout the night, the enemy, so reports had it, had reached the Somme at Peronne and the War Council at home were considering ways and means of maintaining the B.E.F. if the Channel ports fell.

At Orcq the Battalion were only about seven or eight miles north of Rumegies, from where they had started out but ten days earlier, and already were half a dozen miles behind their initial concentration area in Belgium. This day, the 20th of May, was one of order and counter-order. Colonel Steve spent the morning reconnoitring the St. Maur area to the south, only to find on his return, with shell splinters in his car, that these orders had been cancelled. That evening the Battalion carried out a march on three "dog legs" through Ere and Froidmont, eventually arriving at dusk at Taintignies, popularly known as "Tantivy Towers". The move to the canal had been cancelled owing to a party which the Camerons were having with the Boche at Calonne.

Before leaving Tournai the Battalion had been encouraged to kill off some of the wandering cattle in the streets. Whatever success the rifle companies had is not recorded, but Battalion Headquarters appear to have crowned their chase by puncturing the radiator of the office truck. The night at Taintignies appears to have been quiet enough, the Battalion being there for only twelve hours, during which time Peter Brind, the Adjutant, turned up. He had, I believe, heard the news of the German invasion whilst dancing in London and had left immediately, but it was only by his personal perseverance that he ever managed to rejoin the Battalion at all, having finished the last twenty miles from Douai on some other unit's water truck.

Early the next morning the Battalion moved two miles to the east, a refreshing change of direction, and dug in on the line of the Tournai—Valenciennes road about a mile east of St. Maur. They had some twenty casualties from shell fire on the way up to that exposed position, but no one was killed, though the Padre was busy during the afternoon burying some of the Worcesters who had not been so fortunate. There must have been a pretty good mix-up of units milling around in the early morning mist and the Battalion column became involved with a unit of the 4th Infantry Brigade, which took a bit of sorting out.

The Battalion held their position with three companies up and "D" Company and the carriers in reserve. The Divisional artillery came up on either flank, and they, together with the very prominent chimney-stack in our area, drew an unpleasant amount of attention from the enemy artillery, who, though they failed to raze the chimney-stack, managed during the afternoon to score a direct hit on one of the Battalion ammunition trucks.

At about 1800 hrs. the Battalion were ordered once more to quit their present positions and move across country for about two miles to the south to join the Camerons in a position on the Escaut Canal.

The going was not easy, though the march was fairly uneventful until they arrived at their destination, Merlin, where they found the Camerons putting in a spirited counter-attack, in which most of them seemed to have joined, including the Adjutant, who was wounded in this sortie.

At Merlin the Battalion Headquarters shared a château with the Camerons. The Highlanders were there first and had taken over the most desirable accommodation in the cellars, leaving the Dorsets the upper floors. However, the next twenty-four hours were fairly peaceful and the troops had what has been described as the first dull day since the battle began. The Battalion occupied existing trenches with "B" and "C" Companies "up". Major Sam Symes was called to Division to carry out an urgent task of collecting all the keys of the blockhouses on the Belgian frontier from the French Territorial battalions before they were evacuated, to ensure that we could get in when the time came.

At about the time we were moving into Merlin the wireless informed those who had time to listen that the Boche had arrived at Arras and were supposed to have reached the coast at Abbeville, at the mouth of the Somme. At home the Government had taken the decision to evacuate the B.E.F. from Dunkirk or any remaining Channel port, but the Battalion were to know nothing of this for some days yet.

The seeming peace—it could not be called quietness with a 7.2-inch battery position just to the rear—of the Merlin area was rudely shattered by a Messerschmitt attack on Battalion Headquarters and a few casualties from bombing and enemy artillery fire. At last light orders were received to withdraw back across the frontier into France. About an hour or so later the Battalion set off on foot on their six-mile march to Mouchin, just to the north of our old winter positions, and took up a position in the old 1st Royal Welch Fusiliers' area. On the way, as they were passing through Taintignies, they were stonked, but the German gunners were off for line and no damage was done.

Arriving at 0530 hrs., the Battalion held these already dug positions with their blockhouses with "D" Company on the right at Hell Fire Corner, "B" Company in the centre, "A" Company on the left and "C" Company in reserve. "B" Echelon moved back another nine miles to Pont-à-Marcq. The Colonel's orders were to hold this position for twenty-four hours, but during the afternoon the French 131st Regiment began taking over the line in a rather piecemeal manner and by half-past ten, acting on fresh orders, the Battalion had set out for their next rendezvous. They left behind in the Battalion Headquarters area the slit trench to end all slit trenches, a monster of about twenty-five yards long, in which the whole of Battalion Headquarters and some of "C" Company had managed to find cover from the attentions of the enemy aircraft during the day.

This next move was to be a long one: the first seven miles were on foot to Templeuve, where once again they hoped to pick up mechanical transport which would lift them the remaining twentyodd miles to Festubert on the La Bassée Canal. They had been told that they would go into G.H.Q. reserve—and not before time, felt the over-marched and tired 5th Brigade. At Mouchin the weather had clouded over and there was a certain amount of rain about as the Battalion sat waiting in the darkness until six o'clock on the morning of the 24th of May before the long-expected and mostoverworked mechanical transport arrived to lift them and the Camerons, who had joined them at the rendezvous.

Four hours later the Battalion had arrived at Festubert. The later stages of the move through La Bassée were considerably slowed up by refugees, and the scenes of carnage among the civilian population, all casualties from the Luftwaffe, beggared description and made the slaughter at Tournai seem a very mild business in comparison. For a brief twenty-four hours, or rather less, the Battalion went into billets in Festubert as G.H.Q. reserve. A French motorized battalion was holding the canal positions at this time, but began pulling out during the day. In the evening the Carrier Platoon patrolled towards the village of Gorre on the right flank.

The comparatively idle day spent by everyone in resting and refurbishing caused many an empty stomach in the Battalion to realize how very short they were of food. Rations by this time had been halved and most people took an active interest in scavenging off the land and stalking a pig or chasing a hen to step-up the meagreness of the company larders. It was, however, generally a quiet day and, most providential of all blessings, the Battalion had a night's sleep, the first for many a long night and for most of the Battalion the last for some time to come.

The country hereabouts was dead flat, relieved only to the south by the slag heaps in the Lens area, which afforded the enemy such excellent observation posts over the entire country. It was an area which had seen bitter fighting in the Kaiser's War, and there was an Indian cemetery in Festubert as a reminder of those grim days in 1914 when the 7th Indian Division had frozen in the trenches on their arrival direct from a sunnier climate. In that war the battle had been fought from east to west and old concrete emplacements and pillboxes, such as the shelters used by Battalion Headquarters, needed some modification before they could satisfactorily be used in this fight which was raging at this point from north to south.

This area, however, had a very real connection for the Dorsets because it was here, on the very same ground on which the Battalion was now to take up a defensive position for its last and greatest stand in this campaign, that the 1st Battalion had fought probably its severest battle in the previous war, in October, 1914. The very same bridge, the Pont Fixe, which was to be the left of their new position, had been the centre of the most hectic fighting a quarter of a century before. It was here that the 1st Battalion had been especially mentioned by name in Sir John French's despatches for their gallant action on the 13th of October, 1914, where, despite casualties amounting to fourteen officers and over four hundred and fifty other ranks, the Dorsets hung on to Pont Fixe. It now seemed that history was to repeat itself and once again a Dorset battalion was to be called on to fight a desperate defensive action over the very same ground where already a hundred and thirty Dorset soldiers had died in one battle.

During the evening Brigade called up—it must have been from sheer force of habit—warning the Battalion to prepare to move, an instruction which was countermanded thirty minutes later.

Outside the Divisional orbit the general situation was steadily deteriorating. This was the day that Boulogne was occupied by the Germans, although Calais was still holding out by the skin of its teeth.

Dunkirk, which had by now become the main lines of communication port for the B.E.F., was being subjected to intense night and day bombing and the threat of penetration by ground troops, not from the east as might be expected but from the south-west.

Throughout the campaign the shortage of maps had been acute. This was especially the case at Festubert, where there was only one 1/50,000 map in the Battalion, and traces had to be made by the Battalion Headquarters staff and passed down to companies.

Early in the morning of the 25th of May all pretensions at rest were dispelled. The French in Gorre reported that the Boche had crossed the canal and were already in possession of half of the village! Immediately "B" Company, under Major Symes, with "A" Company under command, were ordered to attack and repulse this penetration. The attack was put in by the two companies, but they encountered no Germans. Some very disorganized French troops and a detachment of the Royal Irish Fusiliers from another formation were in possession of the village.

The Dorsets thereupon took over the canal line with three companies "up" on a three-mile front. "B" Company were on the right in Gorre village. Sam Symes ensconced himself in a brewery, which was in an excellent position defiladed from anything except close small-arrns fire. "A" Company in the centre took a mile of front, which included a large wood running down to the banks of the canal, and "C" Company continued the line for another fifteen hundred yards up to and including the bridge over which ran the main road to Festubert, the famous Pont Fixe of 1914. Battalion Headquarters and "D" Company remained in the Festubert area. It was about two and a half miles from Battalion Headquarters to "B" Company and about a mile or so down the road to "C" Company, so it will be realized that the Dorsets were pretty well extended on this their last stand and, for them, the biggest battle of the campaign.

Not only, as has been pointed out, was the country exceedingly open, so flat indeed as practically to deny to the defenders the power of movement in the open by day, but the situation in Gorre was quite tricky. "B" Company were widely extended in Gorre village, with two platoons up on the canal. Owing to the defection of the French and the failure of the Lancashire Fusiliers to reach the canal, their right flank was wide open.

Sam Symes had had, very early on, to send an appeal for more men to cover this front, and by 1100 hrs. "D" Company were on the move to Gorre to stop this gap on the right. Bob Goff's "D" Company had a pretty rough passage across the open, losing fifteen men. The Germans from their excellent observation posts on the slag heaps were able to direct intense and most accurate mortar and gun fire on the company as they moved, deployed, across the open. The Battalion were by now becoming accustomed, if not inured, to the precision of the German mortarmen, and in order to try to combat this menace tried out an old trick learnt when fighting against the Arabs in Palestine. They mounted a 3-inch mortar on a 15-cwt. truck and used this in a counter-mortar role with most satisfactory effect.

The banks of the canal provided some cover and platoons were busy during the morning digging into the bank themselves. However, on the south bank of the canal, opposite the "B" Company front, was a French train which had long been stationary. Into this train the Germans were finding their way, and by taking advantage of the few feet of extra height thus gained were rapidly developing sniper superiority on this part of the front. A call was sent to the Battalion mortars, who brought down a most successful concentration on this train and set it alight. It turned out to be an ammunition train full of all types of ammunition which continued to blaze for the next two days. Unfortunately, when the fire reached some of the more explosive types of ammunition it was not only the Boche but also some of our own men who became casualties from this conflagration.

In the sky above the enemy co-operation planes, not unlike our Lysanders in appearance, cruised around at a very low altitude on their never-ending reconnaissance missions. These ugly-looking planes, hovering like Indian kite-hawks above a unit cookhouse, seemed impervious to small-arms fire, and in the end efforts were made to prop up anti-tank rifles to shoot at them.

Casualties had mounted during the day, and just at about last light Peter Brind, the Adjutant, was wounded and had to be evacuated. This caused a reorganization in Battalion Headquarters: "Oner" Bray left his carriers and stepped into Peter's vacant chair and young Asser, who had joined the Battalion with the last batch of reinforcements prior to the start of the operations, moved up one to command the very hard-worked Carrier Platoon. In the evening "B" Echelon moved back to Delville.

To conclude the second day on the La Bassée Canal the German radio announced that "the ring around the French, Belgian and British Armies was definitely closed".

The next morning all hands were set to deepening the trenches and an order was issued restricting all unnecessary movement in the open by day. The enemy made an attempt under cover of a screen of civilians, pushed in front of them at the bayonet point, to recover the bodies of some of their dead from whom we subsequently gained identifications. Behind the civilians the enemy walked nonchalantly up the canal bank with a handcart, but at one point the Boche themselves became unscreened to one of our Bren guns and the party withdrew in disorder, leaving six more bodies to be collected.

Later in the day enemy armour began collecting on the south bank and the gunners were immediately put on to this target. However, they had run out of ammunition and could do nothing about it. Feelings on this score were by no means relieved when, after investigation, a reported dump of ammunition to the north turned out to be 4.5-inch howitzer ammunition which simply did not fit any tubes we had.

To add to the interest of the day's proceedings, the enemy started dropping invitations to desert: "You are surrounded—why fight on? We treat our prisoners well." Needless to say, this addition of otherwise useless paper was much appreciated by a battalion whose domestic stores were well-nigh expended.

During the same evening Major Sam Symes determined to obtain certain enemy identifications. He offered to swim the canal himself, but this gesture was turned down by the Commanding Officer and Sam called on volunteers for this task. Three men of "B" Company—Sergeant James and Privates Tabb and Sinnott—undertook this dangerous mission. They stripped to the buff and, with grenades tied to their heads, swam the canal, crawled up to the three dead Germans who lay within ten yards of an enemy machine-gun post and obtained the coveted information. All three men were awarded the Military Medal for this gallant night's work. It is sad to relate, however, that Private Sinnott did not live to receive his award, as he was killed the very next day.

On the 25th and 26th the Battalion had over sixty casualties, a total which was immediately augmented when "B" Echelon were badly shelled later in the night on their way to a new location at Lacouture, about five thousand yards to the north of Festubert.

As night fell a warning was received that an enemy offensive was to be expected; fortunately, however, this did not materialize. The Boche generally during this period were strangely inactive at night. It would seem that they were keener on obtaining a good night's rest themselves than harrying a force whose subsequent fate must have appeared to them to be sealed.

The 27th of May was to be a red-letter day in the annals of the Fifty-Fourth—a day of hard and unremitting action that was to extend without a break into five whole days and nights of unending toil, fighting and marching without rest of any kind until the unit embarked under fire at Dunkirk a hundred and twenty hours later.

The day opened at 0430 hrs. with a heavy enemy assault against the hamlets of Loisne and Le Hamel, less than a thousand yards from and rather to the rear of "D" (right-hand) Company's position. There was no doubt about it, the enemy were well across the canal on the Battalion's right flank, and an hour later had penetrated the Lancashire Fusiliers' defences in this locality and were heading for our right rear. Bob Goff immediately sent the two platoons of "D" Company, which had been facing south, in support of "B" Company, together with two medium machine-gun sections of the Argyll and Sutherland Highlanders,[5] to the west edge of Gorre Wood.

This force engaged the enemy infantry who were advancing eight hundred yards away. The Germans immediately retaliated with medium machine-gun and mortar fire accurately controlled by their co-operation aircraft, and caused many casualties. It could be seen that the Lancashire Fusiliers were heavily engaged and further support was rendered increasingly hard by the difficulty found in differentiating between friend and foe. The enemy air forces then turned their attention to the Dorset Battalion Headquarters, which was bombed at about 0730 hrs.

Meanwhile, on the "B" Company front in Gorre village, the enemy were reported to be forming up on a ditch about three hundred yards to their right. This flank was by now completely open owing to the capture by the enemy of the sub-units of the Lancashire Fusiliers which had made their way forward during the previous day.

Sergeant Cooper, of the Carrier Platoon, had managed to get up to "B" Company area with two carriers loaded with ammunition. Captain John Heron, the company second-in-command, volunteered to man Cooper's carriers and counter-attack to break up this outflanking movement. Sam Symes agreed to this, and this attack was a complete success. For this gallant sortie and his general leadership and efficiency throughout the campaign, "Chips" Heron, a Territorial officer, was awarded the Military Cross.

Later in the morning, when the Boche had re-formed in this same area and were attempting to repeat their earlier manoeuvre, Sergeant Cooper once more sallied out and dispersed the attack, returning with bits of dead German in his carrier tracks. Sergeant Cooper's gallantry

---

5 Attached to the 2nd Infantry Division as a second machine-gun battalion for the operations in Belgium.

and initiative during the hectic hours of that morning at Gorre, and his constant and successful management of the carriers throughout the campaign, earned him the award of the Distinguished Conduct Medal. This non-commissioned officer, a one-time machine gunner in peace time, proceeded from strength to strength during the war, finally becoming Regimental SergeantMajor of the Battalion in Burma.

Communication with Battalion Headquarters, as is constantly stressed throughout this narrative, was especially difficult at Gorre. There was very little line left at this stage of the withdrawal, and the German artillery and mortar fire soon played havoc with any that was laid. During the early part of the morning Sam Symes made his way back to Battalion Headquarters and reported personally to the Commanding Officer. Whilst pointing out the seriousness of the situation on the right flank, he emphasized that no Dorset ground had been lost and that, thanks to the efficacy of the immediate counter-attacks with the carriers, the enemy was temporarily disorganized in this sector.

At 1000 hrs. Lieutenant Asser took out a carrier patrol on reconnaissance and this, it is sad to relate, was the last that was ever seen of this gallant young officer; two other carriers in this patrol, though damaged, were able to fight their way back. The Lancashire Fusiliers on the right were at this time commanded by LieutenantColonel Dayrell Stayner, late Second-in-Command of the FiftyFourth, and during the morning it became quite obvious that the Fusiliers had been completely overrun, and, as was learnt later, Dayrell had been forced to surrender with the few men he had left standing. Only a handful of Fusiliers managed to join up with us during the day.

Encouraged by this success, the enemy, at about noon, renewed the attack with ever-increasing vigour and No. 17 Platoon, of "D" Company, were sent hastily to take up a position on the north-west corner of Gorre Wood to break up the attack which was developing against their right rear. The machine-gun section of the Argylls which accompanied this platoon were wiped out to a man by an enemy machine gun as they were moving into position.

It was not only communications within the Battalion which were proving difficult, but by now the Dorsets were out of touch with Brigade Headquarters except by very intermittent wireless. In fact, no one knew exactly where Brigade Headquarters were or what was the situation elsewhere on the Brigade front. Report had it that the Camerons were heavily involved and had been partially overrun, and that the Worcesters on the left were in none too happy a position. Meanwhile, the Battalion were fully extended on their three-mile front on the canal, with the enemy well round to their right flank.

At 1430 hrs. Brigade came up on the air with instructions to stand by for "Jimmy", the code word to withdraw. Still no one knew exactly where Brigade Headquarters was, and the despatch rider sent off on the last remaining motor-cycle to find out never returned. Three-quarters of an hour later the signal "Jimmy" was received, together with a qualifying instruction for the Commanding Officer of 2 Dorset: "You will hold Festubert unless attacked, when you will withdraw fighting." The withdrawal of the 2nd Infantry Division on Estaires had already begun, and the FiftyFourth had been deputed to fight a rearguard action to cover the movement of the 5th Infantry Brigade and the remainder of the Division.

On receipt of this signal Colonel "Steve" ordered his forward companies to close on Festubert village. This order had to be sent by runner and, as will be seen, never reached "D" Company, and the runners encountered "B" Company half-way to Festubert. No one expected that this order would be an easy one to execute. We will now return and see what had been happening during the past couple of hours on the right flank.

All this time the companies in Gorre had been actively engaged, but Bob Goff and Sam Symes, the two company commanders, had maintained close and constant touch and had evolved a plan of withdrawal against such an emergency. Such planning was essential if they were going to be able to extricate themselves without having to fight a running battle. Later, at about 1430 hrs., they received the warning for "Jimmy" relayed from Battalion Headquarters and Goff realized that the successful accomplishment of this withdrawal depended on a fixed time which had to be decided immediately so that the instructions could be passed right down to the junior leaders; no easy task under the circumstances. The unreliability of communications with Battalion Headquarters at this time made it imperative for him to decide on a zero hour for this force, which he fixed at 1600 hrs. on his own responsibility.

The plan itself was simple: all supporting arms and such mechanical transport as remained were to pull out at thirty minutes before zero, followed by the rifle companies at the appointed time. "D" Company were to make for the north end of Festubert by a route to the north of the road from Gorre, whilst "B" Company were to keep to the south of this road, making for the southern exits of Festubert.

Their main concern continued to be the heavy mortaring which intensified during the day as the Boche closed in from the east and the north. Two first-class leaders in "D" Company were knocked out, P.S.M. Meakin being killed and P.S.M. Bowles, who was later to distinguish himself in Burma, was wounded. The latter was subsequently mentioned in despatches for his part in this campaign and awarded a direct commission. Private West, of that noble gang of ever-willing helpers, the stretcher-bearers, so distinguished himself on this day as to earn the award of the Military Medal.

"D" Company's withdrawal went according to plan, and on arrival in Festubert was sent immediately by the Commanding Officer to block the northern end of the village. "B" Company, however, had a much more difficult task to extricate themselves from the canal bank area, as Sam Symes had to execute that timehonoured manoeuvre without which no public school officers' training corps field day was ever complete, the withdrawal across the front of an enemy, dug in in a strongly held position. He accomplished this move by splitting his company into two and making the best use he could of what cover there remained from the copses lying between him and the "A" Company position.

The remaining carriers under Sergeant Cooper managed to extricate the wounded and by a magnificent display of driving over the piled rubble of the church made their way safely back to Festubert. On the way back "B" Company encountered the runners sent to them with orders to close on Battalion Headquarters; "D" Company's runners were not so successful, and bumped into the enemy detachments moving up to occupy Gorre and had a very adventurous time getting back to Battalion Headquarters.

To return to the Colonel, faced with orders to hold on to cover the withdrawal of the Brigade. His plan was to hold Festubert by covering the four main approaches, with "D" Company to the north, "C" Company to the south-east, "A" Company to the south and "B" Company to the south-west. The enemy allowed him no time to assemble his forces, but, pressing relentlessly, launched an attack at about 1645 hrs. with six armoured fighting vehicles against the southeast corner of the perimeter. Regrouping was by no means complete, and elements of "B" Company appear to have been involved in repelling this attack against "C" Company. The enemy were driven off with the loss of one light tank.

Half an hour or so later the enemy renewed their attack. Following up, from the direction of Gorre, they assaulted "B" Company's position with an attack supported by six medium and three light tanks. "B" Company, not properly settled into their new position, had very little left with which to deal with this weight of armour, but after a hectic action the tanks were driven off by the accumulated fire of the two remaining 25-mm. anti-tank guns, anti-tank rifles and Brens. The enemy withdrew to Gorre with the loss of yet another light tank, but their repulse had cost the Battalion one of its precious remaining anti-tank guns and eight carriers.

Some time about now the mechanical transport attempted to set out on a forlorn hope to get away to the north. They had not gone far, however, when they ran into an enemy armoured column, and only two or three of the vehicles at the tail of the Dorsets managed to reverse and get back into the perimeter. The toll of casualties was rising, and in this particular encounter the Battalion lost many valuable and experienced old hands from the Mechanical Transport Platoon, as well as a recently joined officer, Lieutenant Hugh Wylie.

After the repulse of the enemy armoured force by "B" Company and the unfortunate adventures of the mechanical transport, the Dorsets were given no time to lick their wounds. Following up the few vehicles which had managed to return to the perimeter, the enemy, in the shape of six armoured fighting vehicles, appeared on the northern outskirts of the village. They were held up by "D" Company's road block reinforced with some Royal Warwicks and Royal Irish Fusiliers, but continued to fire straight down the village street. The company's one remaining anti-tank weapon, a Boys rifle, was knocked out immediately, but the company commander moved the remainder of "D" Company into an orchard on the left of the road, and for a quarter of an hour an intense close-quarter battle was fought, both sides firing point blank at each other, at the end of which time the Boche decided to pull out. Bob Goff had been slightly wounded in the head before this last attack developed, but, despite this, he continued to fight his company with the utmost gallantry. Any hesitation on his part or lack of steadfastness on the part of the company would have left that part of the perimeter wide open to penetration by the enemy.

Later in the evening, shortly after seven o'clock, the final attack of the day was launched, once more from the direction of Gorre. This time the enemy assaulted with their infantry alone and were repulsed by small-arms fire supported by the one remaining carrier in the Battalion.

In the general disorganization following the hurried occupation of Festubert, and the subsequent confusion caused by the four enemy attacks within about two and a half hours, some men and vehicles were lost owing to fifth-column activity. A German, disguised as a British officer, managed to circulate through the Battalion area and began issuing orders for a withdrawal to the east. In the heat of the moment these orders were not fully checked up and before this spy had been captured and summarily shot he had been able to cause a certain amount of damage.

It had been a heavy day's work, but there was still more to B follow if the Dorsets, now completely surrounded, having hung on to the position a good six hours after the departure of the remainder of the Brigade, were to fight their way out. The Commanding Officer decided to lead the Battalion northwards to Estaires. This involved a cross-country march of about nine or ten miles across territory intersected with canals, as the enemy were by now in possession of all roads leading to the north.

As soon after dusk as possible, at half-past nine that evening, the Battalion was concentrated at a point immediately to the south of the village. It was a sad sight to see how few remained standing after this hard, slogging match of the fight across Belgium and this final stand on the canal. Out of the Battalion which had crossed the frontier a bare fortnight before, only fifteen officers and two hundred and thirty rank and file mustered for this final and hazardous march through country overrun by the enemy. To these were added a handful of Lancashire Fusiliers, about a platoon of the Worcesters under an officer, and some Royal Warwicks, Royal Irish Fusiliers and Argyll and Sutherland Highlanders.

The Battalion moved east for about a thousand yards and then formed up in mass with the Commanding Officer himself in the lead accompanied by the Second-in-Command and a couple of gunmen. Steve refused to delegate the responsibility for navigating his battalion over this very tricky course, avoiding all houses, woods and roads, to anyone but himself and Tom Molloy as his assistant navigator. The course was not made any easier by constantly encountering barbed-wire fences and everlasting stumbling into and crawling out of irrigation ditches filled with warm but stagnant water. Deviations were constantly necessary, but it is recorded that the noise of the frogs croaking in the marshes did much to deaden the sound of the marching columns. The sky all around was illuminated by burning villages and isolated farmhouses, a scene reminiscent of a Dore picture of Dante's Inferno. Hungry as they were, no one had had much opportunity to eat during the day, and belts had to be tightened one more hole before the march began.

Three times during this withdrawal they encountered the enemy. The first occasion was after about a mile and a half, when the Colonel and his gunmen ran into a German non-commissioned officer who was advancing across country from one picket to another. The gunmen were a bit slow with their bayonets and Steve had to deal with this intruder himself, dispatching him with his revolver. It was an awkward moment: a sudden pistol shot might have had serious consequences, and everyone's heart stood still as the late lamented Heinrich's friends or subordinates started to call after him by name. However, it must have appeared nothing out of the ordinary to a German picket for their inspecting rounds to depart to the accompaniment of revolver shots, or perhaps they decided that it wouldn't be a bad thing if something sudden did happen to Heinrich; at any rate, they made no further move and the Dorsets continued on their way, stepping as quietly as possible.

The next encounter was far more serious. After another couple of miles, shortly before passing the outskirts of the village of Vieille Chapelle, the Battalion came across a lateral road, down which was moving from west to east a solid mass of vehicles. To make matters worse, this column, which from all appearances was a motorized formation, was apparently being checked past a trafficcontrol post at which a red light was glowing. Both the armoured fighting vehicles and the trucks showed headlights and there was a considerable amount of stopping and starting and troops debussing going on. There was nothing the Dorsets could do but to freeze in their tracks and lie low, and it is remarkable just how quiet nigh on three hundred British other ranks can keep on an occasion like this. The Colonel appreciated that it was essential to get to Estaires before first light, and as the minutes ticked by and this never-ending column chugged slowly past, with its constant halts and checks at the traffic post, he had awful visions of having to fight his way through this armoured column with his very tired and weak battalion against a lively enemy who not only were vastly superior in numbers but strongly supported by armoured fighting vehicles.

At long last the tail of the column appeared in sight, the last vehicle was checked through and the column vanished into the east.

Cold and stiff after their series of duckings in the various ditches and the long lie-up, the Battalion rose to their feet, crossed the road and continued on their old bearing. After another mile or more the appearance of parachute flares ahead of them caused the Colonel to swing half-left. At about 0230 hrs. they reached a deep-water canal. As they approached, a German patrol proceeded down the canal bank but failed to notice the large body of men waiting to cross, this obstacle. This was thought at first to be the Lys Canal, and everyone's spirits rose at the thought that they were very near to their destination. This guess, however, proved false. In his many deviations Steve had bumped into the Bethune—Estaires Canal which ran approximately north and south and parallel to his original course. There were a number of non-swimmers in the Battalion and these had to be helped across with great care. Two officers, Bray, the Adjutant, and John Peebles, the commander of "A" Company, distinguished themselves on this night by their gallant reconnaissances of this and the subsequent canal crossings, and in their wholehearted efforts to get the Battalion across. For this night's work and continued gallantry in action both these officers were awarded the Military Cross.

No sooner had the Dorsets made one crossing of this canal than they encountered the same waterway again. In the dark they had cut across it at the one place where it made a wide bend to the east and there was nothing to do but swim it once more. Before crossing, those who had not already stripped down to the barest essentials of weapons, ammunition and equipment were ordered to do so. Gas-masks were flung away, the empty haversacks making very useful containers for grenades and other vital equipment. As a result not so many casualties from drowning were experienced on this second crossing. There still remained another couple of miles to go before they came to the bridge over the Lys Canal, as it was deemed expedient to bypass the outlying village of La Gorgue.

At 0500 hrs., soaked through and extremely weary, having been constantly engaged for twenty-four hours without a respite, the Dorsets arrived at Estaires to find that the B.E.F. had already evacuated the town, which had been left in the hands of the French demolition party, who blew the bridge only a short half an hour after the Dorsets arrived.

Here the Commanding Officer called a halt for three hours to enable the Battalion to try to dry themselves out and get some food. As the civilians had all been evacuated this latter task was not as difficult as it sounds, and indeed throughout the retreat, it is said, despite the lack of rations, most people managed to feed themselves to some extent off the country. At Estaires too they were able to gather in some scattered elements of the Battalion which had become separated during the critical hours at Festubert.

The Battalion must have presented a pretty sorry sight in the early morning sunlight of the 28th of May. There had been little opportunity of getting even a wash for the past few days, and the night withdrawal

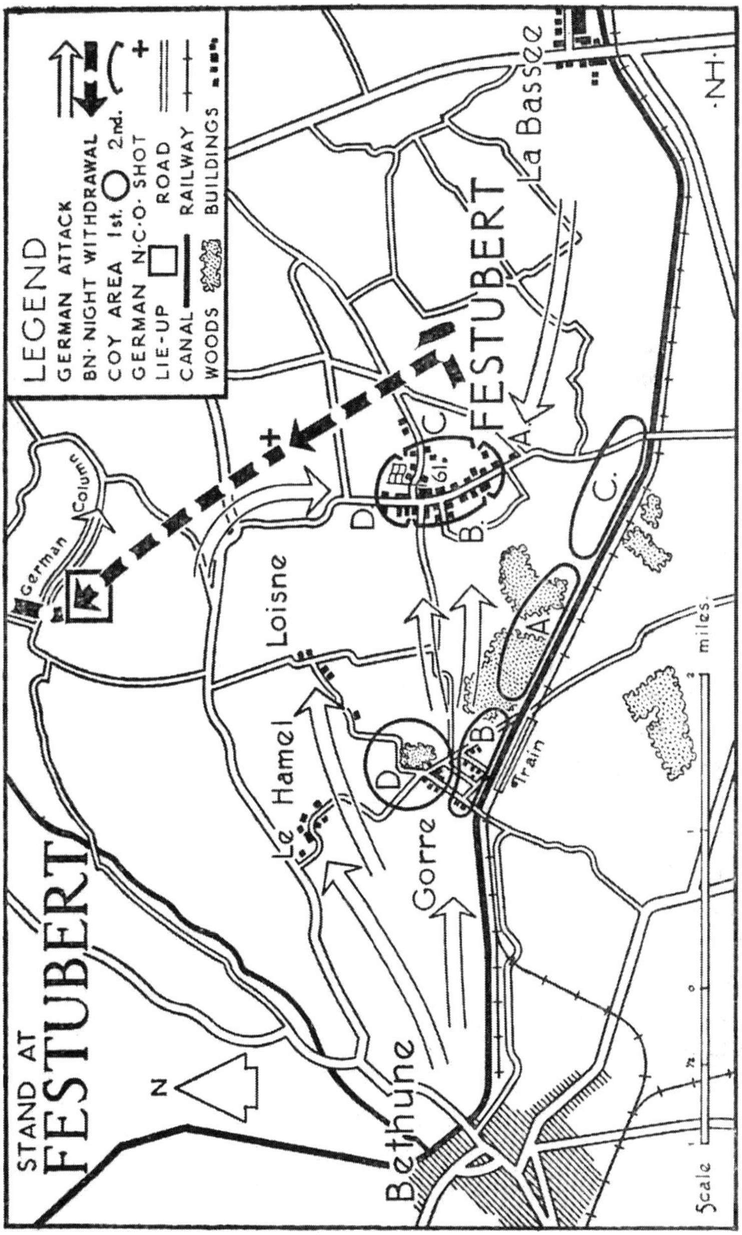
STAND AT
FESTUBERT
LEGEND
GERMAN ATTACK
BN·NIGHT WITHDRAWAL
COY AREA 1st. 2nd.
GERMAN N·C·O· SHOT
LIE-UP
ROAD
CANAL
RAILWAY
WOODS
BUILDINGS
N
German Column
Loisne
Le Hamel
Gorre
Bethune
FESTUBERT
La Bassee
Train
61
Scale
miles
·N·H·

had not done anything to improve their appearance. For example, the Signal Officer, in a sudden access of zeal at Festubert, had ripped off his buttons to prevent identification in case of capture, and with his jacket fastened with string had put the final touches to his appearance by burning a large hole in his trousers in his attempts to dry them off in front of a fire in Estaires.

At 0800 hrs., fairly refreshed and with appetites temporarily assuaged, the Battalion continued its northward march. The going on this day was pure hell. Feet soaked from the drenching of the night before and boots in ribbons after the fierce marching of the past few weeks, and, finally, the rough, hard road down which they now had to continue the withdrawal in torrential rain all added to their discomfort. After an hour they reached Doulieu, where they met the Staff Captain of the 5th Infantry Brigade. This officer expressed his surprise at seeing the Dorsets, who had apparently been written off for lost. They were told to make for Watou, another eighteen miles to the north, where they would contact the Staff Captain of the 6th Infantry Brigade, who would guide them into their new defensive positions.

From Meteren, where Captain Roper of the Regiment had been encountered at the cross-roads, the march was continued by companies independently. A diversion had to be made to the east to avoid the enemy, who were reported to be in possession of Godwaersvelde. This long and exhausting march of twenty miles ended with the arrival of the Battalion at Watou at about 2100 hrs. Of the 6th Infantry Brigade and a defended locality there was no sign— they did, however, encounter Teddy Edwards and the five remaining trucks of "B" Echelon with much-needed refreshment. Here Brigadier Gartland appeared and explained that the latest idea was to push on and rendezvous north of Bergues, some six miles south of Dunkirk, by first light.

It was not until during this long march to Watou on the 28th that the Battalion first heard of any idea of the B.E.F. being evacuated. Up to this point the idea had always been that of "reculer pour mieux sauter", or withdrawal to have another crack at the Boche. But during these long and tiring hours on the march, following so close after a series of strenuous conflicts with the everpressing enemy, various things became clear to the exhausted troops. The feeling of being utterly lost, due mainly to poor communications and lack of information, permeated the Battalion.

Secondly, even the most worn-out soldier, staggering along in the most "browned-off" of all trances, could not but fail to notice the ever-increasing mass of abandoned vehicles. Remember that they were bringing up the rear, and by now not only were the ditches alongside the road filled with abandoned and destroyed vehicles of all shapes and sizes but in many fields whole formations had parked their vehicles in orderly rows, as at a race meeting, before leaving them, rendered as useless as possible, to the pursuing enemy.

The roads themselves were stiff with vehicles jammed head to tail, trying to fight on through the press to the nearest possible point to the coast.

Half an hour after the arrival of the main body in Watou the leading elements of the Battalion were being ferried forward to Bergues, twelve miles to the north-west, and during the night this move was completed, the Battalion concentrating just north of the town.

As has been indicated, the evacuation had, unbeknown to the Brigade, been started from Dunkirk on the 26th of May whilst the Battalion had been fighting at Festubert. The ruins of the town were being held by the remnants of the French Seventh Army, whilst part of the French First Army guarded the eastern suburb of Malo le Bains, to which sector of the Dunkirk perimeter the Battalion was directed from Bergues during the afternoon of the 29th of May. At this latter town they had willy-nilly to abandon their vehicles, as it had been found quite impossible to maintain any vehicles north of this point. Dunkirk itself was in ruins, and the constant day and night bombing was continued by the enemy with ever-increasing energy as more and more shipping piled up in the harbour and off the beaches in their efforts to extricate every man of the B.E.F. The Furnes Canal, which ran behind the sand-dunes on the beaches and parallel with the coast, made an excellent anti-tank obstacle and the Battalion were given an assembly point on the north bank of the Furnes Canal at the bridge in Zuydcoote, about four miles to the east of the Dunkirk mole, with the task of defending this bridge and another one in the vicinity. The Camerons were digging in on their flank. All day long the heavy air bombardment was maintained which greatly restricted movement in the open.

This position was maintained until nightfall on the 30th of May, when the withdrawal to the Mole was started. Second-Lieutenant Stephenson and some twenty other ranks were left to guard the bridges. This party subsequently made good their withdrawal and rejoined the Battalion some days later in Yorkshire. In this way the Dorsets carried out the final movement of this unfortunate campaign. In regular formation, with all their platoon weapons complete, they marched on to the mole under no inconsiderable fire and boarded a

Thames dredger. The sight of this unwieldy craft, which, as first seen in the dark, was apparently half-filled with water, had so appalled Sam Symes when he had been sent forward on the advance party that he had refused to take it over. It was explained to this harassed officer that this was the normal condition of dredgers and actually the craft was quite seaworthy.

Crowded as they were, this night journey across the open sea in a Thames hopper provided no hazards to the exhausted Battalion, who in many cases literally slept standing up. Early the next morning, after some brisk repartee between the "Wavy Navy" SubLieutenant in charge and a Royal Navy Commander on the pier, this unwieldy craft was brought alongside and the Fifty-Fourth Foot marched ashore at Margate to find a welcome meal being distributed by the Mayor and the Corporation officials.

The story of these operations would be incomplete without a further reference to the one man who, from the Battalion point of view, made the operation as successful as it could be in the circumstances. Colonel Steve throughout the short campaign had led the Battalion with great gallantry and audacity. He not only heartened the Battalion throughout the early and confusing days of the withdrawal but when the time came for the final stand to cover the withdrawal of the Division from Festubert, he so inspired them that they put up the fight of their lives against overwhelming odds throughout that desperate series of conflicts on the 27th of May. Where a lesser man might then have well called for slight pause and a refreshing drink whilst donning his sweater between these gruelling sets, Steve realized the gravity of the situation and with his indomitable energy immediately led the Battalion off on the most crucial stage of the journey. Finally, after yet another seventytwo hours of gruelling marching and rearguard action, he led them in formation with their weapons down the mole at Dunkirk to the safety they themselves had so hardly earned and which their efforts had done so much to secure for the remainder of their formation. His award of the Distinguished Service Order, the first to the Regiment in this war, had been well and truly earned.

It was not the wishful thinking expressed in the contemporary cry of our allies, *"Nous gagnerons parceque nous sommes les plus forts"*,[6] which inspired the Battalion throughout this ordeal against overwhelming odds but the indomitable courage and doggedness of the Dorset soldier, fostered on the county motto "Who's Afear'd?"

---

6   We will win because we are the strongest.

This spirit, coupled with a tradition of two hundred and fifty years of campaigning throughout the globe, confounded their exultant enemies. Twice in one generation had a Regular battalion of the Regiment stood its ground and borne the full initial blast of a strong, prepared and overwhelming enemy. La Bassée Canal will ever be remembered in the Regiment as the funeral pyre of both the 1st and 2nd Regular Battalions in successive wars—a Regimental crematorium, from which, phœnix-like, arose, each in its turn, two fresh battalions. These, inspired by the traditions of their predecessors, set out in their time to play their part in inflicting a greater and more overwhelming defeat on the King's enemies.

2nd DIVISION SIGNS

1914-18

1939—to the present day 41

FRANCE, 1940

Lieut.-Colonel E. L. Stephenson, D.S.O., M.C., Officer Commanding 2nd Dorset, 1939-1941

Exercise, Louvencourt area, April 1940. C.Q.M.S. F. Guest issues dinners

Rumegies, February 1940. C.Q.M.S. J. Pratt issues clothing

INTO BATTLE

FAREWELL VISIT OF H.M. KING GEORGE VI TO THE 2ND DIVISION, BANBURY, 1ST APRIL 1942

H.M. The King with the Commanding Officer

A Company jungle training assault course

H.M. The King leaves the jungle assault course accompanied by Lieut-Col. G. N. Wood O.B.E., M.C

CHAPTER THREE

THE BATTLE OF BRITAIN

"They also serve who only stand and wait."

ON THEIR RETURN FROM DUNKIRK the Battalion re-formed at Pudsey and by the end of June had moved to the coast of Yorkshire in the neighbourhood of Hornsea. They took over a nine-mile stretch of coast, with the right-hand company ("B") at Aldborough and the left (H.Q. and "D" Companies) in Hornsea. Battalion Headquarters were at Wassand Hall. Throughout the next six months, and in fact during the remainder of the time they were in England, there was a constant change of personnel. With the initial reinforcements there returned to the Battalion a number of Regular officers, such as Captains Linklater, Laugher and Molyneux, and also Major Peach from the 4th Battalion. They very soon lost Tom Molloy, who in June was posted to command the 7th Battalion The Worcestershire Regiment in the same Brigade.

In common with other formations at home in those days, the 2nd Division spent the winter guarding the coasts of England. They had their alarums and excursions and they shared the momentary excitement of standing-to for "Cromwell", the code word for the invasion. As was the case throughout the country, they helped the Home Guard from the earliest days of the Local Defence Volunteers, until this force was well set on its feet. Many were the problems arising out of those earlier Home Guard exercises. Once they had been called out, who was to feed them and who was to milk the cows?—these and many other equally pressing questions called for constant attention. The Dorsets spent many a long hour erecting coast defences and were by no means the only battalion on the coast at that time to find the results of many hours' labour washed into the sea by the autumn gales. The passion for digging and erecting wire obstacles was not confined to the beaches. Battalion Headquarters was soon able to boast that its "Peach Line" of defences, so called after its designer, was completely impregnable to the normal visitor.

In September they lost three valuable young officers in Bray, Peebles and Heron, all of whom had been decorated for their part in the Flanders campaign, who disappeared a few miles away to become "founder" members of the 5th Commando.

During the autumn the Battalion were honoured by a visit from His Majesty, who decorated a farmer's wife. This good lady had distinguished herself by the single-handed capture of a German airman, who had baled out over the local countryside. The Prime Minister was also among their visitors and the famous picture of him being photographed with a tommy-gun was taken at the time of this visit.

By Christmas the Corps of Drums, which was to play no small part in subsequent adventures, had been revived from old members of the Band and Drums still serving in the Battalion.

Christmas was a great success—probably one of the best wartime celebrations of the Battalion. No small amount of credit for the success of these seasonal celebrations was due to the hospitality and welcome given by the good inhabitants of that part of Yorkshire.

Shortly after Christmas the weather deteriorated badly and for some days outlying companies were cut off and supplies had to be man-handled across the snow.

By March the Brigade had become pretty well embedded in their coastal defences and they were moved to Selby from where they could carry out a certain amount of training. The exercises varied, some were most arduous, and the weather was of such severity as to harden any formation trying to carry out any form of collective training during this time. At the end of March the Commanding Officer departed for a fresh appointment, having completed two years in command of the Battalion. Enough has been said in these annals to show how much the Battalion owed to Colonel Steve and how much they must have regretted his departure. Lieutenant-Colonel P. G. Boon subsequently took over command and must have started off with a very new team. Peter Brind had just recently departed to the Staff College at Camberley and had handed over the Adjutancy to Tony Bridge, who was to hold that appointment until after the Battalion were settled in India. Bob Goff had already departed in January, 1941, and, as we have said, Tom Molloy was next door in command of the Worcesters.

In May the Battalion returned to the coast for a short spell of duty, subsequently returning to Selby.

Collective training at varying degrees of intensity continued throughout the summer and every opportunity was taken to shoot on the limited ranges, and on one occasion the Battalion underwent a "battle inoculation".

On the departure of Lieutenant-Colonel Boon, LieutenantColonel G. N. Wood, O.B.E., M.C., arrived to take over command of the Battalion. Soon after his arrival the Dorsets moved to Boroughbridge from where intense training, involving exercises taking them all over Yorkshire, was continued. Early in the autumn they were under orders with the remainder of the 2nd Division to move south into East Anglia, a move which was soon stopped by the sudden receipt of orders to mobilize and prepare to sail to "furrin parts".

The days of waiting were over, or so they thought at the time. At any rate, after the brief campaign in France and Flanders and the long and dreary period of coast defence, the Battalion were now under orders for overseas and action. At this point we will take up our story, with the Battalion preparing for their long march to Tokyo.

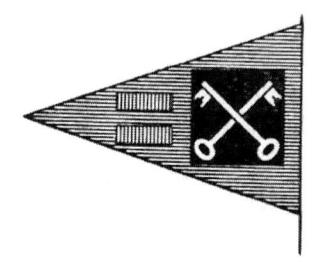

5th Infantry Brigade

What was the end of all the show,
                    Johnnie, Johnnie?
Ask my Colonel, for I don't know,
                    Johnnie, my Johnnie, aha!
We broke a King and we built a road—
A court-house stands where the Reg'ment goed.
And the river's clean where the raw blood flowed...

                                    KIPLING.

The Gateway of India
Bombay

CHAPTER FOUR

IN THE WAKE OF THE SARAH SANDS

What are these fleets that cross the sea
From British ports and bays
To coasts that glister southwardly
Behind the dog-day haze?
They are the shipped Battalions sent
To bar the bold belligerent
Who stalks the Dancers' land.
Within these hulls, like sheep a-pen
Are packed in thousands fighting men
And colonels in command.

—HARDY: The Dynasts.

IN OCTOBER, 1941, the 2nd Infantry Division was suddenly arrested in the throes of moving from Yorkshire to East Anglia and hurriedly mobilized on a war basis for service overseas. Back to the Battalion came Tom Molloy, who had been superseded in command of the 7th Worcestershires by a senior officer of that regiment, and myself from Kent, where I had been acting as Second-inCommand to the 4th Battalion. We arrived to find that those not actually on embarkation leave were up to their eyes in work dealing with all the multifarious arrangements connected with the launching of a battalion overseas. Somehow the fitting of tropical clothing to the shivering bodies of British troops on a freezingly cold day in an English autumn is always fairly ludicrous—this performance, carried out in war time, when the requirements of security demand that the local inhabitants turn a blind eye to the strange sight of British other ranks parading in Wolseley helmets and turned-up shorts on a cold October afternoon is apt to be stranger than usual.

The Fifty-Fourth Foot had already felt the exhilarating effect of their new commander. The recent changes in command during an important stage of their training had had an unsettling effect, and only now were they shaping to the form of the Battalion which was to make its mark in the war in South-East Asia.

Even after two years of war, the Battalion were still very well off for Regulars. We had at this time a very strong team of Regular warrant officers and sergeants, backed up by a strong, though small, nucleus of experienced junior non-commissioned officers and private soldiers.

Some, like Mr. Smith, my old Machine Gun Platoon Sergeant of Dover days, now the Regimental Sergeant-Major, rose to be Quartermaster of the Battalion; others, like Sergeant Cooper, of Festubert fame, who has already figured prominently in these records, rose to be Regimental Sergeant-Major. Each company carried its quota of these "old sweats" who will figure from time to time in these annals—soldiers like Lance-Corporal Woodford, of the Regimental Police, another one-time machine gunner, who became the Commanding Officer's gunman in action and whose devoted service earned him a mention in despatches.

By the end of November it had become obvious that the immediate move was off, and we were ordered to proceed to Banbury, where we went into G.H.Q. reserve. This was indeed a fortunate chance for the 2nd Infantry Division, as we were later to understand that the 18th Infantry Division had departed in our place and sailed, as all the world now knows, straight into the "bag" in Singapore in the following February.

Before leaving the North an event of great significance happened to the 2nd Infantry Division—I speak of the arrival to command of Major-General John Grover. To the historians of the future the 2nd Infantry Division and General Grover must be synonymous. For over two and a half years General "John" led us, drove us and welded us into that extremely efficient fighting machine which was finally to prove itself in action against the Japanese. A great trainer of men, with a capacity for work alarming in the extreme to his subordinates, the General did not, on arrival in the East, confine his attentions to his own division, and even as he flogged us through the heat and the rains over the plains and in the jungle he found time also to assist the armies of India in their efforts to train for the war in South-East Asia.

The good inhabitants of Banbury, overcrowded as they were with evacuees and the opening of war-time plants in their district, were hospitable in the extreme and did everything they could to make our stay of three months as enjoyable as possible. Our sojourn in this pleasant area was, however, not to be protracted. The Dorsets had hardly time to win the Divisional cross-country run (with a surprise individual success by Private O'Reilly, of "B" Company, over that redoubtable veteran international runner C.S.M. Wilson, of the Royal

Scots) and the Divisional boxing championship, when our all-round star, Lance-Corporal John, of "A" Company, took the honours, before we were once more flung into the turmoil of preparation for overseas.

Before our departure we were honoured by visits from the Prime Minister, for whom the Battalion found the guard of honour, and just before we sailed, by His Majesty The King himself. The King spent the day with the Division on the 1st of April, 1942. He started by inspecting the Battalion lined up on the Oxford Road and witnessed a display by "A" Company on the jungle assault course which we had developed high up in the trees in the officers' mess garden.

Before setting foot on H.T. K9 at Liverpool on the 10th of April, 1942, it would be well to take a quick look over the order of battle, which had changed out of all knowledge since that day in September, 1939, when the Fifty-Fourth last embarked for service overseas.

George Wood had as his Second-in-Command Tom Molloy, who the reader will remember had served Colonel Steve in that capacity in France. The Adjutant was Tony Bridge, who had had charge of the mechanical transport in France, and he was assisted by Lieutenant Prebble as Intelligence Officer. Gus Claxton, the Padre, and Joe Chamberlin, the Medical Officer, were by now old hands in the Battalion. Donald Baynes had moved from "A" Company to the command of H.Q. Company. On return to the Battalion I had been appointed to command "A" Company and had a very strong team of assistants in Dick Purser, my second-in-command, Clive Chettle and "Tiger" Havers—all three of whom were to distinguish themselves in their own way in action. Alan Watts commanded "B" Company, whilst Giles, the late Platoon Sergeant-Major, who had earned a Distinguished Conduct Medal on the Dendre Canal, commanded "C" Company, and Tom Hughes, a Territorial officer, led "D" Company.

It is impossible to mention everyone, and those who distinguished themselves subsequently will be referred to during this story, but it would be an injustice to step on board the ship without listing that great band of veterans the warrant officers, whose experience was to prove invaluable and who all subsequently achieved the honour of a commission during the war. Edwards's Regimental Quartermaster-Sergeant was now Warman, Stark had replaced Pratt as Company Sergeant-Major of "A" Company, and with Doughty ("B"), Keegan ("C"), Hunt ("D") and Warren and Towills (H.Q.) we could boast as strong a team of warrant officers as could be found anywhere in the Infantry of the Line at this stage of the war.

The Battalion embarked on the H.T. K9 (*Reina del Pacifico*) and were extremely fortunate in this large ship, built for the tropics. With us were Brigade Headquarters, the 7th Worcesters and the 10th Field Regiment, R.A. The long, dreary weeks of the voyage round the Cape were an experience shared by many who travelled abroad in those early days of the war. The convoy was reputed to be the biggest that had as yet left the coast of the United Kingdom and we were most fortunate in travelling as a formation in our own units and not as drafts. General Grover, with the fate of the 18th Division fresh in his mind, was not one to allow us to slacken off just because we were at sea. Training of every possible kind was the order of the day, and to the astonishment of the boatswain and with the, at first reluctant, co-operation of the captain (who, like all merchant-ship masters, was averse to this wartime practice of wearing boots at sea), we soon rigged up a formidable assault course on "E" deck aft and throughout the day every available inch of deck space was allocated for training.

As I had four years' experience on the Army Physical Training Staff, the Commanding Officer decided to release me for duties as Ship's Physical Training Officer. To my joy I found that C.S.M. Belson, one of my old students at the Army School of Physical Training, was Ship's Physical Training Warrant Officer, and together we were kept busy throughout the voyage. Finding the limitations of deck space difficult, I decided to take the Battalion in mass physical training, half the Battalion at a time. This developed into a great feature of shipboard life, especially when, despite the untunefulness of my voice, we contrived to bend and stretch whilst singing the popular melodies of the day.

Not one of the three thousand five hundred passengers will forget the boxing tournaments on the crowded after deck and the extraordinary performances put up in the tyros' competition, or the controversy that raged over this particular form of combat.

At Capetown we received a grand welcome from the truly hospitable inhabitants of that great city. We had been on board exactly five weeks and the cool of Table Bay was most refreshing after the intense heat experienced during our five days cooped up on board ship at Freetown. The authorities, with previous experience of divisions passing through, decided that, to relieve the congestion, the infantry battalions would have to spend forty-eight hours, in rotation, at a transit camp some eighteen miles outside the city. Here we were welcomed and subjected to those colossal rations to which the South African soldier is accustomed; each of the soldiers' gargantuan meals was topped off with a pound of grapes. It was well that we did not neglect the opportunity to exercise ourselves, and each day we carried out route marches and "dog and stick" walks.

The last night in Capetown was for everyone one of those unforgettable experiences, and when we sailed we all carried with us the deepest thanks in our hearts to those kind inhabitants of the Cape who had so spontaneously gone out of their way to ensure that our brief stay was made as enjoyable as possible.

When we had sailed from England our destination was "X"; we had been cast on the seas to join in the war where we were most needed, and we all, in our hearts, thought in terms of the Western Desert—it was something of a shock, therefore, on rounding the Cape to find that we were destined for India. Undeterred by the feeling of disappointment which pervaded all ranks, Colonel George Wood pronounced his famous dictum: "Gentlemen, you will like India", and immediately set out to teach us Urdu.

The arrival of yet another all-white division in India, though scarcely unheralded in these days of rapid communications, found the administrative authorities hardly prepared. Having been kept waiting in Bombay for a couple of days, the Battalion felt their first real breath of India as they stepped out of the train at Kirkee station and marched three miles to that old stamping ground of the Fifty-Fourth before the First World War, Pashan Camp. What a shock was in store for us! The tents were not all erected, and we all had to set to with immense energy to set up the camp before the rains broke.

How used we were to become in the next few years to these camps set down on cotton soil! Little did we realize as we struggled through the multitudinous problems concomitant with the setting up of a battalion in India how much we were to envy our successors in this very camp a year later. A great feature of our life at Pashan, and one that did a great deal to lighten the burden of those early and uncomfortable days was the kindness and hospitality shown to the Battalion by the Governor of Bombay Presidency and his lady wife. Sir Roger and Lady Lumley, now the Earl and Countess of Scarborough. They took an immense amount of trouble to look after the welfare of the men and to entertain the officers at their nearby residence at Ganesh Kind. Before leaving Pashan we presented their Excellencies with an illuminated scroll setting out our thanks in Dorset dialect.

The unbounded energy of the Colonel needed no encouragement from General Grover to set us off at a very early date on a period of intensive training—training that was to continue with more or less unabated zest for the next twenty-one months. On looking back, I cannot help feeling that our enthusiasm, in those early days (and the Colonel's energy was infectious—all the company commanders catching the bug), laid up for us a store of trouble through our being too active before becoming properly acclimatized. By the time we had been a month in the country, all companies were out doing long three-day treks in the monsoon. The disasters of the campaign then finishing in Burma certainly acted as an impetus, but I am not at all certain that we would not have been wiser to have taken our training a little slower during the time that we were acclimatizing ourselves to the extremely arduous conditions of camp life. If we had done so our losses from disease might well have been considerably lower.

We were not, however, destined to remain long in the Poona area, and by the middle of July it had been agreed that Pashan Camp was, for the time being, quite unsuitable for occupation by white troops, and the 5th Infantry Brigade, always rather independently minded, set off thankfully for Secunderabad. In this delightful station we had one of our really good breaks of the war—for the first time since marching out of Marlborough Lines at Aldershot in 1939 the Battalion were quartered in barracks. Everyone in the Battalion enjoyed the six-week stay in this old cantonment. The barracks were comfortable, the bazaar was handy and good, and, for the officers, the club was easily the best of its kind that we ever encountered on our wanderings. We trained hard and played games hard, but so beneficial was the effect of returning from training to a sound barracks rather than an ill-found camp that we rapidly threw off the effects of our sojourn in Pashan Camp.

This was our first opportunity to smarten the Battalion up, and we attempted with a woeful shortage of dherzis to convert the wartime issue of khaki drill into a smart-looking uniform. Divisional signs appeared on our head-dress, and the officers and sergeants soon put up the peace-time pagris on their helmets with the two green flashes of the Regiment. On the right-hand side we sported our green-and-gold Battalion flashes—a war-time innovation which proved a most useful means of recognition.

Soon after our arrival in Secunderabad the Colonel was promoted to command the 4th Infantry Brigade in the 2nd Infantry Division. It is difficult to assess, in the light of subsequent events, all that George or Sam Wood, as he is known to his many friends outside the Regiment, did for the Fifty-Fourth during his year in command. I am, however, in a position, having subsequently been privileged to command the Battalion both on training and in action, to say that in one year George Wood reinitiated the 2nd Battalion into the art of soldiering. There have been many distinguished Commanding

Officers of the Dorsetshire Regiment, but George Wood deserves a place with the most famous. He never achieved the distinction he so greatly coveted: to lead the Battalion, he served so well, against the enemy. But by his example, cheerfulness, strong personality and leadership, and, above all, his very great sense of duty, he pulled the Battalion out of a period of doldrums and set them firmly on their feet as one of the most efficient fighting units in the 2nd Infantry Division. To him must undeniably go a great deal of the credit for the subsequent performance of the Battalion in action, and we, who were trained by him, were constantly grateful for the spadework he put in during his period of command.

His subsequent career was meteoric. Few knew that he had, on two occasions, turned down the offer to command a brigade in order to take his Battalion abroad: the second time forty-eight hours before we sailed from Liverpool.

He was not destined to remain long with the 4th Infantry Brigade. Before the end of 1942 he had departed to Ceylon as Brigadier, General Staff, to the Ceylon Army. By the end of 1943 he was back amongst us again at Poona, serving in the same capacity to the Commander of the Indian Expeditionary Force. When this became the XXXIII Indian Corps he remained and was responsible to General Stopford for the planning of the Kohima operations which held and annihilated the Japanese army of invasion of India.

During his tour of duty with the XXXIII Corps this staunch Dorset officer maintained a constant touch with his old Battalion.

He visited us in the Kohima perimeter and many a time as we advanced down the road he appeared among the men. On more than one occasion we had hardly occupied a new position before my gunman would say: "Here comes 'Colonel' Wood", and at Maram as we set off on a tricky night march he appeared in the gathering darkness to wish us "God-speed".

Before the advance across the Chindwin, George Wood had achieved his ambition to attain general officer's rank. He left the XXXIII Corps on Sarah Sands Day, 1944, to take over command of the 25th Indian Infantry Division in the Arakan. His success thereafter was unbounded and within a couple of months he was leading them in a series of leap-frogging landings down the coast to Rangoon and subsequently to Malaya. With his two green Dorset stripes in his general's bush hat he led his division with the same energy and enthusiasm that he had earlier displayed with his Battalion, and the award of a C.B., C.B.E. and D.S.O. would seem to be a most appropriate estimate of his great work with this division.

On the departure of George Wood, Tom Molloy assumed command of the Fifty-Fourth. I stepped up to Second-in-Command, and Tony Bridge quitted his Adjutant's chair to take over "A" Company. Tom Hughes handed over "D" Company and moved into the vacancy left by the Adjutant.

Settling down after this game of general post, the Battalion continued to work and play hard during that August and September. "Night weeks" and long Battalion and Brigade exercises took most of the time, but our leisure hours were full of football and hockey tournaments and cricket matches and other athletic activities. We were determined to take full advantage of the excellent games facilities of this station. There was a first-class swimming bath at Trimulgherry, and we rashly invited the Carabiniers (thinking that it was a pretty safe sport in which to challenge a cavalry regiment) to a swimming meeting, only to be soundly and deservedly beaten.

Unconsciously anticipating the shape of things to come, I persuaded the Commanding Officer to allow me to lay on a forty-eighthour "dry-shod" landing exercise. Exercise "Griswold", played out among the peculiar rock formations and red earth of the Central Deccan, was the first of many such exercises that we were to carry out during the following year.

We celebrated Marabout Day with a ceremonial parade and a swimming gala, followed by an officers' dance to welcome the sisters of the 80th British General Hospital, thus starting a liaison which was to recur three years later, when the same hospital accompanied the British and Indian division to Japan.

After duty the troops took full advantage of the amenities of Secunderabad (amenities so outstanding that the General decided to establish his Divisional leave camp here on the racecourse) and, soon learnt, among other things, that the "Dodecanese are NOT repeat NOT two young ladies from Secunderabad".

But all good things come to an end, and none so speedily, so is our experience, as a sojourn in a good station, and in less than two months we were on our way again. The powers-that-be had decided that Secunderabad was to be a big casualty-reception area and our barracks were required for conversion into a hospital. Every other available square yard of suitable camping ground was earmarked for the newly raised Indian Armoured Division.

Half-way through September we left Graeme Gordon Wright, one of the reinforcement officers who had joined us shortly after our arrival in India, to hold the fort whilst the Battalion slipped back to the Poona area for a fortnight's "kindergarten" boating course on the huge lake at Kharakvasla, under the auspices of the newly formed Combined Training Centre (India). Our training as an assault division had started. "KV" was a good spot, and, unlike our experience in Pashan, we found that we could agree with the old "Koi Hais" of Poona, who claimed that this also was a favourite picnic spot in earlier, happier, peace-time days. Here, under the shadow of Sinn Garh the Lion Fort, the scene of one of Shivaji's most outstanding exploits, we practised the art of modern warfare —that is to say, as modern as the Chief Instructor, Major Frank Ingham Clark, of the Argylls, could make it with his very limited equipment and shortage of trained instructors. The passing-out exercise was based on the Bruneval raid, and with great gusto the Battalion worked their way across the lake in Fleming lifeboats and rescued the "scientist" from his "Nazi" guards, found by the school staff. The regatta at the end of the course was most successful. It was here that the Fifty-Fourth first really became acquainted with water, an element in which they were to train for many a long day.

Whilst we were at Kharakvasla (only one battalion could be accommodated at a time, and the Camerons were busy quelling Congress riots in Bezwada and the Worcesters were standing by ready to move), Brigadier Victor Hawkins arrived from a staff appointment in New Zealand to take over the Brigade. Ronny Cavendish, the Commanding Officer of the Worcesters, had been "standing in" during the past couple of months following the departure of Brigadier Aldous, who had brought the Brigade overseas. "The Hawk", who was a son of an ex-officer of the Regiment, the late Captain Montgomery Hawkins of Dorchester, was destined to train us and eventually lead the Brigade in action, until he was wounded towards the end of the Battle of Kohima.

The Hawk had only just time to concentrate his Brigade before taking them off on a big inter-brigade exercise, Exercise "Trek," planned to last a fortnight. The Battalion had exactly two hours on their return to Secunderabad before turning round and setting off to fight their way with the 5th Infantry Brigade across country to Ahmednagar, nigh on four hundred miles to the west. The new Brigadier led his Brigade with great éclat, and, to the joy of us all, seemed determined to hurry us along in mechanical transport whenever possible. What had promised at the outset to be a long test of endurance on our feet rapidly developed into one of the old familiar exercises of Yorkshire days, but on Indian roads.

We were all enthused by our new commander's spirit of "get cracking", and we rapidly closed the gap between us and the defending force found by the 4th Infantry Brigade, who, under the command of our old Commanding Officer, had set out from Ahmednagar to intercept us. On one occasion the Hawk was heard angrily to exclaim: "There are only two things between me and my objective—my own reconnaissance regiment and the umpires!" This was hardly fair to Major Sam Wheeler and "B" Squadron, 2nd Reconnaissance Regiment, who were admittedly slow but were just learning the limitations imposed on their large number of vehicles by the road conditions in the East. Brigadier Hawkins was not the kind of commander to be deterred by mere umpires, and on one occasion, when a certain pass was declared to be blocked, he called up the 208th Field Company, Royal Engineers, who hacked out a detour in no time at all. I should have hated to have been on the directing staff of Exercise "Trek".

As Secunderabad had been the high-light of our tour so far, so were the next two months to be the nadir. After the attractions of Secunderabad, with the privileges of free active service smoke rations and, for the officers, free messing (Deccan Area was, for some obscure reason, considered to be a field concessional area), the 5th Infantry Brigade took unkindly to the discomfort of the converted Indian lines in Stud Farm and a very distant and totally inadequate bazaar. Ahmednagar may have been an excellent onebattalion station in peace time, but was not designed to accommodate two infantry brigades. The 6th Infantry Brigade had already departed to Bombay on the next stage in combined-operation training and were shortly to depart for the Arakan, where they were to become involved in severe fighting before rejoining the Division some months later. Divisional Headquarters, having got two brigades concentrated at Ahmednagar and one in Bombay, promptly moved themselves to Poona. They couldn't have been more right!

Tours in indifferent, as much as in good, stations come to an end, even if unexpectedly, and on the 30th of November, as the Camerons were celebrating St. Andrew's Night, the Dorsets and the Worcesters slipped away to the Ahmedabad area, whither they had been called in aid of the Civil Power.

There is little of interest to recall during the trip to Anand. The year 1942 had been one of unrest in India, and Ahmedabad was a particularly bad area. It was imperative to collect the taxes, without any trouble if possible, and so the Brigade were called out to "show the flag". Actually all went surprisingly smoothly and the Battalion, far from being involved in any frightful Oriental goingson, were entertained royally and spent their first Christmas on this tour under "jungli" but certainly cheerful conditions.

Before we pass on to the next phase in our Odyssey, there are two matters worthy of record. The first was the birth of the Guerrilla (G.R.) Platoon, whose subsequent adventures will figure prominently in our narrative. Whilst at Ahmednagar the Brigade Commander had decreed that all rifle-company platoons in turn would carry out a hundred-mile trek in seven days on their own.

Excellent results were gained from this exceedingly practical form of training. We all felt, however, that we needed, in addition, a specialist platoon on the lines laid down by the present Chief of the Imperial General Staff[7] when he was commanding the XII Corps in Kent. These views were further endorsed by survivors of the Malayan campaign, who paid a very high tribute to the "tiger" patrols furnished by battalions in that initial fight against the Japanese.

So, in Ahmednagar, was evolved the Guerrilla Platoon, which was to prove (under a variety of names) of such inestimable value to us when later we fought the Japanese in Burma. The original platoon, trained by Lieutenant Harold Jones, which made its maiden march across the ghats from Ahmednagar to Bombay in January, 1943, was the prototype of the platoon which was to more than earn its keep on operations just over a year later.

Secondly, just before the Battalion dashed off to Anand, a very strong representative party,[8] together with an equal number of the 2nd Norfolk Regiment under the command of Lieutenant-Colonel George Winter, paid a visit to the Mahratta Training Centre at Belgaum.

The visit was not only a reunion of "Norsets" themselves but both the Norfolks and the Dorsets took the opportunity of making their number with the Mahratta Training Centre, as the representative of the two Mahratta battalions with whom the British battalions had both been closely identified in the 6th Indian Infantry Division in the First World War. We took with us a composite silk flag of Norfolk yellow and Dorset green, superscribed in silver lace with our own pre-Cardwell regimental numbers (when the old Ninth Foot were East Norfolks and the Fifty-Fourth West Norfolks) and the pre-1922 Mahratta battalion numbers. This flag was presented to Colonel Cecil Strong, the Commandant of the Training Centre, at a ceremonial parade held in our honour, and now hangs in their headquarters mess.

---

7 Monty
8 The Dorsets' party consisted of Lieutenant-Colonel T. P. L. Molloy, Major O. G. W. White, Lieutenant (Quartermaster) F. J. Edwards, R.S.M. Smith, C.S.Ms. Warren and Doughty, C.Q.M.S. Penn, Sergeants Cooper, D.C.M., Heathman and Osmond, Corporal West and Privates Valler (our oldest soldier) and Walch.

Colonel Strong and his officers laid on a great reception for the "Norset" party. We were given a demonstration of the Malkamb Pole, the national sport of the Mahrattas, and introduced to their folk dances, such as the Legim. This was followed by the beating of "Retreat," at which ceremony the colours of our "allied" battalions (the battalions themselves being on active service overseas) were marched on to parade in our honour.

This "tamasha" was followed by a most pleasant and very hectic guest night, and on the next day we were shown round the Centre and allowed to inspect every stage of a Mahratta soldier's life. This, as we saw it, was the complete life span, as the regiment provides facilities for its sepoys literally from the cradle to the grave.

We were subsequently to see a great deal of the Mahrattas during our training in the Belgaum forests, and were to continue to be most grateful for the interest and help afforded us by Colonel Strong and his officers. It is sad to relate that, except for a very brief contact, we were not to encounter a battalion of our "allied" regiment in action.

The first ten months of 1943 were to be spent by the 5th Infantry Brigade entirely on combined operational training. Not all this training was carried out by the sea, and as time went on there developed an increasing jungle bent to our exercises. Just as we soon became adepts at practising J.E.W.Ts., or Jungle Exercises Without Trees, so a mere matter of being in a camp a hundred and fifty miles distant from the sea did not prevent us from undertaking many a long and arduous "dry-shod" landing exercise.

Our life became nomadic in the extreme, moving through the whole gamut of good, indifferent and frankly frightful pastures as the months passed. Kipling's acquaintance with the Fifty-Fourth was confined, as far as I know, to his excellent description of the voyage of the Sarah Sands, but had he known us in 1943 he could not have written more appropriate lines than those he had used many years before to describe a regiment of foot on the move through India:

"We're marching on relief over Injia's sunny plains,
A little front of Christmas time an' just be'ind the Rains;
Ho! get way, you bullock-man, you've 'eard the bugle blowed,
There's a regiment a-coming down the Grand Trunk Road."

Probably our three pleasantest months of the war were spent on the coast north of Bombay in the hot weather from January to March, 1943. It would be hard to find any place in the world where combined-operations training could be so pleasantly carried out than on Juhu and Aksa beaches at that time of the year. We worked extraordinarily hard in, out and on the water, and varied the hours spent by the sea with intensive exercises across the mud-flats and into the hinterland of the Bombay Peninsula. The Battalion became wonderfully fit and capable of any exertions, but it was perhaps in the water that they put up their greatest feat, when, after three months at Juhu, I was able to report to the Brigadier that 98 per cent, of the Battalion could swim.

In January Tom Molloy was promoted full colonel to be Second-in-Command of the Brigade, and I was appointed to command in his place.

Throughout this combined-operations training we were always working against time. Life was one constant rush to reach the next stage of training; and each stage was concluded by some gruelling exercise in which the Battalion or Brigade were tried out in some aspect of this new role.

For the first few months we came under command for training of General Festing's 36th Indian Infantry Division, which at this stage consisted only of a headquarters to co-ordinate the combined-operations training in India. These headquarters were the embryo of that famous division which was to fight its way south from Myitkina in the following year, and was subsequently to be amalgamated with the 2nd Division at the conclusion of hostilities.

From Juhu we made our way along the Bombay main watersupply pipe-line (on one of the hottest marches it has ever been my experience to do) thirty-six miles inland to an appalling camp at Bhiwandi below the Western Ghats. Bhiwandi ranks above even Stud Farm as a camp not to return to if possible. I have seen it recorded in an old book on the customs of the white man in India that in the very early days of the East India Company the favourite pastime was to hire a boat and be rowed up the Thana River to Bhiwandi. Maybe to do it that way, with a cask of rum under the seat and a horde of servants to attend to one's every want, may have some attraction—but we could find not one redeeming feature in this pestilential camp tucked away under the hillside. Our only relief was the number of times we were called away from the camp area to continue our training. Two of these exercises involved a trip out to sea for thirty-six hours or more on board the El-Hind, in order to accustom the Battalion to conditions on board an assault ship. These exercises were much enjoyed, and the Battalion put up a very spirited performance on the second of these expeditions, Exercise "Viking", which was considered to be the Brigade's "passing-out" test at the conclusion of their sea training.

In May we had a very pleasant interlude in the hills, moving by comparatively easy stages to Mahableshwar in the heart of the Shivaji mountain country. This was our first approach to anything like jungle, and the Brigadier insisted that we lived, as far as accommodation went, literally on the country. Four tents, immediately appropriated for stores, were the Battalion's allotment, and we all lived in the bushes. All very pleasant until the rains broke prematurely, and Mahableshwar collects three to four hundred inches between June and October. Our brief was a bit conflicting: on the one hand we were expected to get the fullest possible value out of our short stay in this "jungle" area, and on the other hand the General appreciated the recuperative value of this period in the hills after the four months' extremely hard work in the heat of the coastal plain. The result was a compromise; we trained hard from early in the morning until tiffin, and during the remainder of the day played hard at the variety of sports offered during this hill station's brief season. Socially our cricket team, dance band and the Corps of Drums were in great demand for the many functions which the normal visitors managed to cram into these last few weeks before the rains would wash them all down the hill again.

It will always be a marvel to me how the men, and especially the Corps of Drums, who were all ordinary duty men when not drumming, managed under these most "jungli" conditions to keep their best suit of khaki drill clean, pressed and dry. There was nowhere to store these precious garments other than under the dhurries on which their owners slept huddled under their groundsheet bivouacs, reinforced by a covering of the local scrub.

Whilst at Mahableshwar we, trying to profit from the lessons of Malaya, made serious attempts to practise a code of bugle signals to assist us in keeping control in the jungle. Daily

> *"The bugle horn on moor and fell*
> *Was heard continually"*

as I, accompanied by the ever-faithful Private Cripps, tried to locate the companies training in the jungle. We had developed a whole system of signals, based on obsolete routine calls, of which probably the most satisfactory to hear (other than the "Stand Fast" or the "No Parade") was our "success" signal, the old "2nd cookhouse" call of "Pick 'em up, pick 'em up, hot potatoes", used when a company had gained its objective.

Early in June we were virtually washed down the ghats in a torrential downpour and came to rest at what was in effect yet another virgin camp. "Gosh, the Dorsets do pick 'em!" could be heard all round the camp as we took stock of yet another Dorset home set in a wilderness of bare cotton soil, miles from anywhere.

Strangely enough, after we had settled in and celebrated Plassey Day with due pomp and ceremony, and a great deal of gaiety, the Battalion enjoyed Gulunchi Camp, though there was, except for the view, no redeeming feature, other than that we were a hundred and twenty miles from Divisional Headquarters and other outside spheres of interference. The 5th Infantry Brigade were living up to their reputation as an "independent brigade".

A feature of these camps, apart from signing all roads in battalion areas by street names peculiar to the county of the battalion concerned (for example, the space outside my orderly room was always "Top o' Town"), was the very necessary fatigue of clearing stones from the ground to make playing fields of a kind. The men loathed this fatigue for some reason. In one battalion in another brigade the commanding officer overcame this prejudice by selecting as his lesson on church parade the passage from Ecclesiastes which claims that there is "a time to cast away stones and a time to gather stones together"; after hearing the words of the prophet the troops accepted this as sufficient authority, and Michael West, the Commanding Officer concerned, had no more trouble on that score.

Whilst at Gulunchi we were given an allotment of the Wanowrie Ranges at Poona, familiar to R.S.M. Delara and many another Old Comrade of an earlier age. Having classified the Battalion on the ranges, I decided to hold a real "peace-time" Regimental rifle meeting, with competitions framed, as near as we could remember them, to the Bisley matches of old. The Brigadier considered it a complete waste of time. With all deference to a very much more experienced officer, I still do not agree: the one lesson we learnt very quickly in combat against the Japanese was that we beat him because we were the better marksmen. If the Japanese could have only learnt to shoot he would have been an even more formidable enemy. Here was a rifle meeting, designed to give the expert shots the best opportunity and to encourage the unknown marksman, and it was frowned upon as being too "peace-time". Suffice it to say that the Quartermaster, Teddy Edwards, carried the field and retained his position as champion shot in the Battalion which title he had first won before the war on the ranges near Aldershot. He was closely followed by John Bowles in the individual match, and the rifle companies had a very close competition in the team shoot, whilst the open matches provided keen competition from all units of the Brigade Group.

Training at Gulunchi was continued and varied. The companies went out on trek and every available man, who it was feared might be sitting on his backside in camp, was dragged out on periodic route marches, and it was here that we really got down and studied the art of fighting with tanks. Our first collaborators were the 149th Tank Regiment (The King's Own Yorkshire Light Infantry). No sooner had we carried out tactical exercises without troops with their officers and practised climbing on to a Valentine in every conceivable position than they were withdrawn and we welcomed Major Jack Oakey and his squadron from the 150th Tank Regiment (late York and Lancaster) to our fold. It was not until we were in action that we found that, after all, it was Major Ezra Rhodes and his "B" Squadron of the 149th Tank Regiment who were to support us, and whose Sergeant Waterhouse was going to make all the difference between success and failure on the tennis court of the District Commissioner's bungalow at Kohima. Such is the way of preparation for co-operation between the arms.

I do not propose to confuse the reader by delving once more into that permanent headache of all commanding officers, the officers' state, or, as we called it, the order of battle. Suffice it to say that when Lieutenant-Colonel R. H. Linklater arrived from the United Kingdom at about this time to take over command, the Battalion corps of officers presented a very different picture from the gathering which had grouped itself together outside the mess at Banbury for a farewell photograph about fifteen or sixteen months earlier. One reference, however, I must make, and that is to Major Derek Gill Davies, of the Royal Engineers, who had been attached to us since the previous February. Derek, a Territorial officer, had earned the Distinguished Service Order in Norway and had been encouraging the Chinese, through the medium of his guerrillas, to take a more active interest in the war ever since. We, of course, taking the purely infantry view, had assumed that he had joined the Fifty-Fourth to do some honest soldiering, and I would like to place on record how extremely grateful I was, and still am, to Derek for the support he gave me during those long and at times very tiring months. He took over "C" Company and made them do things that even that versatile company had never imagined they could contrive. It was a great blow to us all when, after an eight-month attachment, Derek found the call of the wild too much and returned to his more unorthodox forms of warfare.

This period ended with Exercise "Swordfish," the final passing-out test in combined operations for the 2nd Infantry Division. We all hoped that this was to be the rehearsal for the real thing. The whole exercise had been planned to conform as nearly as possible to a certain part of the coast, further east, which was still in enemy hands. Prior to "Swordfish" we had all marched many miles and spent many a weary hour rehearsing every move—it was a serious blow when we returned to camp and heard that once again the calls of the European theatre were too strong and that the "Supremo" had been overbid in his demands for the landing craft and other accessories essential to the success of our expedition. Once more we had to be resigned to the old business of "They also serve who only stand and wait", though not for the first time for the 2nd Infantry Division the word "train" might easily be substituted for "wait".

We were, however, given no time to sit back and ruminate. Within a very short time of our return from Exercise "Swordfish" the Brigade were on their way south to carry out six weeks' intensive jungle-warfare training in the forests south of Belgaum. In point of fact, the actual area chosen for this first visit to the forests of South India was not nearly so difficult as that encountered in the New Year, but the hardships experienced by all ranks were considerably greater than those usually encountered on service. Three factors ensured this. In the first place, the medical authorities, worried by the incidence of malaria among troops training in India, were most concerned about this project of dispatching troops to a known malarial area. As a result, we had all to submit to the most stringent anti-malarial restrictions which not only greatly restricted our activities but seriously impeded our physical operations as fighting soldiers. Secondly, the Hawk was determined that his Brigade should carry out this period of training under the most stringent operational routine, and as a result we were subjected to a rule of life far more rigorous than we ever found to be the case in action. Finally, it was the era of the "box". At this time, the "box" ruled the jungle war. I was away on a course at the Senior Officers' School at Poona at the time, and found the same doctrine preached there. Everything would be all right, it was argued, when fighting the Japanese, as long as one took up a position at night, or for a series of nights, in a "box". Tactical considerations, such as ground, did not always seem to matter so long as the "box" was designed and laid out on precise geometrical dimensions. The designer of this mathematical exactitude was expected, in those days, to be the wretched commanding officer, who, after having had a strenuous day commanding the battalion through thick jungle, was supposed, with the help of a team of flagmen and a prismatic compass, to lay out a battalion area for the night with the absolute precision of a surveyor.

By Christmas this visit to the jungle had come to an end, and for the first time for many weeks "operational" discipline was relaxed when the Brigade moved to Belgaum for Christmas and our old friends the Mahrattas extended the services of their limited cantonment to the utmost to accommodate a hungry and very thirsty British brigade with its ancillary troops.

The next visit to the jungle was much more successful. By the last day of January, 1944, when the Brigade once again set out on their long and weary journey from the Ahmednagar area to the forests south of Belgaum, all hopes for immediate action were over. The great planning conferences in Bombay had ended in a stalemate only since equalled by a meeting of Foreign Ministers on European affairs. The Supremo had been told definitely that there was just no chance of his launching his long-wished-for offensive, and, to make assurance doubly sure, every conceivable piece of useful equipment had been withdrawn and hurried to Europe. But down in the jungle south of Belgaum, in that impenetrable tract of big-game forest, far thicker and more exacting than anything we were subsequently to encounter in Assam, the 5th Infantry Brigade had profited by the lessons of their recent visit. We were determined now to practise the art of warfare as applied to the individual soldier, the sub-unit and the junior non-commissioned officer. The Brigadier decided to relax the operational routine imposed on the last visit: the battalions stood-to at dawn and dusk only twice a week, and an administrative area, where offices were set up and a canteen was established outside the perimeter "black-out," was permitted. Along hurried Raschid Khan, who once had contracted to serve the Fifty-Fourth when my father was Adjutant, before the Kaiser's War, and in no time at all the troops off duty were filling themselves with "egg banjoes" and other delicacies. Before ten days had passed a cinematograph had penetrated our jungle and had given us a most satisfactory evening's entertainment.

Great days those last couple of months at Jagalpet. We did an immense amount of training, albeit every company commander ensured that his day's exercise ended on the bank of that truly delightful river where, despite the presence of mugger, we all managed to contrive a daily bathe. At Brigade level the Hawk set his staff to working out the ways by which a brigade group, with all its weapons, could reduce a strongly held Japanese bunker position. Little did we think as the demonstration attack went in that in a month's time the Camerons would be the first battalion in the 2nd Division to prove the efficacy of this form of attack against the Japanese.

On the field firing range we had a serious accident which cost us for many months the services of Harold Jones, and for the whole campaign the Carrier Officer, Jock Wilson. It was fortunate that the Medical Officer and Dick Purser, slightly wounded by this unfortunate 2-inch mortar accident, were not more seriously incommoded.

At the beginning of March Lieutenant-Colonel Linklater was posted to a staff job and was succeeded by Lieutenant-Colonel R. S. McNaught, a Royal Scots Fusilier with a very great deal of service. "Jock" McNaught arrived straight out from the United Kingdom and must have found us very "jungli".

We hadn't seen a pamphlet for two years and had acquired the art of living in the jungle from sheer practical experience. We had been through the whole gamut of training—had been experimented upon with every conceivable form of dress and equipment, and had practised every form of living, from existing on roots to the manufacture of even the most essential toilet accessories from bamboo. He must, however, have found a terrific spirit in the Battalion. We knew our strength, and were raring to get at the enemy. Some time later, after he had left us for a more senior command, we were chatting in my command post in Burma and he said that the most extraordinary thing about the Dorsets, when he took them over, was that no one ever seemed to be put on a charge. I took that as a great compliment. By this time we had been abroad for two years, and everyone knew his job and did it. We were, despite the departure of many an old and familiar figure, virtually the same Battalion which had come abroad two years earlier. There was, it is true, in the jungle very little opportunity for infringements of discipline, and crime, as must have been familiar to Jock McNaught, recently out from commanding a battalion at home, was at this time virtually unknown.

Shortly after Jock McNaught had taken over we had an opportunity long awaited to return the hospitality of the Mahrattas. Lieutenant-Colonel Isaacs brought over a team of officers and Viceroy's commissioned officers from the Training Centre. They spent a day with us, studying the latest methods of jungle warfare, and departed after a hilarious evening in the various company messes to the accompaniment of the Mahratta war-cry: "*Chhatra pati Shivaji Maharaj-ki-jai.*" This was our last real contact with the Mahrattas until after the war, when, as we were forming up for Japan with the 1st

Battalion of that regiment, we once again renewed an alliance that has now survived two world wars.

Suddenly, in the middle of our preparations to send the Battalion on leave, after this long and gruelling six months of continual jungle training, the order that we had all been waiting for since quitting Dunkirk arrived: "Move Ahmednagar immediately and mobilize for active service." Those may not have been the exact words, but the meaning was clear. In no time at all the Battalion were on the move. All feeling of staleness and "browned-offedness" was immediately dissipated—we were on the job at last. Within a fortnight the Battalion had moved to their base at Ahmednagar, re-formed, mobilized and were concentrated in action stations in Assam, over two thousand miles to the east. Everything went smoothly: Teddy Edwards, the Quartermaster, was in his seventh heaven as the gates of the Arsenal at Kirkee and the ordnance depots of Western India were thrown open to him. But for the dilatoriness of the Indian railways, to whom a troop train, even under the conditions of extreme urgency, is always fair play as something to be shunted into a siding, we would have been there quicker. As it was, the 5th Infantry Brigade were the first on the scene, the 4th Infantry Brigade arrived by air, and the 6th Infantry Brigade followed us up over that overstrained Bengal and Assam railway. At long last our chance for action had come, and for an account of our campaign against the Japanese we must turn to the ensuing chapters.

Combined Operations training, Juhu

2ND DORSET OFFICERS, MOBILIZATION FOR OVERSEAS, APRIL 1942

Back Row   Capt. H. P. K. Fretts, Lieut. Dupont, Lieut. Randall, Lieut. Davies+, Lieut. Jones, Lieut. Crowther, Capt. Chamberlin (R.A.M.C.), Lieut. Deane+, Lieut. Ward, Lieut. Giffard, Lieut. Haycock.

Second Row   Lieut. Turner, Lieut. Wilson, Lieut. Rolfe*, Lieut. Chettle, Lieut. Hodder, Lieut. Prebble, Lieut. Halahan, Lieut. O'Driscoll, Lieut. Marrs, Lieut. Govett, Lieut. Boyle, Lieut. Highett, Lieut. Morice+, Capt. Bowles+.

Sitting   Capt. Howard, Capt. Giles, Capt. Claxton (R.A.Ch.D.), Capt. & Adj. Bridge, Major Baynes, Major Molloy (2 i/c), Lieut.-Colonel G. N. Wood, Major O. G. W. White, Capt. Molyneux, Capt. Watts, Capt. Hughes, Capt. Edwards, Capt. Purser+.

+ Killed   * Did not accompany the Battalion.

INDIA, 1942-1944

Training with Fleming lifeboats, Karakyasla Lake, Poona, September 1942

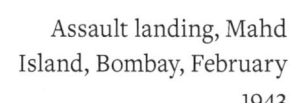

Assault landing, Mahd Island, Bombay, February 1943

Painting road signs, Gulurchi Camp, July 1943

Major D. McLeod-Baynes unveils Dorset bronze, Fort St George, Madras

NORSETS

Visit of Norsets (2nd Norfolk and 2nd Dorset) to Mahratta Light Infantry Training Centre, Belgaum, November, 1942

TWO COMMANDING OFFICERS OF THE 2ND DORSETS

Major-General G.N. Wood
C.B., C.B.E., D.S.O., M.C.,
1941-42

Brigadier R. S. McNaught,
D.S.O., 1944

I have untied against you the club-footed vines—
I have sent in the Jungle to swamp your lines!
The trees—the trees are on you!

—**KIPLING.**

Dorset Memorial, Kohima

CHAPTER FIVE

THE ADVANCE TO KOHIMA

*The grand old Duke of York
He had ten thousand men,
He marched them up to the top of the hill
And marched them down again.*

[*Author's Note* — Throughout this story I will try to simplify, as far as possible, the duplication of place-names. For example, I will always refer to the all-weather two-way road from Dimapur through Kohima to Imphal as the Manipur Road and not the Imphal Road. Likewise, I will always refer to the base of Dimapur as such and not by its peace-time name of Manipur Road!

Milestone (MS) references north of Imphal are given from Dimapur.]

THE TIMELY ARRIVAL OF the XXXIII Corps and the speedy concentration of the 2nd Infantry Division in the Dimapur—Jorhat area were achieved only just in time. Early in March the Japanese Army of Invasion of India, consisting of three Japanese infantry divisions and two brigades of the Indian National Army (former Indian Army prisoners of war forced into fighting with the Japanese), had crossed the River Chindwin with the object of capturing the great British Indian forward base of Imphal and the General Headquarters base of Dimapur and cutting the Bengal and Assam railway which formed the supply line to General Stilwell's forces in the north-east.

By capturing Imphal and Dimapur, and gaining possession of the all-weather Manipur Road, the Japanese would have found themselves well stocked and in an excellent position to interfere most seriously with our air bases in the Brahmaputra Valley upon the continued existence of which our air supply to China over "the Hump" so greatly depended. The loss of these bases could not but have had the most serious political repercussions.

The Japanese Army of Invasion had been subjected to most intense propaganda by means of which their authorities preached a "holy war". By minimizing the opposition likely to be expected and leading their troops to expect overwhelming air superiority, the rosiest prospects of an early and easy victory were painted, provided only that they pressed on fast.

The results of this propaganda in the initial phases must have been most satisfactory to the Japanese High Command. Their advance has been described by one observer as having the relentless momentum of a colony of ants on the move. In the south they had, by the end of March, got two battalions behind the 17th Indian Division, who were withdrawing from Tiddim to Imphal, and had cut the Manipur Road a few miles north of Imphal. Our own particular adversaries were the Japanese 31st Infantry Division, and their extraordinary advance merits some greater attention before we can continue with our story.

The Japanese 31st Infantry Division, with a first-class operational record behind them, crossed the River Chindwin on the 15th of March in the area of Homalin in eight columns, on a forty-mile front. The division at this time were composed of the Japanese 58th, 124th and 138th Regiments. The 138th Regiment on the right were directed on Kohima, with orders "at one fell swoop to fall on Kohima and annihilate the enemy on that front".

The 58th Japanese Regiment, moving farther to the south through Ukhrul in conjunction with the 15th Division, were subsequently ordered "to charge towards Mao Songsang". Some weeks later, in the middle of June, we ourselves passed through Mao Songsang, the highest point on the Manipur Road, pretty fast, on our feet, when pursuing the Nip, but I still doubt whether "charge" is the appropriate word to apply to movement on foot in those mountains. The 124th Japanese Regiment, who were subsequently to be our especial adversaries at Kohima, apparently crossed the River Chindwin four days behind the other regiments, in divisional reserve.

These astounding Japanese moved so fast against opposition that in under three weeks they had covered a hundred miles of some of the thickest and nearly the most mountainous country in the world and had secured a foothold in Kohima.

On the right the 138th Regiment, having encountered the 161st Indian Infantry Brigade, the 1st Assam Regiment and elements of "V" Force, had, as I say, occupied part of Kohima by the 4th of April, and during the night of the 5th/6th of April had cut the Manipur Road between Kohima and Dimapur at MS45 (one mile below Kohima). Meanwhile, the 58th Regiment on the left had, by sheer weight of numbers and after the fiercest resistance, overrun the 50th Indian Parachute Brigade at Sangshak (the latter had been doing some quiet training in the jungle area when the Nip invasion started). This regiment then proceeded to cut the Manipur Road at Tuphema at MS69, where the Somra track joins the road a few miles south of Mao Songsang. From there they divided, two battalions moving north along the main road to join in the Kohima battle whilst the third plunged further into the undergrowth making for Khonoma, about six miles due west of Kohima.

In a surprisingly short time, then, we see that the Japanese had not only achieved one of the more famous advances in the history of warfare but had arrived at their objective of Kohima, and having cut the Manipur Road to the north were even now continuing to encircle the garrison of Kohima and apparently pressing on towards their main objective of Dimapur and the Assam railway.

At this stage we must pause to consider a new figure who has arrived on the scene and whose actions will not only have a very direct bearing on, but one might say will govern, the activities of the Dorsets for the next thirteen months.

General "Monty" Stopford, the Commander of the XXXIII Indian Corps, had paid his first visit to the Battalion in January, 1944, shortly after his arrival to take over command of the Corps. He won our hearts immediately when he was able to give us up-todate and intimate news of our many friends in the 4th and 5th Battalions of the Regiment which had been in his XII Corps in Kent.

On the 21st of March General Stopford had been ordered, as I have described, to prepare his Corps Headquarters and the 2nd Infantry Division for immediate service in the East, whilst he himself, with his senior staff officers and heads of services, had flown to Comilla to be briefed. By this time in the war senior British commanders must have been getting quite used to being presented with unenviable situations, but surely no corps commander since the withdrawal from Burma could have been presented with such an unpromising task as that which faced the Commander of the XXXIII Corps on arrival at Headquarters, Fourteenth Army, in Comilla late in March, 1944.

The Japanese situation I have given. On our side the IV Corps were invested and completely isolated in Imphal, and strong enemy columns were hurrying north to capture Dimapur and cut the vital railway.

A word about our own troops. Corps Headquarters, who were travelling across India in conjunction with the 2nd Dorsets, had not previously taken the field and for some time had to overcome their "teething troubles" in close proximity to the enemy. The 161st Indian Infantry Brigade had been flown in from the 5th Indian Division in the Arakan and put under the command of 202 Lines of Communication

Area for the defence of Kohima and Dimapur. On arrival this brigade had been deployed on a thirtymile front south and east of Kohima. One battalion was already in contact at Maram (MS80) with the enemy, who had cut the road in that area. In addition, the 1st Assam Regiment were in Kohima and the 1st Burma Regiment were in Dimapur. The former had already fought some stout delaying actions on the Jessami track before withdrawing on Kohima.

The Corps Commander was given very definite tasks which were to govern all future operations in this area. It would be well to state this charter before we leave the realms of Corps and plunge with the Battalion into the undergrowth. General Stopford was told first and immediately to prevent Japanese infiltration or penetration into the Brahmaputra or Surma Valleys or the Lushai Hills. Secondly, to open the Manipur Road as lines of communication to the IV Corps. Finally, to be prepared to move to the assistance of the IV Corps and to help in all possible ways to destroy the enemy west of the River Chindwin.

This is not a history of the XXXIII Indian Corps, but the reader will, I hope, see how this redoubtable commander so inspired his newly formed and constantly changing Corps, composed of many and varied nations and creeds that, despite their unpromising "takeover", they had within the short period of thirteen weeks carried out all three of the General's initial tasks.

The General realized that the safety of Dimapur and Kohima depended on a race between the speed of the Japanese advance and the rate at which reinforcements could be rushed across India by rail and air.

At this moment Dimapur was vital, and owing to the few troops available the 161st Brigade were called back and concentrated to guard the Nichuguard Defile, about eight miles to the south-east of Dimapur. Kohima had perforce to be left practically defenceless with only the Assam Regiment, the Shere Regiment (State levies, stout enough men but indifferently officered) and the staffs and patients of the hospitals and convalescent depots to act as garrison.

With the arrival of the 5th Brigade of the 2nd Division in the first few days of April, the 161st Brigade were freed to attempt to reoccupy Kohima. By then, unhappily, it was too late. Only the 4th Royal West Kents managed to get a footing within the Kohima defences before the Japanese finally blocked the road. For fifteen long days this splendid battalion put up a magnificent resistance until relieved by the 6th Brigade, but more of this later.

Before continuing the story of the Battalion it is necessary at this point to say a few words on the topography of the strange land in which the 54th found themselves prepared to embark on their latest operation.

We were in the jungle. Views have become so mixed on jungle, and indeed jungles vary so considerably, that it is difficult to give an apt general description. Perhaps the best way is to compare the jungle with a very beautiful woman, the pin-up dream girl in full technicolour, cool, alluring, beautiful and attractive in the heat to look at but, once approached and negotiated with, full of the greatest possibilities of danger and death to the unwary. This simile is particularly apt because, like the figure of the pin-up girl, the jungle is never flat.

Communications are by Western standards impossible, and to the jungle warrior anything from a native to an elephant may have to be used as a form of transport. It was by no means unusual to employ one's Bren-gun carriers either in their proper role or merely as a means of transport, with one's fighting echelon of bullock carts and "B" Echelon consisting of native porters.

A glance at the map will show the layout of this little-known corner of the world. Dimapur lies in the Dhansiri Valley at an altitude of three to four hundred feet, as hot and unpleasantly sticky as any other tropical land at that height above sea-level. From Kohima to Imphal runs the man-made all-weather Manipur Road.

It was only during the war and by the unexampled efforts of the teagarden coolies that this little-used one-way road was built into a huge two-way road, capable of bearing the lines of communication traffic of a whole army.

Kohima, a second-class hill station, lies at MS46 at about five thousand feet, whence the road continues to ascend a further fifteen hundred feet to Mao Songsang, after which it descends to the Imphal Plain over the last sixty-five miles of its course.

The rains are a very great factor when campaigning in this country. The Japanese never expected us to fight through the rains, whilst they themselves hoped to be tucked away into monsoon billets before the weather broke in June and had made no preparations to fight on during this season—a lack of foresight that they were bitterly to regret.

We left the Fifty-Fourth at the end of the last chapter climbing stiffly out of their cramped railway carriages and plunging immediately into the jungle at Bokajan. The significance of this small village, with its one railway halt, was that it stood at the junction of the Merema track and the main road north from Dimapur, a mere thirty-six miles from Kohima for any force foolhardy enough to attempt its passage. Also at

Bokajan was an important railway bridge which carried this vital railway over the River Dhansiri. This branch of the Bengal and Assam railway, designed for light traffic among the tea gardens of Assam, achieved a notoriety and importance in this war far above the ideas of its original planners or the powers of its personnel to maintain. One of the earlier decisions of the Supreme Commander, Lord Louis Mountbatten, had been to arrange for United States Army transportation personnel to take over the railway entirely from Parbatipur onwards in order to ensure that it functioned at all.

Of the many jungles we have encountered I would say unhesitatingly that the Bokajan species was the worst. It was wet and prickly, dank and gloomy, and it was not only rank but stank. By the grace of God and the Japanese, we were there for only a very short time.

Immediately on our arrival the Dorsets were called upon to join in a riotous game of general post. We know now under what immense difficulties the Corps and Divisional Commanders were labouring. Units and formations arrived piecemeal, often according to no known programme, by land, river and air. To the infantry it appeared, as I have said, to be a colossal game of general post with apparently endless moves. It was not too bad whilst we were still on the flat, but as we approached Kohima, when an order to send a company to a nearby village involved a climb of fifteen hundred to two thousand feet under very full loads, the game lost some of its attraction.

Rumour, of course, was rife: very early on we began to acquire the sense of just how much faith to place in a native report on the number of "japaniwallahs" who had passed through their village. After devious countings on fingers and toes, much rubbing of hairless bellies and the utterance of guttural cries, we eventually (after we had divided the result by ten) got the idea that a Jap patrol was near by. Intelligence summaries and sitreps often made as amusing reading as the news pages of some of our more popular national tabloids.

On the 5th of April, within thirty-six hours of our arrival, the Battalion began to be dispersed over the countryside. This dispersion, as I have indicated, was the most prominent feature of our life at this time. Except for the night of the 10th of April and the advance by mechanical transport to MS32 the following morning, the Battalion were never to be concentrated for anything more than a few hours at a time until our withdrawal to Dimapur for refit on the 15th of May, after the capture of the District Commissioner's bungalow.

On this day the Commanding Officer took Tactical Headquarters, "C" Company and the Carrier, Mortar and G.R. Platoons, together

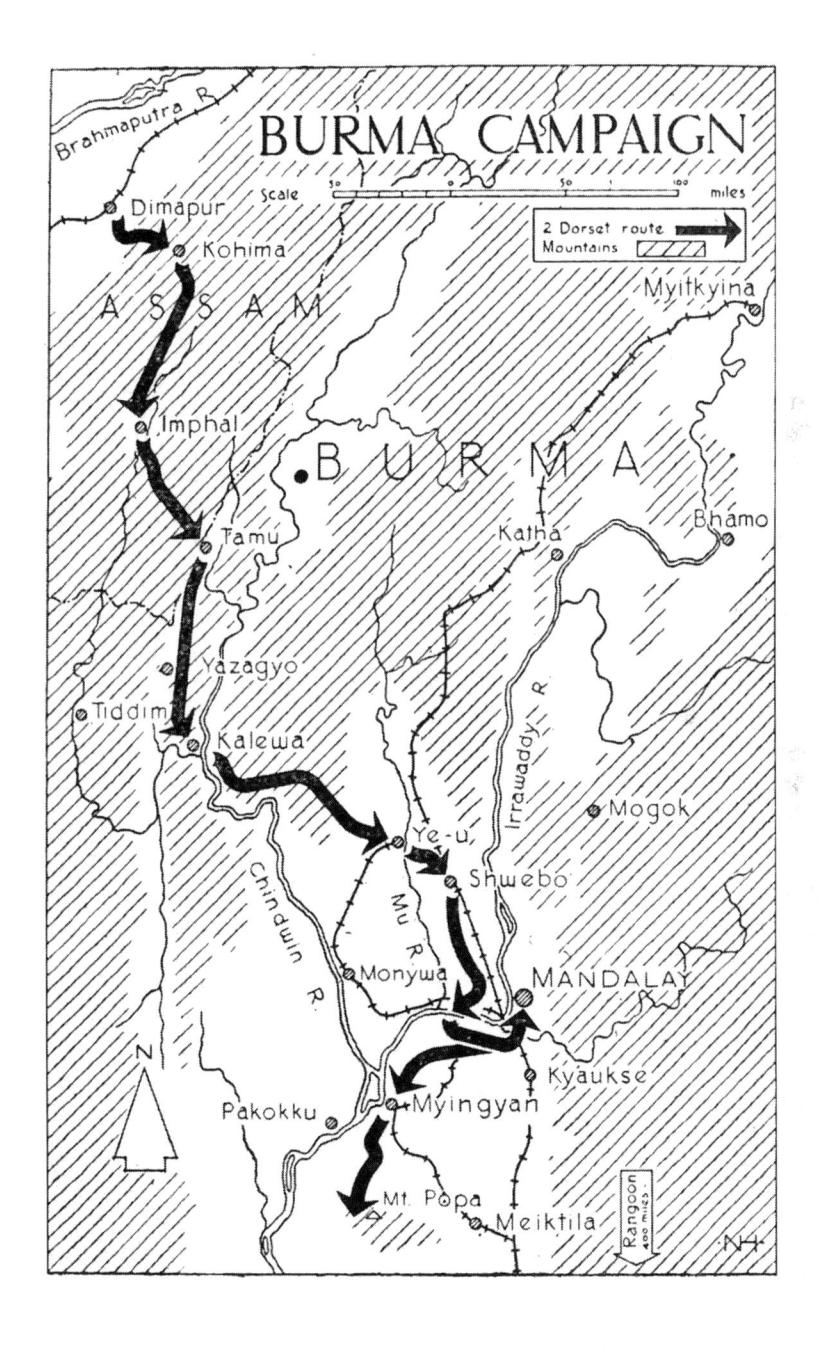

THE ADVANCE TO KOHIMA

with "B" Company, 2nd Manchesters, under command, and set up a block on the Bokajan—Merema track at an important nullah crossing about ten miles to the east of Bokajan.

It seemed that the Japanese were most likely to come romping down this track at any moment, and Dick Castle set his company to dig the most formidable redoubt. It has always been the secret regret of this detachment that they never had to fight in this position. The men dug with a will and it would have been an exceedingly hard nut to crack. The need never arose owing mainly to the dilatoriness of the Jap commander, who, strangely enough, never exploited far beyond Kohima, and also to the fact, which the Japs presumably had discovered, that the famous Bokajan track had for long distances been washed away and was quite unmotorable. Even Private Turner, the Commanding Officer's jeep driver, who subsequently drove me over some most extraordinary tracks, admitted to being beaten. Whilst here, the detachment pushed out patrols and gained much valuable operational experience in this terrain. This view, however, was not shared by the Adjutant, Graeme Gordon Wright, after he had been dragged up some immense mountain by his agile Commanding Officer on a visit to a Gurkha unit.

Left behind at Bokajan, the days seemed to be quite full enough reorganizing the Brigade perimeter as more and more units and sub-units were pushed out on various tasks. On the 6th of April Colin Doran, who had joined us from Headquarters, 2nd Division, in February, took his platoon from "D" Company to Naojan, the next station eight miles north, and from there did some energetic and useful patrolling eastwards for fourteen-odd miles, through thick jungle to the Dayang River. Somewhere they found a man who made kukris, and the platoon eventually returned armed like Gurkhas.

The Worcesters had meanwhile left the Brigade perimeter and had taken over from the 161st Brigade at the Nichuguard Pass south-east of Dimapur. On about the 7th of April I had to dispatch "A" Company thirty miles to the north by rail to occupy the vital railway station at Jamguri and so relieve the Camerons, who were also required in the Nichuguard Defile.

By now the situation in the Kohima area had deteriorated greatly. The garrison were hanging on by the skin of their teeth; the 4th Royal West Kents had managed to get back into the garrison, but were promptly invested in a small perimeter on Garrison and Hospital Hills. On the 7th of April the Nip had cut the water supply and all water, as well as every other commodity, had to be dropped by air.

The remainder of the 161st Brigade had not been able to regain the Kohima perimeter and were themselves surrounded at Jotsoma when the Japanese established themselves firmly across the road at MS32 between them and Dimapur.

On the 9th of April General Grover was ordered to take over operational control of all troops forward of Dimapur and instructed to open the road to and clear Kohima before the monsoon, and secure it as a firm base for further offensive operations.

I well remember the night of the 9th/10th of April. It had been Easter Day and Padre Gus Claxton had had a busy day getting round his very scattered flock. At about ten o'clock that night I was called to Brigade and told that things were happening. I was ordered, in the absence of the Commanding Officer, to concentrate the Battalion by the next evening, handing over our commitments to various columns of the 23rd Brigade. That night I learnt the lesson never to leave a detachment commander to function without some form of staff. The Commanding Officer had taken with him all the important people, like the Adjutant and clerks and the best signallers, and it was only with the greatest trouble that we could find even a message pad, let alone anyone to take down orders.

Early on the 10th of April the 2nd Essex arrived. This battalion, of the 3rd Indian Division, was a long-range penetration battalion and carried a literally staggering amount of kit on their backs and relied for their transport on draught bullocks and pack animals. All that day we worked hard with a minimum of mechanical transport to concentrate the Battalion, now dispersed over a thirty-mile front, at Dimapur, fifteen miles to the south.

The Commanding Officer and Adjutant passed through in the afternoon in their scout car, which they had acquired, driven by Private Johnson, who was subsequently to perform great feats in this vehicle. They hurried straight on to Dimapur for a Brigade conference.

At 2200 hrs. that night I, with the last sub-units of the Battalion, drove into Chatham Lines at Dimapur to find the Commanding Officer's Order Group in full session.

Brigadier Hawkins's plan was to move the Worcesters forward at first light from Nichuguard against the Japanese road block about MS32 (it was quite on the cards that the enemy had even penetrated to MS27 or MS28 during the night), followed by the Camerons, after which the transport would return to Dimapur and ferry us forward.

This was for some of us another sleepless night. A lot can happen to the internal organization of a battalion which has been split up for a week, and the Battalion Headquarters staff were kept busy catching up on the final preparations for the move forward into action in the morning. On top of all this frantic concentration, Pryke Howard, our efficient P.R.I., had found time to unearth a month's beer ration for the Battalion. It may have been more: at any rate, having got the Battalion in and settled down, Jock McNaught, the Commanding Officer, agreed to let the Battalion have their beer. I always accused him afterwards of doing this with his tongue in his cheek. In the same breath he had told me that the Brigadier had decided to leave all Seconds-in-Command in Dimapur, "out of battle", and no one knew better than the Colonel on whom would devolve the responsibility of clearing up after a "night before action" beer issue.

At 1130 hrs. on the 11th April, 1944, the Battalion embussed on the main road outside Chatham Lines and moved off on what was to be one of the most stirring adventures in the history of the Regiment, the eight-hundred-mile advance into Burma by the overland route, an operation of war never before accomplished. Even at this date I feel again the keen disappointment which overwhelmed me as I stood watching the Battalion as they passed over Nichuguard bridge into action. I had stood so often on training as Commanding Officer or Second-in-Command checking the Fifty-Fourth past in their mechanical transport, but this was the second time in one war that I had had to stand and watch them move off into action. The rear details settled down to clear up the results of the hurried concentration. Under the leadership of Brigadier Shapland, Commander, 6th Infantry Brigade, which was arriving, we tried to make some sense of the defences of Dimapur. This was the only occasion during the whole of the campaign that the Brigade had enough men to run the L.O.B. system, and that was chiefly because at this stage we all had trained seconds-in-command, carrier platoons that we did not at this moment really know how to employ, and a wealth of mechanical transport, a legacy from our having come to India two years before fully equipped to European scale.

In this manner the 2nd British Infantry Division were, through no fault of the Corps Commander, committed to action piecemeal, the 5th Brigade on the ground, the 4th Brigade flying in, and the 6th Brigade following up along that same rail route by which we had come. Within a very short time the Saigon Radio announced to the world (despite our elaborate security precautions and removal of signs, it was impossible to disguise a whole division of white faces) that the "Dunkirk boys" were back again at last. Before many weeks were out they were decrying us in the most opprobious terms as "Churchill's butchers".

The 2nd Infantry Division arrived in Assam trained as fully as any formation in the Army, but lacking the experience which four years out of the battle had cost them. Surely, however, never before has a division re-entered the conflict at such a late stage in the proceedings with such a full complement of experienced and seasoned soldiers—men hardened and strengthened by long years of training and with the experience and physical conditioning of two years' foreign service behind them. What we lacked in battle experience we more than made up for in dash and determination, the legacy of long, hard and unceasing training at the hands of our commander, which was now to pay such a magnificent dividend.

It was not for nothing that we were to cause the Saigon Radio to change its tune.

To return to the Battalion as they wound their way up the mountain road towards Kohima. On arrival in the area of MS31 they debussed within sight of the enemy and marched into a battalion position on the left of the road. The Worcesters were in contact farther down the road.

"B" Company were dispatched almost immediately under Major Alan Watts to Kiruphema, a village about three thousand yards away to the south-east (on the right of the road) and about two thousand feet up. On entering the village at dusk after a long and arduous climb the company bumped an enemy patrol and sustained their first casualty, Lance-Corporal Nursaw, of the leading section, being killed.

At the same time, "D" Company, under Major Fretts, was dispatched about eight thousand yards to the north to the village of Khabvuma, also on top of a high hill. Paget Fretts halted at dusk about three thousand yards from the village and patrolled forward. An outstanding feature of this part of the world is the Naga hill village, which is invariably sited on the top of an almost inaccessible peak, and so right from the start we had cause to be grateful for our hard jungle training during the past few months. That night also an officers' patrol under Lieutenant Mayer, was sent forward down the main road towards Kohima.

The next day the Battalion, less "B" and "D" Companies, moved into the Brigade perimeter at Zubza, which was to be the Brigade base and administrative area for the whole of the Kohima battle.

The first real action of the Battalion against the Japanese took place on the 13th of April. On the previous day Paget Fretts had moved forward into Khabvuma village and occupied the village and the spur running due east. From this spur a track ran down into the deep nullah at the bottom of which flowed the Zubza River and thence it rose to

Cheswema on the opposite side of the valley. The Nip reacted strongly on the morning of the 13th of April and attacked "D" Company with vigour. The burden of the attack was taken by No. 17 Platoon, under the command of Sergeant Seale, who promptly showed the outstanding courage and ability which were to earn him promotion and distinction throughout the following year. Lance-Corporal Critchley, afterwards to become Medical Sergeant, displayed great gallantry in carrying out his duties as stretcher-bearer. After four hours the Japanese, unable to penetrate our position, withdrew. First blood to us. This action cost us the lives of Privates Calcott, Bash, Taylor and Atkins, the three lastnamed being stretcher-bearers. That evening the G.R. Platoon of the Royal Berks, who had joined the force earlier, went out on patrol. Whilst guiding them forward Paget Fretts was wounded by a Jap light machine gun. His loss was a serious one to us. He was outstanding as a company commander and the magnificent spirit shown by "D" Company from the start and maintained throughout the campaign was to a great extent due to his leadership and the high standard of training that he had maintained throughout the sixteen months he had been in command of the "Light" Company.

During the past few days both the 4th and 6th Infantry Brigades had been arriving in the area, the latter being flown in by air from Bangalore, whither, you will remember, they had been dispatched on leave earlier in March.

As soon as possible they were hurled into the battle, with the result that brigades, and even units, got hopelessly mixed up. We have seen how the affair at Khabvuma was fought by Dorsets and Royal Berks, and so it was throughout the area. On the 17th of April the Brigadier called all three battalion seconds-in-command forward, and on arrival at Zubza I found Jock McNaught trying to sort out his Battalion. For eight hours we were nearly all together, but early the next morning I was dispatched with "A" and "D" Companies on a mission under the command of the 6th Brigade in the Jotsoma area. The 6th Brigade had taken over from the 5th Brigade after the latter had attacked the enemy position at MS40 on the 15th of April, and the Hawk had motored forward to link up with Brigadier Warren, of the 161st Indian Infantry Brigade. No sooner had my detachment marched out than Jock was told to send another company to the 4th Brigade, and so, within twentyfour hours of my arrival, the Commanding Officer found himself having his first real rest for a week, with two of his companies away under his Second-in-Command with the 6th Brigade, one company with the 4th Brigade, whilst he himself with one company and the bulk of H.Q. Company remained under the 5th Brigade in the Zubza perimeter. Actually it was no real rest, because the Nip took the opportunity to jitter the Zubza area very heavily that night and both sides began to get very gay with their weapons in a sort of Brock's benefit during the middle of the Brigadier's conference.

Meanwhile, everyone was striving hard to get to Kohima and relieve the garrison, which was still holding out but in the direst straits. The state of the wounded in the hospital, many of whom had been left over from the initial evacuation, passed belief. For night after night the gallant garrison had withstood overwhelming attacks and were by now holding on to but a small part of the original Kohima defences, those around Summerhouse (Garrison Hill and the hospital area). The 161st Brigade, with the 1st Royal Welch Fusiliers under command, made a gallant attempt on the 16th and 17th to force their way into the garrison. However, it was not until the Durhams attacked Terrace Hill on the 19th of April that sufficient cover was gained to evacuate the wounded from the garrison. On the 20th of April the Royal Berks, under Lieutenant-Colonel Wilbur Bickford, moved forward and relieved the 4th Royal West Kents in the garrison.

I must spend a moment with the 4th Battalion The Royal West Kent Regiment, who, since the 6th of April, together with the 1st Assam Regiment and every available man of the garrison who could carry a musket, had withstood this remarkable siege against the overwhelming numbers and savagery of the Nipponese attacks.

We, who subsequently took our place in that perimeter, have a very good idea of what Lieutenant-Colonel Laverty and his men went through during these long days and nights whilst the 2nd Infantry Division and the remaining battalions of their own brigade were trying to get through to them.

As the battle moved forward so the Battalion gradually collected themselves together again, and by the 19th of April found themselves finally divorced from their parent brigade and committed to fight the Kohima battle as the guests of Brigadier John Shapland and his 6th Infantry Brigade. For a brief space we hung together by our toenails to some precipitous cliff whilst the Division deployed.

It was during this time that Robert Scott, commanding the 2nd Norfolks, when asked what was happening to one of his companies produced the classic answer: "I haven't got my crystal and can't tell you the something answer."

The "ploy," as Jock McNaught would say, was briefly: the 6th Brigade were to maintain pressure in the centre whilst the 4th Brigade on the right and the 5th Brigade on the left, by dint of stupendous cross-country marches, were to roll up the enemy flanks in order to free the 6th Brigade for the subsequent main effort and break-through. Meanwhile, the 161st Brigade, less the Royal West Kents, who were refitting in Dimapur, were to remain in Divisional reserve at Jotsoma.

On the 22nd of April the 2nd Dorsets were again split. The Commanding Officer was ordered to take over Picquet Hill and sent me off with "B" and "D" Companies to relieve an equivalent detachment of the Durhams. Picquet Hill was an isolated knoll lying immediately west of and covering the approach to the Kohima Ridge from Dimapur. It was a forward bastion of the Kohima defences and from it one could command a great deal of the Jap positions on Kuki Picquet, D.I.S. and F.S.D. Ridges. Why the Japanese did not make more effort to recapture this very important feature I do not know. It may be that by the time we got there they had their hands more than full on the Kohima Ridge itself. From Picquet Hill we obtained a first-class seat in the stalls to watch and observe the fighting on the ridge itself half a mile in front of us.

I had, under command, a platoon of "B" Company, 2nd Manchesters, and with these Vickers guns we were able to hot-up from a flank any Jap activity we saw on the ridge opposite. On the 24th of April a troop of medium tanks of the 149th Royal Tank Regiment came into my perimeter and with them we had great fun sniping Japanese.

A force of Japanese had worked forward over our right shoulder and were digging in on Shrewsbury, a prominent feature lying about one thousand seven hundred yards to our right rear, which was a menace to the Divisional lines of communication. It had not been found easy to attack them up the almost vertical slope on top of which they were digging in, but from where we were we could get them with some direct sniping with the tank 75-mm. gun. There was something intensely satisfying in spotting the Nip digging, silhouetted momentarily against the skyline, site the gun and fire, and see one's target through the tank telescope literally blown sky-high.

I think it was Rex King Clark, Commanding Officer of the Manchesters, who later told me that he subsequently visited this position and testified to the antlike industry of the Nips. They had dug a complete battalion position underground and had not left a trace of spoil, except on the extreme flank, where our tank guns had harried them.

The detachment of the Durhams which I had relieved had moved forward into the Kohima perimeter and had promptly become involved that night in one of the biggest night attacks the Japanese ever made. They had not had time to get their wire out and the Nips made a desperate attempt to overwhelm the battalion. The Durhams stood firm and killed over a hundred of the enemy in close hand-to-hand combat, but with the loss of seven of their officers, including the Second-in-Command and eighty British other ranks killed and wounded.

On the morning of the 25th of April I was very pleased to see Jock McNaught and the Adjutant, who called in on Picquet Hill on their way up to reconnoitre Garrison Hill.

The next day the Battalion, less "Cock Minor" (the Battalion's code name during this operation being "Cock") on Picquet Hill, moved forward into the perimeter on Garrison Hill. They moved by day, and, despite all possible cover being given from Picquet Hill, they were badly mortared going up the road and sniped continually once they had passed the dangerous Mortuary Corner.

This advance to contact cost us sixteen casualties. The Medical Officer, Joe Chamberlin, and the Padre, Gus Claxton, did wonders that day. The Jap sniper, we found, had no respect for the Red Cross, and it was no enviable job to carry the wounded on stretchers up and down those steep slopes under aimed small-arms fire.

Kuki picket from Garrison Hill

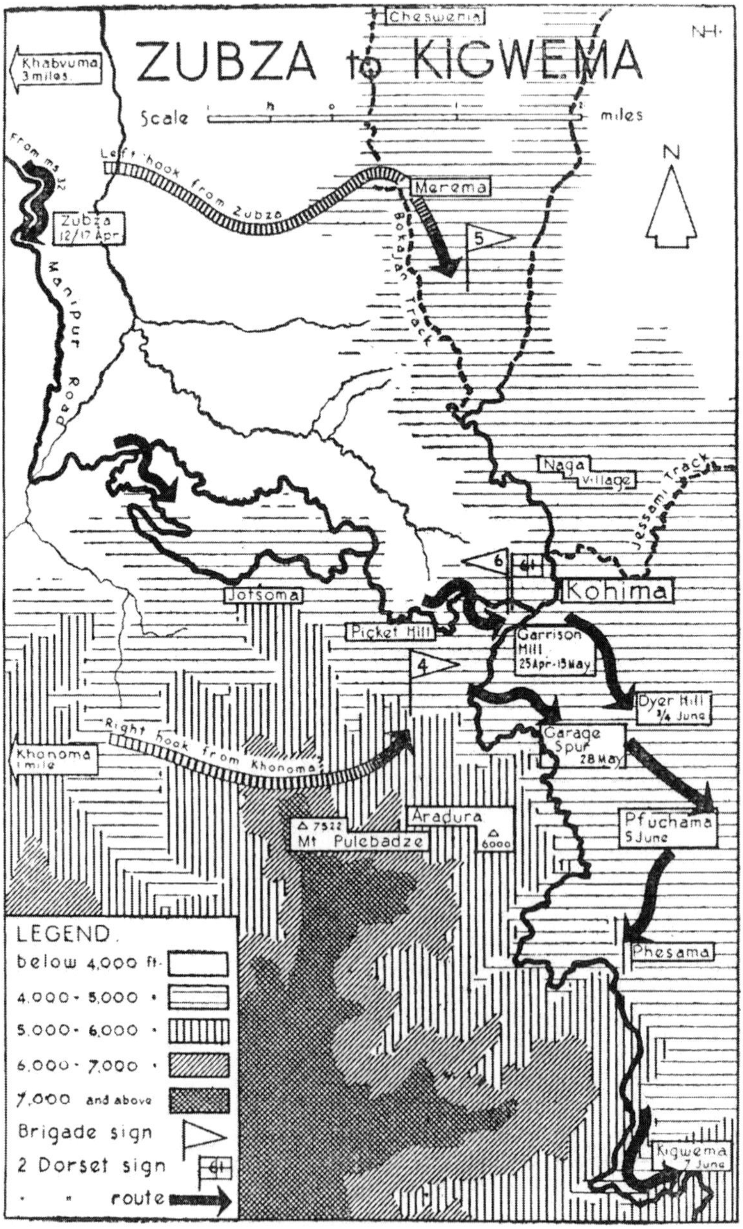
ZUBZA to KIGWEMA
Scale
miles
N
Cheswema
Khabvuma 3 miles
From ms 32
Left hook from Zubza
Merema
Bokajan Track
Zubza 12/17 Apr
Manipur Road
Naga Village
Jessami Track
Kohima
Jotsoma
Picket Hill
Garrison Hill 25 Apr-15 May
Dyer Hill 3/4 June
Garage Spur 28 May
Right hook from Khonoma
Khonoma 1 mile
Aradura
Mt Pulebadze
Pfuchama 5 June
Phesama
Kigwema 7 June
LEGEND
below 4,000 ft
4,000 - 5,000
5,000 - 6,000
6,000 - 7,000
7,000 and above
Brigade sign
2 Dorset sign
route

TWO COMMANDERS OF THE 2ND INFANTRY DIVISION

Major-General J.M.L. Grover, C.B., M.C., 1941-44

Major-General C.G.C. Nicholson, C.B., C.B.E., D.S.O., M.C., 1944-46

TWO COMMANDERS OF THE 5ᵀᴴ INFANTRY BRIGADE

Brigadier V. F. S. Hawkins, D.S.O., M.C., 1942-1944

Brigadier M. M. A. R. West, D.S.O., 1944-1945

COMMANDER XXXIII INDIAN CORPS, 1944-1945

General Sir Montagu G. N. Stopford, G.C.B., K.B.E., D.S.O., M.C., A.D.C. Gen.

KOHIMA, 1944

Dorset war graves below D.C.'s Bungalow – Company H.Q. trench, Treasury Hill middle distance.

SORTIES FROM GARRISON HILL

The attack, May 11th.

Evacuating wounded.

"D" Company mop up the Tennis Court huts. (Capt. Chettle with pistol.)
[Extracted from the War Office Film]

D.C.'S BUNGALOW SPUR AFTER THE BATTLE

The Tennis Court, May, 1944

The Bungalow, May, 1944

The Spur from the Tennis Court, October 1944. (Dorset graves marked by arrow.)

Unveiling of the Dorset Memorial, October, 1944

CHAPTER SIX

THE KEY TO KOHIMA

"Snipers never get me here."

[Famous last words on Garrison Hill.]

BY THIS TIME the 2nd Infantry Division had come up against the main Japanese position, which the enemy had been preparing since their arrival three weeks before.

Ahead of us loomed the series of ridges and knolls running roughly north-east from the lower slopes of the mighty Mount Pulebadze, which stretched to a height of eight thousand feet above us. The Japs held these ridges in the form of a giant horseshoe, with their flanks thrust well forward to Khonoma on our right and as far forward as Khabvuma (the scene of "D" Company's initial action) on our left.

In the centre of this horseshoe General Grover deployed his Division. Already by the 19th of April the Japanese were beginning to withdraw their horns. On that day the Royal Scots had finally turned them out of Khabvuma, and our patrols, penetrating deep into the jungle, found Khonoma clear. The 6th Brigade were established right in the heart of the Japanese positions on Garrison Hill and Hospital Spur. On the 21st of April Brigadier Victor Hawkins, with the Camerons leading, had started out on their great left hook down into the Zubza Valley and up to Merema: a hook that was going to bring them eventually into the Naga village away up on the left flank. The night before the Battalion went into the Garrison Hill perimeter the 4th Brigade had set out on their arduous crosscountry journey, like the 5th Brigade by night, through the dense jungle over the most difficult of hill tracks, in an attempt to work round the right flank of the Japanese positions and descend on them down the massive Aradura Spur.

The Japanese continued to react violently to the presence of the 6th Brigade located inside their own defences. However, it was not merely to reinforce an already overfull perimeter that Jock McNaught had been ordered to lead his Battalion, less two companies, up those difficult sniper-infested sides of Garrison Hill. The 5th Brigade's advance had been retarded on the left and it was absolutely essential for the subsequent speedy prosecution of the operations to pass a troop of medium tanks through to their assistance. The only possible route was by the main Manipur Road.

On the top of the pass over the Kohima Ridge, where the Manipur Road swung right in a hairpin bend for Imphal, a side-road led left-handed up the side of Treasury Hill towards the Naga village. This road junction was dominated by a spur on which was situated the District Commissioner's bungalow. This spur rose roughly due west in four steeply terraced ridges to Garrison Hill, on the extreme top of which stood the Summerhouse which gave rise to the alternative name to this main feature.

The Japanese had been in possession of the District Commissioner's bungalow spur since the first withdrawal of the Royal West Kents to Nichuguard early in April. This spur was to be the centre of our activities for the next three weeks, and I will try to describe it in some detail.

The spur was divided into four main terraces, each separated by a steep bank varying in height from ten to forty feet. Starting from the top, there was the club square on which in happier days the members had played badminton. Ten feet below the club lay the tennis court. On the south side the tennis court was bounded by a large iron water tank and a long tin building which appeared to be servants' quarters. These themselves were sunk so that only the roofs appeared level with the tennis court.

The next drop was a very steep and deep one of about thirty to forty feet to the terrace on which was situated the bungalow itself in its own compound.

Finally, below the bungalow, there was another drop which brought us to the lower garden, which overlooked the important road junction twenty feet below.

Viewed from the eastern side of Garrison Hill, the north, or to the Dorsets attacking, the face of the spur was extremely steep with a fall from the club square to the road of nearly a hundred feet in all.

On the south face of the spur lay various ornamental gardens, a drive into the District Commissioner's bungalow, and the bungalow of the Commandant of the Assam Rifles.

One further feature is of interest. On the south side of the club (topmost) terrace rose a small "pimple" about thirty yards long, fifteen broad and twenty feet high.

An extraordinary feature of this whole spur was the impossibility of being able to see what was happening on the terrace next below. Owing to the thickness of the trees and the conformity of the ground, reconnaissance from a flank was practically impossible. Intelligence about this feature was almost nil. When the Commanding Officer arrived for his reconnaissance on the 25th of April even the Royal Berks, who had been fighting for some days on the club square, could tell him practically nothing of what lay beyond and below them. In fact, it was not until after the initial Battalion night attack that it was finally established that the tennis court was where it was, and not, as we had been led to believe, on the club square. This lack of topographical intelligence played a most detrimental part in the night's operations and definitely led the Commanding Officer to a false appreciation of the enemy position. He was not the only one, and he acted entirely in good faith on what information he was given and could glean. It was not until some days later that Captain Burnett, late Adjutant of the Assam Rifles, who had been quartered for over a year in Kohima, and had been in the beleaguered garrison the whole time, came forward to volunteer information that was to be invaluable to us in the final phases of this battle. If only his presence had been discovered earlier!

To return to the Battalion labouring up the very steep slopes of Hospital Spur into the perimeter laden down with very heavy loads and being sniped and mortared continually. On arrival they doubled up with the Royal Berks and prepared for the attack which was to be put in during the night. Speed was the essence of the contract. The Divisional Commander had said that the capture of the spur to allow the passage of the tanks through to the 5th Brigade was essential by the morning of the 27th.

You will remember that only "A" and "C" Companies were available for this attack. "B" and "D" Companies and the mortars were with me on Picquet Hill, and the carriers were fully employed keeping the road open and acting as a bus service for stores and personnel over the more dangerous parts of the main road.

Whilst the company commanders, John Bowles ("A") and Dick Castle ("C"), were peering through the undergrowth and trying to gain some idea, however hazy, of the ground over which they were to attack, the Commanding Officer confirmed the plan he had evolved overnight. On the right the Royal Berks were to clear the club square and the Pimple which they still shared with the Japanese. "C" Company in the centre were to attack the tennis court terrace (remember at that time it was not known to be the tennis court, only the "centre terrace").

On the left "A" Company were to carry out a tricky approach march beneath the enemy and by climbing out of a steep nullah form up on the north side of the bungalow terrace and lower garden. Owing to the difficult ground and the impossibility of a satisfactory deployment, "A" Company were to lead off, followed by "C" Company. The attack was to go in from west to east and zero hour was fixed for 0300 hrs. As far as possible this tortuous route was taped by lengths of parachute cord, of which there was by now an abundance on the hills, from the number of parachutes used in supplying the garrison. The Commanding Officer established his Tactical Headquarters on a track on the north side of the perimeter, from where at first light he could just get a glimpse of the north-west corner of the tennis court.

"A" Company moved off at 0200 hrs., followed by "C" Company. Shortly after 0300 hrs. the sound of automatic fire and the bursting of grenades indicated that contact had been made. For a long time there was no news at all. It later transpired that once battle had been joined the whole Japanese position of closely interrelated strong-points came alive and the combat developed into such a hand-to-hand mêlée that it was quite impossible for either company commander to get into touch with Battalion Headquarters. Just about first light news came from the regimental aid post that Dick Castle had been wounded and was being evacuated, and the Commanding Officer went down to the club square, where he found the situation to be confused.

On the right the Royal Berks had cleared the Pimple of their unwelcome guests, but had failed to get a footing in the club building on the corner of the square. In the centre "C" Company had come in for some very rough handling. As we discovered later, they had, directly they put their noses over the edge of the north face, hit the very core of the Japanese position centred about the tennis court. The company commander had been wounded, and the commander of No. 14 Platoon, Lieutenant Mayer, together with four volunteers, had been killed in a valiant attempt to storm a Jap bunker which was holding up his platoon. The commander of No. 13 Platoon had been wounded. The only other officer, Lieutenant Day, had been wounded by a mortar bomb during the advance to Garrison Hill the day before. C.S.M. Keegan was trying to restore a not very healthy situation. The Commanding Officer promptly called forward Captain Michael Morice, the company second-in-command, who had been left with Battalion Headquarters for the attack, and ordered "C" Company and the Royal Berks company to reorganize around the club square and Pimple.

On the left "A" Company had fared better. Their initial advance had taken them below the main centre of the Japanese resistance on the tennis court and, once in the open, in front of the District Commissioner's bungalow, they had pressed home their attack in the most convincing manner. A lodgment was effected in the bungalow itself, and on the left Lieutenant Murrills had got his platoon to a position commanding the road junction, and Corporal Softley's section was having a hectic time mopping up Japanese dug in in the steep bank at the side of the road below. At first light the situation deteriorated badly. "A" Company came under heavy fire from the bank below the tennis court, and had to withdraw from the bungalow itself. It was at about this time that Corporal Softley, an old favourite of the Regiment who had made a great name for himself as a boxer in the 1st Battalion, was killed under the most gallant circumstances when trying to reach some of his wounded who had become separated from the remainder of the platoon.

The day of the 27th was not an easy one. "C" Company had, by destroying the large bunker position on the north-east corner of the tennis court, "taken out" a forward position of the Japanese from which hitherto their snipers had definitely made all day-time approach to the main perimeter most unhealthy. But on the club square both sides faced each other, in places only fifteen yards apart, during a long day of grenade throwing and sniping. The Pimple, even though we were now the sole owners, was most unpleasant. The Japanese were very proficient with their grenade dischargers, a spigot device which could throw hand grenades up to three hundred yards, and the Royal Berks that day had seventeen casualties on the Pimple from grenades alone.

Down below the bungalow John Bowles had been ordered to hang on at all costs. How he managed it that day is a marvel. He had been forced to try to reorganize his company on the bottommost tip of the spur, in the open, only thirty yards from and below the Japanese on the terrace above. Furthermore, at that time it was impossible to move in the open by day and he was unable to collect his scattered flock, many of whom had perforce to lie out wounded in the heat of the sun all day.

Countless are the deeds which were performed that night and day, and, despite the continued efforts of the Japanese, "A" Company hung on grimly, though completely isolated from the rest of the garrison. The primary object of the attack had been achieved: the road was kept open and the tanks went through to the 5th Brigade. This night attack had cost us dear, for between them "A" and "C" Companies lost twenty-eight men killed.

During the night of the 27th, after a day of continual sniping and grenading and minor conflicts, the Japs made a determined effort to dislodge "A" Company, but John Bowles, immediately darkness fell, had managed to get his company well, if not happily, organized and stoutly repulsed continual counter-attacks. At about 2200 hrs. the Battalion Headquarters area on Summerhouse Hill was heavily bombarded by 3-inch mortars. This really was the height of annoyance. To be mortared by captured British 3-inch mortars was bad enough, but to receive the bombs meant earlier for the garrison but which had missed the very narrow dropping zone was even worse. To have one's kit set alight in the dark by British phosphorous smoke bombs because the Japanese could not distinguish high explosive from smoke was the final straw.

Following this mortar attack the Japs put in a "Banzai" attack against the summit of the hill. This was driven off except for a small party which had penetrated and were at first light found to be digging in by the summerhouse itself. These were mopped up by the Guerrilla Platoon under Lieutenant O'Driscoll, who had personally distinguished himself by assisting to evacuate the wounded on the march into the perimeter on the 26th of April.

The next day was spent in reorganizing the perimeter and everyone set about constructing head cover. It also became increasingly obvious that, in order to clear the spur and link up "A" and "C" Companies, tank support was essential. We had not at this stage acquired the detailed knowledge of the Japanese positions that we were going to gain during the next fortnight. We had, however, a pretty shrewd idea that if we could only get a medium tank on to the tennis court, serving some pretty fast balls from the north end, the Nip would not stay to finish the set. It was impossible to use our artillery, except in very rare instances, owing to our own troops being so intermingled and "hugga-mugga" with the enemy.

Our little intelligence and the opinion of the tank officers were against the successful chances of driving a tank straight up the drive of the District Commissioner's bungalow and into his compound. The only course seemed to be to bulldoze a track straight up the khudside on the southern face. Lieutenant-Colonel John Garwood, the C.R.E., agreed to try it on, and on the morning of the 28th we were filled with admiration for the sapper bulldozer driver, who, covered by a Lee tank fore and aft, drove his monstrosity clear up the road round the Japanese positions on the spur, and calmly set about trying to drag a Lee tank up this very steep slope. He first dozed out a rough track up the steep gradient and then, hitching on the Lee, tried to drag it up the slope. Unhappily this plan came to naught. The driver had to leave his bulldozer to make an adjustment, and the tank for some reason went into reverse, pulled the dozer down on top of it and was promptly put clean out of action, with no possible chance of recovery after it had crashed down the slope.

Early on the morning of the 29th of April I was called up by the Commanding Officer, with whom I had been in close touch by wireless, and told to hand over Cock Minor to Pryke Howard and come forward myself as quickly as possible. A carrier, I was told, much to my relief, would taxi me forward over the rather more unfriendly stretches of the road. The carriers of the Division had been doing wonders ever since the 19th of April. In conjunction with the medium tanks of our old friends of the 149th Royal Tank Regiment and the Stuarts of the 7th Light Cavalry, they had kept the road open during the hours of daylight. In addition, the carriers had been employed in running a ferry service of stores and personnel continually over the most exposed stretches of the road. Clive Chettle, who had taken over the carriers from Jock Wilson when the latter had been so unfortunately injured at Jagalpet, worked wonders with his platoon. No mention of the carriers is complete without a reference to the scout cars we had acquired at Bokajan. They were in constant use under Lieutenant "Snagger" Highett.

During the whole of the subsequent fighting they were the only means of communicating and supplying the isolated company at the District Commissioner's bungalow spur, and later both Highett and Private Johnson put up remarkably fine shows in maintaining contact with forward elements of the Brigade as we penetrated farther and farther into the enemy positions.

Like all who climbed up Garrison Hill for the first time, I was appalled by the situation. The reader must recall that heavy fighting had been taking place on these slopes, in intense heat, for nearly a month. So close had been and still was the fighting, and so heavy was the sniping, that it had been quite impossible to collect the dead even though, as in many cases, they lay just beyond a section post. Indeed in some places where the Jap had put in a "Banzai" attack his dead lay piled deep where they had fallen in their assault on our positions. In a steep gully not forty yards from the club square, at the top of which lay one of our posts, were piled high the bodies of about a hundred and fifty of the enemy who had perished as they made one of their suicidal attacks against the Royal Berks.

To return to our story. After turning the corner by the appropriately sited mortuary, I left the carrier and, accompanied by the faithful Private Fooks, my batman, and Cripps, my gunman, we set out to climb the hill. Our first greeting was from the outstretched hand of a long-dead Jap, who had been slaughtered in an attempt to reach the hospital and get in among the wounded of the garrison in the earlier days.

Climbing the khudside, grossly overladen (I was not coming into the perimeter without some small comforts for Battalion Headquarters), we were given the tip from time to time which way to go to avoid known sniper beats. The Jap sniper, fortunately, was nothing if not conservative in his methods.

Arrived at the top, I found Battalion Headquarters pretty tired. They had had a rather rough two or three nights, and even Graeme's suavity had been shattered slightly by the destruction of some of his more precious belongings by fire. The smell on the hill and the flies were simply awful. As I have said, no one had yet had a chance to get around and clean up the area. Three battalions, plus a mixed collection of the old garrison, Assam Rifles, who had not been evacuated and a battery of mountain gunners were all herded together round the steep slopes of this conical hill. Washing and shaving were out of the question. There had been no rain for some days to supplement the only means of water supply, which was by air drop. As a result, the garrison was rationed to three pints of water a day for all purposes. The "B" echelons of battalions worked wonders in struggling up the steep slopes of the hill daily, dodging the snipers and the odd enemy 75-mm., to bring up such water as they could to supplement the air drop. However, for a long time we had to keep to a no-shaving rule and beards flourished. The Commanding Officer and the Padre were our two champions in this respect. So fast did the Colonel achieve an excellent "Henry the Eighth" model that after only five days, when the remainder of the Battalion came forward, he was apparently unrecognizable. One of these freshly shaven warriors from Picquet Hill, encountering a magnificently bearded figure whom he should have recognized easily enough, was heard by the Commanding Officer to remark: "Another one of these something sailors."

The Colonel was finishing his breakfast as I arrived. Meals at Battalion Headquarters occurred at the strangest times in those days, and Jock McNaught was trying to figure out whether to finish his half-cup of weak "compo" tea or save the half-inch at the bottom to clean his teeth. We never did find a really satisfactory answer to this problem, which was further aggravated a few days later when neither of us could stand being unshaven any longer and decided to improve our morale by occasional shaves. The only liquid available was the last of one's precious cup of "char".

Jock greeted me with the information that I was to take over command of the Battalion for a couple of days whilst he moved a few yards up the hill to relieve Colonel Jack Theobalds, Second-in-Command of the 6th Infantry Brigade, who had been hard at it commanding the garrison since he had taken over from the Royal West Kents on the 20th of April.

I was taken round the Battalion positions. If the moves of the Battalion up to date had resembled a game of general post, the layout of the Battalion on Garrison Hill seemed to be as inextricably mixed as if the 6th Brigade, for a variation, had gone quite mad and, to the tune of the guns and the cries of "Banzai," had indulged in some colossal game of musical chairs, with poor old "A" Company left out in the open with no chair. The perimeter was exceedingly small, about three to four hundred yards across the hill from contour to contour. Isolated on the left forward position were "A" Company, with the enemy not only thirty yards from them on one side but within easy sniping distance of their backs from Treasury Ridge. "C" Company reigned more or less supreme on the club square, though a platoon of the Royal Berks, until this morning, still occupied the Pimple.

Away on the top of the hill were the Guerrilla Platoon, all lost among the Royal Berks and the Royal Welch Fusiliers. The next day, when "B" and "D" Companies came into the perimeter, the Battalion layout became even more confused, as these two companies took up their positions in the line away over on the right flank, where "D" Company found a most unhealthy position on the left of the Royal Welch Fusiliers. "D" Company did not have a pleasant time up there on the right: they were probably more exposed to snipers than anywhere else, except for the company below the District Commissioner's bungalow. Their forward positions were so open to every marksman that reliefs by day were most difficult.

Joe Chamberlin never moved his regimental aid post from its original position which had been selected for the attack on the night of the 26th/27th of April—that is to say, on the east flank of the hill on the track leading to the club square. Here he built himself a great earthwork, which, however, was not allowed to pass unmolested by the attentions of the Japanese.

My first task, as soon as Jock McNaught had departed with the faithful Harvey to his garrison headquarters, was to lay on the attack with a Honey tank from the club square on to the tennis court.

On the morning of the 30th, even as Pryke Howard was closing up the remainder of the Battalion, less the mortars, who remained on Picquet Hill under that prince of mortar officers Davies, the sappers managed to winch a Stuart tank of the 7th Light Cavalry into the perimeter by the very way that we had failed with the Lee a couple of days earlier. By now our various activities at this very open approach had attracted the notice of the Japanese and they had got up a 75-mm. gun and one or two 3.7-inch anti-tank guns to shoot from somewhere south of Jail Hill, and were paying a lot of unwelcome attention to us with mortars from Treasury Hill. Together with Michael Morice, I made some form of plan and he got "C" Company all teed-up to have a smack back at the Nips after their rather rough passage of a few nights before. By mischance the internal intercommunication of the Honey went completely out of action and this took some hours to repair. Just as we were really ready to go it was found that the tank had run out of petrol. There was nothing to do but say some rather rude things to the British officer in charge of the tank and stand the company down.

The next day we decided to have another attempt at getting on to the tennis court. Oh, how we were to come to hate this tennis court during the next fortnight! It obsessed our minds and controlled our every action. We were determined to get into this position somehow and give the Nip a game of tennis he would never forget. For the moment, however, he had done pretty well in the first set and it was all we could do to play him to deuce games in the second.

The Honey tank commander did not share our faith in his tank's capabilities over the rough ground to the left of the club and just forward of our leading section. Also he, quite rightly as it proved, did not like the look of the drop to the tennis court. It was decided to send Michael Morice forward on a preliminary reconnaissance in the tank to have a look-see. The results were disappointing. Very little could be seen of any value to the attack and the only thing that was definitely established was that it was not "on" to drive a Stuart down the bank on to the tennis court. Owing to the extremely limited area for manoeuvre the tank remained too long stationary in full view of the enemy until a very near miss from a 75-mm. firing at what could not have been more than six hundred yards' range caused him to pull back smartly to the cover of the Pimple. Here the wretched Honey was promptly hit by a 3.7-inch anti-tank gun and put right out of action, fortunately with no loss to the crew. I was not prepared to try this particular attack at this time without tank support, and "C" Company, who had twice been prepared for an attack, were once more stood down. This second disappointment depressed us all immensely. None of us were happy about "A" Company in their isolated position, and the club square area was definitely becoming too unhealthy. The Nips had got on to our activities at the dulldozed ramps and had put a stop to our using this means of approach for getting in heavier forms of equipment such as Honeys, Wasps and 6-pounder anti-tank guns. We had got a section of Wasps in, and one or two 6-pounders, but a gun crew of the Gordon Highlanders (100th Anti-Tank Regiment) had been badly mauled that very morning. We were never able to use the Wasps, owing to the extraordinary proximity of the opposing forces on the club square. It was quite hot enough around that area a few days later when we fired the clubhouse with M191A grenades.

In an attempt to dominate No Man's Land I detailed the Guerrilla Platoon to take over the Pimple position from Colin Doran's platoon of "D" Company which had gone straight there on arrival in the perimeter.

John O'Driscoll and Lance-Sergeant Maule soon got down to business and established an observation post on top of the Pimple, from which a restricted view of the Nipponese "backyard" could be seen. Gradually, by constant observation, we pieced together some idea of the lie of the land and the habits of the enemy. It was not too comfortable an observation post, as the Jap was apt to throw quite a lot of stuff at it, and it was constantly being sniped. However, we found that it was a grand place from which to throw things back and to keep him moving with some good sniping on our part. On his return on the 2nd of May the Commanding Officer had a brilliant idea of fixing a handle, a fuse and a detonator to a Hawkins grenade and chucking them from the Pimple and the forward positions on the club square on to the Nip below. We never discovered if the results of this novel form of attack were as devastating as they sounded. This Pimple observation post became the rendezvous of anyone who felt that he could shoot at all, and I well remember how much better my "M. & V." tasted one evening when I had been down to visit the Guerrilla Platoon and bagged my first Nip.

Meanwhile, the daily toll of casualties continued. Nowhere in the perimeter proper were the troops so thick on the ground as they were in the area of the club square. If in our attempts to dominate No Man's Land we chucked a lot of stuff at the Nip, he for the most part was sitting in his hole only to pop out and fling a grenade or two back over his shoulder on any or no provocation. He was practically bound to hit someone. Another serious source of casualties was from snipers. If I seem to harp on snipers it is because they were our greatest menace at the time. During the Kohima battle the 2nd Division lost four brigadiers, two killed and two wounded. Of these, three were hit by small-arms fire and the other by a grenade. In the same way we, as a battalion, lost a number of men, especially when, despite constant warnings, the soldiers would try to rush out and retrieve valuable air drops which had floated on their gaily coloured parachutes just a few yards beyond the section posts. The dropping zone was incredibly small and difficult to hit, and it was particularly galling to see a nice tin of compo rations or a cask of water fall just out of, but apparently so temptingly within, reach. Lieutenant David Deane, the Mechanical Transport Officer, who had brought the mechanical transport across India by road, was killed by a sniper very shortly after his arrival.

Meanwhile, down in "A" Company's position the Japanese was in his own strange way allowing us to visit and supply the company by day and evacuate the wounded. This was the first time that we really encountered this peculiar habit of the Nip. He would allow us to do practically anything, from brewing-up in "bare buff", supplying isolated units, even to directing battles right in the open and within very close range, but we had only to overstep a certain, unfortunately to us unspecified, line for him to react most strongly. A little more liaison with the Japanese "umpires" and we would have got the whole thing arranged on mutually satisfactory lines. Serving with "A" Company as an artillery forward observation officer throughout this episode was a most gallant Sikh officer, who distinguished himself by his energy, bravery and complete disregard for his own safety, at the same time carrying out his duties under the most unsatisfactory conditions.

At just about last light on the 2nd of May the Japanese brought a 75-mm. gun down the road from Treasury Hill and opened up at "A" Company at about three hundred yards' range. They were pretty well under cover by then, but had no head cover, and this attack from behind them, directed mainly against company headquarters, hit them hard. All communication went, and we on the hill, knowing that they were being stonked badly, could do little to help, though our gunners got on, as rapidly as usual, to the area from where we suspected they were shooting. At about 2300 hrs. Corporal Mansfield appeared at Battalion Headquarters. He had come with two men—Private Morgan I remember was one and, as far as I can recall, Lance-Corporal Breely was the other, all of the Signal Platoon—right through the enemy lines with their damaged 18 set to bring us news and replace their set. Mansfield brought a message from John Bowles and gave us the situation, which was not good. We fixed them a drink of rum and Mansfield set out on his dangerous journey back to tell his company commander that he would be relieved by "B" Company the next morning. Shortly after this Corporal Mansfield was returned to duty with a rifle company: we were fortunate at this time in being well furnished with non-commissioned officers in the Signal Platoon, and Mansfield had shown that he had the makings of a good patroller. For this night's work and his subsequent first-class performance at Dyer Hill and Pfuchama, Mansfield was awarded the Military Medal. Unfortunately, at the latter place, he was wounded and lost to the Battalion for the rest of the war.

The next morning Alan Watts, with "B" Company, took over from "A" Company under the cover of a smoke screen from our own mortars and Divisional artillery. I confess to feeling a large lump in my throat as I watched the twenty-eight survivors of the hundred-odd of my old company, who had swung through the trees at Banbury in front of the King two years before, clamber up the hillside into Battalion Headquarters. Blackened and red-eyed, John Bowles's men had, for five and a half days, hung on by the skin of their teeth against almost overwhelming opposition in the most exposed position. They had fulfilled their task and had not only gained a lodgment on their objective but had kept the road open and had killed a large number of Japanese. Under constant fire by day and continual jittering by night they had fought on with rapidly diminishing numbers. Well had they maintained the stout traditions of the grenadier company.

For a couple of days they were pulled into Battalion reserve, but there was no rest on the hill for men so tired as they, and so we evacuated them to Dimapur to recuperate and there we met them about ten days later after we had completed the job they had done so much to help start.

On the very first night that "B" Company had taken over from "A" Company they too were subjected to the same onslaught from the Japanese 75-mm. Again the heavy toll of casualties in the company headquarters dug-out, more exposed and more easily recognized by the tell-tale 18 set aerial than the remaining slits in the ground which passed for trenches. The night before we had all lost a very old friend when C.S.M. Downton, of "A" Company, was killed, and this night we were deprived of yet another warrant officer. C.S.M. Draper, of "B" Company, had been a very old personal friend of mine. Together we had represented the Battalion in many an athletics competition. During the war he had progressed rapidly and had settled down well as Company Sergeant-Major of "B" Company after C.S.M. Doughty had gone off to become an Indian Army quartermaster. The loss of two such valuable warrant officers in two days was a serious blow to the Battalion.

On the 3rd of May Sergeant Seale, of "D" Company, carried out a very fine patrol in daylight. He attempted to occupy with a section, to be followed if successful by a platoon, the large bunker on the northeast corner of the tennis court. It was this bunker that "C" Company had successfully reduced on the first attack, and we were pretty sure that the Nip had not reoccupied it. By most skilful use of ground and cover, "Yorky" Seale got to within five yards of the bunker, but could not find an entrance. On working round the edge of the tennis court he came under very heavy fire from the area of the water tower and by the shed and had to withdraw. This small action of Seale's produced much valuable information and confirmed our growing opinions of the Jap layout. It would appear that the Japanese were making no attempt to hold the spur in the British fashion—that is, with a perimeter defence. The Japanese commander, whoever he was, must have had a grand eye for ground. He had, or so it appeared and was subsequently proved, concentrated his main defence in the area of the tennis court. With a very strong post dug well in under the water tank at the southwest corner—that is, below the old clubhouse—and strong bunkers along the south end (far end to us) and in the bank which separated the tennis court from the club square above it, he had only to wait for us to emerge on to the tennis court and let us have it good and proper. After Seale's patrol we began to understand a lot of things, mainly why "C" Company had "bought it" on the initial attack, and we were full of admiration for their having achieved so much even after their leaders had all become casualties. One thing stood out a mile: it was absolutely essential either to get a medium tank on to the tennis court or manhandle a gun into such a position as to blow the devils out of their holes at very close range in support of an infantry attack.

On the 4th of May we had another crack at getting a tank into the District Commissioner's compound. By this time the tank experts had agreed that it might be possible after all to drive a tank round the spur and just short of the ramp up which we had dragged the ill-fated Honey, turn sharp right and drive straight up the drive to make a good old-fashioned call on the now absent District Commissioner, or rather on his unwelcome tenants. Our old friend Major Ezra Rhodes, of "B" Squadron, 149th Royal Tank Regiment, cheerfully produced a tank for the purpose, and Captain Jock Murrills, who only two days before had come out of the spur position with "A" Company, volunteered to conduct the tank on this not so social call. Jock, who had so recently fought all

THE KEY TO KOHIMA

over this corner of the battlefield, possessed invaluable knowledge, but his decision voluntarily to re-enter that unpleasant area after so short a respite was one which we all deeply appreciated. As the tank guided by Jock Murrills reached the bungalow, "B" Company rose from their trenches and joined in the attack. The consternation and confusion of the Japs were great and the tank accounted for a large number of casualties. As they moved forward the infantry came under very heavy fire from bunker positions in the bank below the tennis court and had to pull back. The tank also got into difficulties in the narrow area allowed it for manœuvre, and the attack had to be called off. During this attack Alan Watts, commanding "B" Company, was wounded and had to be evacuated. That was the last we saw of Alan, who had been with the Battalion since he joined at Aldershot in August, 1938, and had commanded "B" Company for at least three years.

Profiting from the lessons of the previous day, we were all keen to have another smack at the Nips with this tank. None were keener than Jock Murrills and the tank commander. On their way in they found that the Jap (as was suspected after "B" Company's report of digging during the night) had tried to dig an anti-tank ditch across the drive. Fortunately they had not made it long enough and the driver was able by a brilliant piece of driving to overcome this obstacle both on the way in and out. Once inside, things began to go much better. Both infantry and the tank had a very much better knowledge of the ground than on the day before. The tank made straight for where it considered it could climb the steep bank to the tennis court, and "B" Company, under Dick Purser's (he had taken over from Alan Watts) skilful and gallant leadership, got into the bungalow, where they killed ten Japs. From then on, however, the show again became exceedingly sticky; the Lee could not reach the terrace anywhere and could not depress its gun enough to shoot-up the medium machine-gun post which was by now causing Dick and his gallant raiders a considerable amount of trouble. Once more we had to pull back. This time, however, we reckoned that we had won a couple of games in the second set, and things were definitely looking up. Left behind in the bungalow on this occasion, after having been killed under very gallant circumstances, was that cheerful Irishman Private O'Reilly, whom we have met before in these chronicles. It was the same O'Reilly who had astounded everyone by walking off with the Divisional cross-country championship in 1942. From the moment we went into action, this wild Irishman entered with the same zest into killing Japanese as he had earlier shown for beating an international cross-country runner.

We now settled down to a day or two of attrition and took the opportunity to reorganize ourselves. We kept the Japs on the move as much as possible. To overcome the loss of the observation post on the Pimple, which we had had to abandon, we tried mortaring them with our 2-inch mortars from any position in which we could get a shoot. Intercommunication by day with the company on the spur was good and they used to call us and tell us of any Nip activity, such as brewing-up or, on rare occasions, getting into a huddle, and we tried to shoot them up, not without success. We were not so happy with the new-fangled American M191A grenade after Corporal Bottrill had been killed by one as he was trying to fire it; but we found that it was a good weapon once we had been issued with the correct ballistite. Another source of discomfort to the Nips was the energy of Dick Purser, now in sole charge of the vital position below the bungalow. As the Nip garrison decreased and their energetic efforts to dislodge us slackened, so did Dick's efforts to dominate this particular part of No Man's Land increase. It was Dick's boast that he would bag a Nip before breakfast every morning. It was grand work that John Bowles and Dick Purser, each in his turn, did down there. If ever a commander tried to dominate No Man's Land when everything was against them those two did.

The game of musical chairs around Garrison Hill continued with undiminished zest, and units continued to be inextricably mixed despite the efforts of all battalion commanders to sort out their own particular sub-units. A great deal of this was caused by the necessity constantly to change over sub-units in the stickier parts of the line; whilst, in addition, every small operation made by the 6th Brigade in their effort to break out caused some minor adjustment. To the general confusion was added the arrival of the 4th Rajputs in the perimeter at about this time. The arrival of a fresh battalion was a most welcome relief to the British battalions, who were able to a small extent to close their fronts with the consequent reduction in the number of posts to be manned.

The reorganization of the Battalion in action was becoming quite a formidable task. With my long acquaintance with the non-commissioned officers of the Battalion, the Colonel delegated to me the task of sorting out the Battalion and making the necessary recommendations for promotion for his approval, whilst he continued with the task of harrying the Nip wherever and whenever possible.

By this time our losses were mounting. Three company commanders—Watts ("B"), Castle ("C") and Fretts ("D")—had all been wounded and evacuated. Heaven only knew when we were to see them again. Two company sergeant-majors—Downton and Draper—had been killed. Four sergeants—Adams and Varley of "A" Company, and Clarkson and Messenger of "B" Company— would never lead their platoons again. Lance-Sergeants Cobb and Manning, with Corporals Softley, Berry, Hooppell, Bottrill, Woolford and Plantard, had all perished. Lieutenants Mayer and Deane had been killed. In addition to the three company commanders already mentioned, Lieutenants Day and O'Driscoll had been wounded and of our two "lend-lease" officers from the Manchesters one, Lieutenant Hayward, had been wounded after fighting magnificently in "A" Company's initial attack against the bungalow, and Lieutenant Baldwin had been evacuated sick from Picquet Hill. As a final straw in this rapidly diminishing number of old members of the firm, that grand veteran Teddy Edwards was promoted to Quartermaster of the XXXIII Corps Headquarters. This was a formidable list of vacancies to fill whilst still not only in close contact but virtually besieged. The company-commander problem was answered by promoting Pryke Howard to take over "C" Company, pulling in Clive Chettle from the carriers to command "D" Company and inviting Graeme Gordon Wright to leave Battalion Headquarters, which he had graced so efficiently for so long, for the rather doubtful joy, under the circumstances, of commanding "B" Company, now back on the perimeter on the south-east side of the hill. R.Q.M.S. Goldson became Regimental Sergeant-Major, and C.S.M. Hayward took over Regimental Quartermaster-Sergeant.

The first obvious promotion to Company Sergeant-Major— obvious because of the magnificent form he had already displayed as a platoon commander in the field—was Sergeant Yorky Seale, who went with Clive Chettle to "D" Company. This pair made a grand team from the word "Go," and were to serve together during the next nine or ten months through many a tough affair. We had to pull Sergeant Osmond out of the regimental aid post, where he had been dug in since 1940, to become Company Sergeant-Major of H.Q. Company, which post this redoubtable veteran held through all the chances and adventures of the next few months until after we had reached Mandalay. At this time most of the senior non-commissioned officers in the Battalion were filling "staff" jobs in the Battalion, and we find the Mechanical Transport Sergeant, Pearcey, and his Technical Sergeant, Seward, both laying down their pens and grabbing a musket apiece to become company sergeant-majors. I may be wrong, but I don't believe that either of them had done a day's service with a duty company since those faroff days when the old Machine Gun Company had been disbanded at Dover, but it did not prevent them making a very good attempt at company sergeant-major. Teddy Edwards's vacancy of Quartermaster might have been difficult to fill but for the stout efforts of our friends "at court," chief amongst whom was the B.G.S., George Wood. By some means, fair or foul, he managed to get our own Regimental Sergeant-Major, the inimitable Mr. Smith, posted to us as our own Quartermaster. Whereupon Mr. Smith, or "Bert" as he came to be called very soon, and Private Palmer, his excellent batman, moved from the ammunition three-tonner to the Quartermaster's tent and started "laying things on" with even more abandon than ever.

The departure of Teddy Edwards left a very big gap in the Battalion. He had been with the Battalion as Regimental SergeantMajor and Quartermaster for eight years, and before that had done an incredible number of years as a warrant officer with the 1st Battalion abroad. His knowledge and experience were as invaluable as they were unbounded. In 1943, when I had suddenly found myself at an early age in command of the Battalion, I could have had no more loyal or staunch supporter than my father's one-time company sergeant-major. He did not go very far from us and indeed appears continually in this story, popping up, like all good quartermasters, just when most needed.

The arrival of the Rajputs in the perimeter had two important effects. In the first place, the casualty rate from accidental discharges of weapons increased alarmingly. Let me explain that the Indian soldier was by no means the only offender, but perhaps in this case his enthusiasm had not been curbed by such stringent action as we had been forced to take with the British soldier to eliminate this tendency to shoot blind at night. Throughout the Kohima battle "trigger-happiness" at night constituted a very definite menace. Indeed, on one sad occasion when two "C" Company men had been buried alive owing to their trench subsiding in a very heavy and unexpected fall of rain, it was quite impossible to bring help to them or to dig them out until too late, owing to the very heavy fire brought to bear by our over-enthusiastic allies, who were quite convinced that a major attack was being launched against them. A certain Indian Army brigadier summed up the whole situation very neatly a few days later. He closed an evening conference just about last light with the remark: "Gentlemen, I should hurry home past our lines: our bag so far is three British officers and fifteen British other ranks."

The second, and much more beneficial, result of the arrival of the Rajputs arose from their righteous desire to get well under cover. They had no such inhibitions as we had about felling trees and giving the enemy a better view of our positions. They set about the trees with a will and built themselves some excellent dug-outs. A day or two later, on my way to visit "B" Company, I noticed that something seemed to be different. The forest was much thinner and sure enough, on glancing down the hill towards the club square, I saw a sight which stirred me as much as Cortes must have been excited at his first view of the Pacific—I could see the District Commissioner's bungalow! Shabash! I could not only see the bungalow but vast expanses of the compound! The few square yards thus made visible by the Rajputs' jungle-clearing activities seemed vast to us who had tried every possible way to get just a little peek into this hitherto closed territory.

I promptly sent my gunman to ask the Commanding Officer if he would come on up, and at the same time bade him find the Intelligence Officer, have him send up an observation post with a telescope, and finally to grab a light machine gun as quickly as possible. Now we could outsnipe the Nip.

Jock McNaught, on arrival, was inclined to be a bit peeved at being disturbed (having got me out of the command post he was having a well-earned nap), but when I pointed out what I had seen he immediately shared my enthusiasm for this discovery. Whilst he sat down and started making one of his many "ploys", I proceeded on down through "B" Company area to see what could now be seen from the right or forward flank.

The results were more than gratifying: from a combination of two or three positions we could now have a good "dekho" at the Jap position. Three-quarters of the tennis court, the far end of the lower terrace, the blackened remains of the bungalow (fired by "B" Company on their last visit on the 5th of May) and a great expanse to the south of the bungalow in the area of the Commandant's house and the drive through the ornamental gardens now lay wide open to our gaze.

Ever eager to gain possession of the bungalow compound which had withstood our endeavours for so long (we had actually been ordered to leave the perimeter but requested to be allowed to remain and complete the job), we immediately set about making a plan for an attack on two flanks.

The plan was to launch a pincer attack to gain a footing on the tennis court from which we could loose further attacks against the bungalow terrace and so link up with the platoon of "D" Company under Lieutenant Halahan, which was all that was necessary at this stage to hold the spur position.

One section was to do a long left hook from the club square to try once more to occupy the bunker at the north-east corner of the tennis court. The remainder of that platoon were to execute a short left hook and from the club square drop on to the tennis court and try to demolish the Nip positions below the club and under the water tank. At the same time, Lieutenant Highett, who had returned to duty with "C" Company, was to try to get round the right of the Pimple and attack the Jap from the southern flank. This was an entirely new departure and made possible only by the sudden visual control we now had over the Japanese position.

This attack on the 11th of May was preceded by five minutes' concentrated fire from a 6-pounder which had been man-handled into a position overlooking the long tin shed on the right (southern) end of the tennis court and a bank to its east.

Owing to an unforeseen delay in launching the left hooks the gaff was blown and without further support this attack proved abortive. On the right Snagger Highett's platoon came under very heavy fire from the water tank, which, as it turned out later, was excellently sited for an all-round field of fire, and a very suspiciouslooking clump of bamboo in the ornamental garden to the south.

In this attack yet another familiar figure was lost to the Battalion in the person of Sergeant "Kank" Haddon, who will be remembered by old-timers as one of Major Bolingbroke's "Q.M." clerks. Haddon had during the war been dragged from his ledgers to do various duties from Intelligence Sergeant to platoon commander. To the end his training under "Bolly" persisted, and as he was being evacuated from the regimental aid post he remembered to ask for a signed receipt for his whistle, lanyard and watch, which were being removed from him.

One man was sublimely happy during these last few days. The Intelligence Officer, "Tiger" Havers, practically lived at the new observation post overlooking the Jap position. Woe betide any Jap who moved into the open, for Tiger had a smack at him. At last the Jap sniper and grenade thrower were being sniped in return and our daily casualty rate decreased accordingly. The early morning, we discovered, was the time that the Nip chose to move around, congregate and generally behave as human beings instead of the sub-human hole-dwellers which made him such a first-class soldier in defence.

Passwords were still fashionable in Kohima days and all had to contain the letter "L", being a consonant which the Nip was unable to pronounce (we confirmed this later in Japan). After the favourites "Lilliput", "Lollipop", "Lullaby", etc., had been used *ad nauseam* we fell back on Indian place-names, like "Lahore" and "Calcutta"; but, with so many trigger-happy soldiers of all nationalities around, this custom passed into disuse and we concentrated on restricting all unnecessary movement and firing of rifles by night.

Before recounting the final phase of the Battalion's battle for the District Commissioner's bungalow spur it would be well to spend a few moments considering what had been happening all this time on the remainder of the Divisional front. The plan, you will remember, was for the 4th and 5th Brigades, having worked round the flanks, to roll up the Japanese position from either end whilst the 6th Brigade broke out from the centre along the general axis of the F.S.D. Ridge—Jail Hill.

From the 4th to the 7th of May a very fierce and intense battle was fought throughout the length of the Kohima Ridge. All brigades gained some advantage, but the attack had not been as successful as had been hoped. The 33rd Infantry Brigade from the 7th Division in Corps reserve, had been brought in under the command of the 2nd Division to help out in the attacks on the right in the area G.P.T. Ridge—Jail Hill. The strength of construction and excellent siting of the Japanese defences and the capacity of the enemy to take extremely heavy punishment had made the capture of Kohima a very tough affair indeed. Up to this time three thousand rounds of 3.7-inch howitzer, seven thousand rounds of 25-pounder and one thousand five hundred rounds of medium from our only two 5.5-inch guns had been fired at the enemy, apart from innumerable 3-inch mortar crash concentrations and daily strafing and bombing by our few Hurribombers and Vengeance divebombers. In spite of this and his comparatively little artillery and negligible air support, the Japanese infantry continued with unabated zeal to fight back from his deep and well-constructed positions. Owing to the early rains and steepness of the gradients, it had been found impossible to use the tanks off the roads as had been hoped.

It now became obvious that it was to be a battle to the end and that the Japanese would have to be exterminated before they would run. So after a couple of days' breather, during which the Division regrouped, the final contest of the first phase of the Kohima battle opened on the 11th of May, the day that "C" Company put in their pincer attack. As is always the case, the Battalion never really got the hang of the full operational picture until some time afterwards. Every unit on the perimeter was too busy employed in its own particular tasks to be worried by the outside world.

On the 12th of May the sappers decided to bulldoze a track straight up Hospital Hill Spur into the perimeter from the rear, in an endeavour to push, pull or drag a medium tank up to us. By the evening of the 12th of May they had achieved this miracle—it was nothing less. Every factor, from the steepness of the gradient, the state of the ground and the possibility of the continuance of the rain, mitigated against the achievement of such a task.

That night the tank lay outside H.Q. Company cookhouse—the weapon by which we hoped to achieve success had arrived. No pains were spared to ensure success. After dark the track to the club square was widened and reinforced. A new life and vigour surged through the Battalion as nearly every man who could get away from his post came to look at this monster, this dragon, which was to help us annihilate the stubborn defenders of the bungalow on the morrow. Before sundown that night the Commanding Officer and I, in our new-found elation, recklessly squandered half a mug of water each on a shave!

The plan was simple. We still based our hopes of success on getting a hold on the north-east corner of the tennis court, from where the infantry under the supporting fire of the Lee tank would clear the positions under the club bank, whilst a further platoon working on the right but inside the Pimple would clear the water tank and the long tin shed area. Subsequently a third platoon were to pass through the captured tennis-court area and exploit to the bungalow terrace in conjunction with the platoon of "D" Company still holding the tip of the spur above the road junction. To make assurance doubly sure, we invited the Mountain Gunners, who had a lot of old scores to pay off, to man-handle during the night a 3.7-inch guq up the khudside to the south-west of the Pimple, from where they could get a direct shoot at about a hundred and eighty yards' range into the back of the tin huts and water tank, whilst the Lee hit them from the front. A secondary task was to strafe the bamboo clump and other suspected targets which had proved so difficult for "C" Company on the 11th of May.

For this attack the Commanding Officer decided to use "D" Company, less one platoon, under Major Chettle, who were fresher than "C" Company, supported by "B" Company. We were getting very low in numbers by then, and after their turn at the tip of the spur "B" Company could hardly field more than a strong platoon.

On the morning of the 13th of May, from the Battalion observation post below the summerhouse, which has already been mentioned, we watched anxiously as Sergeant Waterhouse, of the 149th Royal Tank Regiment, waddled his Lee over the edge of the club bank and slid down on to the tennis court. We had done it at last— a tank was on the tennis court and the service was ours! Anxiously we watched for any Jap reaction as the tank slowly, so it seemed, swung round and started to serve. There was no nonsense about foot faults: Sergeant Waterhouse just let the Nip have it with his 75-mm., firing straight into their bunkers at a range of the length of a standard tennis court. On the first round of the 75-mm. gun the infantry moved forward and the 3.7 opened up and let the enemy have fifty rounds fire, at point-blank range, up their sterns. With great skill Sergeant Given manoeuvred his platoon round to the north-east corner, where he deployed and started setting about any opposition he could find. On the right Sergeant Cook waited until the gun fire had switched and then got in among the shellhappy Nips.

On the cessation of the 3.7-inch howitzer fire, forty to fifty Nips were seen to leave their positions legging it for all they were worth, casting away their arms and equipment to make better time down the south slope and past the Commandant's bungalow into the nullahs below. These were pursued by the small-arms fire of anyone in that area of the perimeter who could bring a rifle or light machine gun to bear, which continued even after the enemy were to be seen struggling up the steep slopes of Treasury Hill eight hundred yards away.

Meanwhile, down on the tennis court, Sergeant Given was seen moving around with the greatest unconcern, talking to Snagger Highett, who was in the tank, on the tank telephone and directing his fire on to positions still showing signs of life.

With the tennis court cleared, the tank moved forward to the edge of the terrace overlooking the bungalow itself, and "B" Company went through. It was then that Corporal Siggins, late of the Battalion police, was killed, our only death that day, whilst gallantly leading his section against a pocket of resistance in the immediate area of the bungalow.

The mopping up took some time. Clive Chettle, with his Company Sergeant-Major, showed tremendous dash and determination throughout the whole attack and especially during this latter phase. When he found that the Nips were pulling off the twenty-second fuses on the pole charges so unceremoniously stuffed into their bunkers, Clive merely cut them down to four seconds and hoped his own men would get out of the light in time. The result was most satisfactory except in the case of Lance-Sergeant Shearman, who was incapacitated for a few days owing to an inability to jump aside quickly enough. Not content with mere pole charges, this irrepressible officer was later found stuffing twenty-five-pound tins of ammonal down any hole that looked as if it would conceal a Nip. It was here that we first met Richard Sharp, of the B.B.C., who was to follow our fortunes for the next eight hundred miles or so. With his recording apparatus he gaily joined in the final rat hunt.

So after eighteen days of constant slogging we had gained our objective. The Japanese had been pitched clean out of the position, leaving behind about sixty counted dead, apart from the large number who were completely buried and never recovered. This final attack cost us only one man killed and two wounded.

Mopping up continued right into the night; by which time everyone had visited the famous compound and many a ghastly sight greeted our eyes. For the first time we could really appreciate the magnitude of the task that had been set "A" and "C" Companies nearly three weeks earlier, we could understand how "C" Company had originally walked right into the thick of the fight and realized to the full the magnificent job done by "A" Company in holding on by their eyelids to the vital position on the tip of the spur. If ever there was a feature which should be called "Dorset", it was that spur at Kohima, which was captured by Dorset grit and endurance and at the sad cost of seventy-five Dorset lives in a battle lasting nigh on three weeks.

The 13th of May was a successful day all round, for on that day the 6th, 33rd and 4th Brigades linked up and finally drove the Japanese from the Kohima Ridge back on to Aradura Spur. The next day we set about clearing up the compound and burying our dead. Great work was done by the Pioneer Platoon in locating and identifying the bodies, many of whom had perforce been left out since the 27th of April.

That evening the Padre held a service on the tennis court, still incongruously bearing its white markings, near the spot where "C" Company had their main losses in the initial attack.

No mention has been made of the Mortar Platoon, who throughout this battle supported the Battalion and the Brigade, at first from Picquet Hill and subsequently from a position just behind the hospital. It was here that the value of the long months of training under Davies really showed up to the best advantage. I cannot think how many hundreds of bombs they fired, but I do know that every battalion at one time or another had cause to thank them for their speed and accuracy. The Durhams especially during the time that they were being subjected to heavy "Banzai" attacks had every reason to be grateful for the quick and accurate response of the Mortar Platoon, whose fire did much to break up the enemy's attacks.

I cannot leave Garrison Hill without a final word about our existence during the last three weeks. I have said enough to indicate how "hugga-mugga" we were packed. The B.G.S., XXXIII Corps, our old Commanding Officer, Brigadier George Wood, on a visit to us during the battle, likened it to one of the bloodier corners of the old Somme battlefield in the last war. Amidst all the stench, flies and heat, life continued in the primitive way common to trench warfare. It was surprising how quickly the men managed to make themselves reasonably comfortable, even though their head cover was designed more to be waterproof than shellproof. The command post was a magnificent affair constructed by the Pioneers under the irrepressible Lance-Corporal Cranham and his "Crazy Gang". It was a luxurious abode as those dug-outs went, after we had lined it throughout with disused parachutes. Our white-silk-walled command post became a very popular rendezvous. The filth and the squalor were amongst the greatest of our discomforts. Against filth there was little to be done during the days of the acutest water shortage, save to rig every conceivable bit of tarpaulin, galvanized iron and scrap to collect rain water for a wash. As regards the squalor in general, as the days went by we got around and gradually cleaned up our own areas a bit.

In the main we were supplied throughout by air drop. These redoubtable Dakota pilots flew low over the very limited dropping zone (merely the crest of the hill) most afternoons and dropped us our much-needed supplies. In the course of time more and more stores were brought up by road, but every item that came by this means had to be man-handled up the steep hillside.

The administrative area lay back at Zubza for the 5th Brigade and in the neighbourhood of Lancaster Gate for the 6th Brigade. Separated as we were from our parent formation, I am even at this date still slightly vague as to where Bert Smith managed to conceal himself and "B" Echelon during these three weeks. All I do know is that one had hardly even to think of what one wanted before our demands were immediately satisfied by those magnificent people R.Q.M.S. Hayward, Sergeants Bagnall and Morris, and all the "moles" who went to make up "B" Echelon, ably assisted by the indefatigable mechanical transport drivers.

Throughout the battle we were continually indebted to Captain Norman Swallow and his Light Section, R.A.M.C., who worked so hard and continually to supplement the resources and energy of our own Medical Section.

I have made little reference to the Japanese artillery and practically none to the Jap air support. The former was most limited in quantity but often unpleasant enough owing to the unorthodox means employed by the Japanese in shooting their cannon. They literally were cannon, these old 1905 pattern 75-mm. guns of theirs, for all the world resembling a schoolboy's toy gun, but their results when used direct at close range could be devastating, as the survivors of both "A" and "B" Companies will testify. In the air the Japanese worried us hardly at all, and as a result the Division were able to get away with the most enormous atrocities in the handling of mechanical transport, closely packed gun lines and other concentrations of troops which would have called forth the most imperial rockets on any divisional exercise a few weeks earlier.

It was unfortunate that, for reasons of policy, both military and political, the 2nd Division received such a poor Press at the time of the Kohima battle. In these days of quick communications, when an action is news overnight and of no Press value in a week's time, it is, I am sure, essential that the fullest value be gained from the Public Relations resources, with their active and ever-present reporters. It was especially galling for our men to read in SEAC and hear related over the radio their own deeds ascribed to Indian troops who, however gallant elsewhere, just had not carried out that particular action.

When the ban was eventually lifted, I must say that the 2nd Division received their full share of publicity, but by that time a great many of the deeds performed by the units of the Division were past history and this sudden limelight lacked the authenticity of contemporary accounts, though Richard Sharp, with his immediate recording of the battle on the 13th of May did us an immense service. How much better were these matters conducted during the "second innings," when a reporter, known to the men as a familiar figure around the Battalion, could ensure that his description of a battle would be back in the men's hands not only in SEAC but printed in the home Press within a few days of the action.

On the 14th the 6th Brigade, or those who still remained in the perimeter, were ordered back to Dimapur to refit. Brigadier John Shapland had won his battle against the enemy after just over three weeks of continual hard slogging. We were to return to our own 5th Brigade after refitting, but it was with great pride that we marched out of the Kohima perimeter all freshly shaven—a pride in our having fought this phase of this great battle in such good company and with such a first-class brigade.

General Stopford himself was kind enough to refer to the District Commissioners' bungalow as "the key to Kohima", and its capture as "a turning point in the operations of the XXXIII Corps". I cannot think of a more appropriate close to this chapter than a reference to a report by Brigadier Wood on the Battalion's activities at this time. In writing home to describe the battle for the District Commissioner's bungalow as "the key to Kohima", and its capture. "Well, the Battalion kept on pegging away, cleaning up the Japs bit by bit and beating off their counter-attacks. They were ordered out on relief, but asked permission to remain until they had finished the job. Finally, we got a medium tank up to them and under its fire the Japs cracked and the Battalion did a final assault and accounted for every Jap remaining in the place. They couldn't have done better."

For his gallant and distinguished conduct during the operation Lieutenant-Colonel McNaught was awarded the Distinguished Service Order. For their efforts on the 13th of May Captain Chettle was awarded the Military Cross and Sergeant Given the Military Medal, as well as receiving a direct commission on the field. In addition, Sergeant Seale and Lance-Corporal Critchley, of the Medical Platoon, were awarded the Commander-in-Chief's Certificate of Gallantry.

D·C's BUNGALOW and GARRISON HILL

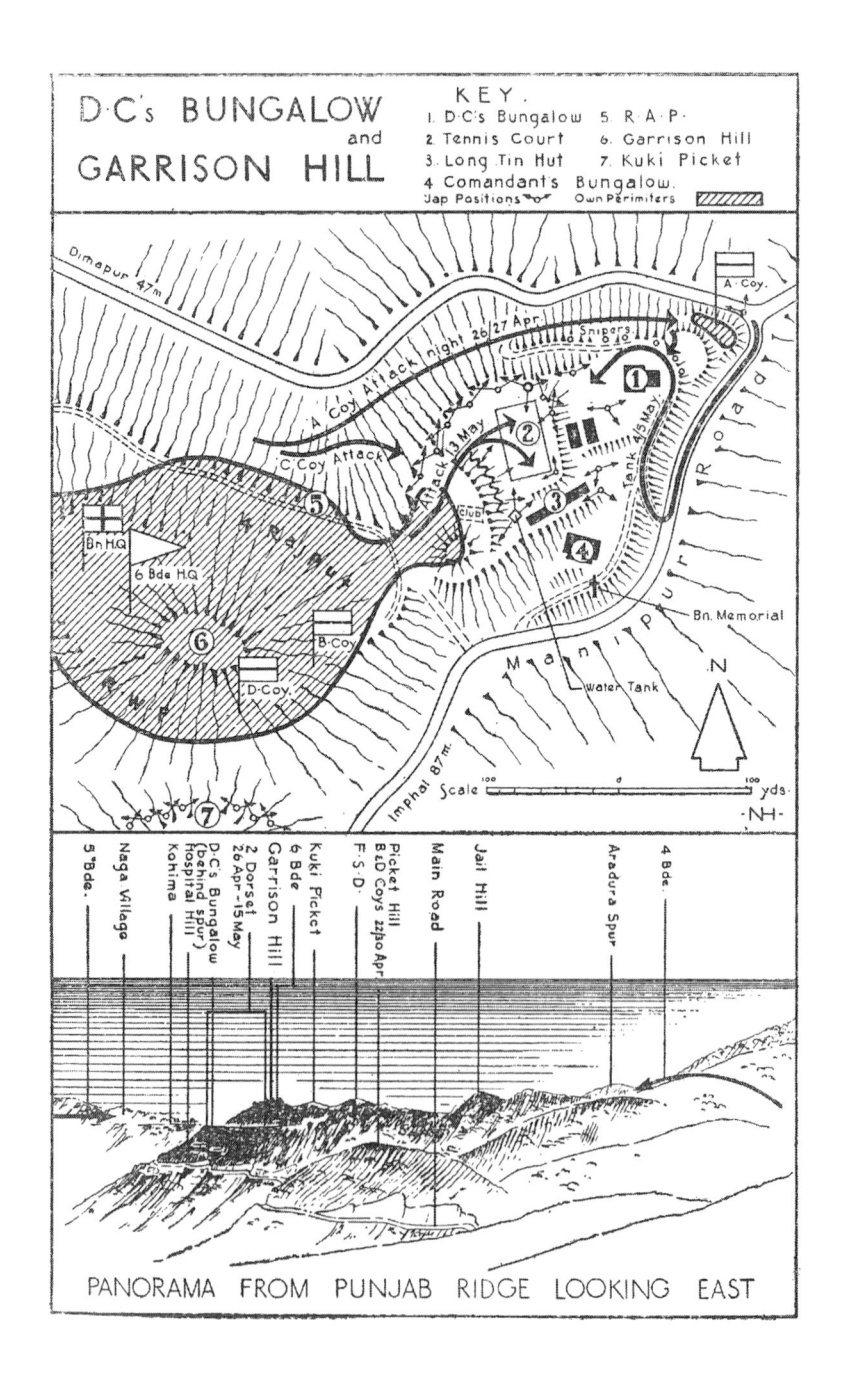

KEY.
1. D·C's Bungalow
2. Tennis Court
3. Long Tin Hut
4. Comandant's Bungalow
5. R·A·P·
6. Garrison Hill
7. Kuki Picket

Jap Positions ⟶ Own Perimiters ▨

Panorama from Punjab Ridge looking east — labels: 5 Bde.; Naga Village Kohima; D·C's Bungalow (behind spur "Hospital Hill"); 2 Dorset 26 Apr–15 May; Garrison Hill; 6 Bde; Kuki Picket; F·S·D·; Picket Hill B & D Coys 22/30 Apr; Main Road; Jail Hill; Aradura Spur; 4 Bde.

Lieut.-Colonel O. G. W. White, D.S.O., Officer Commanding, 1943, 1944-46

BURMA, 1944-45

The Tamu Road

"Sarah Sands" Day, 1944, Maram, M.S. 82.

A Brigade waterpoint in Burma. Such a chaung constituted the entire water supply for all purposes for a Brigade group.

TWO RIVERS—TWO BRIDGES

Bailey Bridge over the Chindwin at Kalewa. The longest bridge in the world under construction.

The Ava Bridge over the Irrawaddy. Blown by 17th Indian Division on the withdrawal from Burma, April, 1942

"SURE BY TAMU AND KALEWA AND THROUGH YE-U WE MUST GO"

The Animal Transport Platoon

Entering Schwebo

CROSSING THE IRRAWADDY, 25ᵀᴴ FEBRUARY, 1945

"A" Company waiting to cross

"B" Company setting off in a Dukw

CROSSING THE IRRAWADDY, 25TH FEBRUARY, 1945

"C" Company in an F.B.E. boat, waterborne

"A" Company press on

SUPREMO VISITS 2 DIV.

The Supreme Allied Commander, S.E. Asia, Lord Louis Mountbatten, talks to men of 2nd Division before the Irrawaddy crossing

Lord Louis Mountbatten and General Nicholson

W.A.S.(B) - Wasbies check canteen stores. Miss P. Tayleur and Miss E. Cheverton.

THE RACE TO MANDALAY

The C.O.'s carrier (Ava) at the Ava Bridge. C.O., L./Cpl. Selby, carrier driver, L./Cpl. Turner, jeep driver

Ava Bridge. C.O. plans future move with Major Fretts ("A" Company). Left: the I.O., Capt. N. Havers.

Mandalay, 1945

How do we know, where the long fight rages,
On the old stale front that we cannot shake,
And it looks as though we were locked for ages,
How do we know they are going to break?

—KIPLING.

CHAPTER SEVEN

THE BREAK-OUT FROM KOHIMA

"On, On, 'Do' Dorset"

[Battalion cry.]

ON THE 15TH OF MAY, 1944, the Dorsets marched out of Garrison Hill, Kohima, and by noon that day were concentrated at Dimapur. The move down the hill past old familiar landmarks had gone well enough, except for a platoon of "D" Company which had had the misfortune to be tipped over the khudside in their Royal Indian Army Service Corps General Purposes Transport Company threetonner. This accident was as serious for us as it was unnecessary. It was this platoon of "D" Company which had, under the command of Lieutenant Halahan, spent the last week in the isolated spur position and during that time had suffered very many fewer casualties than were caused by this one case of negligence on the road.

We were by now feeling ourselves to be quite old veterans and used the old soldier's privilege to grumble heartily at the accommodation provided in this railway siding at Dimapur. This was hardly fair to Brigadier Hayne and his staff of Headquarters, 253rd SubArea, and all those who went to endless trouble to ensure that during our few days' relaxation we should lack nothing that could possibly be produced. Dimapur even at the best could hardly boast an adequate bazaar for a British brigade under these conditions, and amenities were certainly scarce. We were very heartened on the day after our arrival by a visit from General Stopford himself, accompanied by the B.G.S. Few of us had seen our very busy Corps Commander since his first visit to the Battalion in January, and the stout-hearted way in which he set about coping with our difficulties after having spoken with the men did a great deal to encourage the Battalion.

We were forced, whilst at Dimapur, to a reluctant conclusion. In order to continue as a fighting unit we would have to disband one rifle company. The reinforcement situation for British other ranks at this time was paralytic, and we were told that we would just have to make do with what we had. After much discussion the Commanding Officer was forced to the sad decision of having to disband "A" Company. They had lost more than anyone else in casualties, and so for the first time for many years the Fifty-Fourth returned to action without its grenadier company. John Bowles, who had had a very rough time and was not really fit again, was allowed to "swing" for a few weeks.

The days flew past, full of reorganization, promotions, football and visits to various E.N.S.A. concerts and cinemas, and on the 23rd of May I led the Battalion (the Commanding Officer had gone on ahead overnight) back into the hills to about MS45, where we debussed. It was pouring with rain and we were not over-enthusiastic about our new locality away up the side of the mountain well off the road. Here we rejoined the 5th Infantry Brigade, who had, only a day or two before, been pulled back from the Naga village on relief by the 33rd Indian Infantry Brigade. It was good to get back to our old team again, but, oh! what a number of familiar faces were missing! Whilst at Dimapur some of us had been to see our old Brigadier, the Hawk, as he lay in hospital. Up in the Naga village, whilst reconnoitring for a break-through to Treasury Hill, he had been sniped in a most uncomfortable part of his anatomy.

The Hawk had been with us for nearly two years—to him personally must go a great deal of the credit for the performance of the 5th Brigade in action. In India he had taken us, and where necessary flogged us, through all forms of training. His enthusiasm had inspired the Brigade. The son of a retired officer of the Regiment, he always held a high opinion of our capabilities, and I know how deeply he regretted, when the time came for the 5th Brigade to show their true worth in the field at Kohima, that the Dorsets had been divorced from his command.

Brigadier Michael West had in the meantime been promoted from Second-in-Command of the 72nd Infantry Brigade in the 36th Infantry Division, to command the 5th Brigade. He was not unknown to some of us, as years before, in the heyday of our athletics success as a Battalion, he, as a member of the Oxfordshire and Buckinghamshire Light Infantry athletics team and Army sprinter, had been a great thorn in our side. With his arrival the team that was finally going to stick together until the end of the Japanese War was gradually taking shape. Another welcome addition to a much-decimated Brigade Headquarters a few days later was the return of Tony Bridge from the Staff College at Quetta, to take over Brigade Major of the Brigade in place of the unfortunate Ian Thorburn, of the Royal Scots, who had been killed in the Naga village. With Tony

Bridge as Brigade Major and Tom Hughes as Staff Captain the Dorsets were strongly represented at Brigade Headquarters.

On our return we found the 5th Brigade in Divisional reserve in the area of Two Tree Hill, away up on the right flank, ready to be used in the coming break-through the Aradura position and so down the Manipur Road. We ourselves took over from the rear details of the 1st Queen's, who had fought most gallantly during the latter stages of the first phase of the Battle of Kohima when the 33rd Infantry Brigade had been brought under the command of the 2nd Division.

As usual, there was no clear definition of a front line. The Colonel sent Graeme Gordon Wright with "B" Company to take up a position even farther up the mountainside. Above him there was supposed to be a battalion of the Burma Regiment who had fought so gallantly throughout the initial siege of Garrison Hill. Whether they were there in force or not was never fully established; what was, however, quite definite was that just a little farther up was a strong party of Japanese. A telephone ran from Battalion Headquarters up the hill: we always felt that in idler moments Graeme made use of the mysterious prolongation of this line to play a game of bridge by telephone with the Jap company commander higher up the hill!

Generally speaking, this second phase of the Battle of Kohima was proving as difficult a task for two divisions as the initial conflict had been for one. On the 24th of May General Messervy, with his 7th Indian Division, with the 161st Brigade under command, had taken over all responsibility for the left flank from excluding Garrison Hill. The 268th Brigade, from the disbanded 21st Indian Division, had taken over the centre of the line, leaving the 2nd Division free to break through on the right. This was our first contact with the 268th Indian Infantry Brigade. We were to soldier with them in one form or another (they were always changing their composition) for the next three years. At first they followed us up steadily right down to the plains of Burma. After VJ Day, when the 5th Infantry Brigade came to form up for the occupation of Japan, it was the 268th Brigade of the Indian Army who were selected as representatives of the Indian infantry to accompany the force to the enemy's own land.

On the 28th of May, in the pouring rain, the Dorsets advanced once more to the attack. The 5th Infantry Brigade were on the left and below the Imphal Road. Overnight "C" Company had established themselves on Greenfield Spur, and by 0800 hrs. on the 28th were established on the large spur running from MS48, called rather obviously MS48 Spur. The Battalion were ordered to move forward in conjunction with the advance by the 4th Infantry Brigade on the right and occupy a position on Garage Spur East, from which they would be in a position to attack the enemy positions on the crest. By 1030 hrs. "C" and "D" Companies were established on Garage Spur East and Lieutenant Highett was patrolling forward on to the crest. Battalion Headquarters, with "B" Company in reserve, had reached and were digging in on MS48 Spur.

On the right, however, things were not going quite so happily. The 6th Infantry Brigade were finding it most difficult to clamber up the steep slopes to the summit of the Aradura Spur, where the treacherous ground, made increasingly hazardous by the rains, proved nearly as great an obstacle to success as the stubborn resistance of the Japanese. On our immediate right the 4th Infantry Brigade were encountering great difficulty in capturing Basha and Cuckoo Spurs. The same old troubles were encountered. Cleverly concealed and strongly dug Japanese positions in the thick jungle on the steep sides of the hill constantly checked the stoutest attacks. Our orders were not to put in an attack on the crest of Garage Spur East until the positions immediately above the road had been reduced by the 4th Brigade on the right.

In the evening there was a complete checkmate on the right and the 5th Brigade (ourselves and the Worcesters) were ordered to withdraw to our start lines—not, however, before we had lost one of our most popular and gallant officers. Captain Michael Morice, who had already achieved great things at the District Commissioner's bungalow battle, and was a most potent factor in inspiring "C" Company to keep going after their heavy losses in the subsequent fighting, was killed in the forward position of Garage Spur East. He and the company commander, his "mucker," Davies, and C.S.M. Keegan were all considering the situation over a cigarette. They had dug themselves in and were taking a well-earned breather when a Nip opened up from the slopes above and Michael was killed outright and four British other ranks were wounded.

That evening the Battalion pulled back into reserve to a position behind Jail Hill. It was still pouring with rain and I have never seen the Battalion so depressed as they were that night. They had gone into action in great form, refreshed after their interlude in Dimapur; they had performed their own task well and, as is so often the case at the time, could see no rhyme or reason for being ordered to pull back. Finally, Michael's death cast a gloom over the whole Battalion, so greatly was he liked and missed by everybody. I well remember going forward to the Battalion that evening. I had been L.O.B. for the attack, and, although I was bringing up a special meal, the first issue of the much-heralded African ration which was infinitely superior to anything we had yet seen up to date, not even the thought of a good "khana" of steak-and-kidney pie really cheered the men up.

A couple of days later the whole Battalion was ordered back into a "rest" area, away up on the side of the hill above the road about MS43½. By the time we had completed our daily maintenance there was little rest in the mud of these steep slopes, but we were able, in relays, to get the Battalion back to Zubza, where the Brigade "B" Echelon had managed to provide an excellent means of bathing and a change of clothes. We had only a couple of days' grace before the 5th Brigade were launched into the next phase, which was to prove to be the final break out of Kohima.

Despite constant official assurances from South-East Asia Command Headquarters, situated in distant Ceylon, that the monsoon had not yet broken, it was very wet. The rain poured down and these mountain tracks bulldozed out of the khudside to take a jeep were practically impassable. This was our first intimation of things to come. However, the Supreme Commander had ordered and we were all determined to fight on through the monsoon. From intelligence reports the Japanese were already in a bad way, as they had made no provision for the monsoon season and their administrative services seemed remarkably poor.

During these few days Dick Purser was worked very hard running patrols with a battalion of the 4th Infantry Brigade out on the Aradura Spur. With so many "leader" casualties among the junior officers and non-commissioned officers, all battalions were getting very low in leaders capable of taking out patrols. More and more these tasks fell to the few remaining officers, and in many cases company commanders already hard enough worked had to be sent out to obtain valuable information. Patrolling in this area was incredibly difficult. Not only were the Japanese experts at defence but the very terrain militated against successful patrolling except by the most experienced patrollers. Whereas in North-West Europe a thousand-yard patrol would merely mean a stalk over reasonably flat territory, in this theatre it might well involve a climb down and up of a thousand feet or so through dense undergrowth. Too often would patrol leaders report a position clear when they had not even reached it. These false reports were not made with dishonest intent, but a non-commissioned officer, we found, was much less inclined to admit having failed to reach his objective than was an officer. The officer would admit to not having fulfilled his task, but on questioning was able often to state categorically that as far as he had been the ground was clear. This false reporting of positions as being clear was to be a constant source of trouble to battalions until later and wiser we, in the 5th Brigade, evolved our own special technique.

By the end of May the 33rd Indian Infantry Brigade had completed the task begun and made possible by the earlier activities of the 5th Infantry Brigade, and had cleared the enemy from the Naga village. The left flank now lay wide open. On the right the enemy still hung on on the Aradura Spur and so, with the left flank clear, the way lay open to break out by the east, outflanking the enemy in front of the 4th and 6th Brigades. This plan had been considered by the Corps Commander and other senior officers for some time, but it had not been possible to implement until the high ground on the left flank was in our hands.

Accordingly, on the 3rd of June the 5th Infantry Brigade started off on its first proper battle as a brigade rather than as a combination of independent units. Whilst the 6th Brigade were to maintain pressure on the right against the crest of the Aradura Spur, Brigadier West was told to lead his brigade on a long left hook over what was probably the most difficult country we ever tackled. The Brigadier's intention was to capture the Dyer—Big Tree Hill feature and from there press on to the Japanese base for the Aradura operations at Pfuchama, a Naga hill village, and thence descend to the Manipur Road by way of Phesema, to cut it at about MS53. It was hoped that this left hook would tie up with the advance of the 4th Brigade down the road (once they had overcome the two strongly held road blocks which had by now been discovered) and the move forward, through the jungle, of the 6th Brigade still milling around on the hilltops of the Aradura Spur.

Accordingly, early on the morning of the 3rd of June, at a time when in happier days the Battalion would have been preparing to march on parade to celebrate the late King George V's birthday, the Fifty-Fourth left their rest area and took the lead of the 5th Brigade on this arduous advance. They moved by familiar landmarks—Mortuary Corner and the road junction below the District Commissioner's bungalow—turned left past Treasury Hill, now a complete shambles, and after passing through the Assam Rifles' lines plunged downhill into the thick undergrowth. Apart from some intermittent shell fire, the Battalion arrived unhindered in the late afternoon on the lower slopes of Dyer Hill. The Bombay Grenadiers had reported Dyer Hill clear of the enemy. Fortunately, however, the Commanding Officer was induced to take extra precautions after encountering Snagger Highett, who had been sent on an independent mission and had most definitely and but a short time earlier been shot-up both from Big Tree Hill and the Pimple just west of Dyer Hill. Not long before dusk "D" Company, leading, came under fire from the east end of Dyer Hill itself, and Jock McNaught decided to go into a tight perimeter for the night, as the swiftly falling darkness made further reconnaissance with a view to an attack that night impracticable.

During the night it teemed with rain. The Battalion had no cover and had had no evening meal. Of all the bad nights, from the weather point of view, that night on the steep sides of Dyer Hill in close contact with the enemy was one of the worst. Slit trenches filled with water as soon as they were dug, and owing to the extremely difficult nature of the terrain patrolling was reduced to a minimum.

At first light on the 4th of June, cold, soaked through, stiff and breakfastless, "D" Company, under the intrepid Clive Chettle, pushed forward and occupied the crest of Dyer Hill. They found that the Nip had evacuated the position during the night, leaving behind a well-constructed defensive position on the reverse slope.

The Colonel decided to press on towards his objective at Big Tree Hill. At 0810 hrs. a not very accurate ten-minute concentration by the Divisional artillery was put down on the intervening Pimple, after which Captain Davies led "C" Company to the attack with the Guerrilla Platoon under Captain Dick Purser on the left.

On the right the advance progressed without incident until within fifty yards of the top, from which place the nature of the ground caused Davies to call a halt and order one platoon to attack the crest of the Pimple. When within two or three yards of the top this platoon was checked by heavy light-machine-gun fire and grenades from a reverse-slope position some five to ten yards away. A leftflanking movement by one section was also unsuccessful, coming under heavy light-machine-gun fire as it attempted to cross the wire protecting this side of the Japanese position.

At this point Davies put in his second platoon ("C" Company ran to only two platoons at this stage), with orders to work round the right-hand side of the Pimple. The leading section met with great success at first, reaching the top and promptly killing four Japanese. The Japanese, however, reacted strongly, the whole position opening up, and this section were forced back under cover of the crest. Davies now formed up for a second attack with this platoon, again round the right flank, this time with two sections up. This attempt proved to be no more fortunate than the first. Surprise had by now been lost and the platoon found it impossible to penetrate the showers of grenades and heavy light-machine-gun fire coming from the Japanese position as they breasted the crest. When all but one of the right-hand section had become casualties and the remainder of the platoon were finding the going extremely hard, Davies gave the order to withdraw.

On the way back Private Collis was wounded by a sniper, and after two men had tried to get him in, "Dave", as he was so well known by everyone, gallantly went forward to try to rescue him himself. He was killed by a Jap from the Pimple as he knelt beside Collis.

Meanwhile, on the left the Guerrilla Platoon were progressing well under Dick Purser. About fifty yards from the top they ran into trouble, and as Dick was giving out some orders he was mortally wounded through the head by a Jap concealed in the bushes about ten yards away. Sergeant Maule promptly accounted for this assailant, but it was small recompense for the loss of such a fine fighting soldier as Dick.

At this stage, realizing that the Battalion were bumping their heads into a strongly held position, the Commanding Officer called off the attack until he could get some co-ordinated fire support.

That morning's work in the rain on Dyer Hill cost us two invaluable officers killed and sixteen British other ranks wounded. The loss of Dick Purser, a young Regular officer, made a great hole in the Battalion team. By no means outstanding in the humdrum life of barrack and camp soldiering, Dick, from the moment he had achieved his heart's desire of active service, had shown that he had all the qualities of a remarkable fighter. He was never happy but when he was out killing Japanese. He imbued whatever platoon or patrol he was leading with that same indomitable spirit and energy that he always put into his fighting. At the District Commissioner's bungalow, Aradura, Dyer Hill, wherever things were difficult or the odds against us, there would one see Dick's flaming red head moving around and exhorting his men. It was a queer trick of fortune that Dick, always so punctilious in carrying a rifle, save on this last attack, and ever doing his best to disguise himself from being spotted as the leader, should have been killed giving out orders. There is no disguise for such as he, the British officer born and trained to lead men.

The loss of Davies was just as serious for the Battalion. For two years Dave had trained and led the Mortar Platoon, who had up to now produced, and were to continue to produce, such magnificent results. After Kohima he had, perforce, to leave his beloved mortars to take over the task of company commander, and in his leadership during his first battle in that capacity had already displayed what marked ability he possessed. We all knew how deeply he felt the loss of his "mucker," his inseparable comrade, Michael Morice, but a few days before, a few hundred yards farther along the ridge we were now attacking.

Lieutenant Highett, who had rejoined the Battalion overnight after his previous day's patrolling activities, brought "C" Company out of action and took over command as their fifth commander in two months. As a result of the information gained, the Brigadier decided to put the Camerons through the Dorsets, preceded by a very much more accurate concentration of Divisional artillery, mortars and medium machine guns. The Camerons occupied the Pimple in the afternoon and the next day captured Big Tree Hill. The Camerons also had their serious losses on this day, chief among them being their Second-in-Command, Angus Douglas, who had served with the Seventy-Ninth Highlanders for some years and was well known and well liked throughout the Brigade.

Early on the morning of the 5th of June a platoon of "B" Company under Sergeant Mansfield (recently promoted) was sent forward to patrol to the five-thousand-foot-high hill village of Pfuchama, which we had long suspected the Nip to have been using as a forward base area for his Aradura operations. By noon this platoon reported the village clear and the Battalion set off on their tough three-thousand-yard cross-country journey. The order of march was "D" Company, "C" Company, Battalion Headquarters, and "B" Company, less one platoon. The thousand-foot climb down to the Warno Nullah was made without incident. About four hundred yards beyond the nullah "D" Company, on the advice of a friendly Naga guide whose services had been co-opted, took the right-hand fork which led up to a spur running to the south end of the village. "C" Company started to follow. By the time that Battalion Tactical Headquarters had reached the track junction it was hardly recognizable as such and, not realizing that the leading troops had changed direction, they carried on up the left-hand fork on what was the ordered, and on the face of it very much shorter, route to the north end of the village. After a short time the Adjutant, Colin Doran, realized to his horror that Tactical Headquarters, led by the Commanding Officer, were leading the advance up this hill track. They paused for a while whilst "C" Company were discovered, collected and put once more in the lead. It was out of the question to gather in "D" Company, who by now were well on their way up the right-hand track. The whole Battalion was very overladen on this operation, as everything possible had to be carried on the men, and this manoeuvring on the steep jungle slopes after such a gruelling forty-eight hours caused them to overtire prematurely.

All went well until they had almost reached the summit, when the leading platoon of "C" Company came under heavy light-machine-gun fire from such close range that the leading section commander at first thought it was his own Bren gunner firing. It was a nasty place for an ambush, especially with tired men; any movement off the track on those steep slopes was out of the question, and the Commanding Officer ordered the withdrawal of the Battalion to the track junction below to follow up "D" Company. Down the khudside they slipped and fell, eleven hundred feet, to the fork junction and another twelve or thirteen hundred feet up again. Getting the wounded men down was the worst difficulty; three men had been hit and one killed in that brief encounter under the crest of Pfuchama Hill. By 1830 hrs. the Battalion had reached the village and had joined up with "D" Company and the platoon of "B" Company who had been there since the morning.

Clive Chettle had already swept through the village and reported it clear. Earlier the platoon of "B" Company had seen a force of heavily laden Japs marching eastwards away from the north end of the village and had successfully engaged them, killing three and capturing a Taisho light machine gun, some packs and other minor identifications, such as paybooks. It would appear that the light machine gun which engaged "C" Company had been left behind to cover the withdrawal of the main force.

By this time the Battalion were feeling pretty tired. For sixty solid hours they had been advancing against opposition over the most fearsome territory and with little or no opportunity even to brew themselves a cup of tea. For most of the time the rain had poured down on them and, apart from being soaked through, the ground was getting more and more difficult. Since leaving Kohima they had lost two officers and four men killed and another sixteen wounded, a further deficit of twenty-two against our rapidly falling fighting strength.

During the next forty-eight hours, whilst the Brigade closed up at Pfuchama, the Battalion patrolled vigorously towards Phesema. Even during this so-called slack period we were still to have casualties among our vital personnel. Sergeant Mansfield was wounded and was never to return to the Battalion. Another most serious loss at this time was yet another company commander, Graeme Gordon Wright. Wounded in the arm, apparently but slightly, Graeme was evacuated to me with the Battalion "tail" at the Assam Rifles' barracks with instructions to rest for a few days. However, his condition deteriorated and he had later to be evacuated. His description of his subsequent treatment and journey back down the lines of communication to Dehra Dun and thence to Poona makes the grimmest reading. In comparison with their truly expeditious and slick evacuation schemes later in this campaign, the medical services behind Corps were not functioning well at this time, and it was not until October that we were to see Graeme's cheerful smile with the Battalion again.

Meanwhile, the Commanding Officer had left me in charge of the Battalion "tail". I call it this advisedly, as by this time we had to knock up a different organization for each action. The Colonel took with him on his cross-country journey only the bare necessities in men, weapons and equipment. With me he left the mortars, Carrier Platoon and spare files from the Signal and other specialist platoons. "B" Echelon were still back at Zubza (MS36), ten miles from Kohima. I called up the Regimental Quartermaster-Sergeant and a supply echelon, and such mechanical transport as was required and could be accommodated on Treasury Hill, which had for this advance become a gun area and a centre for the forward echelons of the Brigade and Divisional administrative services. After having the privilege of showing General Giffard, the Commander-in-Chief, 11th Army Group, around the battleground of the District Commissioner's Bungalow and presenting to him Sergeant Given, who had been recommended for an immediate commission, I handed over our old rest area to Lieutenant-Colonel Jock Carroll, the new Commanding Officer of the Royal Norfolks, and brought my team forward to the Assam Rifles' lines. From here we had to supply the Battalion with all they required—rations, ammunition and water—by Naga porter. R.Q.M.S. Hayward worked wonders with his team of a hundred porters. With no mutual language except the application of his khud-stick and with but the minimum escort that we could raise from any odd bodies who were not actively employed elsewhere, he drove this party up and down the tenuous lines of communication to the Battalion and back. He would return in the evening soaked through, his bush hat and moustache drooping with rain, tired out but still prepared to work half the night making preparations for the next day.

Whilst here we received a reinforcement officer in the person of Captain A. C. Mackenzie, of the Somerset Light Infantry. "Mac" was one of the first reinforcement officers to come to us direct from home. After a short pause with me I sent him forward with the next supply column and he was posted to take over the Guerrilla Platoon in place of Dick Purser.

Meanwhile, the Brigadier had pressed on relentlessly during the night of the 6th/7th of June. Even as news of the Normandy landings was coming through, news that heartened the tired Brigade to no small extent, the Worcesters under John Brierley were pressing on towards Phesema, and on the morning of the 7th of June they married up with the Royal Scots at about MS53. The Battle of Kohima was over, the last remaining enemy rearguard was pulling out, and the pursuit was beginning.

During the 7th of June the Battalion left Pfuchama and advanced across country to the main road. At Kigwema they encountered some opposition and had to clear the old British Hospital area at MS54 before they could move in and occupy it. The Jap was still selling his life dearly. On the roadside at Kigwema the leading company were treated to another of those astonishing exhibitions of *hara-kiri* by Japanese non-commissioned officers blowing themselves up with their own grenades with which we had grown familiar on the District Commissioner's Bungalow position.

That evening I went up to the Battalion, driven by my old "A" Company driver, Private Wareham, down the recently opened road. Already a long head-to-tail column of guns, tanks and supply vehicles was pouring down the newly opened stretch of this vital road. The Colonel had only one request: fresh clothes. During the two days at Pfuchama they had attempted to avoid the rain by billeting themselves in Naga dwellings and they had suffered bitterly from the attentions of fleas and other indigenous insects.

Owing to the volume of traffic on the road I did not get back to Zubza until after dark, and was most grateful for the rum handed to me by the ever-cheerful Sergeant Stanford.

Early the next morning I was awakened by the signaller and told that the Commanding Officer wanted me on the set. His instructions were quite simple—come forward immediately. "What the hell's happened now?" I thought, as Private Wareham threaded his way through the traffic in the pouring rain. When I had left them the previous night the Battalion were due for a couple of days' rest and I couldn't understand this sudden call.

On arrival at Kigwema I met General Grover, who told me that I was to take over the Battalion immediately and wished me luck. He could promise no long rest, and I must be prepared to move on again pretty soon. In the Battalion Headquarters basha I was greeted by Jock McNaught, who handed me back my old pair of lieutenant-colonel's shoulder-straps which I had presented him with on his arrival to command the Battalion three months earlier. He told me that he had been promoted to command the 4th Infantry Brigade in place of Brigadier Saunders, late Commanding Officer of the Camerons.

Our joy at Colonel Jock's promotion was tempered with the feeling of loss at his departure. Although he had been a Dorset for only so short a time, he had from the moment of his arrival at Jagalpet endeared himself to the Battalion. His cool and calm leadership and his cheerful manner had done more than anything else to bring the Battalion successfully through the campaign to date. He had a very shrewd judgment and the uncanny knack of summing up an officer or man on first acquaintance. His knowledge of regimental soldiering was deep, and he never allowed the Battalion to be bounced. At his request I marshalled the whole Battalion so that he could address them for the last time. To our dismay we found that, so heavy had been our losses, we could easily accommodate the whole Battalion as we then stood in one large basha.

I was fully employed during the remainder of the 8th of June reorganizing the Battalion—first, physically on the ground, to accord with the rapidly changing position, and, secondly, in sorting out the order of battle. Promotions had to be made as a result of our casualties and the promotion of the Brigadier and myself. Clive Chettle got his majority and Lintorn Highett his captaincy, I remember.

By now we could muster six weak platoons and we had to reorganize on this basis for the coming pursuit down the road. Our mechanical transport was limited and we were based on five "tactical" jeeps at Battalion Headquarters and a limited number of 15-cwt. Dodges. On reassuming command I kept Private Joe Turner as Commanding Officer's driver, relinquishing King, who had been Second-in-Command's driver since Yorkshire days, for general duties until such time as we would have a Second-inCommand again (I couldn't spare an officer at present). Turner I promoted lance-corporal and appointed "jeep major" in charge of the tactical jeeps at Battalion Headquarters.

That evening the Brigadier held a conference at Brigade Headquarters and gave us the plan for the pursuit.

A Naga Hut

CHAPTER EIGHT

THE PURSUIT DOWN THE MANIPUR ROAD

"Primus ex Indis" [9]

THE CAPTURE OF the Aradura Spur and the break out of Kohima coincided with the start of the monsoon. The Corps Commander's object was now to follow up the enemy so closely that his orderly withdrawal should develop into a rout and consequently ensure the destruction of the Japanese 31st Infantry Division.

General Stopford's plan was to make the main thrust along the Manipur Road with the 2nd Infantry Division, with the object of re-establishing road communication with the IV Corps. At the same time the 7th Indian Infantry Division were to advance on the left flank, south-east and south, initially astride the Jessami track, thereby causing a constant threat to the enemy's right and closing his communications and escape routes to the east by such ways as the Tuphema—Karasom track. Farther still to the east the 23rd Long Range Penetration Brigade were invited to continue their advance across country to the nodal point of Ukhrul and beyond.

In this way General Stopford planned to use to the best advantage the peculiar characteristics of each of his divisions and the independent brigade—the hitting power of the 2nd Division on the main axis, the ability of the 7th Division to operate on an animal-transport basis, and the strategical mobility of the 23rd Brigade.

General Stopford had moved his Corps Headquarters early in June from Dimapur to MS32, and for the moment had nearly caught up with the 5th Brigade "B" Echelon in Zubza. One of the first things Brigadier West did at this time was to order "B" echelons forward twenty miles to Kigwema as the Brigade advanced, and we tried never again to allow them to get so far behind. At the same time the 2nd Division arranged for

---

[9] 'The Regimental Motto is *"Primus in Indis,"* earned in 1754, when the 1st Battalion (Thirty-Ninth Foot) were the first King's regiment to serve in India. How the 2nd Battalion came to lead the pursuit out of India will be read in this chapter.

the move forward from Golaghat of all our surplus kit that had perforce been dumped when the Brigade went into action on the 10th of April. This closed up yet another echelon; we had quite enough of these already, what with a rear party in Ahmednagar and stores and men scattered along the lines of communication throughout the breadth of India and Assam.

On the 9th of June the Dorsets were put under the command of the 4th Brigade for their advance down the road. Within thirty-six hours of his departure the Battalion were once again serving under the command of Brigadier McNaught. The advance, started on the 8th of June, had gone well for a few miles until the forward troops reached MS59. Here they found the road blocked and extensively mined and under fire from enemy artillery and machine guns in the area of Viswema and the high ground to the west of the road.

This enemy position at Viswema turned out to be strongly defended, and Brigadier McNaught sat down to attack it with all his reserves. No one appreciated better than he did how weak in strength the Battalion, with its six fighting platoons, had become and we were allotted the role of guarding the gun area, which also housed the 4th Brigade Tactical Headquarters, on a small spur at about MS59¼. That evening, just before dusk, I was ordered to send a company and the Guerrilla Platoon to join the 2nd Norfolk on Shaving Brush Spur.

Shaving Brush Spur was a very thickly wooded and steep spur running down on to the road from the west. It completely covered the village of Viswema and the enemy positions. Unfortunately, owing to the inaccuracy of the maps and the very limited visibility of about ten to fifteen yards, the Norfolks had the day before reached only a subsidiary spur and had not in point of fact reached their objective. They were heavily counter-attacked, and it was in answer to their call that the Brigadier had told me to send up reinforcements.

I received the order at about 1730 hrs., but there was some delay in launching "B" Company and the Guerrilla Platoon owing to the extra stores that had to be collected in the way of ammunition and extra digging tools for the Norfolks. Consequently, when the force arrived at the foot of the jungle track which led off from the main road, Peter Feeney was faced with that most difficult of operations, a night climb through jungle up a steep mountainside on an impossibly slippery and practically non-existent track with very heavily overladen troops. The situation was not improved by the encounter, at the foot of the track, with the supply party of the Norfolks, who, on their way down, had found the track cut by the Japanese and had escaped only after a brisk skirmish which resulted in several casualties.

However, their orders were clear and everyone understood the necessity of getting through to the Norfolks as soon as possible.

Feeney ordered the leading section to dump their packs and tools in order the more easily to deal with any emergency, and the company started off up the track in the dark, led by one guide of the Norfolks. So bad was the going that each man was forced to hang on to the water-bottle of the man ahead, and the climb up was made literally on the remaining hand and knees. Constant breaks occurred. It was found impossible for the stretcher-bearers to carry their stretchers under these conditions and they had to be jettisoned until the next day. The signallers also found the going practically impossible. Fortunately the Jap block had moved off, possibly considering that we had closed the lines of communication for the night, and at about 0300 hrs. on the 10th of June the long column arrived dead beat at the Norfolks' position.

This position was not an enviable one: the perimeter, already extraordinarily small, could not absorb the extra troops who had now arrived. Lieutenant-Colonel Carroll dispatched the Guerrilla Platoon on an independent mission, but even this did little to decrease the congestion. At first light the Dorsets realized that the Japanese position was only three to four hundred yards away and above them. The Nip found it very much easier to mortar the very "hugga-mugga" "Norset" position than it was for the latter to retaliate. These difficulties, however, were eventually overcome by the excellence of our support fire. The forward observation officer with "B" Company quickly got the range of the Nip position and soon a Japanese had only to show himself for a crump to be brought down on him with incredible accuracy. Our infantry-artillery cooperation in fire control in this thick country was improving rapidly.

Meanwhile, the Guerrilla Platoon were, as I have said, sent to occupy a small feature about seventy-five yards outside the "Norset" perimeter, from which they could command a view of the Japanese positions. Excellent work was done by Mackenzie and his platoon that day. Not content with merely plotting what he could see, Mac tried, with small patrols, to niggle forward and find out even more about the enemy position. Their platoon position, owing to the strangely scant cover in this particular area, was soon discovered and they were subjected to heavy sniping throughout the day. At about 1530 hrs. Mackenzie pulled in his platoon and reported to Colonel Carroll with some invaluable information which enabled the Norfolks' Commanding Officer radically to alter his plans for his projected attack. The Guerrilla Platoon had four casualties that day.

On the 11th of June Colonel Carroll, still under the impression that he was on Shaving Brush Spur, attacked eastwards downhill with "C" Company, 2nd Norfolk, and the Guerrilla Platoon, 2nd Dorset. This attack, however, was met and held by heavy enfilade fire from the Japanese position on the Shaving Brush Spur proper, a ridge to which the "Norsets" had not penetrated and to which they exposed their flanks on turning to the left to carry out this attack. Owing to the mist artillery support was difficult and tank support was out of the question. It was not until they had reached the road that it was finally discovered that they had attacked down the wrong spur. The Dorsets Guerrilla Platoon were promptly ordered to attack uphill and gain a foothold on Shaving Brush Spur proper, which attack they made under intermittent small-arms fire. "C" Company, 2nd Norfolk, were then guided up the spur in an attempt to "beat" the odd sniper posts in the vicinity. No sooner, however, had this attack started than the whole force bumped into a strong Japanese position with at least four light machine guns, and a withdrawal to the road was ordered. This had been an expensive afternoon's work with nothing to show for it, the Guerrilla Platoon losing another five men and the Norfolks twelve. In addition, Mac lost his platoon packs, which they had discarded when they started to attack up the hill. The loss of those packs worried Mac for a very long time afterwards. No wonder Michael West always referred to Viswema as the place where no one seemed able to read his map. It was admittedly extraordinarily difficult, but what a saving of life and trouble there would have been if only the force had got on to the right spur originally!

This was the only occasion in this war when history repeated itself and Norfolks and Dorsets actually fought together as a "Norset" force, as had their forebears in the Kaiser's War fought against the Turks at Kut al Amara. Colonel Carroll was full of praise for the conduct of both "B" Company and the Guerrilla Platoon, and it is unfortunate that our combined efforts did not achieve the success they had hoped for and thereby shorten considerably the Battle of Viswema.

Meanwhile, back in the gun area the remainder of the Battalion had not been idle. To us was allotted the daily task of opening the lines of communication to the Norfolks, which duties were shared by "C" and "D" Companies alternately. The weather was appalling: it poured with rain incessantly.

The first night, to get under some cover, the Adjutant, Colin Doran, and myself had shared a bivvy tent. In fact, for some hours after dark, as we conferred, we had taken the acting Intelligence Officer, Prebble, in as well. I considered that two six-footers in a bivvy tent was not the ideal habitation and the next day Bert Smith produced a forty-pounder tent. From then on I never moved without this invaluable piece of equipment. Folded, it fitted nicely on the bonnet of the jeep. So satisfactorily did it function that very soon we had organized three or four of these small tents for the signal office, "G" office and other essential personnel who had to work under cover and after dark.

When I look back at those days I am staggered by the number of liberties which the Japanese allowed us to take. On this small spur, jutting out of the side of the road, no more than two to three hundred yards wide and about the same number of yards deep, and within eight hundred to a thousand yards of the Japanese positions, the enemy allowed us to concentrate an immense amount of hitting power. At one time just before the final attack on Viswema, which had now become a joint effort of the 4th and 5th Brigades, run apparently as a condominium between Brigadiers McNaught and West, we harboured as guests in our perimeter the 4th Brigade Tactical Headquarters, the 16th Field Regiment, a battery of 3.7inch howitzers from the 99th Field Regiment, a squadron of Lee tanks, and over fifty 3-inch mortars, all with their gun-line dumps of ammunition. Nor was our list of V.I.Ps. any less formidable. On the 11th of June we were visited by the Army Commander, the Corps Commander and the Divisional Commander, all of whom came into our perimeter to have a "dekho" at the Japanese from really close quarters.

Apart from the operations already mentioned, the Battalion were not further actively involved in the Battle of Viswema other than in the continuance of their garrison role. At one time there was a distinct possibility of our being requested to do a long right hook three thousand feet up round the mountain of Tarhazu, in an attempt to encircle the Japanese. The Brigadier—I forget for the moment which, as one got quite confused as to which master one was serving at this time—went so far as to ask me to set about planning this operation with the use of Naga porters. However, fortunately for us the Camerons managed on the 13th of June to climb a precipitous slope on the east side of Tarhazu and so get above the Japanese on Shaving Brush Spur.

On the 14th the big attack went in, with the Camerons descending from the mountain on the right, the Royal Scots pushing up the centre and the Worcesters, supported by the massed Divisional artillery, tank, machine-gun and mortar fire, attacking round the left flank. For the first time we used the Bofors red tracer from a flank, with the result that the Worcesters were able to get up to within forty yards of their own supporting fire.

At first light the next morning the 6th Brigade passed through with an armoured column which had been formed and made for Mao Songsang, where we felt that the Nip would hold out in strength on this high watershed between Assam and Manipur.

This armoured column was to be the main feature of our advance down the road from now on. By European standards it must seem a very puny force, but it was much more than the Nip could muster and its effect on their rapidly diminishing morale was great. It is worth quoting the composition of this column in detail in order of march, as, though its infantry composition varied from day to day, its form was generally on these lines:

> One troop of armoured cars with a Royal Engineer officer.
> One troop of the 149th Royal Tank Regiment (Lees).
> Tank commander.
> Vanguard commander in Bren carrier.
> Infantry commander in carrier.
> One section of carriers loaded with infantry.
> Two armoured observation posts for forward observation officers.
> One troop of the 149th Royal Tank Regiment (Lees).
> One section of carriers loaded with infantry.
> Two carriers carrying Royal Engineer party.

This column was followed by the remainder of the leading infantry battalion which had found the personnel for the infantry element of the armoured column, and then the remainder of the Brigade.

As this column was pushing slowly down the road, owing to demolitions and isolated enemy resistance, the 5th Brigade were fully employed in mopping up and reorganizing. The 4th Brigade were taken out to rest.

By this time the 5th Brigade team were fully established. Michael West commanded the Brigade with great energy and had as his three commanding officers Angus McAlester (Camerons), John Brierley (Worcesters) and myself. All three of us had served together in the same brigade since 1941 in Yorkshire. All three had successively risen from company commander to second-in-command, and in the case of myself and Angus to a six-month period of command in 1943 together. We all knew each other, and when it came to mutual support in action we all knew how each of us would make his individual play.

Early on the morning of the 17th of June the three commanding officers met the Brigadier at the road junction, where the track to the village of Viswema met the main road. Looking back at it, we must have presented a strange sight that morning as we stood in the unexpected sunlight in the shadow of a 5.5-inch gun which had just been installed approximately on the site of a very cunningly concealed Japanese anti-tank-gun position. It had rained solidly for ten days and we were no copybook plates as we gathered together. John Brierley approached, making his way through the blackened ruins of Viswema, Angus appeared out of the jungle at the right of the road, and the Brigadier and myself arrived, slightly fresher but just as mud-stained, from the rear.

The pursuit was on—from now on there was to be no rest. Already General Grover was forward again with the leading battalion, urging them on and fretting at the delays imposed by Nature and the enemy. The 5th Brigade Order Group was short that morning: "On, on!" was the cry, and by noon the Battalion were on their way to Khuzama at MS64. We took over from a battalion of the 6th Brigade, who had patrols forward at MS65½. The Brigadier was still nursing the Dorsets, as we were still very much below the strength of the Camerons and Worcesters. On arrival at Khuzama the Brigadier decided to commit the Camerons and the Worcesters to a night encircling movement to get round the Japanese positions at Mao Songsang.

Mao Songsang was a nodal point on the route. Not only was it the frontier of British India and the native state of Manipur, but it was the highest point on the road and the place where the advance of the 2nd and 7th Divisions should converge. We had all fully expected the Japanese to hold this naturally strong position in strength, and had been led to believe this even before the Battle of Viswema, when a captured Indian National Army officer had disclosed what he knew of the enemy's plans.

However, during the night of the 17th/18th June our artillery heavily pounded the Japanese positions which had hitherto held up the 6th Brigade, and in the face of the two encircling attacks by the Camerons and the Worcesters he unexpectedly pulled out without further resistance.

The 18th was to be a very memorable day in the history of the Battalion. Leaving Khuzama early in the morning, we had our first party with the armoured column. With two squadrons of the 2nd Reconnaissance Regiment to boost our armoured column, we set out for Mao Songsang in the pouring rain—and how it did rain! For the whole of that day we splashed along in about two inches of water which could not clear itself off the road quickly enough.

Our first halt was at Mao Songsang, where we encountered John Brierley and his battalion, having done a magnificent night's work. Here on the frontier of India in a narrow defile one of those inevitable huddles started: the Divisional Commander, the Brigadier and two battalion commanders—no, three, as Jack Stocker and the Royal Welch had moved forward into Mao earlier in the morning —all collected together to discuss the situation in the pouring rain. Suddenly through the mist I saw a face I hadn't seen for over three years, the large, smiling face of Roscoe Turner. Back in 1940, when the 43rd Infantry Division had been sent to Dover, Roscoe commanded a battery in the Dorsetshire Yeomanry (141st Field Regiment) and so continued a connection he had made with the Dorsets when his regiment had lain alongside the 1st Battalion in Nowshera in 1939. Now he was to pick up the connection again and was to soldier on with us as battery commander and second-in-command of the 10th Field Regiment, right through to Japan.

But to return to our story. The upshot of the conference was that the 5th Brigade were to press on down the road. "Crack on, Geoffrey" said the General. I was allowed to retain my armour, my two troops of tanks and, fortunately, as will be seen later, a "mock-up" armoured bulldozer that the R.E.M.E. workshops had fashioned from a spare blade and a Lee tank. Peter Wells and his reconnaissance squadrons were to be side-tracked at Tuphema to close the Kharasom track and generally search the area.

All through the morning we marched without let or hindrance, through the rain and muck, until we reached a bend in the road at about MS73. Here we did come up against it. A large landslide had freshly dropped, completely blocking the road. I pushed the leading company (Clive Chettle) over the block and round the corner, from where they could look down into a deep nullah and away across to where the road curved in a steep incline up the other side, but for the moment we couldn't get the tanks through.

I reported back to the Brigadier, who, realizing that there would be a couple of hours' delay, decided to whistle up the Worcesters in mechanical transport to go through us and continue the advance once the road was opened again.

It was here that I had my first drink of zu, the local Naga ricebeer, from a friendly headman who came hurrying down from his village once the news got around that the British were back again. He also brought a couple of chickens. "D" Company grabbed these, but somehow my batman, Fooks, managed to scrounge some further local produce from another party of natives.

THE PURSUIT DOWN THE MANIPUR ROAD

I was personally disappointed at the Brigadier's decision to pass the Worcesters through us, but I am sure that he was right. They had had a few hours' rest after their exertions of the night before and we had by this time been on our feet marching under the most appalling conditions for ten hours.

In remarkably quick time a track was bulldozed through the landslide, unfortunately at the cost of the bulldozer, which had to go back for urgent repairs, and after the Worcesters had passed through we rose wet and stiff from the halt to continue our advance.

By the time that we had got to MS77½, overlooking Maram Spur, the Worcesters had been checked by enemy opposition and the Brigadier decided to call it a day.

A great day! Never before had an advance of sixteen miles been made against the Japanese Army in one day. For us it was especially significant, for we had earned the right to add "Primus ex Indis" to our already proud motto, as that day we had been the first British or any infantry to lead the pursuit of the Japanese out of British India over the frontier of Assam at Mao Songsang.

Later that evening the sun shone palely for a while, and as I was organizing the defence of the Battalion Headquarters position – without a Second-in-Command it was surprising how many odd jobs fell to the Commanding Officer – my gunman, the faithful Woodward, said, rather surprisingly: "Here's the Colonel, sir."

Looking round I saw the familiar figure of George Wood, who had come up with the Corps Commander to see for themselves what advances we had made. They were thrilled with the day's work, though I remember General Stopford being a bit impatient at the Worcesters stopping short of Maram. The events of the next day proved that with the best will in the world any further advance that night was simply not "on". We had run up against another of those prepared Japanese positions with which by now we were so familiar.

I can't say how much the appearance of the Corps Commander and two senior staff officers here in the front line at the end of a long and tiring march bucked up the troops. We were all feeling pretty flogged and the men greatly appreciated it when the General took some time off to speak with them. Shortly after his departure the cooks' trucks appeared from "B" Echelon, twenty-odd miles to the rear, with a hot meal. Good for the Quartermaster! He never let us down on that score, and how we needed that meal that night.

Later that evening Brigadier West held an Order Group in his headquarters by the roadside in the Battalion area. The Camerons were still at Tuphema, the Brigadier having decided to motor them forward the next morning to arrive fresh for the battle.

It rained harder than ever during the night. Colin Doran, the Adjutant, shared my forty-pounder tent erected on a bank just off the road. We were completely flooded out and spent a miserable night and just waited for the dawn to break.

The 19th of June broke fine and clear. Soon after first light patrols of the Camerons and Worcesters moved forward to try to locate the enemy positions. At 1000 hrs. the attack started. A great part of the Divisional artillery had come forward with us the evening before, and with the guns, the machine guns of "B" Company of the Manchesters and the mortars of the Brigade the enemy was being hotted-up to no mean extent. We had arrived the evening before so close on his heels that we had been able to observe him working at a number of his positions, which he was not allowed to do unmolested. This was a most unusual state of affairs, as one seldom saw the Nip at all.

On this day Brigadier West tried out a technique that later was to become common practice in the Brigade. Whilst the battalion commander, with his tactical headquarters, was plunging through the undergrowth close behind the leading companies, with his reserves behind him and under control, he was quite unable to direct his fire. This task the Brigadier, from an observation post sited to get the best view of the whole battle, undertook. This "5th Brigade system", as we called it, though we can't claim any particular originality, worked like a charm. On this day further little points of technique were improved. At various times during the Worcesters' attack the supporting arms had to cease firing owing to not being able clearly to spot our leading troops. John Brierley was asked by the Brigadier to make his forward sections throw No. 77 smoke grenades at regular intervals, and from then on the supporting arms had no difficulty in spotting how far the forward platoons had reached. Once again we were able to use our Bofors from a flank and their red tracer once more proved to be a great help to the infantry as a means of showing the near limit of the artillery concentration. Finally, on this day, whilst climbing up the steep khudside under the guns, the Worcesters displayed for all to see the most satisfactory keenness to get right up under their own artillery fire. The air was a great help that day also, and, supported by a great weight of fire from the ground and the air, the Worcesters by the middle of the afternoon had reached their objectives on Maram Ridge on both sides of the road. High up on the right flank the fighting patrols of the Camerons, having much farther to go in their enveloping sweep, were still mopping up some time later as we went through the Worcesters to exploit the attack. Under cover of a smoke screen and tank fire two road blocks at MS80 were removed by a bulldozer.

At about 1700 hrs. I was ordered by the Brigadier to advance in mechanical transport to MS80, debus and make hell for leather for MS82. We thought that once the Nip had broken he would try to make for Karong, an important junction and bridge about twelve miles farther on. MS82, with its spur sticking out over the road and tracks running out from it to the east and down on to it from the huge Maramei feature in the west, seemed to be an obvious rendezvous for the Nip. I was told to advance through the night and secure this feature as a firm base from which the 4th Brigade could pass through us and continue the pursuit in the morning.

I reached the Worcesters' objective at about 1745 hrs. and after a quick reconnaissance decided to put the Guerrilla Platoon over the top of the ridge to the right of the road, whilst the Battalion, debussing at MS80, could proceed round the corner by the main road and meet the G.R. Platoon at a point where a steep nullah met the road at MS80½.

The order to move had arrived whilst we were getting the evening meal out to the companies, and, realizing that there was not enough time to complete the job by daylight, I concentrated on getting the company commanders forward for a reconnaissance from the Maram Spur before dark.

Actually, by 1915 hrs., with about half an hour of daylight to go, the Battalion were ready formed up at MS80 and off we went. Brigadier Wood suddenly turned up in shorts and green hose-tops to see us on our way and to wish us "God-speed". When he reached me we had just turned the corner, and as we were talking an impertinent Taisho opened up on the group which we must have been making at the roadside. The irrepressible Joe Chamberlin claims that Brigadier Sam took cover with his accustomed dignity. Farther on there was more firing as Mac and his guerrillas flushed some Japanese lying up, presumably waiting for dark before they made their get-away.

By nine o'clock we had reached MS81, where a prominent spur ran down to the road from the huge Maramei feature on our right. Here I had been ordered to drop a company to clear this particular area and secure the road. Accordingly I dropped off "B" Company, and "D" Company took the lead. We went on steadily enough for another half-mile, when, coming round the corner of the road, our leading section bumped a Japanese patrol led by an officer. Sergeant Cook accounted for the officer, but also received a casualty in his leading section.

I realized that this particular spot, with a steep perpendicular fifty-foot cutting on the right and a three-hundred-foot drop on the left of the road, was no place to run into a Jap ambush, and so decided to pull back a quarter of a mile and went into a tight perimeter covering a road bridge at MS81½. "C" Company I sent up on the high ground to the right, and "D" Company I disposed about the bridge with one platoon forward on a bump overlooking the road, the scene of this last encounter.

When, in Kohima days, General Stopford had issued an awful decree expunging the word "box" from the military vocabulary of the XXXIII Corps, he did a most immense service to British arms in the East. A "box", he rightly maintained, was a container with a cover into which one climbed and pulled down the lid. From the moment that the term "box" as indicating a defensive locality was verboten all commanders down to the lance-corporal in charge of a section group began to revise their ideas about night defence in the jungle and thought in terms of offensive defence. So it was this night. Having been checked on the road, with one company committed at MS81, I was not in a position to indulge in any ambitious night operations. However, I could patrol offensively, which I did throughout the night, especially towards Point 4643, our objective.

At first light I sent Clive Chettle with "D" Company forward to occupy a small knoll to the right of the road immediately alongside the spur on which was Point 4643, which lay on the left of the road. Clive got there round the right flank and occupied this position without any trouble. I then, in view of the patrol reports, ordered "C" Company and Battalion Headquarters to advance along the road and move on to Point 4643 covered by "D" Company. No sooner had we turned the corner where Sergeant Cook had dealt so effectively with the Jap officer a few hours earlier than we came under intense enemy medium-machine-gun fire. The luckiest people to escape damage were the tactical jeeps and their passengers, who were following up my carrier too closely and had to bale out very quickly. Under the shelter of the bank I was able to recall "C" Company and back we returned to our overnight positions to moisten our lips and start again. We were exceedingly fortunate in that there was only one casualty from this heavy machine-gun fire, which caught us on a narrow road between a steep bank and a deep drop. Snagger Highett, who was hit in the hand, was the third officer commanding "C" Company to become a casualty in this campaign.

Leaving C.S.M. Bond temporarily in command, I sent "C" Company on to the right flank with orders to join up with "D" Company. The coming of daylight involved us in a further task of watching the right flank and rear where odd parties of Nips were spotted breaking away from the high Maramei hill to our right rear. With only three companies, all of them by now committed, I reckoned that I was in no position to complete my task and regretfully reported this to the Brigadier.

Brigadier West soon summed up the situation, and it was arranged that the Royal Scots, who were to lead the advance of the 4th Brigade, should come forward and take Point 4643 on the way. Accordingly, around noon Lieutenant-Colonel MackenzieKennedy put in an attack following a twenty-five-minute concentration from the Divisional artillery and the medium regiment on the enemy positions on Point 4643 and captured the hill without any further worry.

The 4th Brigade were in a great hurry to get on and we took over as soon as Brigadier McNaught had dispatched his armoured column in pursuit of the enemy, in order to release the Royal Scots to catch up with their brigade. "D" Company immediately became involved in mopping-up operations to the eastern end of the spur.

Two months later we returned to MS82 to live for some time. 6th Brigade Headquarters established themselves on the knoll which "D" Company had occupied that morning. We settled down on the main feature and many a time have I thought that the Japanese position, at the very door of my tent, may well have harboured the medium machine gun which had caused us such an unpleasant five minutes during that dawn advance.

The night of the 20th/21st of June was particularly hectic. I had arranged for patrols from "B" Company to work round the base of the hill and connect up with a standing patrol from "C" Company at a place where, from the map and after having viewed it with glasses on the ground, it seemed likely that any stray Nips trying to move by night would have to pass. However, things went badly with this plan. The patrol seems to have gone a bit adrift and the "C" Company patrols must also have been out of station. This story ended most tragically when the patrol leader, working completely round the flanks of the position, encountered an unexpected 149th Royal Tank Regiment sentry post at about MS82, with fatal results to both sides.

The next incident was a personal call from the Divisional Commander, who wanted to know why the hell my medium machine guns were shooting-up his Divisional Headquarters. Unknown to me, Divisional Headquarters had deployed quite a way to the east down Maram Spur. During the night the Manchesters, under my command, got an SOS call from my G.R. Platoon, who were guarding the eastern part of my defensive locality and had opened up. Owing to the curve of the hill and the sweep of Maram Ridge, the "overs" were cracking apparently uncomfortably near Divisional Headquarters.

So ended the Battle of Maram. The Japanese, we learnt from captured orders and the statement of a second-lieutenant captured in the battle, had tried to hold Maram with a whole battalion, with orders to delay us for at least ten days. In fact, to make it a second Viswema. The speed with which we had followed him up from Mao Songsang, the swiftness and energy displayed by Brigadier West in his deployment of the Camerons and the Worcesters, and the determination of both these battalions, supported by an overwhelming weight of artillery, some of the guns firing over open sights, had together resulted in the capture of this strong position within twenty-four hours.

This stand at Maram was the enemy's last attempt to stem the tide of our advance. From now on the tempo quickened and we swept all before us.

For the 5th Brigade this action was virtually our last fight in this particular campaign. We took over the defence of the road, involving mopping up pockets of resistance for the next forty-eight hours, and on the 22nd of June we were rushed forward eighteen miles by mechanical transport to MS 100. I personally, with my Intelligence Officer, got as far as MS 106 on this great day, on a reconnaissance with the Brigadier. Great day, I say, because this was the day that the 6th Brigade, now in the lead after Karong, joined up with a brigade of the 5th Infantry Division advancing north from Imphal at MS 109. The road was open and we had completed our task.

As soon as it became obvious that the opening of the road was only a matter of time, Corps had started collecting large quantities of stores to rush through to the beleaguered garrison. Prominent in an early convoy which moved forward into Imphal on the heels of General Stopford himself was a large quantity of beer!

On arrival at MS 100 I was instructed to send two companies immediately up to the mountain village of Mayankhang, five thousand yards to the east and two thousand feet above us, which was believed to be a Japanese rendezvous for their scattered forces in their wild flight eastwards. John Brierley and the Worcesters took the right of the road and the Camerons took the left of the road farther south than us. All three battalions were actively engaged during the next few days in mopping up. There was no future in capturing a Japanese position. No army with a role such as theirs and travelling light through a country as barren of luxuries as was Burma could be relied on to provide its conquerors with adequate booty. As always, the most prized trophy was a Japanese entrenching tool, though "poached-egg" flags and swords were eagerly sought after.

Some people recovered possessions lost earlier on, such as the gunner officer who retrieved a map-case which he had lost in a struggle on Aradura Spur.

The condition of the Japanese captured and killed at this stage was pitiable in the extreme. They seemed to be thoroughly demoralized, physically wrecked, covered with sores and riddled with disease. So urgently did they appear to require clothes that they even stripped their own wounded and left them to die naked. They had no compunction about leaving a wounded man to fend for himself. Most unforgivable of all was the state in which they left their animals, mostly our own and native ponies captured from us earlier in the campaign. Stragglers gave themselves up for a crust of bread or crawled into ditches alongside the road to die. Hardly a sub-unit of the Battalion, even down to the ration-store team, but gathered in its Nip on the rush through. We did hear that the B.G.S. claimed to have bagged one. It was a colossal rat hunt, with the rats running into the open and hardly ever biting back.

Throughout the campaign the Battalion had fought admirably. The traditions of the Regiment had been nobly maintained and fresh lustre added to their Colours. There was never any need to encourage the Dorset soldier to destroy the enemy: the main difficulty was to secure a live Japanese. The battle honour "Kohima" had been won at no mean cost: the going was hard, the fighting grim and earnest, the country formidable and the monsoon conditions after the end of May terrible. As Wellington was supposed to have described the Battle of Waterloo, it was "a great slogging match with neither side giving quarter".

By a happy coincidence, the day following the opening of the Manipur Road was the anniversary of the Battle of Plassey. The President of the Regimental Institutes, Major Pryke Howard, managed to produce a bottle of beer for each man "out of the blue", and every man in the Battalion, including those on detachment at Mayankhang, was able to drink his Plassey Day beer. The few officers remaining in Battalion Headquarters and "C" Company were able to throw a small rum-and-beer party by the roadside.

We sent out our usual Plassey Day signals to our various commanders. The replies of Generals Stopford and Grover and Brigadier Wood bear recording in these annals.

From General Stopford came the personal reply:

"Greatly appreciate your kind message and have complete confidence that your Battalion will always live up to its high traditions wherever it may be sent to fight the King's enemies. Am deeply appreciative of the splendid work done in recent operations, particularly in the final action in D.C.'s Compound, which was a turning point in the operations of XXXIII Corps. Best wishes to you all and may many more successes come your way in exterminating the Jap."

General Grover, the Divisional Commander, replied:

"Please convey to all ranks, 2nd Battalion The Dorsetshire Regiment, my thanks and warm appreciation of their most kind message on the one hundred and eighty-seventh anniversary of the Battle of Plassey. It is only fitting that the final success of today of the Divisional operations to open the Imphal Road should have culminated on the anniversary of the battle which was the foundation of our Indian Empire. The 2nd Battalion The Dorsetshire Regiment may well be proud of their own share in the Divisional operations of the last three months. They have fulfilled all tasks asked of them in their best regimental tradition and may be especially proud of their fine success in the operations for the capture of the D.C.'s Bungalow at Kohima, as a result of magnificent tenacity and determination and an indomitable fighting spirit. My best wishes to all ranks of your Battalion for today's anniversary and for continual success."

In paying our Plassey Day respects to our old Commanding Officer, Brigadier Wood, the senior Dorset officer in the East, I emphasized what a great debt the Battalion owed to him personally for his skilful rebuilding of the Battalion after the Battle of France and for setting our feet so firmly in India. In his reply Brigadier Wood signalled:

"I have received Plassey Day greetings from you and all ranks with great pleasure and am most grateful for your kind personal references. During the whole of the period of the recent heavy fighting I have heard with the most profound pride innumerable comments from all ranks, from General to

Private, on the repeated fine performances of the Battalion. Our newest battle honours have been won at the cost of gallant comrades, and I join you in honouring their memory. Please convey to my friends of all ranks my best wishes and my confidence that more victories await them."

Since the 11th of April the Battalion had advanced seventy miles, mostly on their feet and mainly against opposition. They had fought through the heat of the hot weather and the rains of the monsoon over some of the most difficult territory in the world, or so we thought at the time. A month later we were going to gain even further experience in weather and terrain. On the 3rd of April we had crossed the Brahmaputra River, twenty-three officers (including the Medical Officer and Padre, out of an establishment of thirtyeight) and eight hundred and six British other ranks strong. By the time we reached MS 100 at the completion of this operation, eighty days later, we had lost five officers and eighty-seven British other ranks killed, and in addition a further three British other ranks had died of disease. Eight officers and two hundred and twenty-seven British other ranks had been wounded, and sickness, in the form of malaria and various kind of tummy trouble, had necessitated the evacuation of an appreciably larger number in addition to the wounded.

Excluding Brigadier McNaught, who was busy commanding the 4th Brigade, only fourteen officers (including the Medical Officer and the Padre) and three hundred and forty-two British other ranks remained at duty of those who had crossed the Brahmaputra with the Battalion that night early in April.

In addition to the honours and awards already mentioned, the Quartermaster, Bert Smith, had been awarded the M.B.E. in a periodical honours list for his distinguished services as Regimental Sergeant-Major in India.

The fate of the Japanese Army of Invasion of India

STRAIGHT ON FOR TOKYO

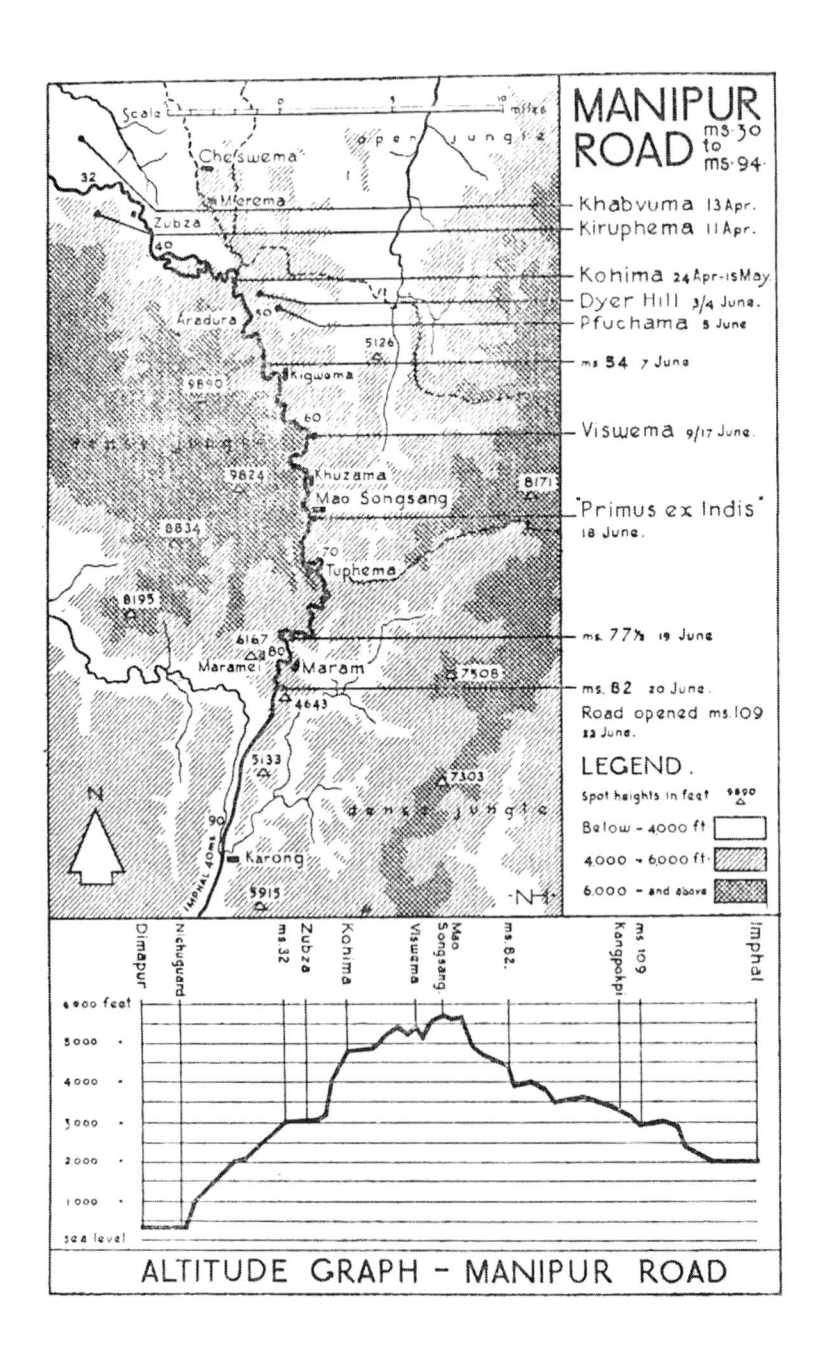

CHAPTER NINE

FORWARD INTO BURMA

"It never rains but it pours."

ON THE 27TH OF JUNE the Battalion embussed in mechanical transport and drove thirty-five miles down the hill through the plains of Imphal to the great town itself. This was our first campaign visit to a "town". The Battalion had accepted Kohima as being a shambles (after all, we had done a lot to make it so), but Imphal was different, and I think that everyone in his own special way expected something bigger and better than the collection of bashas in this hot, malarial plain which we found to be the capital of Manipur State. The 5th Infantry Brigade were allocated the area of the reception camp, where there were a few straw bashas, but the Battalion as a whole lived under canvas. I have met many people who think that Imphal is a grand place, and no doubt in the cold weather, and provided that one is well "dug in", it may have its points. To us, fresh from the higher altitudes of the hills, it had very little to offer.

One of our first visitors was the Corps Commander, who insisted on seeing for himself how we were getting on. His visit was, as usual, quite unexpected, but from that day he always accused the Quartermaster of keeping one platoon permanently waiting, naked and shivering, at the side of their cut-down oil drums in our "mockup" bath-house in order to produce a party of men in "full bathing order" for his, the General's, edification!

Our next V.I.P. was none other than the Supreme Allied Commander himself. Lord Louis Mountbatten visited the Brigade Group on Sunday, the 2nd of July. After meeting the commanding officers and certain selected soldiers, such as, in our case, C.S.M. Seale, he gave the Brigade one of those inspiring speeches of which he was the master.

During his talk the Supremo referred to captured Japanese documents, one of which was a special army order by General Mutagichi, Commander of the Japanese Fifteenth Army, who had been entrusted with the invasion of India. To quote this order, General Mutagichi told his troops:

> "After a month's desperate and courageous fighting we had surrounded the strategic position of Kohima. In three months we had the enemy hemmed in round Imphal and the battle situation stabilized. That all this has not been fully up to the expectations of our nation is indeed a most regrettable matter."

The Japanese army commander continued:

> "Withholding my tears, painful as they are, I shall for the time being withdraw my troops from Kohima. It is my resolve to reassemble my army and with one great push to capture Imphal. ... You must fully realize that if a decisive victory is not gained we shall not be able to strike back again. On this one battle rests the fate of the Empire."

The commander of the troops fighting the 17th Indian Infantry Division at Bishenpur was even more explicit, so quoted the Supremo, especially as regards the fate of the not-so-keen-to-die Nip. Having used valuable paper to deliver a pep talk and put his "group" in the picture, this general officer commanding went on to say:

> "You have got to expect that the division will be almost annihilated. ... But should any shirking occur you have got to understand that I shall take the necessary action."

This commander, who wrote this order as far back as the 2nd of June, went on to explain further:

> "In order to keep the honour of his unit bright, a commander may have to use his sword as a weapon of punishment; exceedingly shameful though it is to have to shed the blood of one's own soldiers on the battlefield, it is better so when one shirker is no better than a horse's backside."

The Supreme Allied Commander went on to explain that these orders had been published at least five weeks before, since when the Japanese had lost both the Manipur and the Ukhrul Roads, and from the appearance of the prisoners of war there were many signs to indicate that the heavy losses suffered at our hands by the Japanese 31st Division had carried the progress of demoralization and disintegration still farther.

That evening the Brigade held a memorial service. This service, most impressive in its simplicity, was undenominational. An old friend of the Brigade, our original Roman Catholic priest, Father O'Callaghan, was missing. A descendant of that remarkable warrior who had commanded the Thirty-Ninth (1st Dorset) a century ago, he had unfortunately been killed early in the conflict at the very first engagement near Zubza.

On arrival in Imphal we were given to understand that we were there to rest, refit and, as we hoped, absorb reinforcements. As the reader will have gathered, we were pretty well flogged out. Physically we were very tired, but probably on that score alone no more so than any other brigade of the Corps who had just completed three months' hard fighting. However, with no reinforcements, we were very much more tired than we should have been, and in a far worse position to carry on. When there is no possibility of one's strength being even "topped up", every casualty means extra work for the survivors. I have never found that there has been any noticeable decrease in routine chores owing to lack of numbers. As long as a battalion continues to function as such, so does it have to find the "duties" accordingly.

For my part I found myself harder at work than ever. I was beginning to get the hang of this "one-man band" principle on which it was so often necessary to run the Battalion, not only during the war but immediately afterwards. Of my company commanders only Bowles, who had returned to the fold, had had any previous experience of the job out of the line. Clive Chettle had been a platoon commander before we went into action, and, although magnificent at drawing his sword in action, he found to his dismay that there was a great deal besides tactics for a company commander to think about when "at rest". The third company commander, Peter Feeney, had joined us at Kohima straight from G.S.O.3 at the 2nd Divisional Headquarters, to which appointment he had gone direct from the Staff College at Quetta. My Adjutant, Colin Doran, had taken over from Graeme Gordon Wright in that dug-out on Garrison Hill and had not yet really had the opportunity of settling down to learn his job. He had his chance now. Finally, I had a brand-new Battalion Headquarters staff. Mr. Goldson had been promoted Regimental Sergeant-Major at Kohima and was very busy trying to get the Battalion quarter-guard back to our own special standard; my faithful Vaughan had not only been promoted

Company Sergeant-Major but had been evacuated sick, and I had to train Sergeant Vine as Orderly Room Sergeant. Luckily, Vine, my one-time Mechanical Transport Corporal in "A" Company, had had some experience of the orderly room when I had dragged him into the office at Bhiwandi fifteen months earlier.

To our great joy it was decided to reopen leave for the Brigade. We were given very good vacancies to fly out from Imphal. Not everyone flew: many had to make the awful trip back down the one hundred and thirty-five miles of the Manipur Road in a threetonner to Dimapur, from where they made their way in leisurely stages to India. There was a subtle difference between officers' and British other ranks' leave. The latter were allowed twenty-eight days clear in India, but so short were we of officers that we were allowed only twenty-eight days in all, including travelling time. In order to save the officer spending anything up to three weeks of his twenty-eight days in travel we tried every wangle to get him flown out.

The 6th of July was a very sad day for the 2nd Division, as on this occasion General Grover paid his last visit to the Brigade as Divisional Commander, prior to boarding a plane for England. The reader of these annals will have appreciated by now how much the 2nd Division owed to General Grover. From the very first day that he assumed command in Yorkshire he had invested the Division with his own great personality and drive. On arrival in India he found that we were not to be used in an operational role immediately. No one could have been sorrier for this decision than the then Commander-in-Chief, General Wavell, himself a former commander of the 2nd Division. General Grover, far from being dismayed at this ruling and content to sit back in the comparative luxury of Western India, continued to drive his Division with everincreasing energy. Not content with purely domestic training, he established a battle school at Ahmednagar which must have been of the greatest value in the training scheme of the Army in India as a whole. When finally our turn came for action General Grover was able to produce a highly skilled and trained division, fully capable of taking their place in the line and inflicting, as they did, great loss and an outstanding defeat on the enemy. His departure in the moment of his triumph was a loss felt personally by every man who had served under his command.

So short of reinforcements was the Division that every man who could be spared from the supporting arms and services was pressed into the infantry. One morning we received a draft of 2nd Divisional R.A.S.C. and sufficient redundant gunners to enable me to re-form "A" Company. Apart from the purely personal pleasure at being able to re-establish the grenadiers, I was overjoyed once more to have four rifle companies in the Battalion. Anyone who has ever tried to fight a battalion with only three rifle companies will appreciate fully what the deficiency of one company means. It is like trying to box an opponent with one hand tied. So it was a great occasion when, one Monday morning during our tour in Imphal, the revived "A" Company paraded and I was able to present John Bowles with the "A" Company flag which I had kept in safe custody with my personal possessions during that company's temporary suspension.

Despite the return of various officers from hospital and special duties, such as Major Donald Baynes, we were still woefully short when, one afternoon, concealed behind the most immense moustache, a brand-new Regular major arrived. Major Tommy Tucker, of the Hampshire Regiment, had come a very long way to join in this Oriental conflict. I immediately told him to carry on and act as Second-in-Command, and with his twelve or so years' service he was of the greatest assistance to me in those Imphal days. Tommy was to stay with us until the end of the campaign, and in time was to perform sterling work in command of "C" Company, but we see more of him later.

Meanwhile, only a few miles outside our camp, a very bitter struggle was being waged. In our own parochial manner we realized that there was fighting going on, but I don't believe that the average soldier really considered why. For him it was good enough that we had knocked the 31st Japanese Division out of the ring and had opened the road. To the British other ranks there didn't seem to be much of a war on, what with redcaps in perfectly "dhobied" and, what is more, "conjeed" khaki drill all rushing around the town with apparently nothing better to do than to take the names, at sundown, of soldiers who had not rolled down their sleeves or otherwise disregarded anti-malarial rules. No; as far as the Battalion was concerned, the IV Corps seemed to be having a pretty cushy time, and what was all this talk about a siege and why had we flogged ourselves silly to get to Imphal?

However, outside the Imphal perimeter a fierce and stern battle was still being fought down three of the four roads that led to Imphal. At Bishenpur General Cowan, with the 17th Division, was fighting as bitter a battle (so the General later, when we were in Japan, confided to me) as ever he fought. On the Ukhrul Road the 20th Indian Infantry Division, under General Gracey, were fully employed, and away up on the heights of Shenam Ridge the 23rd Indian Division, under General Roberts, were trying to push the Nip back over the Burmese border in the direction of Tamu.

It was when we visited our sick and wounded (our later casualties had been evacuated to Imphal) in hospital that we saw the latest battle casualties and really appreciated what a dour conflict was still being fought around us.

The continued waging of the battle with such unabated vigour was to have an immediate effect on two of the brigades of the 2nd Division. First the gunners were called on to join the battle with one or other of the Indian divisions, and suddenly, about the 15th of July, the 5th Brigade were called out and told to take themselves with all speed to join in the 23rd Indian Division's battle on the Tamu Road. Shortly afterwards the 4th Brigade were sent to join in the Ukhrul battle.

This order was received with mixed feelings, but mainly I really believe with relief. After a fortnight's rest the Battalion had "had" Imphal and its heat and bugs and restrictions and boredom, and were quite prepared to have another crack at the yellow perisher.

Battalion Headquarters were the least prepared for such an eventuality. With the Brigadier's approval I had sent my Adjutant and new Orderly Room Sergeant on leave. After some discussion Colin had proved his right to a place at the top of the leave roll, though we considered that his former life at Divisional Headquarters whilst we had been flogging through the jungles and across the plains of India had constituted permanent leave. One company commander, Peter Feeney, with his contacts in India, had also departed for Calcutta and Delhi to prepare the way for those who might follow. However, we made one of our rapid reorganizations and fell in for Palel, with John Bowles commanding "A" Company, Tommy Tucker dispatched from my side to take over "B," Donald Baynes back with his old company ("C") and Clive Chettle remaining with "D" Company. At Viswema in June we had had to disband the old Anti-Aircraft Platoon (No. 2), the Carriers, superfluous Pioneers and most of the Mechanical Transport Platoon and turn them into riflemen. It was a great waste of trained specialists, as we found to our cost, but there was no help for it. At Imphal we had to go even farther and disband the Mortar Platoon to swell the diminishing ranks of the rifle companies. At Imphal, too, I had to leave quite a strong rear party of storemen and sick and sorry who had the important job of acting as reception unit to the 23rd Brigade, who had been out on our left flank ever since they passed through us at Bokajan early in April. They had had a really rough time and had existed for over a hundred days practically on "K" rations alone. It was very much a battalion of riflemen who moved out of Imphal on the 19th of June, bound for Palel at the foot of an immense range of hills at MS29 on the road from Imphal to Tamu.[10]

At Palel we waited for a few days until the 23rd Division had completed reorganization on the heights above us. We were in Divisional reserve, having been brought in to make four brigades in the Division. The Dorsets were leading the 5th Brigade.

Whilst at Palel I took the opportunity to go and "make our number" with the 4th Mahrattas, who were bivouacked quite close. I did not see the 6th Battalion, who were already on the move. This was the only occasion in this war, as far as I know, that a battalion of Dorsets fought in the same battle with their traditional allied regiment of Indian infantry. Even our encounter was but the briefest. The 49th Brigade, in which there were two Mahratta battalions, was sent off on a long left hook to cut the road beyond the Japanese, and so, except to wish them "God-speed" at the start, and to pass through them at the conclusion of their operation, we saw but little of them.

Palel seemed to be full of incident. First of all, Brigadier John Shapland, recovering from a wound received at Kohima, sent us the news of our immediate decorations for Kohima, which have been mentioned in an earlier chapter.

The next day an unfortunate accident with a Sten gun put Lieutenant Percy Schuster, a reinforcement officer, who had joined us just north of Mao Songsang, out of action for some time. I cannot think how many accidents were caused in the 5th Brigade by careless handling of this particular mark of Sten gun. All units had to have very strong orders that the magazine was not to be adjusted until the bearer of this weapon was actually in contact advancing to meet a Japanese. In the enthusiasm of moving once more "into action", though the enemy were at least ten miles away, a keen Sten gunner had adjusted his magazine during a company lecture and was most grieved when in the bustle of squeezing through the door of the basha at the conclusion of the lecture his firearm went off, injuring his platoon commander.

It was a strange feeling to come straight from a speedy and successful pursuit of the Japanese to a state of attrition resembling very closely the European Western Front in the First World War. The 23rd Division were very tired, having been fighting the Jap continually for about two years, and they were temporarily bogged down in the monsoon on the Shenam feature, which rose two thousand feet above the Imphal Plain. Over this huge ridge wound the road to Tamu and the Kabaw Valley,

---

10 For this campaign all milestones will be reckoned in terms of distance leading from Imphal and not to Imphal as we have done hitherto.

which at the beginning of the war had been but a hill track. On these perpendicular ridges both sides faced each other, waiting for the mist and rain to lift sufficiently for the opposing guns to open up. Visibility during the whole time we were there was about fifty yards, clearing for short periods at a time only. These periods occurred normally at first light, and so early every morning at first light the Brigadier would rush me up to Reconnaissance Hill on Shenam Ridge to have a "look-see".

Despite our enthusiasm for these early morning reconnaissances and the strong desire to get away from Palel, with all its heat and bugs, it was not until the 23rd of July that General Roberts had completed the deployment of his division and was ready to advance and thus make room for the 5th Brigade on Reconnaissance Hill.

I took over positions from a battalion of the 5th Royal Gurkha Rifles, with two companies ("B" and "C") on Reconnaissance Hill.

I sent "A" and "D" Companies to the left flank to take over from another battalion of Gurkhas on Patiala Ridge. Although we moved into very strong and magnificently constructed dug-outs, reminiscent of Sherriff's play "Journey's End", it was not quite as simple as all that to take over from the Gurkhas. Dug-outs, we found, constructed for four of these Nepalese hillmen would by no means take an equal number of our own "swede bashers".

We were beginning to think that we had become inured to rain, but we hadn't experienced a thing until we got to Shenam Ridge. It never stopped: the mud was not only over our ankles but well over our knees. It was miserably cold up there at five thousand feet, and for about six days, until we advanced through the Division to take the lead, our existence was comparatively uneventful.

Not that we were idle during this time—far from it. We had taken over all patrol commitments from the Gurkha Brigade and these included some strenuous two or three-day patrols. The moment a patrol left the crest of the ridge on one of its expeditions it plunged into the thickest undergrowth we had yet encountered and slithered up and down slopes by which, in comparison, the climb to Pfuchama appeared in retrospect as a mere stroll on a maidan in a far-off cantonment in India.

The general situation at this time and General Roberts's plan were after this fashion: the two sides were deployed in defensive positions facing each other along the very narrow spine of this huge ridge, which rose to five thousand two hundred and thirty-nine feet at Reconnaissance Hill, where we were, and continued at about this altitude to the Japanese positions about three thousand yards to the east. The fight had raged back and forth for some weeks among these steepsided pimples, ridges, crests and "tumps," as we would call them in Dorset. This ground had been much fought over in the past three years and most features bore the name of some regiment that had distinguished itself in a bitter fight on the steep hillsides.

Owing to the limitations of his artillery until this last attack, and the difficulty in deploying his division along the ridge, General Roberts had hitherto not been able to make the progress he would have liked. However, now that he was strongly reinforced with field artillery from the 2nd and 20th Divisions, and medium guns released after our opening the Manipur Road, he felt that he was in a position to make his grand attack. Only the weather was against him. Like all the divisional commanders, however, acting on the Supreme Commander's instructions to fight on regardless of the weather, General Roberts was determined to convert "General Monsoon" if not exactly into an ally at least into a friendly neutral.

On the right he deployed the 1st Indian Infantry Brigade, under the command of Brigadier Robert King (who had come to India with us as Brigade Major of the 5th Infantry Brigade), on a short right hook to deal with the Japanese positions to the south of the road. The Gurkha Brigade was to attack frontally down the middle and take the enemy positions immediately astride the road, including the redoubtable position on Scraggy. On the left the 49th Brigade, in which were the two Mahratta battalions to whom I have referred, were dispatched on a very wide left hook designed to bring them right round the rear of the Japanese positions to cut the road to the east of the Lokchau Chaung, a very deep and formidable obstacle.

This latter move was the most ambitious of the three, involving a cross-country march across very difficult thick jungle country over a period of about ten days. This brigade were also following up a withdrawal route used by the Japanese and were constantly faced with the possibility of having to fight their way through.

The enemy, the Japanese 33rd Division, one of their crack formations, had not as yet had the hammering that their colleagues of the 31st Division had received, and were still comparatively full of energy. They had some guns, both field and medium, and a little armour, though the formidable nature of the ground and the weather precluded the use of the latter except on the roads.

The enemy reacted violently to any move on our side, and only a short time before had counter-attacked and gained a footing on the crest of the impregnable Gibraltar feature, with its sides rising perpendicularly for fifteen hundred feet on its northern side, up which the Nips had swarmed from the nullah below.

The rate of advance of the Division was to a great extent controlled by the amount of time in any day that the guns could obtain visibility enough to shoot and support the infantry. But steadily the two brigades in the centre advanced as the 49th Brigade continued its flanking move. As the Gurkhas moved forward so we stepped up into their shoes, and Clive Chettle moved "D" Company on to Gibraltar, to be followed for a short space by Bowles on to Malta.

At about this time we very nearly lost the Brigadier for good. Anticipating our early advance, he had gone forward on a reconnaissance. The Gurkhas had assured him that they had cleared the road; they certainly had cleared the hills on either side, but not the road itself, and Michael West ran straight into a Japanese road block. He, the Intelligence Officer and the driver baled out of the jeep and over the khudside, but the gunman, Private Hill, of the Worcesters, stood his ground and was killed covering the escape of the others.

By the 29th of July the advance had quickened and in one fell swoop we advanced seven miles in the pouring rain to MS46. There was a very bad landslide at about MS41, where the road had gone completely. It was only with the greatest difficulty that we could get even essential vehicles down a bulldozed track, and I had to leave "B" Company in this area for some days. They had the task of ferrying all supplies and ammunition past this block. This was done by means of a huge chute from one road to its continuation farther down. The company worked magnificently and gained great praise for the speedy manner in which they passed all supplies for two brigades through this block. They did not neglect this opportunity to look after themselves. After all, tins of rations and bales of socks are apt to break open if thrown down a hundred-foot slide, and for many days I did not have to worry about dry socks for Peter's company.

The advance of the 23rd Division had not been speedy enough to prevent the Japanese from blowing the vital bridge over the Lokchau Chaung. Unfortunately, though the 49th Brigade had emerged from the bush at the right place, owing to some misunderstanding they had failed fully to exploit their success and had thereby allowed a large number of the enemy to slip through their hands back into Burma.

What with the delay imposed on us by the difficulties of supply, despite the efforts of "B" Company in their role of a labour unit, and the destruction of the bridge, it was not until the 4th of August that the 5th Brigade were able to continue their advance. Away back in June

I had requested permission from both General Grover and Brigadier West, on the strength of the Regimental motto, "Primus in Indis", and because we were the only battalion in the Division to bear a battle honour for a previous campaign in Burma ("Ava"), that in the event of an advance over the frontier we should be allowed to lead the Brigade.

Unfortunately, this was not to be, for before we crossed the Lokchau the Worcesters had moved up to take their turn in the lead and owing to the nature of the road and the speed of the advance the Brigadier never had an opportunity to put us through into the lead again before the Brigade had crossed the frontier into Burma at Tamu.

Just before we handed over MS46 to a battalion of the 11th East African Division we were visited by our new Divisional Commander. General C. G. C. Nicholson, C.B.E., D.S.O., M.C., had paid a flying visit to us in Imphal before we left, but apart from meeting the acting Adjutant and myself he had not until this occasion had an opportunity of meeting the company commanders. A gunner himself, General Nicholson was never grudging in his praise of the work of the foot soldiers, and, though we were divorced from his command for this battle, he was full of enthusiasm for the work done by the 5th Brigade since leaving Imphal, though this had consisted mainly of marching and patrolling.

On the 4th of August we set out on our eleven-mile march to Bulldozer Ridge on a sizzling-hot day. The sun had come out in its intensity, especially trying after the wet cold in which we had lived for the past fortnight. This march was made additionally trying by having to descend a thousand feet to the Lokchau and up again another thousand-odd to Bulldozer Ridge. The 208th Field Company, helped by an East African field company, had done wonders in repairing the Lokchau bridge, and we pressed on, our essential vehicles, such as they were by this time, accompanying the Battalion. The climb up on the east of the chaung was gruelling, and the general unpleasantness of the march was further aggravated by the unusually large number of dead Japanese littering the roadside. The 49th Brigade had certainly made a killing after their long walk.

Bulldozer Ridge had an unenviable reputation. Hereabouts the Devons had lost a large number of men from the dreaded scrub typhus. This disease, with an unusually high mortality rate, is miteborne and extraordinarily localized. One small area may carry the dreaded mites, whilst a few yards away the ground is immune. We did not stay here long, merely overnight—a night not made any easier by a violent thunderstorm just about the time of the evening meal.

By this time the pursuit was well on. The Japanese we were picking up began to resemble those scraps of humanity we had gathered in in the last lap of the race down the Manipur Road. Their resistance had been broken and they were making for the Kabaw Valley literally as fast as they could crawl. The plight of the men of the Indian National Army brigades was even worse. The Japs certainly were not good at looking after their allies. These "JIFs" were not the solid sepoys, still loyal to the King-Emperor who had joined the Indian National Army in order only to get away from Singapore and go into action in the hope of escaping, whom we were to encounter nearly a year later. These were the real traitors of the Gandhi and Bhose Brigades, who had early turned to the Japanese with the full intention of having a smack at the White Raj and had fought amazingly hard until disease, privation and neglect on the part of their yellow masters had turned them from soldiers into disease-ridden, starving creatures who could hardly crawl into our lines to give themselves up.

On the 5th of August the advance continued, still with the Worcesters leading, followed by the Camerons, with us bringing up the rear, and so we came to MS62, about four miles north of Tamu. That day the Worcesters advanced into Tamu and occupied it.

The scene of desolation in Tamu was indescribable. Dead and dying Japanese lay everywhere as the result of our air strikes and artillery concentrations. Here for the first time the Brigade was able to augment its equipment from enemy sources. With their experience of jungle warfare, the Nips had a certain amount of equipment that was especially useful to us. I have already referred to their entrenching tools. I can't think how many times we submitted requests during the war to be equipped ourselves with similar picks and shovels. India's only reaction, every time, was to send us larger and more cumbersome tools with softer and softer metal heads which just buckled when we tried to dig with them. The Nip also had a most useful pattern of communal mosquito-net. After we had been to Japan we realized that he always equips his own houses with these huge nets, under which the whole family sleep. To us, in Tamu, they came as a godsend for our cookhouse and food stores. The Mechanical Transport Section ran amok among a large workshops area and for days the silence of the jungle was shattered as the jeep drivers, encouraged by Private Dickinson, liberated all sorts of strange electrical horns from discarded staff cars. Fitter tools! Fitter tools! I thought that I would never hear of anything else as each day the mechanical transport drivers returned with some extraordinary machine which they insisted was invaluable.

Tiger Havers, who, after a long bout of sickness after Kohima, was back on the job, and in Colin Doran's absence was doubling up the duties of Adjutant with his old task of Intelligence Officer, completely forsook the office and set his section on a wild chase for captured documents and flags. A patrol of ours captured a Japanese flag inside Burma which I promptly sent to the Mayor of Dorchester as a gift to the county. My accompanying letter was the first news the county town had had of the 2nd Battalion for some time, and I understand aroused a great deal of interest.

We stayed at MS62 for four days, busily employed in patrolling the locality, mopping up and generally destroying Japanese. By this time, as the troops said, one did not have to waste ammunition on the Nip: one just grabbed a passing one, shook him and he died in your hands.

The weather continued to be perfectly frightful and the heat as we descended into Tamu at only five hundred feet above sea-level in the dreadful Kabaw Valley, the "Valley of Death", as its name implies, was intense. We were all most glad when orders came for us to hand over to the Askaris of the 11th East African Division, and, leaving them to plunge farther through the undergrowth of the Kabaw Valley, started our long march back. The first day we did sixteen miles in two stages; we completed seven miles before first light and after lying up continued after dark down to the Lokchau and up again to MS46. The last nine miles, though taken in the comparative cool of the night, was, in the teeming rain, one of the grimmest marches I have ever done. The mechanical transport had great difficulty in getting up the hill and we nearly lost our faithful water truck, which by now had emblazoned on its radiator the proud words "Kohima to Tamu". It is extraordinary, on looking back, to think that battalions of infantry fought all through those campaigns in a tropical climate with one water truck. The mileage that truck did and the hours that the drivers put in were truly phenomenal.

That night we lay up in bunkers along the roadside below our old Battalion position, and the next morning were overjoyed to find mechanical transport ready to lift us back over the ridge at Shenam and down to Palel. We had had awful visions of the Brigade being ferried, which in the case of the Dorsets bringing up the rear would have meant that we would have had to climb at least another three thousand feet to Shenam Ridge before the lorries could have got back to lift us.

We did not linger in Palel, and the next day continued back through Imphal on an eighty-mile drive right through to our new concentration

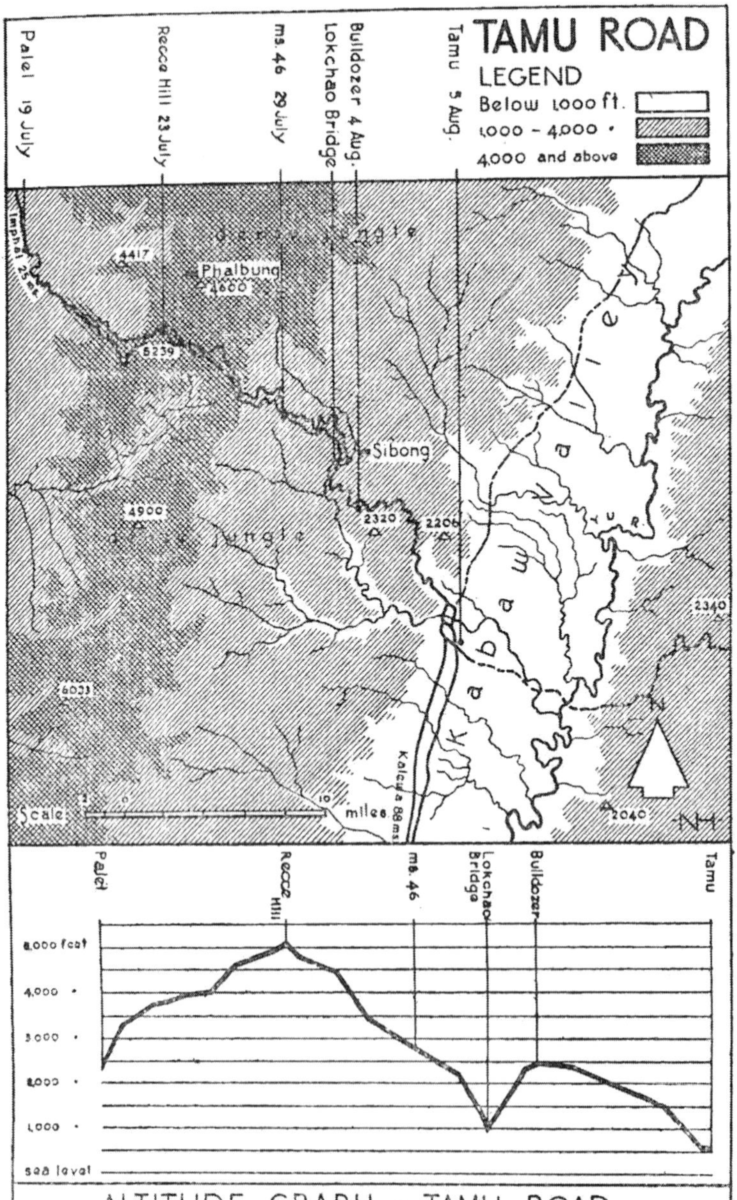

ALTITUDE GRAPH - TAMU ROAD

area at MS82 on the Manipur Road; back to the scene of our last battle on the way down.

We found the 6th Brigade in situ doing very nicely, thank you. They had been there practically ever since the road was opened and had managed to scrounge every available bit of corrugated iron and everything that went to make a waterproof shelter. We ourselves and the Camerons were superimposed on the same feature, already occupied by the Royal Welch Fusiliers of the 6th Brigade. The Worcesters and Brigade Headquarters returned to the same ridge which the Worcesters themselves had so speedily captured at the Battle of Maram.

Here we were told that we had come to roost for some time. The Division had to do a great deal of reorganizing before it was fit to go into action again, and we all felt that we had earned a rest.

We had, unfortunately, returned just too late for the visit of the Viceroy to Imphal. Field-Marshal Lord Wavell had spent one day motoring up the Manipur Road to Kohima. At Maram he had stayed for some hours with his old division, of which he must be one of the most famous commanders in the long and illustrious history of the 2nd Infantry Division.

After presenting decorations to members of the Division, earned during the recent fighting, the Field-Marshal congratulated the Division on its magnificent work and claimed that this campaign in Assam and Manipur had been one of the turning points of the war.

'D" Company will parade for baths.

CHAPTER TEN

MILESTONE 82 AGAIN

THE ESTABLISHMENT OF Marabout Lines on the hilltop at MS82 presented a number of difficulties. Two battalions had to be superimposed on what our neighbours of the 6th Infantry Brigade looked upon, quite rightly, as a pasture adequate only for one battalion. Roads had to be built, hewn out of the hillside, and shelters constructed from tarpaulins and any other form of waterproof—spare the word! —material. All this was done in pouring rain, with movement restricted to slithering around on our hands and knees. I can assure anyone who has seen the film "Burma Victory" that the opening monsoon scenes were no exaggeration, and I continue to marvel at the manner in which the Quartermaster's staff, backed up by the never-flagging efforts of the mechanical transport drivers, managed to maintain the Battalion during this period.

Leave, which had continued during the Tamu expedition, reopened with increased vigour, and by the end of August members of the Fifty-Fourth were to be found scattered throughout the subcontinent from Srinagar in Kashmir to Madras in the south. This leave did us all a power of good and we must be for ever grateful to the Royal Air Force Transport Command and the Movement Control staffs, who got us away and returned us, sadly out of pocket but refreshed in spirit.

A Second-in-Command, Major Mervyn Jones, M.B.E., a Territorial officer of the Monmouthshire Regiment, had been posted to us during the advance to Tamu. Mervyn had come direct from an appointment on the XV Corps Headquarters in the Arakan, and, hardened campaigner as he was, he had been visibly shaken by the conditions on Shenam Ridge which resembled those on the Western Front in the First World War.

During September we received our first reinforcements. These were by no means trained infantrymen but redundant anti-aircraft gunners, who looked with dismay at the surrounding hills, which we cheerfully told them, on arrival, that they would have to climb and train over before we took them into action. It is hard to find words strong enough to commend these erstwhile anti-aircraft gunners of ours, who in a few short weeks became first-class foot soldiers. When they had enlisted, most of them early in the war, nothing had been farther from their minds than the prospect of swarming over some jungle-covered mountain in far-off Burma. They set to with a will and a spirit to master their new trade, and by their example did much to revive a tired battalion, and subsequently they put up a great show in action.

With the reinforcements arrived some first-class officers, full of life and vigour, who set about training with the most commendable energy. Jack O'Donnell (Vishnu's "Little Ray of Sunshine", as he came to be called); Johnson and Willcox, who joined together and were promptly christened "Roger" and "Willco"; John Main, who took over the Mechanical Transport Platoon and had no sooner mastered the technicalities of that job than he found himself saddled with forty-odd mules; John Joslin, who was to prove himself invaluable as a platoon commander; and others—all arrived during this period.

Old friends gradually floated back, happy to escape from the hospitals of India and be back once more with the men they knew. Graeme Gordon Wright, Paget Fretts, Lintorn Highett, Harold ("Jonah") Jones and Dicky Boyle were among those who returned to us at Maram.

In September also our war establishment was changed. At long last the 2nd Infantry Division shook off the old European establishment and we adopted officially an organization more suitable to our current tasks. On the personnel side, the "standard" battalion organization gave official recognition to the long-established custom of divorcing the administrative echelon from H.Q. Company. David Harris took over command of the new Administrative Company, or as it was called in those days "Admin" Company, with its Quartermaster's, Medical and Transport Platoons. H.Q. Company became virtually what was now called the Support Company in Europe, though its composition was different, as we confined ourselves only to a Signal Platoon, a Mortar Platoon and a Pioneer Platoon. Provision was also allowed for a Defence Platoon at Battalion Headquarters, which, though not adopted as such in the 5th Brigade, at least gave us official sanction for the hard-working Guerrilla Platoon. Still retaining our basis as an "all-white" division,[11] we were never allocated our scale of sixty-odd native followers allowed to British battalions on the same establishment in an Indian division.

---

11 'During the ensuing campaign the mule companies of the Royal Indian Army Service Corps allotted to the 2nd Infantry Division actually wore our sign, the only non-European troops ever to attain that distinction.

On the equipment scale we were reduced to a minimum amount of mechanical transport, which is discussed more fully later on, and an issue of unit mules to step up our "F" Echelon. The arrival of the mules caused a great stir. A few survivors of the old horse transport days were still around, but most of these, like Sergeant Sturmey, had become much too senior to revert to their old duties of "drabby" or muleteer.

There was only one solution: just as nearly a decade earlier Colonel Charles Woodhouse had converted, by a stroke of a pen, the old Horse Transport Platoon into a Mechanical Transport Platoon, so I, in an even more illegible hand, signed the decree that converted the long-suffering Carrier Platoon into the Animal Transport Platoon. In carrying out this measure I was extremely fortunate in my three chief aides. John Main, the Mechanical Transport Officer, willingly assumed the dual responsibilities of Animal and Mechanical Transport Officer. As assistants he found Lance-Corporal Park and Private Churchill; the former had arrived with a batch of gunner reinforcements and to our joy we discovered that Park was an ex-Regular cavalryman in disguise. Not only had he done his colour service with horses but had been actively employed in training and racing stables for the past twelve or thirteen years. Churchill had also, in peace time, been completely tied up with horses and was overjoyed to find some animals in the Battalion lines.

Under this expert leadership the Carrier Platoon rapidly transformed themselves into a very efficient collection of muleteers, whose boast was, and later proved, that they would out-walk the Battalion at any time. So quickly and efficiently did John Main and the newly promoted Sergeant Park function that at the end of October, when the Army Commander, General Slim, visited Marabout Lines, he was able to give us a special "shabash" on the state of our latest-formed platoon. John Main always insisted on the highest standard of animal management, and except for a few inevitable casualties from a virulent indigenous disease we never had a mule placed "B.L.R."[12] or even sent back to the Veterinary Section as a "workshops job," as one is inclined to call such an evacuation in these more mechanized days. But we will hear more of the "donkeys" as we march into Burma.

As regards our living conditions, the Battalion settled down rapidly,

---

12 "B.L.R." —a term used in R.E.M.E. circles when it is necessary to evacuate a vehicle damaged "B.L.R." or "Beyond Local Repair." In the case of an animal such an action would result in shooting the beast, as there is obviously no "B.L.R." for a broken leg or similar ailment.

and the men showed the greatest ingenuity in erecting home-made shelters in which to live. The inevitable "Bellevue" and "Kozy Kot" villas sprang up around the lines—the most famous of these was "Zu Villas," where the senior warrant officers lived. On the top of the hill we erected the latest of our churches dedicated to the patron saint of Dorset—Saint Aldhelm. The founder of Sherborne Abbey and School would have been extremely surprised —and, I hope, gratified—to find the latest of his churches constructed of bamboo with a large vehicle tarpaulin to serve as a roof, set up six thousand miles from St. Aldhelm's Head in Dorset. "St. Aldhelm's-in-the-Jungle" was complete with its verger, Private Hounsome, the Padre's batman, and organist, Private Stroud, of the Mortar Platoon, who every Sunday knocked hymn tunes out of the Padre's portable organ, known as the "assault organ".

A great feature of our life at Maram was the appearance of a detachment of the Women's Auxiliary Service (Burma). These gallant ladies, under the leadership of Mrs. Alison Maclaren, came to live within our perimeter. For some reason they were administered by the Royal Welch Fusiliers but they had become an integral part of the 2nd Division and before long were seen to be wearing our crossed keys as they went about their daily task of running mobile canteens for the Division. These girls not only shared our discomforts of weather and terrain, and isolation at Maram, but later when we once more went into action they followed us across the Chindwin and Irrawaddy, continuing to carry out their much-needed tasks of welfare.

Facilities for sport were extremely limited on these hills, but the sappers managed to bulldoze out a couple of grounds and during this rest period the Division not only played a visiting team of international class at Imphal but visited Kohima, and there, on Treasury Ridge, the scene of such bitter fighting a few months earlier, won a great game against the 7th Indian Division.

In October the Divisional Commander unveiled the Battalion War Memorial at Kohima, erected in memory of those who had lost their lives in the fighting in the Naga hills.

A few days later a strong representative party of the Battalion went once more to Kohima, to attend the unveiling of the 2nd Infantry Division Memorial by General Slim, the Commander of the Fourteenth Army. By happy circumstance the site selected for this memorial, consisting of a huge Naga stone, was at the head of the club square, but a few feet from the old "C" Company headquarters, scene of some of the hardest close-quarter fighting in the whole campaign.

On the face of this stone are engraved the words credited to

Leonidas, the Spartan commander at the Battle of Thermopylae, four hundred and eighty years before the birth of Christ:

> *"When you go home*
> *Tell them of us and say*
> *For your tomorrow*
> *We gave our today."*

Apart from the Regimental detachment, the Fifty-Fourth found one of the sentries on the memorial, Private Wiltshire of the Mortar Platoon, and Corporal Cripps sounded "Reveille" and "Last Post".

During October the 2nd Norfolks held a "Norset" Day and entertained a large party of the Battalion in their lines at Kigwema at MS54.

Brigadier Michael West decided that it was impossible to do much higher training during the short time at our disposal. We all concentrated on ensuring that our technique at section level was as perfect as it could be made. However, it was, we found, necessary to hold at least one exercise on gunner "drill order" lines, on which we could take out the whole Battalion with their mules. The course I selected was over the high Maramei Hill, over which the Brigadier had just held a Brigade signal exercise. The results were most satisfactory and we were all able to patch up defects in our machine before we were called forward into action once more.

One of our chief worries at Maram was the incidence of scrub typhus, that dread disease, so localized that in our limited training areas at MS82, whilst the Camerons and ourselves were sorely smitten, the Royal Welch next door escaped. Although Paget Fretts and Sergeant Maule recovered fairly quickly from the disease, we were, despite the first-rate arrangements made by Lieutenant-Colonel Lowe and the advanced dressing station of the 4th Field Ambulance, to lose Captain Smith, a promising young reinforcement officer, and a number of other ranks.

Meanwhile, on the road through Tiddim to Fort White and down the Kabaw Valley, the 5th Indian and 11th East African Divisions had been steadily pushing the Japanese back over the Chindwin.

This campaign, conducted by General Stopford under the most unfavourable conditions of weather and terrain, had been so successful that by the end of December the two divisions had linked up and it was time for them, in their turn, to be relieved and the rate of advance maintained.

At 0400 hrs. on the 29th of November, our "works" creaking somewhat from such a prolonged period of immobility, if not inactivity, the Fifty-Fourth set out from Maram at the head of the 5th Infantry Brigade. It had by now become bitterly cold in the hills and for a change we were glad, after a couple of days of travelling down the old familiar road, through Imphal, past Shenam Ridge, through Tamu, to find ourselves in the comparative warmth of the Kabaw Valley. This area, which we had dreaded in August, now appeared under much more favourable conditions, and for many days we lay up in the jungle at Yazagyo, waiting for the bridgehead to be cleared and the signal to break out across the Chindwin.

Even here we were about three hundred miles beyond railhead at Dimapur, and the success of our advance—nay, the entire possibility of the operation being carried out at all—depended on our conserving every drop of petrol. On the new establishment our mechanical transport was limited in the extreme, but seldom have the mules been used so hard as they were in this jungle camp. Every possible load that could be broken down to mule loads was handed over to the Animal Transport Section to transport, and outside my Battalion Headquarters the ponies stood ready for an immediate "taxi" service, in place of the usual jeep.

Christmas was a great success. In fact, of all the festivities of that season I have ever spent with the Battalion I rate this "false" Christmas, celebrated some days before the official date, as the most successful and enjoyable. It was remarkable, considering the difficulties with which the administrative authorities were faced in launching the operation, that we had any kind of celebration at all, let alone an abundance of fare which we were to remember for many a long month ahead. Teddy Edwards came over from Corps Headquarters and celebrated his twenty-second Christmas abroad with his old Battalion.

Just before leaving Yazagyo we received a new draft of officers, including Gerry Overman, who was to distinguish himself on patrol in the forthcoming operations, and Colin Beale, who was unfortunately to be wounded in his first battle. The significance of these arrivals lay in the fact that they were the first Dorset officers to arrive as reinforcements for a very long time, actually wearing our badge in their caps.

To us, also at this time, arrived Major James Heath and a platoon of the 1st Battalion The Gloucestershire Regiment, who were to be attached for a period of battle training. Many of this platoon had taken part in the 1942 march out of Burma, and, with them, we shared the thrill of retracing their steps along the old route by which they had come out, and the search for their missing mess silver. They were a great band of fighters and I can never be too grateful for the immense aid they gave to me by becoming an extra platoon in our forthcoming operations.

Three days after our premature celebration of Christmas the Battalion embussed at 2200 hrs. on the 20th of December, 1944, and set out in the lead of the 5th Infantry Brigade on the next phase of the recapture of Burma.

The Church of St. Aldhem's-in-the-Jungle, Maram, 1944.

CHAPTER ELEVEN

"THE DUKE DESIRES THE INFANTRY WILL STEP OUT."

MARCHING SONG OF THE FIFTY-FOURTH

1. There are new faces on the narrow forest track
And the choking dust engulfs the weary road,
Whilst the sun that shines on Burma seems to flourish in the day,
So at night the gloomy jungle's our abode.

Chorus
Sure by Tamu and Kalewaand through Ye-U we must go
Down the emerald-green pagoda-studded way;
If it's only home and comfort and kind, happy things you know,
You've never trod the road to Mandalay.

2. O'er the wide Chindwin the path is to the East,
By Meiktila and by Toungoo to the sea,
By the broad Irrawaddy, still the peasants till the fields,
While the leafy palm trees sing their song to me.
Chorus

3. Oh, the far city is calling us along
And the hazy, far-off mountains do the same;
The white pagodas seem to mutter "Mandalay"
And the fields reflect the magic of the name.
Chorus

[To the tune of "The Road to the Isles", with words by Captain L. T. Highett, 2nd Dorsets, 1945.]

DURING THE EARLY PART OF DECEMBER, whilst the 2nd Infantry Division had been concentrating in the Yazagyo area thirty-five miles from Kalewa on the Chindwin, the 11th East African Division had been putting the final touches to the magnificent job of work they had been doing since they passed through us at Tamu in August. The Askaris had crossed the Chindwin and were making a bridgehead through which the 2nd Infantry Division were to pass.

General Stopford's forceful advance down the Tiddim Road and through the Kabaw Valley had been prosecuted with such vigour that the Japanese had had no time to rest, re-form or even put up a resistance on the east bank of the Chindwin opposite Kalewa. Had they been able to do this they would have proved a very formidable obstacle to our advance, as the east bank in this area was not only covered with thick jungle but made up of a series of very steep hills and ridges. It was hereabouts that the 17th Indian Division made their famous rearguard stand with the 7th Armoured Brigade on the withdrawal from Burma in 1942.

To the foot soldier views on the future were limited to considerations of how much we could carry and how far and fast we would have to walk to the next line on which the Japanese would try to hold us. We know now that at higher levels our commanders were already considering the campaign in terms of Rangoon before the monsoon. We, who expected to have to walk the whole six hundred miles, thought in terms of the more limited target of Mandalay to be reached as fast as we could march.

The men were in great fettle—it was virtually a new battalion which was taking the field in this second innings, but fortunately very much strengthened by a hard core of battle-experienced, fit and refreshed veterans of the Kohima campaign. Our successes of the summer and the continued advance of the XXXIII Corps had so heartened everyone that, although we realized it was to be no cake-walk, the 2nd Division set out on their long advance with great élan.

Our earlier planning had been deep and detailed. Opinions varied greatly on the jungle conditions we would find east of the Chindwin. Not much was known of this very sparsely populated area even before the war, and except for patrolling and the activities of the Chindits farther to the north in 1943 little fresh information had been gained.

One factor was abundantly clear: we were hundreds of miles south of our railhead at Dimapur and we would have to rely mainly on air supply. The shortage of petrol would play an enormous part in any operation and we foot soldiers were reduced to an absolute minimum of transport. Further, we were to advance for a hundred and fifty miles through the dreaded "dry belt" of Burma where the supply of water at the best was extremely limited and the prospect of watering an advancing army was causing everyone furiously to think.

Finally, the success of the operations depended on speed, speed and more speed. That is to say, in this form of warfare the infantry had to march farther and faster than ever. This was to be no armoured rush through to Brussels on the European scale; however, the same principles applied and, comparatively speaking, we were to move just as fast, and, as it turned out, arrive at Schwebo with as comparatively little petrol and supplies as the Second Army had when they reached the Belgian capital.

The factor of the enemy in our appreciations at all levels was rather unknown. He did not seem to be playing his usual game at all. There were three possible lines on which he might hold us: the east bank of the Chindwin, the hilly jungle country around the nodal point of Pyingain, or "Pink Gin" as it came to be called, or on the River Mu at Ye-U.

He failed to hold us on the Chindwin, he was outmanoeuvred by the 2nd and 20th Divisions in the "Pink Gin" area, and how we dealt with him at Ye-U on the Mu, I will presently recount.

Opposing the XXXIII Corps were the 15th, 31st and 33rd Divisions of the Japanese Fifteenth Army. The 15th and 31st Divisions, which had been virtually disintegrated at the Manipur and Kohima battles, were re-formed or in the process of being re-formed and, as we were soon to find out, were not of the same mettle as the original divisions. The 33rd Division had borne the brunt of the entire withdrawal, excellently executed as it was, from Imphal, and as far as could be gathered numbered only about four thousand effectives.

On the 19th of December General Stopford received orders first to capture and construct airfields in the area of Ye-U—Schwebo (one hundred-odd marching miles to the east) with all possible speed. Secondly, to capture Monywa, which doesn't affect our domestic story, and finally to capture Mandalay.

To do this General Sir "Monty"[13] ordered the 2nd Division to push on to Ye-U—Schwebo as quickly as possible down the main axis—that famous track along which an army had withdrawn and down which a victorious army was now to set out on its relentless pursuit; that dusty track which was marked on the map with the ominous words "motorable in the dry season," and even this warning was optimistic. The 19th Indian Infantry Division, which, some weeks before, had crossed the Chindwin at Sittaung and set out on their memorable two-hundred-mile left hook, were to advance and capture Schwebo and cross the Irrawaddy due

---

13 The Army Commander and Corps Commanders of the Fourteenth Army had been knighted by His Excellency The Viceroy, Field-Marshal Lord Wavell, at an investiture held in Imphal on the 16th of December, 1944.

east of that town, with the subsequent intention of capturing Mandalay from the north. The 19th Indian Division, which had only recently come from India, had originally been in the IV Corps. When General Slim, in planning this operation, decided to take the IV Corps right out of the Mandalay battle and swing them in away down on the Irrawaddy on the right flank of the Fourteenth Army and make the decisive move for Meiktila, he passed the 19th Division to General Stopford with instructions to keep up the bluff that the "Dagger" Division were still in the IV Corps. This deception plan worked magnificently for a long time.

The 20th Division were ordered to advance south-east and capture Monywa whilst our old friends the 268th Brigade, completely reorganized and very much on a bullock-cart basis, were to operate between the 2nd and 19th Divisions.

This line-up, with the 20th Indian Division on the right, the 2nd British Division in the centre and the 19th Indian Division on the left, was maintained throughout the operations for Mandalay. Brigadier Dyer, with his 268th Brigade, continued to play his usual fine game of full-back to the infantry divisions' three-quarter line.

On the 19th of December the leading elements of the 2nd Infantry Division (6th Infantry Brigade) passed through the East African bridgehead on the east bank of the Chindwin. The next night, at 2200 hrs. the 2nd Dorset, with Brigade Tactical Headquarters, left their concentration area at Yazagyo and advanced by mechanical transport to the banks of the Chindwin at Kalewa. It was a bitterly cold night as we drove down through the jungle. The dust was so thick that we found that we had to roll the canopies of the threetonners back to prevent the dust being sucked into the back of the trucks, and without greatcoats or blankets we were all very cold. At first light we crossed the Chindwin at Kalewa. The sappers had put up a magnificent show by constructing the largest Bailey bridge in the world, eleven hundred feet long, on the Myitha River and had floated it down to Kalewa and stretched it across the nearly four-hundred-yard-wide River Chindwin. At Kalewa the Battalion separated for a few hours, the fighting echelon vehicles crossing by the bridge whilst the marching troops were ferried eight miles down-stream to Schwegyin, on the east bank, from which point they set out on a twelve-mile march to Chaungzon, where we took over from rear details of the 6th Brigade.

"The Duke desires the infantry will step out": in 1711 the Duke of Marlborough's Chief of Staff put rather more pedantically the very same request that General Nicholson now made to the British 2nd Division. We learnt on that first day's march in the intense heat something of

"THE DUKE DESIRES THE INFANTRY WILL STEP OUT."

the conditions which were to lie ahead of us in this advance through the dry belt. In fact, we appreciated very quickly, whenever possible, never to advance by day but always to take advantage of the cool of the night for our marches.

Throughout this day our advance lay along this track littered with grim reminders of the 1942 withdrawal. It was at Schwegyn that all vehicles that had managed to get so far had finally to be abandoned. Here was a second Dunkirk, with tanks, cars, private and military, and lorries littering the roadside. The Nip had managed by a process of cannibalization to put into service some of these old Honey tanks and a few trucks, and occasionally we were to come up against our own vehicles, both hard and soft-skinned, in action.

At Chaungzon we waited for a couple of days whilst the Brigade caught up. Troop-carrying mechanical transport was so scarce that the Brigade had to be ferried forward from Yazagyo to Kalewa in dribs and drabs. The Brigadier never knew from day to day what force he would have "up" by the evening. However, by Christmas Eve the Brigade were firm in the Chaungzon area and our animals had caught us up, having marched from Yazagyo. The 4th Brigade had to be left behind in the Yazagyo area for some days before they were ferried forward.

The Battalion machine still creaked a bit after the reorganization at Maram and we were glad of this forty-eight hours to get ourselves organized for battle. We were on the barest minimum scale of equipment and vehicles.[14] Each man carried a large pack and some form of entrenching tool. Bush knives or machetes were theoretically section stores, but there were very few men who had not acquired one of these most useful items of kit. We still carried our toggle ropes and

---

14 On conversion to the Indian Army "standard" battalion, modified for a British unit, we should have been reduced to twelve jeeps and trailers as the complete scale of unit transport for all echelons, as were the British battalions in Indian Divisions. Fortunately, however, there was a shortage of jeep trailers in Assam at the time and the 2nd British Division, having already in other regards modified the standard-battalion establishment to suit themselves, were allowed to retain a proportion of Dodge 15-cwts. in place of jeeps—a bargain of which we were not slow to take advantage. Experience had proved that the Dodge 15-cwt. could go anywhere that a jeep could, except on the narrowest mountain tracks, and was a much better load carrier.

We actually took the field with nine jeeps (including two with trailers) and six 15-cwt. Dodges in place of jeeps, one water cart and four carriers. For communication we were allowed to retain two motor-cycles. In addition, we had "made" a jeep from somewhere and built a "G" office trailer from the chassis of an old 8-cwt. P.U. To supplement the very limited mechanical transport, our scale of mules was officially forty-one unit mules led by Dorsets; and attached to us for all purposes was a troop of the Divisional R.I.A.S.C. Mule Company of fifty-nine mules led by Indian other ranks. These latter included six so-called "riding" mules for the evacuation of casualties.

usually a "dhurry" line, that invaluable length of cord which is an issue in the East and is put to so many more uses than its specific purpose of securing a "bed roll".

My Quartermaster's main worry was to ferry forward our secondline stores—the men's second packs, containing change of battledress, spare boots and other valuable possessions, the blankets and the "bivvy" tents. These three items caught us up whenever possible, but I always tried by hook or by crook to get the blankets up. At this time of year, though it was intensely hot by day, the thermometer would drop thirty or more degrees by night, and, clad in tropical kit, with only a cardigan and gas-cape to keep out the heavy morning dew, we found that few of the Battalion obtained any sleep unless we had our blankets. There was little enough sleep in all conscience with all the night marches we were to do, but if those not on "stag" could snatch an hour or two's sleep between two o'clock in the morning and dawn it made all the difference.

The one Dodge 15-cwt. per rifle company which was all that we could allow a company for its cook's truck was invariably heavily overloaded, and at Chaungzon I had to order a lot of stores to be jettisoned. I do not know what we would have done without our captured Jap three-tonner, "Tojo", which we acquired at Yazagyo, and its mate, "Tokyo", which we "won" farther down the road. These two vehicles, maintained throughout by Sergeant Smith and his fitters and flogged to death ferrying stores up and down that terrible road, made all the difference. We could carry just that little bit extra, and of course, with an extra vehicle, could ferry quicker and thus get things like blankets up in reasonable time. "Tojo" and "Tokyo" were also invaluable in lifting the "non-marchers", those invaluable storemen and vital personnel, excellent men at their jobs but unhappily ill-equipped with marching feet, who simply could not have done the march, but whose evacuation would have meant a serious loss to us in experienced personnel who, behind the scenes, always kept the unit functioning.

At Maram the Brigadier had always insisted that we keep our training down to section level; he maintained, and quite rightly, that our reinforcements would shake down into their component platoons and companies as we moved down the road. How right he was! If our joints creaked a bit as we set out after our long rest, and if the company commanders, tired after a long march, had to take time off to check up on points of minor training, and if the Brigadier himself at stand-to on Christmas morning found cause to chase that excellent Provost Sergeant, Sergeant Fincham, who seldom laid himself open to attack from anyone, we soon learnt by experience, and by the time we

"THE DUKE DESIRES THE INFANTRY WILL STEP OUT."

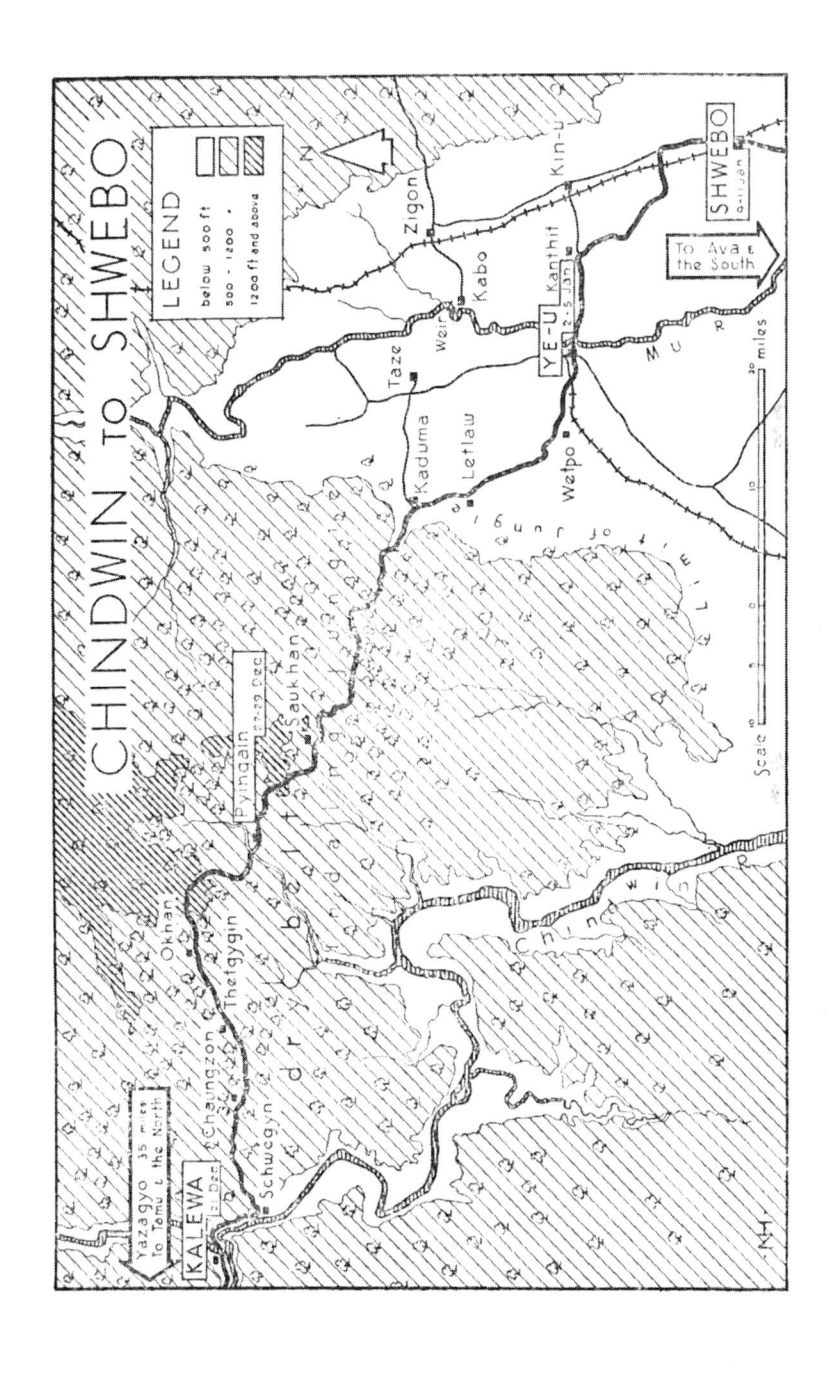

reached Ye-U the Battalion had settled down with remarkable rapidity as a fighting unit.

It was on Christmas Eve, 1944, that the Fifty-Fourth really got going on this hundred-mile race through the thick indaing jungle across the "dry belt" to Ye-U. Our marches varied in distance: some days we would be content to walk all night, and on other occasions we would do a comparatively short march, lie up and then continue the movement. Our bounds were restricted by the location of suitable water points, the congestion at these points as well as the tactical situation ahead. Although we were not to move into the lead until after Kaduma, it was essential that the 6th Brigade moved on before we could get at the water. I say water advisedly—at this season of the year even the largest chaungs carried only a mere trickle, at most two inches deep in the deepest part, and invariably we had to dig for our water supplies.

These night marches are firmly embedded in our memories. The road was so uneven, the dust so thick and the weight the men carried so heavy that we used to halt for fifteen minutes in every hour with a three-quarter-of-an-hour rest every three hours. This latter was originally an hour's halt, but with the drop in the temperature at night we found that the cold stiffened us too much and used to hurry on as soon as we were adequately rested.

Whilst we were still following the 6th Brigade I could afford to send the motor transport on ahead to prepare the bivouac area, the only snag being that the "B" Echelon trucks used to come back down the column on their never-ending ferrying journeys and cover us with still more dust, but all this was bearable so long as we arrived at our destination to find hot tea and blankets awaiting us.

The most difficult feature of these night marches was the column of mules we had to trundle along with us. In addition to our fortyone unit mules we had taken under command our affiliated troop of the R.I.A.S.C. Mule Company, with their further sixty donkeys. In the column also were Brigade Headquarters, with their huge signal mules. The R.I.A.S.C. mules were always strung together in twos or threes, with the sepoy driver tied on somewhere about the sharp end of the leading donkey (many of these R.I.A.S.C. animals were little bigger than donkeys), and this system worked until there was a fork in the road, when an Indian mule driver could usually be guaranteed, unless carefully watched, to lead off down the wrong track, or when the second or third mule on the string decided to liven the night with some antics. Our own drivers plugged steadily on, punctuating the night with cheerful repetitions of the monotonous military monosyllable which goes for the English language as it is spoken by the soldier. Herding the Battalion tail along would be Sergeant Park, on one of our so-called riding mules, of which we had half a dozen issued in the hope that they would be useful for evacuating casualties. He also assisted the officers and Viceroy's commissioned officers of the mule company, riding the most immense chargers, to keep the unwieldy column in order. All the animals did a great amount of work on these marches, the chargers covering many more miles than anyone else up and down the column, whilst the mules carried their heavy weights as patiently as these animals always do. The object of the long halts was really to rest the mules more than the soldiers, and part of the game was to load and unload the animals at these halts. This unenviable job, as far as the R.I.A.S.C. mules were concerned, fell to the lot of the rearguard company. It was obviously impossible for the Indian driver, with two or three mules "under command", to do more than hold the leading animal by the nose and make soothing noises at him in the hope that it would encourage his "string" to stand still; meanwhile, the rearguard company would, in accordance with a prearranged drill, assemble round the mules and remove the loads. At first this was all quite chaotic in the dark, but it is surprising how soon even the most town-bred soldier would get accustomed to dealing with these animals in the darkness, and after a night or two our halts went through with great slickness and lack of fuss. This business of doing rearguard-cum-mule party was never popular, as it involved taking over and loading the mules prior to departure; escorting them the whole night at the tail of this long and dusty column; unloading them and loading them up again at the long halts; and, after the Battalion had arrived, long after the head of the column had had their "char" and were settled down for the remainder of the night, the wretched mule escort were still completing their job and supervising the delivery of the precious water, carried by the mules, to company "cookhouses" for the breakfast meal.

As we continued our way through the jungle we began to find that, as so often happens, the problems ahead of us had been exaggerated. The weather was most pleasant and this indaing jungle, with its huge trees and not so very thick undergrowth, was not nearly as formidable as we had been led to expect. We were on short commons, it is true, but the supply services with all their worries just could not keep us up to full scale. Our cigarettes were not yet cut, but we began to have forebodings of a state of affairs later to come about when ammunition and petrol had to be flown in on a higher priority than cigarettes.

On the third night we arrived at Pyingain, thirty-odd miles to the east of Chaungzon. We arrived at 0215 hrs. and went into a bivouac area about two miles to the east of the town, which, except for some elaborate defensive positions, showed little sign of its recent occupation by the Japanese.

I do not know why this night's march had been so particularly wearisome; perhaps we were feeling the serious water shortage at our last halting place at Okhan, or was it that the mules had been especially "bobbery" that night? At any rate, I remember being more than pleased to turn off that dusty road into the shelter of the trees and find the ever-cheerful Fooks with my tent up and a bowl of water to wash in and a steaming mug of tea ready. At that moment Tony Bridge, the Brigade Major, showed up and said that owing to some fracas ahead in which the 6th Brigade were involved, we would not be moving on the next day.

Jimmy Heath, the attached Gloucestershire Regiment company commander, was overjoyed, as it gave him an opportunity to set out the next morning in search of his battalion's mess silver. This silver had been buried when the 1st Glosters and 1st K.O.Y.L.I. marched out of Burma in 1943. At "Pink Gin" they had been told to dump all their battalion stores. Accordingly they buried the silver; the Colours had already been flown to safety, but except for some valuable and very small pieces they had had to leave all their treasured possessions and trophies, gathered in two hundred and fifty years of soldiering, in a chaung in the middle of Burma. Those responsible had made a sketch which Jimmy brought back into Burma with him. We all took a great interest in the Glosters' silver, but unfortunately the time at our disposal was very limited and only a hurried reconnaissance was possible. Enough, it is true, to show us that the chaung, which was one of the landmarks, had altered its course in subsequent monsoons and the Japs had developed another road round "Pink Gin" as a "motorable" road, and so I don't think that Jimmy really got much value for his efforts. We heard later that the site of the buried treasure was subsequently discovered, but that the native Burmans and not the Japanese had dug up the silver some months after the withdrawal and had sold most of it. Some pieces were discovered subsequently in places as far away as Rangoon, silver plates from sports shields and some valuable trophies were re-collected, but unfortunately very little of their magnificent set of mess silver is now back with the battalion.

At "Pink Gin" I ordered out Shamus, my pony, and with Mervyn Jones, the Second-in-Command, went for a ride around the really beautiful hill country round the town and had a look at the temples and pagodas in the village itself. On this ride I was more than ever filled with admiration for the regiment of foot—I forget the particular one—which about fifty or sixty years ago came rushing up through what must have been practically trackless jungle from Mandalay to Imphal to quell a rebellion in Manipur State.

We, by modern standards, were poorly enough supplied at all costs, but what of the hardiness of our forebears who marched, through this practically unpopulated zone, in their red coats and carrying equally heavy packs? The natives on whom they must have depended for replenishing supplies could not always have been as friendly as we found them and with a much greater tendency to use their villainous-looking long "dahs" which can inflict such unpleasant wounds.

On my return I found that a reinforcement officer had arrived in the person of Captain Bartrum, of the King's, a Regular officer of some quite considerable service but with no battle experience. Brigade sent over a very charming Australian officer who was doing an exchange visit. He told us something of New Guinea and the Pacific War, and I tried hard, but without success, to persuade him to part with his Australian gaiters, which are so much better than our pattern.

After a wait of a day and a half we set off at about 1700 hrs. the next evening on our next bound to Pauktha Saukhan, the next water point, about ten or twelve miles down the road.

The Battalion were by now well under way. We were shaking down under the new organization of six companies, and so far I had been able to keep my "B" Echelon up with me. I was always much happier when "B" Echelon were at hand. In this war, where the possibility of enemy infiltration and "jittering" was much greater by night than was the case in Europe, we could never afford to have isolated detachments unless they were quite capable of looking after themselves. Except when "B" Echelons were brigaded I always preferred to have mine up with me in the Battalion defensive locality.

We had set out across the Chindwin with most of last season's "colours" in the team. Mervyn Jones had joined me as Second-inCommand in July, 1944, at Shenam on the way to Tamu and had seen the Battalion in action and already knew our ways. Graeme Gordon Wright, on his eventual return from a tour of the hospitals of India, had, to my great personal relief, accepted my invitation to reoccupy his old chair as Adjutant in place of Colin Doran, who had left us at Yazagyo to go to the Quetta Staff College. "A" Company, as of old, was commanded by John Bowles, "B" by Peter Feeney, who had taken over from Graeme Gordon Wright as far back as Pfuchama, "C" Company was led by Tommy Tucker, who had already done a great deal to reorganize and retrain them after the gruelling knocks they had received in the Manipur Road campaign, and Clive Chettle was still in charge of his beloved Light Company, assisted by his old Company Sergeant-Major of Kohima days, C.S.M. Seale.

Lintorn Highett had returned some time before and had taken over the Defence Platoon—such an inappropriate title for the old unofficial Guerrilla Platoon, who, despite their new name, were to continue to be much more guerrilla- than defensive-minded. Mackenzie had taken over H.Q. Company and was itching to get at the Nips again. The many reinforcement officers were settling down well in their various jobs, and every day I could feel the Battalion gather strength as we pushed down this interminable road.

After Saukhan we got a lift for a few miles in mechanical transport, suddenly released by the 6th Brigade, which brought us to Letlaw, about a dozen or so miles short of Ye-U.

Two things happened during this particular afternoon, the last of 1944, as the Battalion sat crowded uncomfortably in their three-ton lorries enjoying the unexpected if qualified comforts of a third-class ride instead of a first-class walk. At Kaduma the road split and, whilst the 6th Brigade hurried on to the Kabo Weir to try to get there before the Japanese wrecked the water supply for the whole of this part of Burma, we led off right-handed, going flat out for Ye-U. So on New Year's Eve, 1944, the Dorsets came once more into the lead of the advance of the 2nd Infantry Division against the Japanese. Secondly, at Kaduma, we suddenly broke out of the jungle and found ourselves back on the plains. For two long years we had concentrated our thoughts and training and had fought exclusively in jungle lines, except where this conflicted with landing from the sea. Now, suddenly, we found ourselves in the hot plains with no wood to brew-up our tea and no convenient hook on which to hang our shirts. This last passage through the jungle had proved so pleasant in comparison with some other types we had encountered previously that we all, I think, regretted the sudden change to the blinding sunlight and heat of the open plain. As far as fighting went, there was little change: the unending banana groves and miles of eight to ten-foot-high jungle grass could prove, as we soon found, just as difficult country to work through as the thickest of jungle.

We spent the first day of 1945 advancing to contact down the road from Letlaw to Schwebo. Ahead with the leading company worked the ubiquitous sapper reconnaissance party, with their armoured car and their inevitable pot of paint to mark up the bridges. By this time the Nip seemed to be moving back so fast that we were not encountering the mines and the barricades of felled trees which the 6th Brigade had met in the initial stages of the advance from the Chindwin.

During the advance down the Manipur Road the Royal Engineers had, with great foresight, provided themselves with a blue-print of every bridge on the road, with the result that they were able to anticipate the probable damage to any bridge which might have been destroyed by the enemy. Whether they did so or not on this occasion I have not been able to find out; the variety of roads used by the many divisions advancing on different axes in the Corps area would have made this task most difficult. However, just as in our earlier campaigns, so during the advance to Mandalay the Royal Engineers were invaluable. The C.R.E. of the 2nd Division was now Dennis Calvert, one of the many Calvert brothers who made such great names for themselves in Burma in this war. Dennis we used to see a very great deal: General Nicholson, the Divisional Commander, never spared himself in his efforts to get around to see his battalions, and encouraged his staff to do likewise. By far the most frequent and always welcome visitors at my headquarters were the C.R.E. and Eric Cleeves, C.R.A.S.C. One of Dennis Calvert's main worries after we had reached anywhere was to get the local irrigation system working again. Once we had arrived in the plains we encountered the excellent canals and waterways constructed by the British Raj to irrigate these naturally dry plains of Burma. Fortunately, the Japanese, relying as they were on a vast yield of rice from Upper Burma, had tampered little with the canals and had left too hurriedly to wreck this water system. However, Dennis had one or two difficult moments in his enthusiasm to reopen the waterways before he had collected together the old prewar native teams to run them once again.

In my enthusiasm for the work of the Royal Engineers, to which I have paid little enough attention to date, I find I have left the Fifty-Fourth slogging along on their feet on New Year's Day, 1945, advancing confusingly enough from Letlaw to Letlan. Our advance was slow that day, as it was very much a case of "soflee soflee catchee monkey"—we had not yet gained contact, but all local reports pointed to the possibility of immediate resistance. During the day these confusing and often conflicting reports gradually clarified themselves into a definite tale that the Nip had pulled out about twenty-four hours ahead of us, preparing to fight a delaying battle on the Mu River. The Burmese "umpires", as we came to call the local informers, were a bit vague at this stage and were still too cowed by recent overlordship of the "master race" to give us really accurate information. We could gain a lot of knowledge, however, by inquiring how many bullock carts the Nips had commandeered from the villages through which we passed, to lift their kits to the rear, and at what time Farmer U-Sin, or whatever his name was, was expected to return.

For the first time in three years the soldier was up against the language difficulty. Hitherto he had been able to get along with the few essential words of Urdu backed up by some pretty strong pronouncements in Dorset dialect. In Burma, at any rate during the early stages, this did not carry us far. We had all been issued with a little yellow pamphlet called "Rubbing Along in Burmese", and for many weeks the evening bivouac was greatly enlivened by the pantomimic efforts of the British other rank to describe just particularly which form of livestock, whether in the shell or on the hoof, he wished the grateful natives to liberate for his own especial benefit.

Early in the afternoon of the 1st of January the leading company ("A") reached the Ye-U main canal at Letlan about five miles due east of Ye-U, and found the bridge blown. From my map I could see that there was a viaduct at Wetpo, a mile to the south, with a railway bridge a quarter of a mile farther on. I sent a company hurriedly in this direction to confirm the native reports that we could still cross there, and, leaving "A" Company at Letlan, followed up as fast as possible to liberate Wetpo. Here the Brigadier decided to halt for the night.

Wetpo definitely gave us a welcome as the first British troops to return. The head of the welcoming committee appeared to be a Sikh who had been left behind in 1942 and went to great pains to run in all his pet enemies on charges of collaboration. Further, he also took trouble to see that the local inhabitants did the right thing by us in the way of eggs and what have you.

After dark I unloaded the mortar carriers and made up a couple of sections from the Defence Platoon and bade Snagger Highett to mount and ride off: "Go view the land, even Ye-U."

Meanwhile, the Brigadier called an "O" Group at his headquarters at Chaungzon (these Burmese village names recur with an unvarying monotony), about three miles to our rear. His opening remark was characteristic. Placing a finger on the rather rude name of Wetpo, he merely said: "Geoffrey, we knew back at Maram (before we had ever seen a map) that we just had to come to a place with a name like this."

After laying down various night patrols, which still had to be done, he ordered me the next day to advance and occupy Ye-U, with a view to crossing and establishing a bridgehead over the Mu. For the first part of the operation we would be on our own whilst the remainder of the Brigade caught up. He laid down certain instructions regarding route

"THE DUKE DESIRES THE INFANTRY WILL STEP OUT."

which precluded my going flat out across country, but confined me to the main axis.

When I got back to my headquarters at about 2330 hrs. I found the whole of the camp discussing the disused small-gauge railway which ran through our defensive position. This may seem strange, childish talk for grown men, but except for those who had been on leave none of us had seen a railway or a train since May of the previous year. For the men this was a great step in the right direction—obviously a country which ran to trains could not be so uncivilized after all, and—pious hope!—there might even be a cinema in Schwebo!

Highett returned during the night, having had a good look round the town, but had encountered no opposition at all. As far as he could make out, Ye-U was lying open for our occupation. Unlike Joshua, the son of Nun, he had had no exciting adventures and could expect no red cords to be dangling from Ye-U windows on the morrow.

Ye-U, itself an important town in this part of Burma, second only to Schwebo, which lay about thirty miles farther east, was a great road centre. Apart from our west-to-east axis, down which we were advancing, important roads converged here from the north and south. Along both of these roads the Japanese were retreating hard, and I could anticipate encountering quite a number of isolated parties, especially on the north road, having been driven down from the race-course airfield and Kabo Weir direction by the advance of Jan Bradford's 2nd Reconnaissance Regiment and the Royal Welch Fusiliers in their successful rush for Kabo Weir.

Early the next morning, the 2nd of January, the Battalion Group, which included our machine gunners from "B" Company, 2nd Manchesters, started out northwards from Wetpo, following the road to Letlan. Here we were joined by "A" Company, who had got themselves across the canal, and set out on our final advance due east down the road to Ye-U. At Point 348, where the railway crossed the road in its course to its terminus at the north end of the town, I sent John Bowles with "A" Company to follow the line of the railway with three tasks: first, left-flank protection; second, to clear the north end of the town; and, third, to put a block on the northern exit, to gather in any Nips closing in on Ye-U from the north and north-west.

Shortly afterwards firing broke out ahead of us as "C" Company, under Tommy Tucker, in the lead, flushed some snipers. This particular conflict put us all on our toes, because among the party left to hold us up were figures in civilian dress. We couldn't at this stage determine whether they were the infamous Burma Traitor Army or Japanese disguised in native dress. At any rate, from then onwards we always treated all natives found in No Man's Land with the greatest caution until their bona tides were established. It was a very simple matter for the Japanese to wrap a native lungyi (a cotton skirt-like garment affected by the Burmans of both sexes) around their loins and with the similar features and colouring of their skins it was impossible to determine the difference except at very close quarters.

On arrival at Ye-U we found that the town had been deserted by the enemy. I pushed two companies down to the river bank and kept one in reserve. To the north we could hear John Bowles busily engaged in flushing Japs in the area of the railway station, which lay about a mile from the centre of the town. We could not cross the river at this point without some assault equipment, as the bridge had been blown, and we could see quite a lot of Jap activity on the far bank. I got the machine gunners of the Manchesters down on the right of "B" Company, where they started to hot-up the enemy with the help of our field artillery. This activity on our part brought instant reprisal in the form of 75-mm. and 105-mm. shell fire, which showed us that we had come up against a strong Japanese position. The walk through Burma was over and we now had to fight for our bridgehead across the Mu River, the banks of which at this point were six to eight hundred yards apart.

"A" Company continued to fight and scrap until nearly sundown, by which time they had completed all their tasks and had got a substantial block across the road from the north.

The town of Ye-U lies on a bend of the River Mu, which formed a salient of land on the far bank, on which the Japanese were preparing a defensive position.

The remains of the bridge were at the south end of the town and on the opposite bank the main road continued due east from Ye-U. At about half a mile inland lay the village of Thayetpinzu. Running due north from Thayetpinzu across the base of the salient lay two copses which we called, for obvious reasons, Gun Copse and Pagoda Copse, and farther north still the village of Yadaw. From what we could make out, the Nips were holding the whole of this position, which was about two thousand yards long, with some form of defences, continuing south for another thousand or so yards to the village of Indaing.

During the night of the $2^{nd}/3^{rd}$ of January Snagger Highett, with his Guerrilla Platoon, did a magnificent bit of patrolling. They crossed the Mu River and reached Yadaw, which they found occupied. They then left the village by a track running due west to the river and shot-up a Jap vehicle which they found near the stream. We guessed, I think correctly, that this vehicle was collecting Nips withdrawing from our bank at one of the few fordable places on the river. They then made their way back, contacted a patrol of "C" Company, the left forward company on the river, and brought back much valuable information.

Meanwhile, the enemy artillery continued to shell us throughout the night.

In making my plans to cross the Mu and establish the bridgehead which was my object, I was restricted by the Brigadier's insistence that I maintain a sufficiently large force on the west (near) bank to hold Ye-U against any infiltration from the north until he could bring up the Camerons or the Worcesters. Time, however, being the essence of the contract, not only to get a bridgehead to allow the 2nd Division to carry on on their race for Schwebo but also to deny the Nip a moment longer than absolutely necessary to prepare his positions, I was determined that we should have a smack at this crossing the very next day.

The Brigadier promised me a troop of Grants from the Carabiniers, who had become for this campaign our affiliated armoured regiment, and strong support from the very mixed Divisional artillery we had in support. I had call not only on the 25-pounders of the 10th Field Regiment and the 3.7-inch howitzers of the 99th Field Regiment, still equipped for the jungle, but also on—wonder of wonders in this theatre! —a battery of Priest self-propelled guns of the 18th Field Regiment. In addition to this very mixed bag of artillery support, the Brigadier was most hopeful that I could call on a pretty substantial air strike to cover my crossing. Owing to a large number of other calls on the very wide Corps front and the long distance the Air Force had to come, Brigadier West's promises in this respect could not be so definite as usual.

I saw little future in trying to cross the Mu frontally and assault the Nip in his strong Thayetpinzu position from the direction he was expecting me, with the totally inadequate resources at my disposal. If I could only cross from Kyabunni, three miles to the north, where the river was reported to be most shallow, and make a bridgehead at Yadaw, I could descend on the Nip from the north and roll him up from his right flank to his main position at Thayetpinzu.

As I was determining this plan, the Brigadier called me up to confirm that he could let me have a troop of Carabiniers from 0800 hrs. the next morning. I welcomed the offer. Three Grant tanks would be of the greatest value: even if we could not get them across the Mu, they could at least support us to Kyabunni, through as yet uncleared territory, and could shoot us over the river to Yadaw.

Accordingly, I divided the Battalion into two parts, named,

with a shocking lack of originality, Force Major and Force Minor (I remember that I had been looking at the pictures of the Ginger Rogers film in an old copy of Life in the command post the night before). Major, which I was to take off on this left hook, consisted of a small Tactical Headquarters, "A" and "D" Companies, the Pioneer Platoon and a detachment of mortars with, under command, a troop of "C" Squadron of the 3rd Dragoon Guards under Captain Archie Ware. The Carabiniers had been very busy supporting the 6th Brigade throughout the advance and had hurried to join us in answer to the Brigadier's request for assistance. I left Mervyn Jones, the Battalion Second-in-Command, in Ye-U commanding Minor, consisting of "B" and "C" Companies, the remainder of H.Q. and Administrative Companies and the Machine Gun Platoon of the Manchesters. His tasks were to hold Ye-U against all comers, including certain staff officers who would insist on strolling down to the river bank and draw unwanted attention from the Japanese gunners. Also, with the Manchesters, he was to be prepared to give us all possible support on to our successive objectives as we progressed down the east bank. Finally, he was to dispatch an officers' patrol of one platoon to land on the east bank, to gain as much information as possible to assist me on my advance and to link up with me after Yadaw. The dispatch of this patrol under Lieutenant Dicky Boyle was to be co-ordinated with the arrival of the air strike.

At about 0830 hrs. on the 3rd of January, Force Major set off northwards towards Kyabunni. At Ye-U-gon, about a mile from Battalion Headquarters, we picked up John Bowles and a rather tired "A" Company. They had led all the way from Kaduma and had had a pretty strenuous twenty-four hours' mopping up. Breaking out of the thick treed area of the Ye-U "oasis", we deployed into open formation in true Certificate "A" style to cross the open plain to Kyabunni. Our "guest artists" at Tactical Headquarters presented a formidable body on their own. The gunner party included not only the usual complement of armoured observation posts but, owing to the different types of field artillery, we had not only one but two battery commanders (from the 10th and 99th Field Regiments) and a Sherman observation-post tank of the 18th Field Regiment.

Whilst ever appreciative of the results they produce, I have many a time cursed this unwanted increment to my already overloaded Tactical Headquarters. However, the battery commanders of the 2nd Divisional Artillery were by now quite accustomed to the views of the infantry battalion commanders and fully appreciative of the necessity to keep their conglomeration of armoured observation posts concealed. Quite apart from the invariably excellent results of this most intimate support, our gunners were always most hospitable. Realizing that they had a means of carrying that little extra denied to the foot soldier, they never failed to produce a cup of tea from the bottom of their monstrous machines at the most opportune moments, and for some extraordinary reason always had a wireless set that worked. Finally, I felt that the presence of such a strong "carrier" force moving astern of the leading companies, apart from presenting a large target, must have completely confused the Nip as to the strength of my "armour".

We found Kyabunni only just recently evacuated by the Nips and the inhabitants greatly thrilled by our return. Lacking the amenities of the "comfort platoons" supplied for service in their army with the forward units, the local Japanese commander had tried to satisfy the appetites of his garrison troops during the occupation with local talent, stepped up with the occasional visit of a "comfort" detachment from Army sources, and his enthusiasm for his men's welfare in this respect had not gone down too well with these Burmese peasants.

I was all ready by 1400 hrs. to carry out a daylight crossing under the cover of smoke to Yadaw, provided that I could get the air strike I wanted. Then came one of those delays so irritating to the ground troops but so unavoidable in this theatre. The Royal Air Force and the Royal Indian Air Force worked wonders in this campaign, overcoming the greatest difficulties to give the necessary support to the troops on the ground, and we all owe them a great debt of gratitude. However, on at least two occasions, and this was one of them, they did not make it on time, and I had to postpone my attack. Our hours of daylight were greatly restricted at this time of year, being only from 0615 to 1745 hrs., and unless an attack were launched in these thick plantations in time to enable us to mop up before dark one was liable to let oneself in for all sorts of trouble. At any rate, on this occasion I was not prepared to make an opposed crossing and arrive on the enemy bank without plenty of time to reorganize before last light.

The air strike was eventually put in during the afternoon and was most effective. It was the first time we had seen rocket-firing aircraft and the moral effect, however depressing to the Japanese, was terrific for our soldiers. They had never seen anything like it. The accuracy of this strike as we were to see the next day was most impressive. Under cover of the strikes I was able to filter "D" Company (Clive Chettle) across the river that evening and he established a small bridgehead. After dark this company moved forward and occupied Yadaw and patrolled south to Pagoda Copse and east to a reported gun site, finding both unoccupied.

Meanwhile, back in Ye-U, Force Minor had been subjected to continual shelling which in two days had accounted for about a dozen casualties mostly in "B" Company. But their presence there had apparently deceived the Japanese into thinking that a frontal assault across the Mu from Ye-U was to develop under cover of the air strikes. This became obvious from the events of the next day, and had we not been delayed until the morning of the 4th of January in delivering our left hook with Force Major across the Mu I feel that we might have wrought even greater execution than we did on the enemy.

I cannot pass this night without mentioning the "burrah khana", or big meal, provided by the headman of Kyabunni. Owing to various other appointments only John Bowles and I were able to slip away and enjoy for a few moments our host's excellent curried duck. This meal was especially memorable to me as being the last I was to share with John, who was killed the next day. In the twelve or so years I had known him, since as a recruit he had joined my platoon, the old pre-Belisha No. 1 Platoon of "A" Company, we had had many parties together, but we both felt that night, during a brief moment of reminiscence, that that curried duck tasted better than anything we had ever before enjoyed together.

The 4th of January was to be a most energetic and memorable day in the history of the Battalion. It started bright and early at 0400 hrs. when John Bowles led "A" Company splashing across the Mu. We had found a place where it was fordable even for our most short-legged men, and so the main danger was not being caught in boats in the river but being caught in this wide open, thousand-yard stretch heavily laden, wading through water nearly up to our waists. This would seem to be the main difference between crossing minor chaungs in Asia and the smaller rivers in Europe. Both are equally unpleasant, but the Asiatic variety has such a wide river bed, with quite undeterminable depths of water, that one is in the open for a very much longer period than in Europe.

As we tried to get the tanks across we encountered our first setback. The Sherman observation-post tank bogged in the sandy nullah leading down to the river and successfully blocked the only approach for the Grants. However, encouraged by the success of "D" Company and the safe arrival of "A" Company in the bridgehead, I decided to press on, hoping that Archie Ware, helped by the Pioneer Platoon, would find some way out of his predicament.

We re-formed in Yadaw, not looking its own bright self by any means after the air strike of the evening before. Clive Chettle was able to give me a deal of information, mostly negative but which was cheering despite the fact that at least two still-unlocated enemy 75-mm. guns continued to fire vigorously for some time.

The country hereabouts was not easy. We were either feeling our way through thick jungle grass away up over our heads or padding through banana groves. These latter were just as restricting to the vision, owing to the huge size of the leaves, as the thickest jungle. Progress was necessarily slow.

Encouraged by Clive Chettle's patrol reports, and with an eye on the clock, I decided to press on southwards from Yadaw with the minimum of delay. I left "D" Company in the lead, as they had by now got the feel of the ground.

As the head of the column was leaving Yadaw we met head-on a party of about sixty Japanese "bumming" down the track into the village. I don't know who were more surprised, the Japanese or ourselves, and both sides deployed rapidly. I was most impressed by the battle drill of the enemy—perhaps because we were at the receiving end, but in a very short time, before even Tiger Havers, the Intelligence Officer, had established Tactical Headquarters in a convenient village air-raid shelter in a nearby garden, the Nips had fanned out and were trying to get round our flanks. Leaving Clive Chettle to deal frontally with the Nipponese, I deployed John Bowles's "A" Company to cover the right flank, detaching a platoon of his to cover the left of the village.

Our gunners were excellent: both battery commanders outvied each other in getting a shot on the ground first. Within a remarkably short time there was a heavy concentration of both 25-pounder and 3.7-inch howitzer landing on the Japanese. This quick concentration was all the more remarkable for the extremely narrow confines of the target area, bounded on the near side by the very noses of the leading sections of "D" Company and having a depth of only two hundred and fifty to three hundred yards. If we had been impressed by the swift battle drill of the reputedly slow-minded Japanese, they must have been astounded by the speed and accuracy of our artillery reprisal. Fire support from the self-propelled guns was for this conflict out of the question, and I very much regretted the absence of Archie Ware and his three Grants lying back at Kyabunni just out of view of this battle.

It took about two hours to clear up this skirmish, delayed by the persistency with which the enemy would try to bring up a medium machine gun to about one hundred and fifty yards' range. At about 1100 to 1130 hrs. "D" Company had cleared the field and the Nips had withdrawn. The bag was six killed, including one officer, and various bloodstains through the plantations found by our patrols testified to a few more Nips who had little chance of ever seeing Dai Nippon again. As I have already mentioned, their medical setup was so paralytic that we used to reckon that a wounded Nip was as good as a dead Nip, his chances of survival among his more fortunate comrades being extremely small.

The identifications gained were extremely valuable. These Japs were found to belong to the 124th Regiment of the old 31st Division, annihilated at Kohima. They were obvious reinforcements, big chaps but seemingly overfed and from their showing of that morning lacking the guts of their predecessors, our old opponents of the District Commissioner's bungalow.

Meanwhile, the Brigadier was waxing impatient. Whilst I was talking to him over the air during the conflict he asked me to say definitely whether or not I could get Thayetpinzu and secure the bridgehead by nightfall. As we seemed to have bumped a quite formidable party, at any rate in numbers, and knowing from experience how long it took to dig the little devils out, I had to say that I did not think I could, but asked for a little while longer to give him a clearer picture. However, in order that there should be the minimum delay at the Mu River, he had to be prepared to try to push across elsewhere. In order to do this he had to move some way downstream south of Ye-U with the Camerons and the Worcesters in order to find a suitable crossing. If I could get Thayetpinzu by last light all would be well; if I was doubtful, then he must start now to do his crossing and work up northwards during the night.

Having given my answer, the Brigadier decided to put in his right hook, leaving me, with the Battalion astride the river, to clear up and try to reach Thayetpinzu by first light the next morning at the latest.

Having cleared the Japanese, I took stock of the position. Not having been able to bring on the tanks, I reckoned that with two companies I was too thin on the ground. Any sort of advance against opposition in these thick plantations—and this morning's foray had shown that the Jap had not pulled out—simply ate up men, and I must have a reserve. Also "D" Company had managed to fire off a remarkable amount of ammunition, especially with their automatic weapons, in this thick country, and so we needed more men and more ammunition before we could advance. I called up Mervyn Jones and ordered him to send up Tommy Tucker with "C" Company via Kyabunni as fast as he could with as much extra ammunition as they could carry. We were also running short of rations. Mervyn was quite cheerful despite the increased amount of shelling they had had in the past twenty-four hours, and promised to get "C" Company up to me with all I wanted by 1600 hrs.

We did not spend our time idly whilst waiting for "C" Company and the replenishments to come out. Both "A" and "D" Companies were kept busy patrolling and trying to link up with Boyle's platoon out on the right flank. This officer, I gathered from speaking to my Adjutant on the wireless, had patrolled right up to the enemy position at Thayetpinzu during the previous night and could, I am sure, have given me most useful information. However, by one of those vagaries of wireless sets, I could not talk to him direct, although he was only about a thousand yards away, and could reach him only through Battalion Main Headquarters three or four times that distance in the same direction.

I was greatly encouraged by the patrol reports coming in and accordingly amended my plan. I had intended to make two or three bites at the cherry, having regard to three possibly defended localities ahead of me. The extra time given me by the Brigadier, which had, as you now remember, been extended to give me time, if required, to get into Thayetpinzu at first light on the morning of the 5th of January, would allow me to do this. When, however, "D" Company reported Pagoda Copse, six hundred yards to the south, clear, I immediately sent a platoon of this company to hold it and decided by using Pagoda Copse as a jumping-off ground to attack Gun Copse as soon as "C" Company were up, and follow up to Thayetpinzu if there was sufficient daylight left.

A friendly inhabitant of Yadaw had by now returned to the village and reported that about sixty Nips had, when the air strike started, evacuated the village the previous afternoon for the greater security of more deeply dug positions at Thayetpinzu. This cleared up the mystery of our encountering them in the morning. The same party were obviously moving up to reoccupy the village or perhaps even try to cross to Kyabunni, and they had not expected to find the British already on their bank.

Oh, where were "C" Company? We were all impatient to start. Poor Tommy Tucker had not even had time to remove his steel helmet and mop his brow before I had grabbed him and was telling him in no uncertain terms to drop the stores he had brought up (these were already being divided by the grateful "A" and "D" Companies) and join in the forthcoming attack just as fast as he could. On more than one occasion I had to rush Tommy a bit, and this was no exception. At 1620 hrs., after he had been about thirty minutes in Yadaw, the column began to move off: I reckoned that there was just time, but only just, to put in this attack before the tropical night clamped down upon us.

There had been no time to make an elaborate plot, and I am sure that our success was the result of the extreme simplicity. One thing worried me: both battery commanders, Graham Pank, of the 10th Field Regiment, and Brian Bonsor of the 99th Field Regiment, assured me that their allotment of ammunition was very restricted and that we had used or very nearly used up our day's supply already. With the Brigadier away on his right hook, and certain technical hitches on the radio, there was no Caesar to whom I could appeal. The Divisional Commander the next day, when I took him on a battlefield tour of the enemy position, was most firm in proclaiming that in an emergency such as this I could always have that little extra, and we never had a repetition of this difficulty.

The plot, as I say, was simple: "C" Company were to move forward into Pagoda Copse and "A" Company were to move up through some plantations on the left (or north) of the wood to a start line which was the front edge of Pagoda Copse and the track extending in prolongation of it. "C" Company had to make this attack, as they were the only company with three full platoons (having the platoon of the 1st Glosters to make up their complement). "A" Company were still just functioning with three platoons, but "D" Company, who had been going flat out for twenty-four hours, were hard put to it to raise this number. "D" Company were to close up on its leading platoon in Pagoda Copse in Battalion reserve, where I was to establish Tactical Headquarters.

At 1654 hrs. a very strong artillery concentration came down for three minutes on the front edges of Gun Copse and other located enemy positions. We had the full resources of the 10th Field Regiment, a battery of self-propelled guns (firing in a normal field role) and a battery of the 99th Field Regiment. The guns were all ideally situated, being on a flank to our advance, firing from their gun positions on the main axis somewhere between Letlan and Ye-U.

The concentration was followed by smoke, during which the two leading companies advanced across the five hundred yards of open country (tomato fields) between the two copses. At first things were quite sticky and "C" Company were checked for a time on the right. Tommy Tucker soon proved what a grand leader he was in action, ably assisted by the imperturbable Jock Given (you will remember him as the platoon sergeant moving unconcernedly about the tennis court at Kohima, now an officer platoon commander), who put down a most effective smoke screen from the company 2-inch mortars to cover the advance of the company against a hitherto unknown and apparently unaffected enemy position. Tucker, with great energy, kept the momentum of his attack going, despite the heavy small-arms and mortar fire put down by the Nips, who had reappeared after the artillery concentration. On, on they went, right into the wood, where to their joy "C" Company found that they could use their bayonets. There was a fierce competition between the Dorsets and Glosters on this company front and the Nips suffered severely from their rivalry, which was directed mutually to the greater destruction of the enemy.

In Pagoda Copse we were getting a number of "overs" and a great deal of direct fire from the enemy, who, deceived by the smoke, fired into the wood as the most obvious target. I was personally lucky in this battle when my carbine was hit and the bullet deflected over my shoulder. Just at this moment "A" Company came up on the set. It was the gunner forward observation officer, Jimmy Thom, from the 99th Field Regiment, who gave me a reasonably clear picture of the situation on the left flank. "A" Company had advanced a certain way across the open when company headquarters and the rear platoon came under very heavy mortar fire from a position in a banana plantation to the east and slightly forward of Gun Copse. John Bowles had been killed instantly, and this platoon (No. 9) temporarily disorganized. The leading platoons (Nos. 7 and 8) were, however, pushing on towards their objectives.

I asked Jimmy Thom if he could command foot soldiers, and, receiving a reply to the effect that he would have a "bloody good try", I instructed him to take over "A" Company and press on. This remarkable yeoman of Buckinghamshire,[15] not only took over "A" Company and reorganized the reserve platoon, which had suffered some few casualties, but continued to direct his own guns and brought down most effective fire from his battery on the very mortar position which had been so troublesome. For his gallant part in this battle Jimmy was awarded an immediate Military Cross. There were other sterling characters in "A" Company that day. C.S.M. Bedlow was sent by Thom to give me a more detailed account of what was happening. We did have an indifferent day on the wireless that day, and Sergeant Smith, an old Devon who had joined us in Gulunchi, and had already shown his true worth in the District Commissioner's

---

15 99th Field Regiment, R.A., Royal Bucks Yeomanry.

bungalow action, was Thom's great standby. Under Thom's direction he really got the tail of "A" Company going again and led them successfully into the woods. Meanwhile, the leading platoons of "A" Company, despite two officer casualties (Colin Beal and "Sunshine" O'Donnell, both platoon commanders), under the leadership of "Roger" Johnson, the company second-in-command, swarmed on to the objective with bayonet and grenade. It was a most fortunate decision on John Bowles's part that, owing to the conformation of the ground, he had sent his second-in-command off with Nos. 7 and 8 Platoons in the lead, as this resulted in this gallant officer finding himself in an excellent position to control the fight once the company had been split.

Meanwhile, on the right, "C" Company had cleared up to the edge of the wood, causing great slaughter. I don't think that we had ever found so many Japanese ripe for bayoneting, and the Dorsets that evening had every opportunity for some real practice. It was really good ding-dong, hand-to-hand fighting. One eager Gloster, it is said, with his eye on a Japanese officer's Mauser automatic, dodged by his opponent's sweeping sword and brought him down with a good rugger tackle before dispatching him by more orthodox means. Elsewhere, before he was wounded Colin Beal is reputed to have tried out his recently acquired kukri on a Japanese pate. Lieutenant Pullin, of the Glosters, greatly distinguished himself in leading his platoon that evening and was subsequently awarded a mention in despatches for his continued gallant conduct during the eight weeks he was with us in action, of which this attack was his most outstanding performance.

As ever, the stretcher-bearers were magnificent. There was no covered line of withdrawal for them. On the right Lance-Corporal Jesty organized the evacuation of "C" Company's casualties to Pagoda Wood, ably assisted in an unofficial capacity by Private Bishop, Tommy Tucker's batman, who temporarily deserted his master in order to help out the stretcher-bearers.

It was nearly dark by the time the wood was cleared, which proved deeper than we had expected, and I called a halt to reorganize. The resistance had been quite strong enough in Gun Copse to make me think twice about streaming on into Thayetpinzu with a consequent six-hundred-yard advance across the open without organized support.

I just had time for a reconnaissance throughout the Battalion position in Gun Copse and a quick "dekho" towards Thayetpinzu before it became too dark to see. I had ordered up "D" Company and the Battalion went into a locality in the wood, with, facing south, "C" Company on the right, "A" Company on the left and "D" Company in the rear.

The wounded I had ordered to be evacuated from Pagoda Copse by a track down to the Mu, where Mervyn Jones had meanwhile fixed up a ferry by means of the few assault boats which had by now been brought up.

Joe Chamberlin, the Medical Officer, had been kept busy until well after dark, and either not trusting Boyle's report that the river bank was clear, or for some reason of his own, determined to evacuate by the way he knew. Only two casualties, one of them an officer, returned by the correct route, having missed the regimental aid post in the dark, and Joe started off on his long trudge back the way we had come through Yadaw to Kyabunni, carrying with the very limited personnel at his disposal his fifteen-odd casualties. Somehow I got wind of this and was able to warn the Second-inCommand in Ye-U, who organized every available bit of transport to Kyabunni and set out to meet Joe. By the greatest of good fortune the two parties encountered each other literally in mid-stream, both parties being perfectly sure for one awful minute as they were standing up to their waists in water that those on the other side were Nips.

Back in the Gun Copse area we settled down for the night all very tired and hungry. I kept patrols going throughout the night towards Gun Copse. I always kick myself that I did not put out a stop on the Schwebo Road to the east that night; if I had done so I would have got a number of infantry at least, even if not a gun or two. I had not got the men available, with the Battalion split as it was, but it would have made an even better ending to the party than our subsequent advance the next morning. Our dawn patrol brought us news that the position at Thayetpinzu seemed to be remarkably quiet, even for a Japanese position. The appearance of the odd native approaching in the distance seemed to indicate that things were pretty peaceful, and I set the Battalion in motion for their final advance. We felt our way forward with leading sections well up, prepared to launch a proper attack if necessary. However, very soon after first light the leading companies were in Thayetpinzu and the bridgehead was ours.

With the remainder of the 5th Brigade advancing northwards 1 had received strict orders through my Adjutant at Main Headquarters not to advance south of the Schwebo Road. On arrival at this road at Thayetpinzu I took very good care to get a message through to Brigade to say that the Dorsets were now on the road, and ask that the Camerons and Worcesters be requested to direct their fire eastwards.

During the morning the remainder of the Battalion closed up on Thayetpinzu. The weather had changed suddenly and it was raining for the first time for about six weeks.

With the arrival of the remainder of the 5th Infantry Brigade during the day, and the establishment of the Brigade Group on the main axis east of Thayetpinzu preparatory to the advance of the 7th Worcesters the next morning, the Battle of the Mu was virtually over. As far as the Battalion were concerned it had been a great battle. We had been given our opportunity for a fight after the long march across Burma. It was most encouraging, with such a large proportion of hitherto untried reinforcements in the ranks, to have scored a real hit so early in the second innings. The Battalion had been well and truly blooded and had ended the attack with that most satisfactory of all conclusions, the actual bayoneting of the enemy in their positions. The Fifty-Fourth had seen for themselves, as had their predecessors often in the past, that there are no soldiers in the world who can stand up to the British bayonet. Within fortyeight hours of our arrival at Ye-U we had not only crossed the River Mu but had ousted a strong Japanese force which had had strict orders to hold the 2nd British Division indefinitely on the line of the Mu River. They had not only been defeated in battle but had, contrary to their custom, abandoned their position hurriedly, leaving their packs and much valuable equipment behind. Thirty-three counted bodies of the enemy were found in the Gun Copse—Thayetpinzu positions the next day. There was plenty to indicate that their casualties had been still heavier. We had not gathered any prisoners: this was always an unlikely eventuality, especially after the troops had seen the results of the Japanese handiwork in the form of a badly mutilated Burman corpse, freshly expired, found in Thayetpinzu Wood.

Our own casualties had been comparatively slight; during the advance on the 4th of January we had lost one officer and two British other ranks killed, and two officers and fifteen British other ranks wounded. The loss of a company commander in John Bowles was serious, and his death a sad blow for us all. I had known him longer than most. Prior to the outbreak of war he had entered whole-heartedly into the life of the Battalion, rising to the rank of platoon sergeant-major. He was an outstanding marksman and had represented the Battalion at Bisley. He was mentioned in despatches for his work in France and Flanders in 1939-40, and on arrival home he received a direct commission from the ranks. At Kohima he had led "A" Company in their very hard fight for the District Commissioner's bungalow, and had, by his leadership, inspired them to hang on, during those vital early days, to the spur above the road junction.

The officer situation as we reorganized ourselves on the east bank in the pouring rain did not look too encouraging. Strong as I was in "first eleven" company commanders, I had very few "second eleven" in the team, although one or two of the "colts", such as Roger Johnson, had shown outstanding ability in action. I was fortunate in having a spare player up my sleeve in Major Jimmy Heath, of the Glosters, who took over "A" Company for the time being. In addition to the two officer casualties on the 4th of January, three other officers—"Jonah" Jones, Fawcett and Smith of "A" Company—had to be evacuated from Ye-U. In addition, three valuable sergeants—Fox, Nott and Hector—were all wounded in this battle. We were suffering again from the old trouble of casualties among commanders at all levels.

General Nicholson paid us a visit during the afternoon of the 5th of January, and congratulated the Battalion on their performance. He insisted on being shown round the Gun Copse and Thayetpinzu positions on a private battlefield tour.

It took longer than was expected to get the whole Brigade Group firm, with all their vehicles and supporting arms, on the east bank of the Mu River, and it was not until the early morning of the 7th of January that we set out on the final stage of our advance to Schwebo.

On the 6th of January the Jap Air Force had paid us a surprise visit when their objectives were the Mu bridge and the concentration of men and material piling up in Ye-U. They repeated the performance on the morning of the 7th just as the Brigade were getting under way. This time they devoted their attention exclusively to the leading battalion, the 7th Worcesters, and their troop of tanks, who reported these Oscar pilots to be unusually indifferent marksmen. This is the last occasion on which the enemy air arm was in any way hostile to the 5th Brigade in the present campaign, although we were to witness the unfortunate attack by Japanese fighters on Dakotas flying into Schwebo a few days later.

We moved at the tail of the 5th Brigade in reserve for the next two days and so missed the Worcesters' skirmish and the extraordinary sight of the suicide attack by a platoon of Japanese who poured out of a wood in line, led by an officer with a sword, and charged across the open paddy against the Camerons, who were proceeding cheerfully on their way in the Brigade column.

On the 9th of January, a few miles north of Schwebo, we encountered the 2nd Royal Berkshires of the 19th Indian Division, which, the reader will remember, had crossed the Chindwin some weeks before us and had carried out a wide left hook through the jungle.

During the evening of the 9th of January, passing through the Camerons, who were still mopping up north and west of the town, the Battalion entered the moated city of Schwebo. Our first impressions

STRAIGHT ON FOR TOKYO

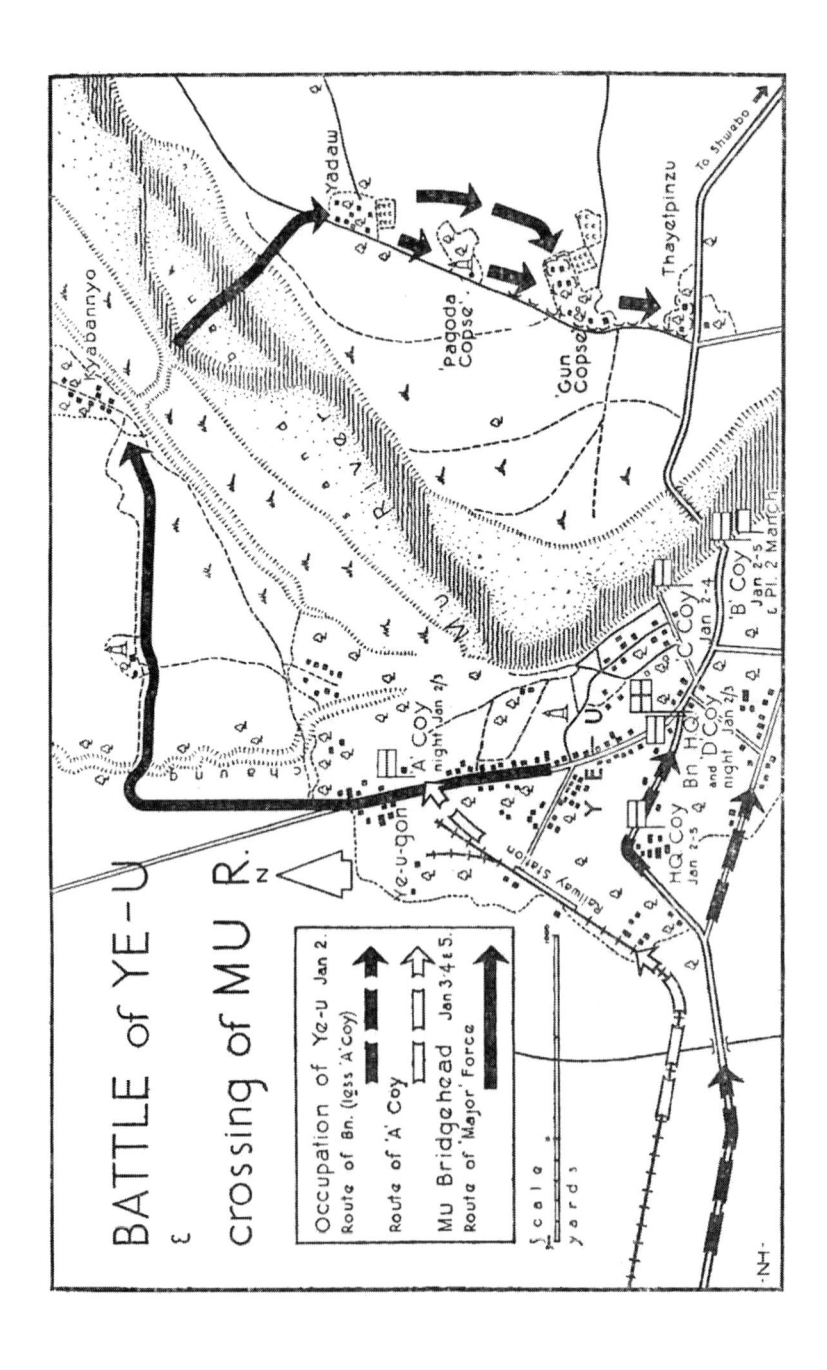

were good. We went into a position astride the road at the north end of the town in a most delightful area, clean and pleasant, with not too unpleasant bathing in the moat, where we could wash off the accumulated sweat and dust of three weeks of hard footslogging. Unfortunately, we suffered a couple of casualties in "B" Company that evening from cornered Nips fighting back like rats.

We had reached the "big city", we had advanced more than a hundred and thirty miles in nineteen days, a hundred and eighteen of which had been on our feet, and over the last thirty miles we had been in contact and had taken time off to fight the battle of the crossing of the Mu River. Our casualties had fortunately been slight with one officer and ten British other ranks killed and two officers and twenty-two British other ranks wounded. This was not quite as simple as it sounds. There was, at this time, a steady stream of about five men or so a day going sick, all of whom added up to a steady drain of manpower in a theatre where there were virtually no reinforcements and battalions had to fight on with steadily declining numbers. On the credit side, however, Paget Fretts suddenly reappeared, apparently unharmed by his bout of scrub typhus, and took over from Jimmy Heath the command of "A" Company vacated by John Bowles.

After a second look at Schwebo, the city did not come up to expectations. By European standards it should have ranked as a city about as big as Amiens: it was the most important town north of the Irrawaddy. Very soon our patrols had discovered the same collection of burnt-out "bashas" and depressed-looking natives, which did nothing to inspire the men as to the possibilities of the town as a possible leave centre, despite its tarmac roads and well laid-out parks.

Battle of Ye-u. Evacuating wounded across the River Mu at night.

The word of a scout—a march by night—
A rush through the mist—a scattering fight—
A volley from cover—a corpse in the clearing—
A glimpse of a loin cloth and heavy jade earring.

                                        -KIPLING.

CHAPTER TWELVE

"HOW BARE WAS OUR BUFF?"

"The men can chew their belts, but I must have gas."

[GENERAL PATTON, U.S. Army.]

WITH THE FALL OF SCHWEBO, the 5th Infantry Brigade found themselves having their only lucky break for many a long month. The weather at this time of year was excellent, and the pastoral tour through the villages of the Schwebo area, if it did not exactly reduce the infantryman's mileage on his feet, was a period to be remembered among the pleasanter aspects of this campaign.

We spent the whole of the 10th of January in Schwebo, busily mopping up. Companies in their own way found excitement and interest in this the largest city any of us had seen since leaving India. The enemy were not entirely inactive, but we all had the feeling, familiar to Dorsets of any battalion, that the set-up was too good to last: we were all too comfortable; digging in was easy in these compounds of large houses where so many local as well as Nipconstructed air-raid shelters existed; the water supply from the large moat surrounding the town was close at hand; there must be a catch somewhere. We were not surprised, then, when, on the evening of the 10th of January, Tony Bridge, the Brigade Major, rang up from Brigade and said that the Brigadier had orders for me, and meanwhile there would be no move before the morning of the 11th of January.

At Brigade Headquarters, on the banks of the moat, Brigadier Michael West explained the situation to us. The Division had gone so fast—in fact, all divisions had gone so fast—that we had outrun our supplies. It seems incredible, in these mechanized days, that a mere man on his feet can so easily outrun his supplies, but that is exactly what did happen. Despite all efforts of the "Q" boys at Corps and Fourteenth Army to maintain us under very great difficulties, we had arrived at Schwebo so fast that we had quite outrun our supply echelons. The speedy advance certainly paid dividends later on, in that we had presented our own side with ready-made airfields at Ye-U and Schwebo, but meanwhile, like General Patton's Americans in the Ardennes a few weeks earlier, we were left to chew our belts whilst the available transport, both land and air, was used for petrol and ammunition.

The immediate tasks of the Division were roughly as follows: the 4th Brigade was to take over the lead and push on down the main Schwebo—Mandalay Road, with the 5th Brigade moving south on a limited front to mop up in the immediate neighbourhood of Schwebo, and at the same time the 6th Brigade was to come forward from the Kabo Weir and concentrate around the town. Meanwhile, the 19th Indian Infantry Division, which had penetrated beyond and south of Schwebo, was to hand over to the 5th Brigade and concentrate in the west preparatory to making its crossing of the Irrawaddy due west of Schwebo. The 20th Indian Division, on the right, was to continue to press on towards Monywa and the Irrawaddy.

The Dorsets once more went into the lead at Schwebo and accordingly, on the 11th of January, we marched out, following the line of a canal southwards for about eight to ten miles as far as the village of Moksogyon. This really was a day of "soflee soflee catchee monkey": we advanced incredibly slowly, having first had to take our turn with the Royal Scots, of the 4th Brigade, at the only exit out of Schwebo which had not been destroyed by the enemy. We had with us a troop of Carabiniers and must have seemed a very formidable army until about three miles from our objective we encountered Major-General Rees, Commander of the 19th Division, driving back towards us in his jeep after having visited his leading brigade!

Around noon we met this brigade and started taking over from it immediately. At Tactical Headquarters that night, in the garden of the gasworks, or some sort of factory, at Moksogyon, we produced a bottle of Mariners gin to toast our feet on the completion of a hundred and fifty miles since crossing the Chindwin. Suddenly, out of the darkness, appeared Lieutenant-Colonel Sam Symes, of the Regiment, whom we had last seen on the morning of Sarah Sands Day plus one. Sam turned up at my headquarters and claimed that he and his 2nd Worcesters had just completed three hundred miles on their feet! The next day the two battalions of the Worcestershire Regiment, the 2nd from the 19th Division and the 7th in the 2nd Division, took time off to celebrate a reunion on the banks of the Moksogyon Canal. I believe that around this time the 1st and 2nd Battalions of the Royal Berkshire Regiment also staged a reunion.

On the 12th of January we advanced into the really delightful village of Hallin Twinma. The tanks had gone back overnight, but as no one from the 19th Division could tell me whether this village was occupied or not I decided to take the approach steadily.

Our welcome was almost embarrassing in its intensity. This was the first village we occupied in Burma that had not felt the heavy hand of war. It was delightfully situated and completely rural in that pleasant sense with which we connect the remoter villages of our own country. What struck us all most forcibly after a prolonged sojourn in India and Assam was the cleanliness of the natives. The Burmans seemed to have organized some form of sanitation, pretty primitive I will say, but so infinitely preferable to the universal and indiscriminate defecation of the Indian. It did not take us long to find out that Hallin Twinma must have been a very exceptional village and, taken by and large, the Burman does not score many points on cleanliness and sanitation over his opposite number in an Indian village.

Having disposed the Battalion around the village as tactically as possible and at the same time trying to allow the men the fullest advantage of our hosts' generosity, I set up Battalion Headquarters in the P.W.D. bungalow, again remarkably clean, and the Pangyi Kyaung. This latter building must be explained, as it will appear frequently in our narrative. In Burma, like many other countries of the world, the priests are the most educated section of the rural population, and thereby exercise great control. The pangyis, or priests, dressed in their yellow robes, live, I believe, on the charity of their flocks. That may be, but, however they contrive to feed, they actually dwell in the best house in the village—the best not only in build but in design, the most suitable therefore for that rather extraordinary formation of very independent sub-units, an infantry battalion headquarters. On our entry into Burma, General Slim had laid down very firmly, in accordance with traditional British policy, that the various shrines, pagodas and pangyi kyaungs were not to be interfered with, and so we relied to a great extent on the hospitality of the local priest. His attitude was a good guide, anyhow. These pangyis were notoriously pro-Japanese; that may be an unfair generalization, but shall we say that of all the classes of Burman they had shown up least well as protagonists of the British Raj both during the earlier battle for Burma and throughout the Japanese occupation of the country. To the advancing battalion commander the local pangyi and his influence on his flock were always a very definite factor in one's appreciation. A pangyi who would come forward and offer his house or kyaung (confusedly enough pronounced "chaung," the word for a river course) was obviously likely to be better received than the yellow-robed priest we sometimes saw slipping out of the back of the village across the fields as we entered by the front.

The six days we spent in Hallin Twinma will always be well remembered. Our animal transport caught up with us; in fact, owing to the extreme shortage of petrol it played a very important part in our daily lives. Here in the village of the hot springs we raised the "Dorset Yeomanry"—a mounted-infantry reconnaissance party, led by myself, mounted on ponies and riding mules, which scoured the country, and, apart from, as we fondly imagined, taking weight off the infantryman's feet, provided us with a great deal of amusing hacking. Shamus, my pony, started his life as a jeep-taxi in earnest. Whenever I was called to Brigade I would ride Shamus, and it was Private Fellowes, the groom, and not LanceCorporal Turner, my jeep driver, who had to turn out. "Goggles" was our champion. A mule herself—or is it himself?—he/she was quite determined that he/she would make a way in the world and end up as a handy hunter. Nothing pleased Goggles more than being taken out, ridden by Corporal Churchill, on a reconnaissance or as escort to myself on Shamus. For some time before we set out and for hours after our return Goggles could be heard telling his/her companions in the mule lines what it was to be a charger and not a mere pack mule.

We even opened up a shoot on one of the local lakes. The duck hereabouts were plentiful and in season, and it was not long before Brigadier McNaught took a night off to come and stay with us for a shoot over the home ponds.

But once again the set-up was too good to be true, and as the advance continued the 5th Infantry Brigade were ordered to concentrate on Wetlet, a town and what used to be called, in our old "Home Guard" days in the United Kingdom, a nodal centre, about twelve miles to the south.

Wetlet, because of its military importance, had been badly strafed by the Royal Air Force, and on arrival, quite apart from losing our sudden access to extra food in the form of poultry and eggs, we found an area almost devoid of habitable buildings. However, we made up for the loss of extra rations by being able to give the Battalion a few days' complete rest. I say complete advisedly, because hardly a day went past without some sub-unit being called out, either the carriers to the Irrawaddy on patrol or a whole company to Schwebo. Generally speaking, however, we had ten days' "rest" at Wetlet, a rest that we were to remember well, as it was the last we were to have during this campaign.

The Battalion was centred around the old police barracks at the north-east end of the town. Within reason we made ourselves most comfortable and the lack of full rations was soon forgotten in the abundance of things to do—things that the soldier likes, games to play, few guards and duties, and a certain amount of entertainment.

Whilst at Wetlet we had a visit from the Divisional cinema with one of the best and most up-to-date films we had ever seen. I do not believe that any one of us had ever seen it before! The next night we were entertained by Forsythe, Seaman and Farrell—a grand trio, the first of the all-star E.N.S.A. teams to come out East. This scheme, which promised much, never really lived up to expectations except for the teams like this one, who fought their way against innumerable difficulties to the front line. This team, it is worthy of note, had left the United Kingdom on the same day that we crossed the Chindwin, and as we had marched east they had played in Karachi, Bombay, Calcutta, Colombo and Comilla. This night they played to us only a few miles behind the so-called front line. Of front line there really was none. A few nights later our successors in Wetlet were raided by a strong party of Japs whose "umpires" had not really been put in the true picture.

The next day we held a transport day—a real Animal Transport Platoon "At Home". In the morning we held competitions for turnout and mule drill for our own unit mule teams attached to each rifle company, and also for the Royal Indian Army Service Corps troop attached to the Battalion. We also held the preliminary rounds of the mule wrestling competition. In the afternoon we held a real old-fashioned Dorset point-to-point. John Main and the Animal Transport Sergeant, Sergeant Park, worked wonders not only to organize the race meeting at all but to produce the animals for a succession of well-contested races.

For the success of the meeting we relied to a very great extent on the co-operation of Major McArthur and his R.I.A.S.C. Mule Company affiliated to the 5th Infantry Brigade. Most of the ponies and mules had to run twice if not three times with different riders. Everyone who could claim to be able to stride a horse or mule had a chance of riding, and some very good races resulted. The betting was tremendous, and not only the Battalion but anyone else in the Brigade who could get away came to the meeting, which was graced by the presence of the Divisional Commander. Thirty-five hundred rupees passed through the tote and the two bookies that afternoon, and a very substantial sum was eventually paid towards the welfare of the Tonga ponies in India, through the R.S.P.C.A. (I.), and a cheque for fifty pounds was sent to the Regimental Old Comrades Association. For myself the meeting ended well, as in the last race I was able to flog the long-suffering Shamus past the post ahead of Lieutenant-Colonel Charles Street of the Worcesters. Poor old Shamus had already run two races that day, finishing second in each case with my groom up. The trophies, the Mandalay Bowl, the Plassey Gold Cup, Sarah Sands Gallop and the Wetlet Stakes, were all manufactured out of ration tins by that most efficient craftsman Sergeant Smith of the Mechanical Transport Section.

Peter Feeney had hardly finished counting up his winnings as a bookmaker when, early the next morning, in response to an SOS, I had to rush him and "B" Company into Schwebo on a security role—security against the Japanese. So fast had the fighting troops passed through the city and so keen was everyone to get on to the Irrawaddy that our supply echelons found themselves sitting in the big city with but a handful of soldiers to guard them against wandering columns of Nipponese. Just how nearly our old friends of the Women's Auxiliary Service (Burma) had been slaughtered as they slept I never quite found out, but fortunately for the limited garrison the Japanese is a conservative soldier. Having caused a stir, he decided to lie up on the position he had reached overnight, and lying up proved to be an easy mark for "B" Company when they were called in to clear up.

Before we left Wetlet the three commanding officers made their first reconnaissance of the Irrawaddy from the back seat of an L5 light plane. My pilot, an American sergeant, had, the day before, lost himself over Wetlet and had landed, much to his relief, on our "racecourse", as he had lost his bearings and did not really know whether he was landing amongst British or Japanese. The next day he took me up on this flight and, to save me a thirty-five-mile drive back in a jeep, landed me again on my own racecourse-cum-airstrip. We really began to feel that we were getting modernized.

On the 28th of January the Fifty-Fourth set out on their next and what proved to be the final innings against the Nip. This was going to be a long match, though we did not realize it at the time: from now until the end of April we were to be almost continually in the leading brigade with never another break.

The Camerons had been sent off due east a few days earlier to harry the Japanese on their rearward journey across the Irrawaddy, and the main part of the Worcesters followed them, so when, on the 27th of January, an urgent call for one more battalion came from the 4th Brigade, the Brigadier had no option but to send us in to bat, though we had hoped to join in the fun and games that the Camerons were having on the Irrawaddy a few miles to our east.

We arrived in Ondaw to find that the 4lh Infantry Brigade had been heavily involved in clearing up Japanese resistance as we pushed the enemy relentlessly towards the Sagaing foothills. I say "had been" because by the time we arrived most of the fun was over. The Norfolks subsequently had some serious battling to the east on the left flank near Saye, south of the vast Yemet Lake, and the Royal Scots had a good battle for Ywathigi on the Irrawaddy, but for us during these few days there was little to do but to establish a series of firm bases from which battalions of the 4th Brigade could push forward.

Much as we enjoyed coming under the command of our old Commanding Officer again, the restriction on our employment (we were being saved to take part in the 5th Brigade's crossing of the Irrawaddy) irked us a lot and we were very glad when, early in February, we received orders to leave our foster-parents and rejoin the 5th Brigade.

We rejoined the 5th Brigade on the banks of the Irrawaddy at Maundaung, a village lying about four or five thousand yards due north of the mighty Irrawaddy. We really had reached this great river at last, and immediately joined in the active preparations for the crossing. Before continuing our story it would be well to pause here and consider for a moment the general situation, with particular reference to the ground at this bend of the Irrawaddy and the movements of the enemy and other formations of the XXXIII Indian Corps on the Schwebo Plain.

The XXXIII Corps theatre of operations at this time was the Schwebo Plain, a rectangle roughly thirty miles wide by about fifty miles deep, bounded on the east and south by the Irrawaddy, on the west by the River Mu, and on the north roughly by the road down which we had advanced and its prolongation due east from Schwebo to the Irrawaddy. The Irrawaddy takes a sharp turn to the west a few miles south of Mandalay, which lies on the east bank, and continues running practically due west for some thirty miles before it is joined by the Mu River at Myinmu, when it swings sharply southwards and pursues its course to Rangoon, some four hundred miles to the south.

The country generally is flat plain. Heavily cultivated and intersected with water-courses and interspersed with abundant copses, this country generally helped us in our mopping-up operations against the enemy whilst denying him any real line on which to form. Only in the south-east was the Jap in a good position. In the south-east corner of this square lay the huge lake, the Yemet-In, about eight thousand yards wide and fifteen thousand yards long. Behind this, running up the west bank of the Irrawaddy due north for about twenty miles from Sagaing, the big town on the west bank at the bend of the Irrawaddy, was a line of hills. These hills formed an ideal defensive position for the Nip, studded, as they were, with caves and rising in places thirteen hundred feet above the river. The main road from Schwebo to Mandalay runs roughly south-east through Ondaw to Sagaing, where at one time one could cross the river by the huge Ava bridge, turn sharp left in Ava and reach Mandalay from the south. The bridge had been blown by us on the way out in 1942 and had not been repaired by the Nips.

The average width of the Irrawaddy was about fifteen hundred yards, studded with sandbanks and falling at the rate of three to six inches a day—all very confusing for planning crossings under the primitive conditions from which we all suffered, as we will see later.

In this square, where, for the first time, the XXXIII Corps could make full use of its mobility, three infantry divisions, an independent infantry brigade on a bullock-cart basis, and a tank brigade were deployed against the Nip with certain great restrictions on movement which we will discuss in a few moments.

As regards the enemy, he was being pressed back rapidly and, in order to maintain his hold on Central Burma, and the Lashio Road in particular, he decided to hold the line of the Irrawaddy.

To cover his one hundred and twenty miles of river front from about Thabeikkyin, due east of Schwebo, to Sammaikkon, on the east bank about opposite to Myinmu, the Japanese Fifteenth Army could deploy at this time only four divisions, our old friends the 15th, 31st, 33rd and 53rd Divisions, about ten thousand men, and with the all-over pressure by the Allies he could see little chance of any reinforcements coming up.

The Japanese High Command at this time still considered the possibility of a double counter-offensive across the Irrawaddy from Thabeikkyin and Sammaikkon—an optimistic view, written off by a Jap battalion intelligence officer as "mere pipe dreams," considering that within a very short while after the fall of Schwebo they were already confronted with the fait accompli of two bridgeheads in the 19th Division area in the north-west and the immediate possibility of a third in the Sammaikkon area.

Deployed north of the river in the 2nd Infantry Division area the Nip had three battalions, one of the 58th Regiment and two of the 138th Regiment, with a proportion of field and anti-tank artillery. His forward elements were gradually being forced back by the 2nd Division on to the really strong position in the Sagaing hills.

For the rest the Nip contented himself with sending across raiding parties of varying strengths to the north bank.

Before returning to the Battalion it is necessary to have a quick look round the Corps area. Despite the capture of the Ye-U and Schwebo airfields and the subsequent capture by the 4th Brigade of the Sadaing airstrip, it became necessary for General Stopford to slow up the Corps operations for an immediate administrative build-up before setting out on his final advance to Mandalay.

We were by this time four hundred miles beyond our railhead and were practically entirely dependent on air supply. This, for various reasons, had to be reduced and General Stopford could allow only one brigade of the 2nd Division and two of the 19th Division to be maintained by air. The 254th Tank Brigade were not expected up until early in February, which again delayed any immediate advance. As a result, the divisional commanders were given the following tasks for the period from the middle of January to about the middle of February.

The 2nd Infantry Division were to clear the Schwebo Plain and locate Japanese defensive positions north and west of the Irrawaddy. They were to be prepared to cross later. Meanwhile, the 19th Indian Infantry Division were to establish two bridgeheads in the north-east of the Corps area in the area of Thabeikkyin and Kyaumyaung and patrol vigorously, with a view to an advance on Mandalay from the north. In the south-west of the square and on the west of the Mu River, which was the inter-divisional boundary, the 20th Indian Infantry Division were to operate one brigade group about the confluence of the Mu and Irrawaddy Rivers. This was all part of a deception plan to lead the Nip into thinking that a crossing would be made from Myinmu. They were to be prepared to cross subsequently to the west of Myinmu and isolate Mandalay from the south and west.

The Carabiniers were allotted to the 2nd Division as the affiliated armoured regiment to assist in clearing up the Schwebo Plain.

To prevent further recurrence of isolated cases of enemy raiders damaging rear installations, the 268th Infantry Brigade was brought into Corps reserve, and the Commander of the 254th Tank Brigade was appointed, upon arrival, Garrison Commander of Schwebo.

It was on the 4th of February that the Battalion rejoined the 5th Indian Brigade on the Irrawaddy. The move from Ondaw had of necessity been very complicated. The Divisional Commander was at the time laying on a very thorough deception plan to make the Japanese think that we were attacking in the south-east, i.e., the Sagaing hills area, preparatory to a crossing on the axis Sagaing— Ava. It was obviously wrong, therefore, to concentrate the 5th Brigade, or even one battalion, in the south-west corner of the Divisional area by simply marching the troops south from Ondaw and thence due west across the enemy front, and, incidentally, in full view of the enemy and within field-artillery range. Therefore, to make this move we had to go northwards to the area of Sadaing and thence to take a "chukka" through the paddy fields and move south to our concentration area down the east bank of the Mu River.

On arrival we found the Brigade deployed on a front of eight thousand yards with a depth of about the same distance. Our right rested on the Mu River, but our left was rather in the air, there being some distance between the left-hand company of the Camerons and the right-hand battalion of the 6th Infantry Brigade, which had moved forward into the Ywathigi area after the capture of that river port by the 4th Brigade. We moved into reserve at Maungdaung alongside Brigade Headquarters, in a very pleasantly wooded area. By now the weather was getting hot and we were beginning to yearn for shade. The Worcesters and Camerons were deployed forward on the river bank, with the Worcesters on the right and the Camerons on the left. The Brigadier had been briefed by General Nicholson and was busy making his plan for the eventual crossing of the river.

The task of the reserve battalion at Maungdaung was, as we soon found, no sinecure. Both the Brigadier and the General were most keen on the successful development of the Divisional deception plan to confuse the Nip as to our intended crossing place. In the Cameron and Worcester forward-company areas very strict precautions were taken to prevent unnecessary movement, and sentries were even dressed as natives pounding maize, to fit in with the picture of peaceful village life for the benefit of any prying Japanese with a telescope on the south bank. Farther back, east of the 4th Brigade and around the Yemet-In, Jan Bradford's 2nd Reconnaissance Regiment were deployed as a dummy division, with a completely bogus wireless set-up to make the Japanese think that the 2nd Division were concentrating in that area. To further the confusion, I was invited to take the Dorsets out on a series of deception operations. I could think of no better example to follow than the deception plan before one of the battles for Gaza in the last war, when units were moved one way by day and returned under cover of darkness by night.

Accordingly, we mounted Operation "Gaza". Early one morning the Dorsets, trying to make themselves look as big as possible, with every available vehicle trailing large branches of trees to create even more dust than usual, set out on a ten-mile march from Maungdaung due east to Natkayaing railway station, where we lay up for the day and marched back at night. To add to the confusion, I mounted every available pony and mule that was rideable and took the "yeomanry" on a demonstration across the foothills on the left flank of the Battalion, following a course which we hoped would be observed but not fired upon by the Japanese artillery, who were quite active enough in these parts.

How successful these efforts at deception were I do not know. I am afraid that this extra exercise was not too popular in the Battalion, but it did keep us fit. Some weeks later, after we had captured the headquarters of the 2nd Indian National Army Division at Popa, we found a large number of copies of a broadsheet called Greater Asia, a news-sheet written in English and produced by the Japs for the enlightenment of their Indian soldiers. It was an interesting document, with such glaring headings as "Nippon Bombers in Burma score Record Results". One paragraph in particular, under the heading "Central Irrawaddy Front", concerned us. "The British 2nd Division in the Sagaing sector", wrote the Nipponese author, "which from the latter part of February have been showing little signs of active movements, are now carrying on futile underground activities in that district." So much for Exercise "Gaza"!

This sector of the front was fairly quiet for a few days except for the evening "hates", when the enemy opened up on any located position with his field and medium artillery. Both the leading battalions held their localities with two companies up on the river, and it was these forward companies which took what punishment was going. The Nip, however, is a very conservative man and we were usually able to set our watches by the time of his stonks.

The Worcesters on the right held the villages of Tadaing and Dawete, with a company in each about a thousand yards apart and right down on the bank of the river. Early on the morning of the 8th of February—I remember we had got in very late the night before from Operation "Gaza"—we were awoken by the noise of battle from the direction of the Worcesters' forward companies. We all stood-to, until Brigade told us it was only an isolated raid and that we could stand-down, it now being daylight. The Brigadier and all commanding officers were due to attend the 2nd Divisional administrative conference for the crossing of the Irrawaddy and advance to Mandalay, and, leaving Charles Street to deal with the intruders in his area, and the Brigade Second-in-Command, Cecil Mitford Slade, at Brigade Headquarters, the Brigadier, Angus McAlester, and I set off for Divisional Headquarters, which at that time was located about twenty miles to the north. During the conference the Brigadier received an urgent signal to the effect that Charles Street had been killed and that the Worcesters had become involved in a battalion battle. I was ordered to return as quickly as possible and hold my battalion in readiness to join in the fray if necessary.

On my return I found the Battalion on the move. I hurried forward to the battle area and found the situation a bit mixed. It seems that a raiding party of the Nip had crossed the river and stumbled upon the Tadaing garrison (the most westerly of the Worcesters' company positions). The intruders were confused and, turning right, found the telephone line to Dawete and had followed this up (after cutting it) and launched an attack on the garrison of Dawete. That was the battle that had caused us to stand-to in the small hours. After day had broken, Charles Street found that the two forward companies were pinned down and he had put in a counter-attack with his two remaining companies. They had reached the village and the Commanding Officer himself had been killed when personally leading an attack against a Japanese position in one end of Dawete village. They managed to fire the village, or rather the eastern end of it, and had driven a party of Nips into a pagoda area about four hundred yards to the east.

During the afternoon and evening I was able to get two companies forward, one into Tadaing and the other one, the left, opposite Dawete. Battalion Headquarters was set up in a nullah and by last light I was all set for a fully supported attack on Dawete with my reserve companies in the dried-out paddy fields just behind Battalion Headquarters.

Early the next morning our patrols got into Dawete and found that the Jap had pulled out, leaving a number of dead.

The immediate effect of this raid was that we relieved the Worcesters in the forward area whilst they pulled back to Maungdaung to reorganize themselves.

On the reorganization on the 9th of February "B" Company (Peter Feeney) moved into Tadaing and "D" Company (Clive Chettle), which had taken over Dawete, remained in that not-too-salubrious spot. A great number of cattle and some Burmans had also been killed and most of the village had been burnt down by our smoke grenades. "A" Company (Paget Fretts) I sent to Schwele, a village about twelve hundred yards north-north-east of Tadaing, on our right front, which, as part of the Brigade plan, was to be developed into an administrative forming-up area for the crossing. Battalion Headquarters and "C" Company I moved into a copse about a thousand yards north of

Schwele, an unintentionally crafty move as I discovered later, as this copse was not marked on any map and therefore received no attentions from the Japanese artillery. Into the Battalion Headquarters area I also moved my "B" Echelon and animal-transport platoons.

When the documents captured from the Dawete raid had been deciphered we found that this raid had not by any means been directed on these villages, but on another task well inland. However, they had met with the same difficulties that we were subsequently to encounter in crossing fifteen to eighteen hundred yards of water with a three or four-knot current in primitive craft, and had landed in the wrong place and bumped opposition. Our sentries a few evenings later saw a Nip appear from the south bank eighteen hundred yards away, walk down on to the beach opposite Dawete and start praying, presumably for those lost in the raid.

The Japanese were making a number of these raids to our side of the river, there were frequent alarums and excursions, and our patrolling activity was redoubled. To the east Clive Chettle carried out nightly patrols at varying hours to link up with the right-hand Cameron company, and to the west Paget Fretts patrolled across the Mu to link up with the 1st Devons, the left-hand battalion of the 20th Indian Division.

At one stage in our wanderings we had received a number of Devons as reinforcements, most of whom had found their way to "A" Company. As a result there was great competition with our fellow West Country regiment to do these patrols, and the same Sergeant Smith who so distinguished himself at Ye-U found one or two old friends in his old regiment.

As a brigade we now settled down to plan our crossing, assemble our stores and equipment, and generally get ready for D Day, which, for the 2nd Division, was planned for the 24th of February.

Petrol was still in short supply and every possible supply task was carried out by unit and R.I.A.S.C. mules. In the case of battalions with companies scattered as ours were, our mules were used to supply our own companies and we collected our bulk supplies from the Brigade supply point by mechanical transport. However, the R.I.A.S.C. Mule Company were used, as far as I can remember, from the Brigade "B" Echelon area at Nyaungbinwun forward to Maungdaung. During January and February all three battalions became quite accustomed, owing to the petrol shortage, to employing as "B" Echelon vehicles the traditional bullock cart of the East. It was here also that I found the greatest use for my home-made breeches. A non-commissioned officer in the Mortar Platoon, Corporal Packham, who in peace time had been a tailor in a firm of ecclesiastical breeches-makers in Savile Row, one day forsook his mortars to convert an ordinary pair of jungle-green drill slacks into a most serviceable pair of jodhpurs. With some leather, scrounged from the Quartermaster, for strappings, these essentially "jungli" breeches rendered me yeoman service.

We became very horse-minded at Battalion Headquarters those days. Every day I rode Shamus out, usually with Corporal Churchill on Goggles as escort. We made our tour of the forward companies and invariably visited Brigade by this means. Riding became quite fashionable in the Brigade Group, and it was nothing to see a string of assorted ponies tethered outside the Brigadier's caravan whilst he was holding a conference. It was to be our final fling with animals. They never crossed the Irrawaddy with us. It was one of those tragedies of war that the fine team that John Main and Sergeant Park had built up over a period of six months was of necessity dispersed and handed over to other divisions and formations. One is very inclined to think that other people do not look after animals quite as well as one's own team, and it cheered me up a lot to find that my efforts to keep Sergeant Park with our animals were not wasted. Sorry as I was to lose him, he was obviously of much greater value with the animals, wherever they went, and I was very pleased when Lieutenant-Colonel Todd at Corps Headquarters was able to accept and keep Sergeant Park with the animals. The Battalion owe a very great debt of gratitude to John Main, Sergeant Park and all the Animal Transport Section, who, by their enthusiasm and keenness, kept the Battalion supplied, sometimes under most trying conditions, and always lived up to their boast that they could and did outwalk the rifle companies. At the last veterinary inspection in this position on the banks of the Irrawaddy I am glad to record that the Battalion earned an excellent report on the state of their animals.

During this time the company commanders and I were given the opportunity of flying over our beaches on the south bank of the Irrawaddy in an L5 or Auster. There was little to be seen, however, except to emphasize the depressing fact which we knew already, that we would plunge directly from the beaches into jungle grass well over our heads.

From our observation posts in the forward company positions we could get a very good view across the Irrawaddy and any movement seen was reported immediately. There was precious little activity, however, the main subjects of our reports being the noting the next morning of any additional foxholes and noticeable fieldworks dug by the enemy during the night.

Our concentration was still secret, and for this reason we, in the 5th Infantry Brigade, were denied the chances of patrolling over the river to the south bank.

We had with us a section of the Sea Reconnaissance Unit. These officers would plunge into the Irrawaddy night after night, spending hours in the stream with their "flippers" and flat boards and appear at dawn at Dawete, where we would take them in. The river, we found, was most confusing. The rapid fall at this time of year of about three to six inches a day made great changes in its current, and sandbanks would suddenly appear right across a proposed route. It was enough to have to paddle one's way across the Irrawaddy in an assault boat, anyhow, but to be stuck on some sandbank within close range of the enemy's small-arms fire was a prospect we did not relish.

I have referred to the Japanese propensity for raids. Though we never again had anything on the scale of the Dawete show, we were constantly kept on our toes by reports of raids and patrols wandering around the country which had to be mopped up. An E.N.S.A. concert party had to spend one night in a unit area forward of Corps Headquarters owing to the presence of a raiding party. I think that it was the same patrol which, in the process of being eliminated on the "ten little niggerboys" principle, bumped into the 5th Brigade Workshops, where they were given a very warm reception.

One most comforting sight at this time, as one made one's way to Brigade Headquarters of a morning, was to see, to us, large formations of heavy bombers of Eastern Air Command flying over on their way to soften up Mandalay or, more usually, bent on targets even farther afield.

Whilst we had been clearing the Schwebo Plain and waiting our turn to cross, other divisions had been more actively employed. I have already referred to the most northerly crossing by the 19th Indian Infantry Division north of Mandalay, and by the 25th of February it was ready to advance on the big city.

During the night of the 12th/13th of February the 20th Indian Infantry Division had crossed the Irrawaddy in the Lingadippa area to our right and just round the bend in the river where the Irrawaddy turns south after it has been joined by the Mu. The Japanese reacted fiercely to this new bridgehead, and the 20th Division had some fierce fighting for a few days.

Just as we were to set out on our own crossing we received the magnificent news of the IV Corps' advance. As far as any of us, and certainly the Japanese, knew, the IV Corps were resting back in India. Not a bit of it! As I have explained earlier on, the IV Corps, under the redoubtable General Messervy, was very much in action. Now it suddenly appeared on the left rear of the Japanese with infantry and armour. The 7th Indian Division, our old friends of Kohima days, crossed the Irrawaddy with the utmost dispatch, having made a magnificent secret advance, and before the enemy could retaliate adequately their armoured columns were hurrying on to Meiktila, away down in the south.

The time had come for us of the 5th Infantry Brigade to don our shirts and gird on our equipment over our well sun-tanned bodies and in our own turn cross this huge obstacle, which, as so often happens, became daily more and more formidable the longer we were forced to sit and look at it.

"Let's have a Dekko."

How do we know, by the bank high river,
Where the mired and sulky oxen wait,
And it looks as though we might wait for ever,
How do we know that the floods abate?
There is no change in the current's brawling—
Louder and harsher the freshet scolds;
Yet we can feel she is falling, falling,
And the more she threatens the less she holds.

—KIPLING

THE ADVANCE TO MANDALAY, 1945

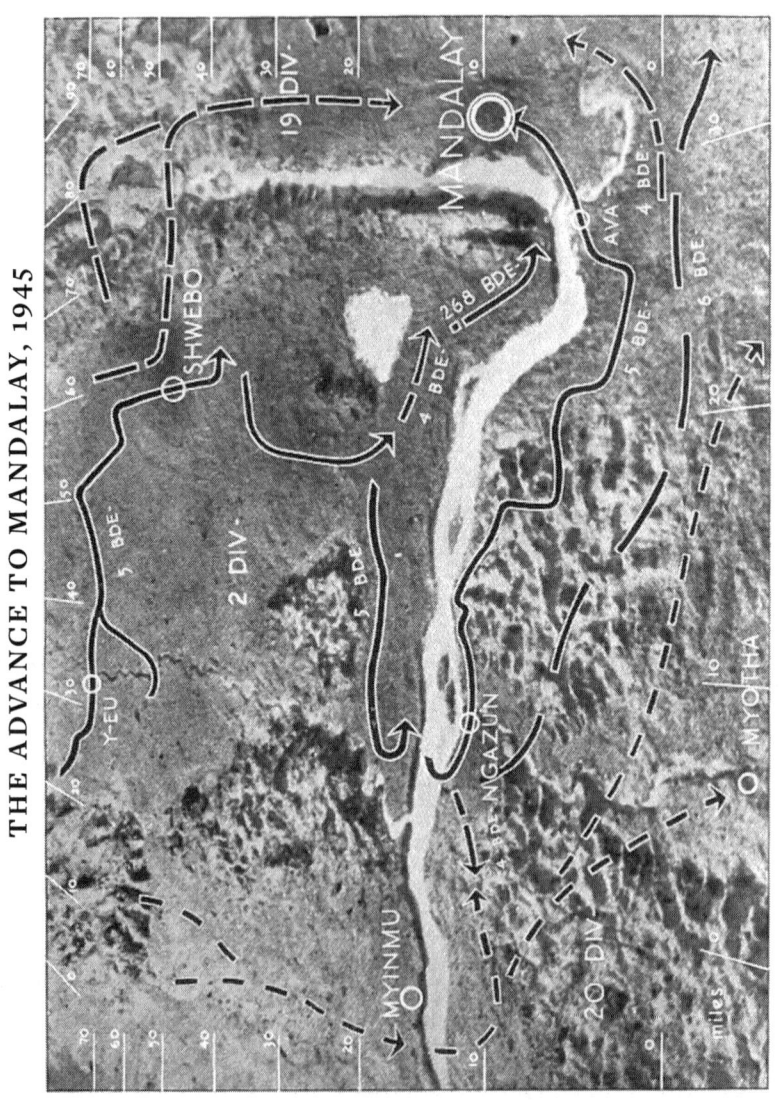

Schwebo Plain and River Irrawaddy

CHAPTER THIRTEEN

"WHERE THE FLYING FISHES PLAY"

If you've 'eard the East a-callin', you won't never 'eed naught else.
No ! You won't 'eed nothing else
But them spicy garlic smells,
An' the sunshine an' the palm trees an' the tinkly temple bells:
On the road to Mandalay.

[RUDYARD KIPLING]

TO BRIGADIER MICHAEL WEST, Commander of the 5th Infantry Brigade of the 2nd British Infantry Division, sitting in the sunshine with the never-ending tinkle of bells from the pagodas in the village of Maungdaung ringing in his ears, the problem of setting his brigade on their next and final stage of the road to Mandalay must have seemed most formidable.

He not only had to make an opposed landing across fifteen hundred yards of open river (we never really felt that we would be unopposed) but once over he had to establish the bridgehead and make provision for the passage of the Divisional administrative echelons in a trackless desert of jungle grass and steep watercourses.

His planning was further complicated by the vagaries of the Irrawaddy, and before we actually set out all three leading battalions had had to select the most tortuous of routes to avoid bogging down on sandbanks which daily became more numerous.

To assist in the assault, the 1st Royal Welch Fusiliers, from the 6th Infantry Brigade, were put under command. Despite the fact that we had taken over the forward positions from the 7th Worcestershires, the Brigadier decided that they should continue to take their turn, in accordance with the established Brigade custom, and would be one of the assault battalions; we were to revert to reserve as the Worcesters passed through us.

Accordingly, the Brigadier decided to cross with three battalions up. On the right the 7th Worcesters were to cross from Dawete and make for a wide, sandy strip immediately to the south of us, and to the west of Mud Point. The sandbank about three hundred yards off the southern bank was increasing daily, especially on the east end, and this was a point of especial worry to Tom Irvine, the late Second-in-Command of the Camerons, who had taken over command of the 7th Worcesters on the death of Charles Street.

In the centre the Camerons were to cross from Myitha and make for the opposite bank to the east of Mud Point. Again owing to the presence of sandbanks, Angus McAlester had to choose a very circuitous route which caused him to paddle very much farther than the fifteen-hundred-yard direct north-to-south crossing.

On the left Jack Stocker was ordered to land the Royal Welch Fusiliers on Ngazun Island, which they were to occupy and hold to cover the remainder of the Brigade across. Ngazun Island was a large "permanent" island on which cultivation could be seen. We suspected and subsequently proved that it was possible at this time of year to ford the river between the island and the south bank, and it was essential that this feature was held to cover our left flank.

The 2nd Dorsets were to cross behind the 7th Worcesters and open up the west beach as the main beach for the future administrative build-up.

In the Dorsets' area on the north bank plans were made for the few Dukws allowed to us and other vehicles, such as the flotated carriers, to be collected prior to being rushed over once the infantry were firmly ashore. This administrative build-up on this flank is important in the light of what subsequently happened.

The most depressing feature, from our point of view, was the extreme shortage of boating equipment. With a four-knot current running, and such a very wide river to cross, it was not really possible to toggle or propel ourselves across on petrol cans and bamboo poles, though the Brigade had, in the past, achieved some pretty staggering feats of watermanship. The 7th Worcesters were allotted four Mark III and thirty-two Mark II infantry assault boats, whilst the Camerons had the same number of Mark IIIs and were completed with an issue of the rather better American Ranger boats. The Royal Welch Fusiliers were similarly short of craft. There was a proportion of outboard motors. Most of these boats had come out after the Division from the United Kingdom three years earlier. In fact, I am not at all sure that some of them were not our original issue after Dunkirk. They had seen much hard service throughout our combined-operation and jungle training, and had been used in turn by the 19th and 20th Infantry Divisions. The Divisional Engineers made every effort to patch up these boats and make them waterworthy. They were all we had. Finally, owing to the shortage of boats, none of the three leading battalions was able to cross in one flight.

The 24th of February was selected as D Day; and H Hour, the time at which the leading battalions were due to touch down, was to be 2230 hrs. There was very nearly a full moon, which in Burma means a very bright night: this was unfortunate but unavoidable. We had, for reasons already explained, been delayed long enough and no one was prepared to wait a few days extra to allow the moon to go down.

On the evening of the 24th I closed the Battalion up behind Dawete and Tadaing, leaving my "B" Echelon in the Battalion Headquarters area. We had prepared our positions, which were very much the same as those occupied on the night after the Dawete raid. In order to help the Worcesters in their initial stages we carried their boats for them over the six hundred yards or so of open sand between Dawete and their jumping-off area.

Having seen the Worcesters on their way, I went back to my command post, where I found a very welcome present, a bottle of whisky, sent down by Teddy Edwards from Corps Headquarters with one of the Pressmen. The Battalion were in colossal form that evening and not a few wished that we had been allowed to make the assault landing. This waiting in reserve did not please us in the least, especially as the number of assault boats likely to return was most problematical.

The subsequent events of the night were most confusing. Surprise was lost with the starting up, or attempts to start up, of the Seahorse outboard motors. The Worcesters got into mid-stream and soon found themselves in difficulties. Some of the boats began to fill and as they approached the south shore they came under small-arms fire which holed the surviving boats. The Commanding Officer found himself swimming about in the water and by his own personal gallantry saved a number of lives. The opposition on the far side being stronger than had been expected, and the difficulties of navigating these obdurate craft by paddle in the four-knot current proving much greater than had been anticipated, the Worcesters were back again on the north bank by midnight.

In the centre, also, things had not gone well. The Camerons came up against strong opposition and could get only about a company and a quarter across, with the Commanding Officer and a very small tactical headquarters. They had to land under and assault a cliff, but had gained a precarious foothold in the thick jungle grass on the top.

When, however, they tried to get their assault craft back again they failed completely. The current was much too strong and the Nip was picking off the boatmen at his leisure. Oh, for a few modern stormboats! On the extreme left the Royal Welch Fusiliers were also finding enough difficulties to keep Jack Stocker busy. We heard that he himself was across but with only two platoons.

At about midnight the Brigadier had to make a big decision. He had failed to make a landing on his main beach and so decided to develop what little beach he had got. He couldn't reinforce the Camerons without some better form of craft than the assault boats and so obtained authority to unload the few Dukws and rush them round, a ten-mile journey by the only bulldozed lateral track which had been developed out of sight of the Japanese from the south bank.

Meanwhile, he called me up and ordered me to move across country for five thousand yards to Myitha and be prepared to cross behind the Camerons and develop their bridgehead.

This move we managed to do comfortably in our own time, losing only our two Pressmen, who, falling asleep at one of the innumerable checks in the column, woke up at first light to find themselves quite alone in a strange world. It took a long time to get the Dukws round and meanwhile Allan Roy, the Second-in-Command of the Camerons, whom I contacted at Myitha, was busily trying to ferry his battalion across by any possible means. It seemed that the Nip had got a strong position dug into the cliff at Mud Point from which he could enfilade the river approach and at the same time be covered from attack by us.

It was not until noon on the 25th that the last boat-load of Camerons left the north bank on their journey across the stream.

Meanwhile, I had been called back to Brigade Headquarters next door to my old command post of the night before, and had received further instructions.

I do not know why the Nip did not shell us that morning when the best part of two battalions with every kind of supporting arm and a variety of craft were concentrated in that narrow nullah leading down to the river at Myitha. We were spared his air, I think, only because he had made his last all-out air effort against the 20th Division bridgehead a few days earlier.

With the departure of the last of the Camerons at about noon I took my Tactical Headquarters down to the river bank with the leading company ("B"), and we prepared for our own crossing. During the morning the Royal Welch Fusiliers had all crossed to Ngazun Island and so an alternative route was now open to us.

Between Myitha and the Camerons' bridgehead there was a large uncharted sandbank, around which the Camerons had had to manœuvre. Their main route had been round the western tip of this sandbank, which, if the boats got into trouble with the current, led under the strong Japanese position on Mud Point. We hoped, by using F.B.E. boats with outboard motors on a left-handed route passing under the west tip of Ngazun Island, that we would escape the attentions of the Japanese machine gunners in this very slowmoving form of craft.

To lift the first flight of the Dorsets I was given two Dukws and two F.B.E. boats. As the new proposed route had never been reconnoitred and the possibilities of a Dukw grounding seemed more than likely, we decided to send half the first flight round by Dukw on the old right-handed route whilst the F.B.E. boats tackled the new, and as yet uncharted, route.

I loaded Tactical Headquarters into an F.B.E. boat with "B" Company headquarters and a number of "B" Company, and off we set. It was a memorable voyage: if for us on the left the enemy provided little thrill, we had plenty of excitement from the sapper driver of the F.B.E. boat. He had little or no experience of piloting such a cumbersome craft across a stream on a circuitous course of well over two thousand yards in a strong current. We progressed in a series of ever-decreasing circles, bumping from one sandbank to another. My last memory of the north shore was the agonized look on General Nicholson's face as he saw us depart in this manner, strangely reminiscent of the tale of "The Owl and the Pussy Cat". However, we made it without any casualties. The remainder of "B" Company in Dukws were not so fortunate; one of the amphibians drifted just too close to the Nip medium-machine-gun position and came under fire.

Our arrival in the Camerons' bridgehead is a memory I treasure more than most. The British soldier does not often display his feelings, but when the Camerons lined the south bank and cheered us ashore I felt that all our years of training and action together meant something very real.

I found Angus McAlester in the thick jungle grass on the top of the cliff. So thick was this grass at this point that the 79th Highlanders had been able to extend their bridgehead only a very little way, and the Commanding Officer was greatly cheered by our arrival. They had had a difficult night, having first had to fight their way ashore and then suffer some brisk counter-attacks. Angus's idea was to invite me to move in on his right flank, where the grass was much thicker.

This idea did not appeal to me and, having had a quick look round, it struck me that the ground to the left was much more open and easily defended as well as being more suitable for exploitation than milling around in the long grass which reached over the heads of even the tallest of us.

Accordingly, I decided to exploit to the left, and as each successive company came ashore I built up my own bridgehead to a depth of about four hundred yards, the Camerons pushing forward on the right with their latest-joined companies to fit into the picture.

The first flight of the Dorsets had not set off from the north shore until 1330 hrs., and so it was getting dark as the final elements of the rifle companies and the Mortar Platoon arrived. The Nip position on Mud Point had not yet been captured by the Camerons and our last flight of Dukws of the day fell into the same old trap. Those Jap machine gunners certainly deserved a very high award for their day's work. They had had a troop of Grants, divisional artillery and a private air strike of Hurribombers all trying to winkle them out, but they hung on. The trouble was that, being positioned as they were behind a large bank, they were virtually unassailable from the front—that is, the north shore—and they were finally destroyed only when a company of the Lancashire Fusiliers of the 4th Brigade, supported by a troop of tanks (Carabiniers), managed to get round behind them, but not before the troop leader of the Carabiniers had been killed. The Nip seemed to play very definite rules of his own. He let us cross and recross the river and build up on our beach well within range, but should a boat drift to a certain point in the water he opened up with deadly accuracy. Unfortunately for us and those very gallant men the Dukw drivers, our amphibians were by no means the latest models, and stoppages and breakdowns always seemed to occur just before reaching or immediately after quitting the south shore. The moment the engine stopped the current swept the craft down-stream into the Japanese E.B.Z.. In vain we would stand on the bank waving and signalling to an approaching craft to keep up-stream, and one if not more Dukws ran into trouble on every trip. I think that there were only five Dukws altogether, and the drivers were getting very tired by the evening of D plus one Day.

Our casualties during the crossing were four killed and nine wounded, the greater number being in the Mortar Platoon and in the attached Gloster platoon on the last trip of the day. This was not the same platoon that had marched across Burma with us, but its relief, which appeared an equally fine platoon, even though it did not contain so high a proportion of Burma veterans of 1942. The platoon commander, Lieutenant Collister, recently commissioned, had, however, made the retreat in 1942 as a young soldier.

By the evening of D plus one we were firmly ashore, across the Irrawaddy, and the battle was definitely looking better. At dusk the Brigadier called me up on the 48 set, actually whilst Angus was at my headquarters, and he sounded very much happier than when I had last seen him earlier in the day. I told him what I had done to open the left flank and he approved. He ordered Angus to send a company out again and try to get Mud Point, and instructed me to send a company about a thousand yards up-stream, i.e., to the east, to cover the western tip of Ngazun Island from any attempt by the Nipponese to cross to the island and attack the Royal Welch Fusiliers.

I sent "A" Company (Paget Fretts) off on this mission, and after detailing some last-minute patrol chores given me by the Brigadier and re-forming the locality slightly, we settled down for the night.

"Settle down" is quite the wrong term. The Nips took this third intrusion across the Irrawaddy very badly and the whole night they jittered our bridgehead, not very effectively but enough to spoil any possibility of rest. Our pleasure at having something very soft, such as sand, instead of the usual hard-baked earth in which to dig was somewhat tempered when the blast from enemy mortars caused some of our slit trenches to cave in and Corporal Reynell was smothered in his sleep. The main worry that night was from the Japanese grenade dischargers. Our bridgehead was so small that the little devil could reach nearly every corner of it from just outside our forward positions.

Those of us who remembered our Kipling found much to recall his words. During our peregrinations on the river we had, amongst other things, definitely established the fact that there are flying fish on the Road to Mandalay. These little creatures may hardly have qualified for their "wings", but the way they skimmed across the surface of the water proved them to be definitely "airborne". Again, on the morning of the 26th of February, as "the sun rose up like thunder" in one of those superb Burmese dawns which never failed to refresh us, our tail crossed the stream, bringing with them many odd bits and pieces which we required. For the crossing we had travelled light, or as light as possible, with our packs only, and it had become pretty cold in the small hours just before dawn. After stand-to, when sections were brewing-up their "char" and what was left of the compo rations, the Brigadier called me up to tell me that the Worcesters were on their way across, and bade me consider how best to attack Ngazun.

This instruction cheered me up immensely, as it meant that for the time being at any rate we were not going to be asked to continue to push forward into this impenetrable jungle grass towards our original objectives of the White and Blue Chaungs, but were going to turn left and make for the town of Ngazun.

Ngazun was the largest town on the south bank of the Irrawaddy between us and Ava, about twenty miles to the east. It was an important roadhead for one of the few routes south, and obviously a one-time ferry point on the river. It lay about two or three thousand yards to the east of our bridgehead, with nothing but open, flat, cultivated fields interspersed with a few trees. The Brigadier's idea was to attack and capture it with two battalions.

Lying in mid-stream immediately north of Ngazun town was the island of that name, already occupied by the Royal Welch Fusiliers. Early on the 27th the Brigadier moved his Tactical Headquarters on to the island with "B" Company of the 2nd Manchesters and a troop of the 3rd Dragoon Guards (Carabiniers), which had been ferried across. The Divisional Artillery was deployed on the north bank, roughly in line with Ngazun, except for the 18th Field Regiment (self-propelled), which was still deployed west of the River Mu, from which position it had been supporting the 20th Indian Infantry Division and from where it could continue to support us. It can be seen, therefore, that the Brigade was in an excellent position to put in one of its "special" attacks, under very favourable conditions, with supporting arms on a direct flank, at right angles to the line of advance. Further, the Brigadier himself was in a position to control the fire from an observation post *in line with the objective.*

To show how good the co-operation between the various commanders in the 5th Brigade was, I would remind the reader that, prior to this attack, I had not seen the Brigadier for twenty-four hours. The attack such as we intended had not been laid on, as we had never expected to do it this way at all, and I did not meet the Brigadier again until after we had captured the objective. Everything was arranged on the radio, with 1/25,000 maps and an excellent gridded, though two months out-of-date, air photograph. So featureless, however, was the ground that we could definitely detail at which particular tree I would halt the foot soldiers until the completion of the air strike, followed by the advance to another tree for the artillery concentration.

The plan briefly was this. On landing Tom Irvine was to lead his Worcesters inland to a tree line that my patrols had reported free, and there form up. Together we were to turn left and move forward about a thousand yards into line with my "A" Company, who, you will remember, had been sent to a position on the south bank opposite the western tip of Ngazun Island.

From there we were to deploy in good old Lallan's Plain style and advance against Ngazun.

The Brigadier promised us the best air strike we had yet seen, followed by everything we could get from the Divisional Artillery stepped up with medium guns. It seemed all so simple and so very like laying on a fire-power demonstration for General Grover in Ahmednagar days. Today, however, our main worry was not in making arrangements for the spectators but in finding out just where the Nip was holding. Again we received unexpected assistance. We could see one gun position on the river bank, which caused us some worry, but our gunners reckoned that they had got it taped. We were busily contemplating another position when a friendly native appeared from Ngazun and from the air photograph (once he had learnt to hold it the right way up) he was able to point out a very strong infantry position on the eastern edge of the town. The correctness of this information was amply proved later, but owing to this unexpected assistance from a Burman "umpire" we were able to get the information to the air boys before they went in and the strong-point was very definitely smartened up for us.

Leaving the Brigadier to tie up the final details of the fire plan with the supporting arms and to try to hurry up the air, Tom and I sat down on the river bank to decide on detailed objectives. The eastern flank of the town appeared to be about twelve to thirteen hundred yards long, but there seemed to be no obvious way of dividing it other than for me on the left to take the northernmost eight hundred yards, leaving Tom a narrower front but with more possibilities of exploitation round the southern flank.

All was now set, and the air was confirmed for 1300 hrs. Our ground-to-air co-operation at this time was first class, but to lay on a big show meant bringing planes in from airstrips far away in Assam and even Bengal, and this always took time.

The day was by now, to put it mildly, stinking hot, and, anticipating some hard fighting in the town I ordered the Battalion to dump their packs on the start line. Promptly at 1300 hrs. the air strike went in, and I must say that the R.A.F. and, I believe, the U.S.A.A.F. did their stuff for us that afternoon. For thirty minutes they pasted the village and seemed to be hitting the targets we had given them. At 1330 hrs. the air moved off and down came the guns; it was a grand show to see, and one could feel the Battalion's spirit rise with every pace we took forward to the artillery-concentration line, about six hundred yards farther on. I had hoped to get even closer to the objective, but the enthusiastic S.P. gunners firing air bursts from behind our left shoulders retarded the progress. As it was, we received casualties from this form of supporting fire. I could see that the Worcesters on our right were going well. Suddenly, to my horror, I heard the noise of mortars being fired from somewhere over my right shoulder. "Hell!" I thought. "Are the Nips counter-attacking us?" I then noticed that the Worcesters' mortars had halted and were in action (we both of us were taking along our mortars man-packed in the Battalion "square" for the subsequent reorganization), and I learnt later that Tom had spotted some enemy in the south end of the village trying to pull out in mechanical transport, and was trying to get them.

During this last advance there had been a certain amount of odd firing with bullets whining overhead, and, observing the leading companies, I was startled to see so many men stooping as if hit. This worried me until I realized that we were advancing over tomato fields and that the Dorset soldier, even on such an earnest occasion as this, could not resist stooping down, overloaded as he was, to snatch a few handfuls of tomatoes. If the brigade at Minden in 1757 earned the traditional right to wear a rose on Minden Day, the emblem of the 5th Infantry Brigade after our advance through Central Burma should certainly be a ripe tomato.

At 1350 hrs. the artillery concentration ceased and the Battalion went in in magnificent fashion under the really close support of the troop of tanks and Manchester medium machine guns, who from their position on the flank could continue firing right up to the time the infantry entered the thickly treed village and even for a few yards beyond.

It was really a most inspiring sight to see two battalions of British infantry advance with bayonets fixed right up under the support of the tank 75's and the machine guns.

The attack could not have gone better if it had been rehearsed for weeks beforehand, and as a demonstration of fire and movement it was splendid. This feeling of a staged show was further enhanced by the knowledge that the Divisional Commander was among the spectators in the "gallery" on Ngazun Island, and, as we subsequently heard, the Corps Commander had witnessed the conflict from an L5 over our heads.

The effect of the air and artillery concentration on the Battalion was dynamic. It was the first occasion on which we had been treated to a really good "conk" before we went in to the attack. Dorset soldiers, unlike Scottish and Indian troops, do not normally shout and yell as they attack, but prefer to do their bayonet work silently. But on this occasion the advance was reminiscent of a peace-time Army Cup match as "A" and "C" Companies closed on the town with cries of "Up, the Five and the Fours!" and "On, on, 'Do' Dorset!" answered by "Up, the Twenty-Eighth", from the Gloster Platoon in the van of "A" Company.

Paget Fretts and Tommy Tucker, with their companies, swept through the village, and any sign of movement from a basha or hut called for a No. 77 grenade, which promptly ignited the building.

The going was quite thick and the fire started by the air strike slowed up our advance considerably, and it was not until close on three o'clock that I could report to the Brigadier that our section of the village had been cleared.

On the right the Worcesters progressed steadily before coming up against a strong Japanese position in a pagoda near the police station at the south end of the village. Here a suicide party of Nipponese hung on until they were finally exterminated the next morning.

Just as we were checking up, the Brigadier appeared from the island, having waded ashore, and was most pleased with the show. After giving me instructions for the night he moved on to Tom Irvine.

Our casualties had been very light, with only five British other ranks and one officer wounded. Unfortunately the officer was the invaluable Jock Given, who, whilst gesticulating during the attack had apparently pulled a bullet out of the air. It is extraordinary to relate that all the casualties in this attack, except for one man hit in the head, had been arm or hand injuries.

For the rest of the day I left "A" Company acting as escort to the sappers as the latter cleared away booby-traps and mines in the eastern end of the village and started tidying up Ngazun for the morrow, when the 6th Brigade would pass through us. The remainder of the Battalion I pulled back to the open plain to the west of the town over which we had advanced to attack.

We had learnt never, if possible, to occupy a native village for reasons both tactical and hygienic, and so deployed ourselves in the open to prevent any Japanese counter-attack to the river and to cover the Dakota strip which we knew would have to be put down the next day. Tommy Tucker I put into a zareba on the south-west limits of the village to link up with the Worcesters. "D" Company was sent to the right flank to secure Brigade Headquarters, and "B" Company was set down in the open maidan to cover our front. "A" Company I pulled back in the evening to the river bank to stiffen up the defence of Battalion Headquarters and give us some depth.

"C" Company, though they were farthest from the river, became very fond of their zareba. It was very "P. C. Wren", and whenever I visited them I half-expected to find Tommy Tucker and his Company Sergeant-Major having a quiet dose of "cafard", with Private Foot, the company runner, propped up in death in a loophole of the zareba, Corporal Cripps, the Battalion bugler, sounding a trumpet, and a ragged tricolour flag fluttering from company headquarters.

Tiger Havers, the Intelligence Officer, immediately set his minions to work to see what they could find from the relics of Jap occupation. Their search was enlivened by the discovery of a live duck in a Japanese foxhole. Apparently the late owner had departed so hurriedly that he had left his food behind. It confirmed our suspicions that we were not the only troops to carry our livestock around with us. By now all sorts of people had acquired a hen or a duck, and these used to be carried on the Battalion vehicles. At one time they had been carried on the man, until I put my foot down and said that owners of livestock really must find some form of conveyance other than their own left arm or shoulder when on the line of march.

What interested us most was the report of a survivor of the Japanese garrison captured by the 6th Brigade a couple of days later. He was an old long-service soldier and claimed that our air strike was pretty effective and our gunners horrifying, but what had really scared his commander and forced him to pull out with most of his force, leaving only a suicide garrison behind, was the sight of two battalions of British infantry deploying in the open for the attack. This Japanese claimed that he had never before seen so many men coming at him with such a purposeful air. It was most gratifying to receive this testimonial to the efficacy of British infantry from a man who, after all, was in a very good position to judge.

On the 28th of February the 6th Infantry Brigade passed through us whilst the Worcesters completed mopping up at the south end of the town and the Camerons continued to enlarge their bridgehead while the Divisional administrative build-up continued with all speed. To ease matters, work was started as soon as possible on a Dakota strip to the south-west of the town, and within a few days we heard the familiar roar of planes as these invaluable machines landed with their precious loads right in the front line. Constructing airstrips had become by now second nature to us, and the men, however tired they were, always set to with remarkable energy: it was something that very much affected their stomachs.

One of the most outstanding achievements during this period was the construction of the 5th Field Ambulance's advanced dressing station. Lieutenant-Colonel "Pooh" Baker, the Commanding Officer, had asked me to lend him a few pioneers and I was amazed at the results he produced. Within forty-eight hours of the capture of Ngazun, the 5th Field Ambulance had erected a very fine advanced dressing station on the banks of the river in the northwest corner of the town. It was Pooh Baker's boast that his hospital could produce service equal to that of the finest London hospital. Fortunately I never had cause personally to test the truth of this claim, but I was most impressed by the appearance of this advanced dressing station, and the Brigade in particular, as well as the Division generally, owe the doctors and R.A.M.C. personnel of the 5th Field Ambulance a great debt of gratitude for their energy on the banks of this river.

For the 5th Infantry Brigade this was a period of "rest". We, in particular, as we were on the banks of the Irrawaddy, could take the greatest advantage of this respite. In a very short time this bridgehead resembled more a Scandinavian bathing beach than a hard-fought-for front line. I released as many men as possible to bathe, and the whole day the river banks were covered with naked bodies as the men swam and sun-bathed and did their "dhobi". The enemy gunners did not always enter into the spirit of this massed nudism and used to stonk us from time to time. It is extraordinary how completely defenceless one feels under shell fire without even a towel, and how reminiscent of the brigaded grenadier companies at Maida in 1806 the Battalion looked, as, on the first round falling, we all dashed for our tin hats and weapons and, with no other form of clothing, closed in under the lee of the bank.

Our visitors during this stage were innumerable. Dennis Calvert, the C.R.E., and Eric Cleeves, C.R.A.S.C., as always, were well up in the van and I think the very next day were sitting chatting outside my dug-out, which my gunmen had called "Fort White."[16] They were followed by many high-powered doctors who came to admire Pooh Baker's handiwork. Among these was Colonel John Bruce, the eminent surgeon from Edinburgh, who eighteen months earlier had taken out my cartilage. It was grand to see him again, and, although he had by now moved high up in the medical hierarchy and was senior consulting

---

16 A famous stronghold between Tiddim and Kalewa.

STRAIGHT ON FOR TOKYO

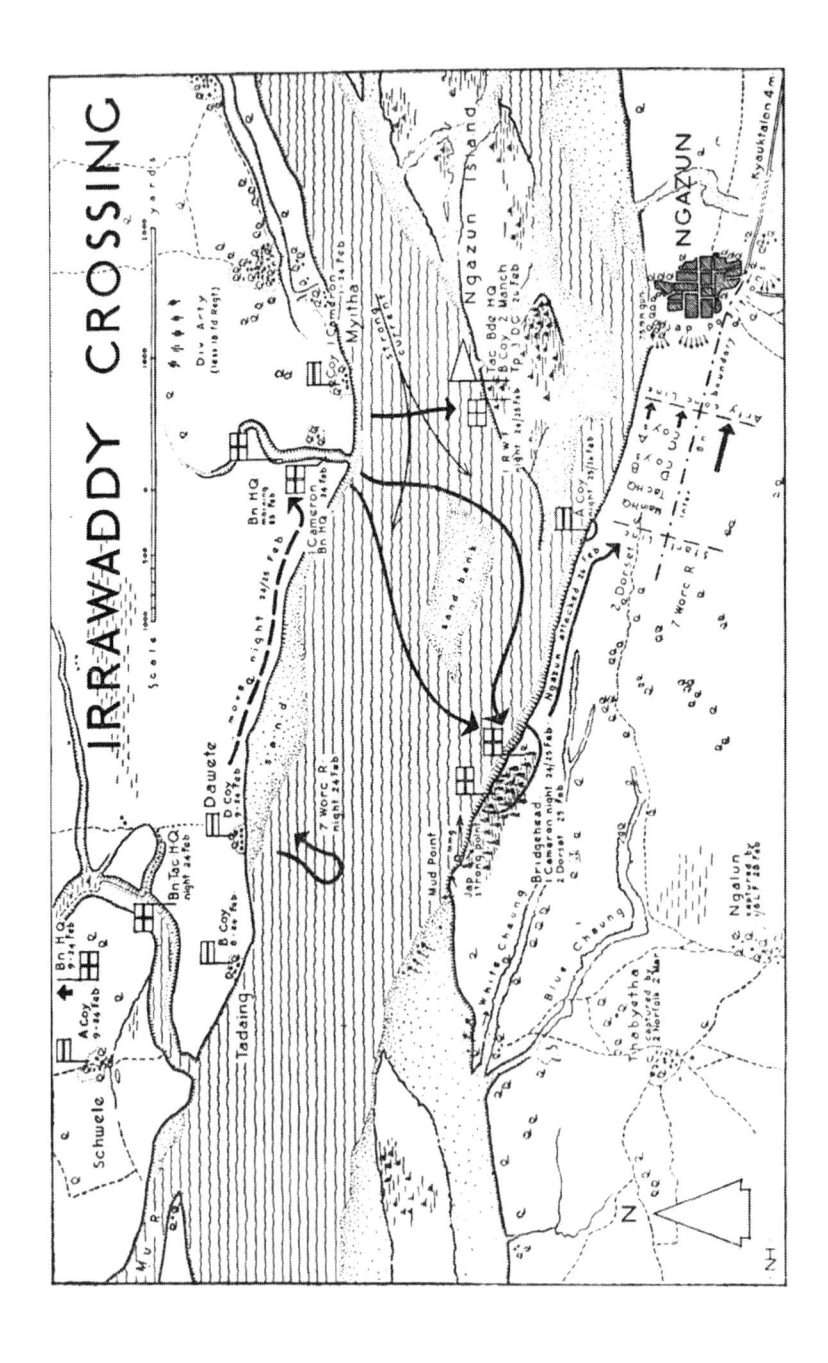

surgeon of the Fourteenth Army, he was still employing his great surgical abilities to the best effect. This was the third time he had crossed the Irrawaddy and had assisted in operating urgent cases in all three divisions during the fighting for the respective bridgeheads.

Other visitors included a team of American airmen, amongst whom were some of the Lightning pilots who had strafed Ngazun before we went in and who had come to visit the results of their handiwork. They spent some time with us and went forward to witness an attack by the 6th Brigade. They left, saying the nicest things about the infantry but very happy that they did not have to fight the war on their feet.

A visitor we would have welcomed on our side of the river was Miss Frances Day, the actress. During the winter of 1939-40 she had formed a great attachment for the 2nd Division in France. Hearing that we were in Burma, she had come out and, breaking away from her conducted party, had "thumbed" her way forward until she found us. It was our loss that we in the 5th Brigade were fully involved in crossing the river and could not see her concert.

She, however, must have seen everything of us, if the report was true that, being forbidden to cross to the southern bank, she had managed to persuade an airman to fly her over the 5th Brigade in an L5 as we were sun-bathing on the banks of the river.

Floated carriers crossing the Irrawaddy.

CHAPTER FOURTEEN

"COME YOU BACK, YOU BRITISH SOLDIER. COME YOU BACK TO MANDALAY."

"There's a dirty white pagoda to the east of Payadu."

[2ND DORSET CRY]

BY THE BEGINNING OF MARCH General Stopford could congratulate himself that the XXXIII Corps was across the Irrawaddy. Over all, the Japanese reaction had been most strong and, not yet appreciating the strength of the IV Corps' "right flanker", the enemy was still fighting hard to hold the Irrawaddy line at the very moment that General Messervy was thundering towards Meiktila, set upon cutting the enemy forces in two.

The result of this resistance to the XXXIII Corps' advance over the Irrawaddy was that, at the turn of the month, no great territorial progress had been made. The 19th Division in the north had not yet crossed the Chaungmagyi Chaung, north of Mandalay, and the 2nd Infantry Division had managed only to clear to about four miles south of Ngazun. On our right the 20th Indian Division were still confined to a relatively small area around their bridgehead and there had as yet been no link-up with the 2nd Division.

In their regrouping against the XXXIII Corps the Japanese had set their 15th Division against our 19th Indian Infantry Division. Our old opponents the 31st Division were holding the Sagaing bridgehead on the north bank and were deployed along the south bank between Ngazun and Ava. The 20th Indian Infantry Division had received very special attention from the 33rd Division and the remnants of the 14th Tank Regiment. That the Japanese still had tanks was amply proved on the day our air forces brewed-up thirteen of them. When the Japanese found that they could not push the 20th Division back into the river they whistled up elements of the 53rd Division from their army reserve in the area of Myotha, a few miles south of Ngazun. This reserve division must have found life most confusing because, before they knew where they were, an Allied corps had roared past behind them, hell-bent for Meiktila.

By the 4th of March, however, the XXXIII Corps were all set, regrouped and administratively prepared as far as the conditions would permit for the final stage of the race to Mandalay.

The 19th Division started south in earnest for Mandalay at breakneck speed. The 2nd Division had turned left and set off on a two-brigade front (the 6th Brigade on the right and the 5th Brigade on the left) due east along the linE of the Irrawaddy for Ava and Mandalay. The 20th Division swung farther out and were echeloned on the right of the 2nd Division on an axis Myotha— Kyaukse.

For the 5th Brigade the next fortnight was to be hectic in the extreme. It was on the thirteenth day after leaving Ngazun that the Dorsets found themselves scrapping inside the municipal boundary of Mandalay. A great deal of the advance was across country, and only for the last twelve miles after Ava did the road become recognizable as such. In addition, we had to clear most of the way, and at a rough estimate each battalion had about half a dozen actions during this advance of nearly forty miles.

Well might General Rees, the Commander of the 19th Division, signal back to Corps Headquarters during his rapid advance on Mandalay from the north: "Enemy resistance has practically ceased to be coherent." That was quite true, but when related to the foot soldier ploughing through the tall jungle grass or searching the many copses and villages on the way, the picture was not quite so simple. To the Japanese on the run this very lack of cohesion was one of their greatest assets. Indifferent as their tactics were in the attack, the Jap was a very fine individual soldier in the defence. He possessed the ability to break up into small packets and had the suicidal courage of the fanatic to hang on in vital positions until exterminated. This beating-up of the Japanese after the fashion of a pheasant drive could at times slow us considerably, and unfortunately could also prove exceptionally costly. Unlike a pheasant, a Japanese when beaten out of a copse or rustled in the elephant grass still retained his weapons and the ability to use them. Many a time we wished a Japanese "umpire" would appear on the scene and explain to his soldiers that they were beaten and really must withdraw elsewhere. However, I don't think the Japanese knew where their men were towards the later stages of this advance, and I am pretty sure that the ordinary Japanese other rank had no idea where he "be to", as we say in Dorset.

Against the 2nd Division the Japanese had the remains of the 124th Regiment, about a thousand men, and elements of the 58th Regiment.

Not many men; but, especially in the early stages, they had the advantage of prepared positions in rocky, low-hilled country eminently suited for defence. Furthermore, they had always expected us to make our crossing from Ywathigi and to establish our bridgehead in the hills south of Kyauktalon astride the Myotha Road, an artery more important than the road out of Ngazun. He had prepared his positions accordingly and it was through this defensive crust that our way now led.

The advance of the 5th Infantry Brigade started really on the 7th of March with the capture of Letpantabin, three miles to the east of Ngazun, by the Camerons, and the concentration of the Brigade Group east of the town. On the 8th the Worcesters on the right came up against a strong enemy position on Dirty Pagoda Ridge, about a mile to the east of Payadu, a village to the south of Letpantabin. The Worcesters attacked this position on the morning of the 9th, but could make no progress. It was very difficult going for the infantry and quite impossible for the tanks to move up in support. Furthermore, this position covered the main road, which, incidentally, was liberally mined, and the Camerons on the left could make no progress either. We had obviously bumped the western end of the main Kyauktalon position. On our right, a few miles to the south, beyond the "coastal crust", the 6th Brigade were making better progress, though they were finding the advance across these foothills difficult enough.

There seemed to be only one thing to do: this must be a night advance. The Brigadier was being encouraged to press on without delay, and as a daylight party had proved unsatisfactory he ordered me to lead the Dorsets on what was nothing less than a fifteenhundred-yard advance through and behind the Japanese position in the dark. I do not like operating against a savage enemy in the dark across unknown country with a large number of British soldiers. Perhaps we are over-civilized, but against the Japanese who suffer from such a slight veneer of civilization I feel that by operating as a battalion at night we give him too much of an advantage. In Europe, where white man fought white man and both sides were presumably equally as noisy and both suffered from common faults of noisiness, rattling equipment, clattering of boots and an inherent tendency to a continual muttering and coughing, matters might have evened themselves out and no such advantage might have accrued to the enemy.

However, there was nothing to be done about it and, casting back in my mind to all I had ever been taught about General Wolseley and his famous advance by night across the desert at Tel el Kebir, I accepted the assignation and set about trying to simplify what promised to be quite a complicated operation.

My task was to pass through the Worcesters' position in the dark and occupy the high ground of Dirty Pagoda Ridge, which extended in depth to about twelve hundred yards. Owing to the high frontage of this position, on which stood the, by now, famous "dirty" pagoda, it was not possible to obtain a view of the rear of the position, and for this conflict we had to plan entirely off a 1/25,000 map, which was not entirely accurate.

I planned to form up in the Worcestershire area, pass through that battalion and use as a start line a very prominent nullah which ran most conveniently at right angles to my line of advance and stretched across my front. The Worcesters promised not only to reconnoitre this nullah beforehand but to secure it as a start line until I passed through.

After this nullah we were faced with a steep climb, which by daylight had proved unassailable but which we hoped to be able to make at night. On arrival at the top I must perforce split the Battalion and deploy it over an area roughly a thousand yards long by five to six hundred yards wide and overcome the resistance from the Japanese positions on this feature, and thereby open the road to Kyauktalon, along which the Camerons would pour the next morning.

"B" and "C" Companies were to lead this advance and on arrival at the Dirty Pagoda were to press on for another thousand to twelve hundred yards and occupy a ring contour marked on the map. In reserve "A" Company were to occupy the immediate area of the pagoda, with its command of the ground to the south, whilst "D" Company, with Battalion Headquarters and mortars, were to occupy a ring contour on the left about five hundred yards north of the pagoda.

At 0045 hrs. the Battalion moved forward from its lying-up area in a treed area about a mile west of the Worcesters' position which we had occupied during the day. Everything went smoothly for a while. We passed through the Worcesters' position and advanced in square formation to the nullah. This proved to be a far more formidable obstacle than I had been led to believe by the Worcesters. The banks were very steep and covered in thick thorn scrub and, in point of fact, it took three-quarters of an hour to pass the Battalion through. The loss of thirty-five minutes at the start line, although a mere irritant at the time, was to prove most important in the morning when the leading companies had little enough time to get settled on their objectives before first light.

To our surprise, the advance up the hill went extraordinarily smoothly. I say "surprise" because, instead of meeting Japanese opposition, all we encountered in the dark were the traces of stillwarm fires in the cracks and crevices where the Nip had obviously only recently finished cooking his rice. These signs of the Nip pulling out were most encouraging and the Battalion pressed forward in grand style, keeping their formation very well. On arrival at the pagoda, which stood out most eerily against the black tropical night, "B" and "C" Companies pressed on to their ring contour, a further three-quarters of a mile ahead, whilst Paget Fretts deployed "A" Company in the pagoda area. Clive Chettle led off left-handed towards his objective, another ring contour, and "D" Company and Battalion Headquarters were settling into their positions at the head of a re-entrant by about 0430 hrs. I had selected this particular position because it seemed to be defiladed from the south and the west, and in fact seemed to be a most suitable position for the reserve company and Battalion Headquarters. Soon after we had settled down I ordered Clive Chettle to send out a patrol down to the main road to see if all was clear.

Just as it was getting light, pandemonium broke out on all sides. It all started with the patrol of "D" Company. It seems that on their way down to the road they had passed by a Japanese medium machine-gun position situated on a wee bump farther down the hill, away on the flank of the main position. The Jap had not reacted very quickly, but, having been awakened, he must have had a look round. After a bit, when it began to get light, he saw and heard the unmistakable sounds of men digging in at the top of the re-entrant above him and he started to shoot us up. The position in the rapidly brightening light, from our point of view, was not good, and after a quick reconnaissance I decided to reorganize the reserve company and Battalion Headquarters in the rough country on the eastern slopes of the hill up which we had advanced overnight. In the meantime, "A" Company found themselves being counter-attacked by a force of Japanese which had been lying up to the south of the pagoda and had resented this intrusion into their territory. Fretts fought his company very well and the Japs had every reason to regret their early morning enthusiasm. Unfortunately, in this action "Roger" Johnson was severely wounded in the head. This was the officer who had done so well as second-in-command of "A" Company in his first battle at Ye-U, and his loss to the Battalion at such a time as this was unfortunate.

Just as these two actions were getting under control, the sound of very heavy firing came from the forward positions. Their last calls on the wireless had been most cheerful and I wondered what sort of mischief they had got into now. As so often happens, just when one wanted to hear more they both went off the air.

What had happened transpired later. "B" Company took up a position on the north side of the objective, but, finding the area too constricted for two companies, Tommy Tucker had pushed forward into a position from which he hoped to command a re-entrant immediately ahead of him. When dawn broke, the Japanese reacted most fiercely to this penetration so far inside their position. "C" Company came under very heavy fire from a strong bunkered position immediately in front of them. With the help of "B" Company, Tommy Tucker was able to re-form the whole position with the exception of one platoon of "C" Company who were in a very exposed spot and had perforce to remain under heavy fire for some hours before we could get a tank up to them.

"C" Company's wireless had been hit in the fracas and "B" Company's set took this opportunity to go "diss", and so I was completely out of touch with them at this most crucial period.

Meanwhile, back in the rear position, we had had a short but hectic period of fighting. "A" Company had done well and the situation was soon under control. Outstanding this morning was the gunner battery commander from the 10th Field Regiment, Major "Barney" Brooke Fox. Barney was absolutely irrepressible, and whenever a target presented itself he was there to examine the possibilities, quite regardless of personal danger, and he brought retaliatory fire down on the Nips in the shortest possible time.

During the morning the Nip reactions against this force which had arrived in his midst continued. He still held the high Kanywa Ridge to the south, our right flank, and throughout the morning he launched a series of counter-attacks. This, once we were settled in, was just what we wanted, the chance to catch the Nip in the open in daylight. After a few desultory efforts against our widely scattered positions he decided that after all we were a mistake and weren't really there at all, and formed up to attack the Worcesters! To the Jap that must have seemed a most reasonable thing to do. After all, he had fought the Worcesters the day before on the ridge they were holding and so it must have been them who had had the insolence to advance during the night. They can't possibly have remained in the forward position, argued the Nip, and so let's attack them back in their old positions. To the Worcesters on the ridge behind us this came as a heaven-sent opportunity to pay off some old scores, and that counter-attack melted away under their fire.

Meanwhile, our casualties had been mounting up. It had been an expensive morning for us, with twenty-five casualties in the two skirmishes we had had in the rear position, not to mention what had been happening forward. Behind us Lieutenant Chichester-Constable, with his pioneers in carriers, had opened up a line of communication down the mined Kyauktalon Road, to where our famous nullah of the night before joined the road, and then across country to the pagoda. He brought up a welcome replenishment of water and various stores, and continued the good work all day, carrying back casualties on his return.

This was the same Chichester-Constable who had left us as a sergeant at Bhiwandi in 1943 to earn his commission on service. A veteran of the last war, with certain commando-type exploits to his credit in this, he had not only fought with distinction and earned a mention in despatches in the Arakan but had won his commission into the Regiment. At Deolali they had told him there wasn't a hope in hell of his getting to the front. By means fair or foul he had made the trip and duly reported to me on the banks of the Irrawaddy. I had put him in charge of the Pioneer Platoon and a remarkably fine job of work he did. The pioneers needed no encouragement at any time to put on a good show, especially when the Battalion were a bit "pushed", but Basil certainly made them dig bigger and better holes and carry larger and heavier loads than ever before.

A welcome visitor that morning was the Divisional Commander, General Nicholson, who arrived at my headquarters under the pagoda at about 1100 hrs. I understand he had been told by my traffic post at the nullah road junction that he could not go forward. "Nonsense!" the General is reported to have said. "If the Dorsets can get there overnight I can go up to see them in the morning." His visit cheered us up immensely. We had had a very hectic few hours after a long and tiring night, with the prospect of continued battling, and the presence of the Divisional Commander during the morning did a great deal to dissipate the feeling of tiredness, and put new life into the Battalion.

During the morning Tommy Tucker, finding that he could not communicate with me on the radio, made his way back to my tactical headquarters across the thousand yards of No Man's Land.

This was no small effort and quite in keeping with Tommy's great performance that day. He gave me the general picture and related what had happened since the time he had left me and pushed forward with the two companies from the pagoda in the early hours of the morning. He had as yet been unable to evacuate his casualties and still had a platoon pinned down in the open. He badly needed some extra support. I got on to the Brigadier and asked for a troop of tanks. As carriers were by now coming up to me from the rear, and we had, as far as we knew, cleared the north side of the ridge, it would seem that we could get tanks up to Tommy. The latter assured me that the going for tanks up to his position was all right. The Brigadier told me that he was pushing Camerons up the road towards Kyauktalon, and as soon as they were abreast of "C" Company's position he would release a troop of tanks.

Eventually two Grants arrived and with the support of a battery of field guns Tommy Tucker set about the Nipponese positions in earnest.

It was during the subsequent operation that Lieutenant Robin Cuthbertson was killed under circumstances of extreme gallantry. Throughout the battle he had led his platoon with complete disregard for his own personal safety. Time and again he had tried to extricate the section which had become pinned down and to get in his casualties. When finally he was able to re-form and get the badly wounded men to safety he decided to have a final look round to see that no one had been left out. He went from body to body, well knowing there was little chance of his own survival, and found them all dead. As he was coming in to the safety he had so disregarded and to the security he had so hardly won for his platoon, this gallant officer was killed by a burst of machine-gun fire.

There are many deeds in war which go unrewarded, and Robin himself would certainly never have expected the highest award a soldier can receive, but his deeds that day certainly placed him in a very high position among those famous men who throughout the long history of the Regiment have distinguished themselves by their personal valour in action and have laid down their lives that their men may live.

"C" Company certainly had a bumper day that day. They fought hard and earnestly and not without casualties. It was a great day for the Battalion when, a few weeks later, we heard that His Majesty had awarded three decorations to us for the night advance to the Dirty Pagoda, and on "C" Company in the van of the Battalion fell the honour of receiving all three. Tommy Tucker, the company commander, earned the Military Cross, Sergeant Seale, whom we have encountered before in these annals, though wounded, continued to fight his platoon with the utmost gallantry and was awarded the Distinguished Conduct Medal, and Corporal Warren received the Military Medal.

By noon we were established, the position had been gained and the Japanese opposition eliminated. The Camerons had come up on our left and the way was open for them to fight their way into Kyauktalon, against the remaining Japanese opposition, in this their main position, the next morning.

The hazardous night advance had proved entirely successful. This expedition through the Japanese lines had been costly, but we had achieved our object and had opened the road by carrying out an operation against a position which but twenty-four hours earlier had seemed to be the toughest we had had to crack since Kohima. The Japanese in a prepared position in which he had been allowed some time to dig was, as we knew by experience, no easy nut to crack.

Our casualties that day again involved a high proportion of leaders at platoon and section level. Lieutenant Cuthbertson and twelve British other ranks were killed, among the latter being some very old and familiar characters, such as Private Merchant of "A" Company, and Private Easter of "C" Company. Our losses in wounded were heavy, totalling one officer (Lieutenant Johnson) and forty-eight British other ranks. Among the latter were Sergeants Lee, Wells, Williams, Seale and Beasley (Gloster Platoon). Seale was only lightly wounded and was back at duty in a day or two, only to be wounded again in the next engagement. Perhaps the loss which hit "C" Company especially hard was the temporary disappearance of that imperturbable "swede basher" Private Foot, the "C" Company runner. Foot for years had held this very special job and had accompanied a series of company commanders through the Kohima and subsequent fighting when this particular company had been so unfortunate in their officer casualties.

The next day we moved up in line with the Camerons and took up a position astride the Myotha Road well satisfied that we had undertaken and executed a first-class job.

Perhaps the most distressed person, other than the casualties, was Tommy Tucker, who at some time during the battle left his equipment by his slit trench. On his return he found that it had been set alight by a No. 77 grenade and his precious stock of cigarettes destroyed.

I can't pass by this battle without paying a tribute to the medical services. That day they were terrific. Oh, what a happy comparison with the conditions obtaining in the Kohima battle a year earlier! This time all our casualties were evacuated with the greatest promptitude. Once we could get them into the Battalion aid post they were hurried back to the advanced dressing station, from where they were flown away by light plane. So speedy was the evacuation, and so excellent the medical arrangements forward, that many of the wounded recovered and were healed in record time and were back fighting with us by the time we had finished the race for Mandalay. Even the more serious cases, like Roger Johnson, were rushed back to Comilla, and in a very short time were well on the way to recovery. Once again we could not be too grateful for the support of the 5th Field Ambulance.

The advance of the Camerons into Kyauktalon itself was opposed and it was not until the evening of the 11th that the 5th Brigade were firmly on the line Kyauktalon and the southern road through to Myotha. That evening a patrol from "A" Company on the high ground on the left linked up with the 6th Brigade at about MS3 on the Myotha Road. The next day the Dorsets were allowed to rest in Brigade reserve at Kyauktalon whilst the Brigade pushed on, and on the 13th we moved up, still in reserve, to a position just west of Letpanzin (not to be confused with Letpantabin), which had just been captured by the Worcesters.

The 14th of March was to be a busy day for the Battalion. Although the Brigade were destroying the enemy on their line of advance down the river bank, too many were escaping southwards into the foothills, and, apart from it being bad policy to allow any Japanese to live, these were tending to pile up in front of the 6th Brigade on our right. Accordingly, the Brigadier decided to send the Dorsets on a "right-flanker" through the foothills, fielding on the boundary, as it were, to the Brigade advance round the bend of the Irrawaddy. I had collected in Kyauktalon a battery of mortars of the 100th Anti-Tank Regiment, the Divisional antitank regiment. These Gordon-Gunners were equipped for any eventuality, having a dual role of anti-tank gunners and mortarmen. This vast increase of sixteen mortars under command enabled me to dispense with my own "tubes" for this operation. I therefore unloaded the mortar equipment from the carriers, and mounted part of the Defence Platoon in a carrier platoon role. Lintorn Highett did a grand job with his carriers on this show: his reconnaissances of villages off our axis were thorough and energetic, and later in the day, when we were allotted a troop of Carabiniers, he proved invaluable in guiding the tanks through the long grass and acting as infantry escort against concealed Nips.

This day we advanced fourteen miles across country which varied from wood to rock to open paddy, ending up finally in tall jungle grass. It was a long and tiring day, during which we had to mount a "T.E.W.J." against Sinde, a large village in which the natives reported Japanese. A T.E.W.J., or Tactical Exercise Without Japanese, was a form of operation daily becoming more common. So often had units bumped resistance and become heavily involved before they had time to deploy, especially against the disorganized enemy we were now fighting, that we developed the T.E.W.J.. It started normally with patrols going forward, followed by a section, platoon or company, until finally the

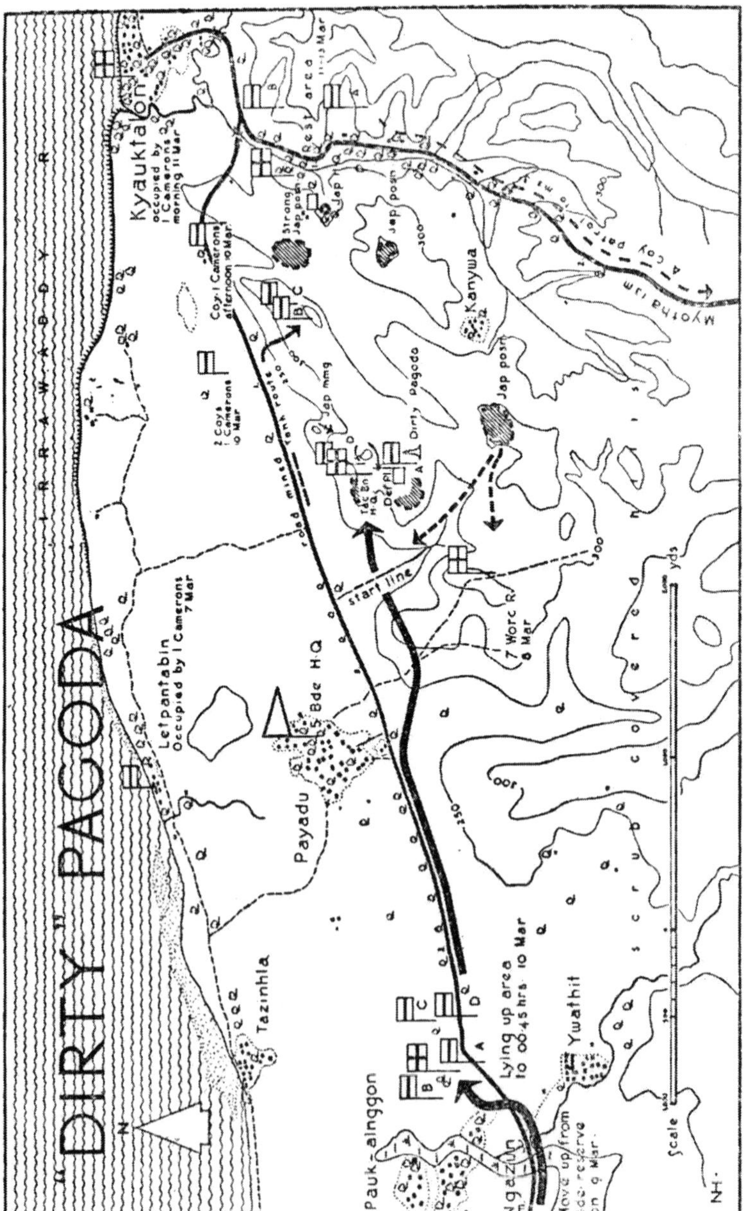
"DIRTY" PAGODA
IRRAWADDY R
Kyauktalon
occupied by 1 Camerons morning 11 Mar
Rest area 11-13 Mar
Strong Jap posn
Jap posn
Coy 1 Camerons afternoon 10 Mar
Kanywa
Myotha rd
A coy patrol
2 Coys 1 Camerons 10 Mar
road mined tank route
Jap mmg
Dirty Pagoda
Tac Bn HQ
Letpantabin
Occupied by 1 Camerons 7 Mar
start line
7 Worc R. 8 Mar
5 Bde HQ
Payadu
scrub covered
Tazinhla
Lying up area 10 00.45 hrs 10 Mar
Ywathit
Ngazun
Move up from Bde reserve on 9 Mar
Scale
yds
NH

Battalion had built itself up on the position. Another form of T.E.W.J., which we carried out that day, was to deploy the Battalion and advance on to the objective ready for anything that might happen. Sometimes nothing did happen and the operation developed into a T.E.W.J.. It was a slow form of warfare, but the insurance was well worth while in view of our dwindling numbers and the extreme difficulty which all units of this all-British division were finding in obtaining reinforcements.

Between half-past four and five o'clock, after the Battalion had passed through Sinde, the leading companies rustled the Nip in the jungle grass about a mile to the east of the village. Again the Nip reaction was surprisingly quick. He managed to sling a number of grenades from his grenade discharger amongst the leading platoons before he was adequately pin-pointed and dealt with.

Just as we had eliminated the enemy, the Brigadier called me up to tell me to halt for the night, as dusk was not far off and he wanted to get the Brigade firm before continuing the march the next day.

On the 15th the Brigade continued to press on. Retaining our flankguard role, we made for Kadozeik and the Worcesters for U-yin, to force a crossing of the Tayok Chaung at the spot where it entered the Irrawaddy. To our right the 6th Brigade were pushing on towards Tada-U.

At about 0830 hrs. "B" and "C" Companies, who were leading on this day, ran smack into enemy positions about half a mile west of the village of Kadozeik.

The country around the village was thickly cultivated with banana plantations and the areas that were not cultivated were thick grass—an unpleasant place in which to search for this very well-concealed enemy. Two of the three tanks were immediately put out of action by some form of hollow charge grenade, fired from a rifle, which we had not previously encountered. One of these grenades penetrated the 75-mm. ammunition bin of the troop commander's tank and brewed it up immediately. The carriers did a fine job of work in rounding up the Nips and escorting the second tank, badly damaged as it was, out of action. Meanwhile, reports from the leading companies and the degree of firing indicated that we were up against a prepared position. I decided that it was the occasion to hit the enemy as hard as possible, and called up Brigade and asked for an air strike and all the artillery the Brigadier could raise. It was our unlucky day for air. They had a great number of calls and for some reason these fighter-bombers had to fly in from an especially long way. I was told that I could not have my strike until the afternoon. In the meantime, I patrolled as actively as possible and began to get a very good picture of the enemy position. John Joslin, of "D" Company, did a good piece of patrolling that day and was able to give me a very clear picture of the enemy positions in a wood in which stood a pagoda on the west edge of the village. Our Burma Intelligence Corps team at the same time managed to collect some valuable details of the enemy defences from the locals. These positions appeared to be concentrated around this pagoda and at the western entrance to the village.

We were all "teed-up" ready to attack at 1300 hrs. when we were told that the air boys would be an hour late. Three times the attack was put off because of the non-arrival of the air, and when they did finally come it was too late to put in an attack. That wasn't all. On their arrival over the target, which was the clearly defined wood in which the village stood, they swooped down and attacked us! By the greatest good fortune the first two two-hundred-and-fifty-pound bombs, which landed bang in the middle of "D" Company's area, failed to explode. We fired Very lights, waved those damned orange umbrellas which we had toted around with us all this way, waved our arms and did everything to try to deflect this downward swoop of a squadron of Hurribombers coming in on their second run to open up with their guns. Fortunately the contact car got through in time and the planes pulled out of their dive and passed harmlessly over our heads. No, it was not a good day for the Royal Air Force. These things happen in the best-regulated families, and I must say that it was the first time that it had happened to us. As I have said before, the ground-air support throughout the campaign was first class, and despite the great distances over which they had to come in most cases, the airmen usually were up over our heads in very short time.

We had lost Jonah Jones and ten British other ranks wounded in the battle in the morning, and half a dozen men had gone down with fever and heat exhaustion, and so I was quite glad when the Brigadier ordered me not to press in an attack following the air debacle, but to content myself with the artillery concentration at last light and press on in the morning.

We strafed the known enemy positions thoroughly that evening — how thoroughly we were able to see the next morning, when a very satisfactory number of dead Japanese were found in their positions. That night, to encourage the Nip to continue on his "advance back to Rangoon", as his masters so nicely put it, we employed all sixteen of our mortars to try to burn him out of the village and harassed him with artillery and mortars. The Japs did not have a very quiet night.

On the 16th we patrolled into the village and found that the remaining

Nips had pulled out, only to be scotched by the 6th Brigade in the area of Tada-U. We did not stay long in the ruins of Kadozeik, but, turning due north, marched to the Irrawaddy and, following up the Brigade, made along the river bank to the quite unpronounceable village of Ngayabaya, where we deployed into Brigade reserve. Meanwhile, the 5th Brigade had been pressing on remarkably fast and even now the Camerons were hammering at the ancient moated defences of Ava.

It was a great relief to get back to the river, where we could wash and bathe and have a short rest. This proved to be a very short pause, less than twenty-four hours, but to us it was a lot. We were getting pretty tired and our casualties were mounting steadily. We had covered the two hundred and fifteen miles between the Chindwin and Ngazun on the south bank of the Irrawaddy with only one officer and sixteen British other ranks killed and four officers and thirty-three British other ranks wounded. In the last ten days, following up the Nip in this jungle grass, we had, including the battle for Dirty Pagoda Ridge, already lost the same number killed in officers and men, and two officers and sixty-five other ranks had been wounded. In addition, there was a steady trickle of a daily average of three or four men being evacuated for fever, septic sores or heat exhaustion. These last recovered quickly enough to rejoin their platoons, but it was a constant drain on our man power which was likely to increase rather than diminish the longer we were kept "out of stable".

At Ngayabaya there was little to do except to prevent the Japanese from the north bank landing in the Brigade area and trying to break out to the south. Our B.I.C. Corporal fell in the local villagers and allotted them their tours of duty "on stag" to help us out, and I must say they were most willing to collaborate. We had swung round into a friendly Burman area again, after having lived among a rather unfriendly section of the population in the south-west corner of the Schwebo Plain.

I took the opportunity at Ngayabaya to hold an "inquest" with the company and specialist platoon commanders on our performance up to date. My aim was to try to see where we could improve our battle technique and try to eliminate as far as possible our battle casualties. The discussion proved most interesting and I think we all learnt a lot that morning on the banks of the Irrawaddy. At any rate, there was a marked improvement in our various drills. Not that I was dissatisfied with our performance—far from it—but I felt that a good overhaul was necessary if we were to continue fighting without being pulled out to refit.

By the afternoon of the 17th the Camerons had captured Ava Fort and the Worcesters had advanced through them and were even now planning to cross the Myitinge River, which was three hundred yards wide at this spot, about half a mile south of where it flowed into the Irrawaddy.

Even as I was moving the Battalion up to its new position in the south-east corner of Ava on the banks of the Myitinge, the Brigadier decided to send the Worcesters over straight away by any means they could. He was dead right: the Worcesters' crossing itself was unopposed and by last light after a slight skirmish they had got a patrol to the east end of Ava bridge.

Meanwhile, we had sent out a carrier and tank patrol to the south to try to link up with the brigade in Tada-U. This patrol returned in the evening, having successfully accomplished its task.

At first light on the 18th the Dorsets crossed the Myitinge in Dukws. The number of Dukws was extremely limited and it took some time for the Battalion to concentrate on the east bank. We then pushed forward and took over the east end of Ava bridge from the Worcesters, who, the evening before, had had a skirmish with the Japanese in the ruined fort at the east end.

The Fifty-Fourth really had reached Ava this time. A hundred and twenty years earlier our predecessors had earned the battle honour "Ava" for their part in the Burma War of 1824-26. In common with the remainder of that force, they had never reached the ancient capital of Burma. The award of "Ava" had been a general honour for the campaign. A much more appropriate one for the Regiment would have been "Arakan", in which province the Fifty-Fourth fought, and in the capture of the capital city of the same name had played such a prominent part.

We had been denied, owing to our fighting at Kadozeik, the honour of the assault on Ava and the Worcesters had beaten us to the bridge. All we could do was to get the first man (Clive Chettle) across the bridge to the north bank and take advantage of the appearance of certain Pressmen to have my own carrier, appropriately named "Ava", photographed on the Ava bridge.

The Japanese had not done much to repair the two spans in this thirteen-hundred-yard bridge across the Irrawaddy which we had blown on our withdrawal out of Burma in 1942. They had, however, managed to rig some crazy catwalk which was suitable for pedestrians and just passable for bullock carts. On his arrival on the north bank Clive found our old friends of the 268th Brigade. Brigadier Dyer had been given the task of mopping up in the Sagaing hills after the 2nd Division had crossed the Irrawaddy. He had carried out this formidable task with only the minimum of support. The Brigadier himself came over to see us later in the morning and met Brigadier West at my headquarters. With Brigadier Dyer was his Brigade Major, Major Robertson of the Indian Cavalry, who had done his attachment with the 1st Battalion in Nowshera in 1938 and was very pleased to meet some old friends such as Corporal Wood of the Regimental Police.

We remained in the area of the Ava bridge for the rest of that day, covering the crossing of the river by the remainder of the Brigade, and early the next morning moved off once more in the lead of the 5th Infantry Brigade on the last lap to Mandalay.

Our way lay for six or seven miles along a main tarmac road banked up practically the whole way. On either side of us the country was flooded and it would have been difficult, in the earlier stages, to have deployed if we had bumped trouble. Clive Chettle was leading with "D" Company, and the "Light" Company were certainly determined to waste no time in getting to the city. On arrival at the north wall of the ruined Hmandan Fort, where the road actually pierces the ancient defences, the leading platoon came under fire from a pagoda compound ahead.

Clive Chettle quickly deployed and within a very short time he had attacked this pagoda, crossed the garden wall, and the Dorsets were fighting within the municipal boundary of Mandalay. Having brushed aside this opposition, we were all for pushing on and trying to link up with the 19th Division, which was fighting hard for Fort Dufferin in the middle of the city, a couple of miles farther on. However, the Brigadier called a halt. We had not got all our guns up, our supply line across the Myitinge was tenuous in the extreme, and we were not in a position on this day to become embroiled in street fighting.

During the afternoon I deployed and occupied a wide front, with my left company at Atwin Thayagon covering a possible escape route for Japs crossing the Irrawaddy. I sent "A" Company to the pagoda area at the north-east corner of Hmandan Fort which gave a commanding view of the south and south-east exits from Mandalay. To this position I sent the Manchester machine gunners, and they subsequently had a grand shoot across the Kyaukse Road.

Meanwhile, astern of us Brigadier West deployed the Worcesters to the south of the fort and Tom Irvine put out a block across the Kyaukse Road, for which he had to fight. It was at about this time that we were horrified to hear of the death of Major Jack Boyt, of the Worcesters, a very old friend of the Battalion, who had been in the 5th Brigade since 1940.

Early the next morning, the 20th, "A" Company and the Manchesters had a field day—one of those grand moments unfortunately so rare, when the machine gunners have an orgy of firing. A convoy was seen breaking out of Mandalay and driving rapidly southwards. As it passed the fort we opened up at about a thousand yards' range. The results were most satisfactory. Some of the vehicles got through, but these were scuppered by the Worcesters at their road block farther south.

In order to clean up the resultant mess and find out what this convoy was, and also to collect any more, I persuaded the Brigadier to let me put a block across this road in a wood due east of "A" Company's pagoda position. When we had strafed this convoy the survivors had been seen to disappear into the village of Ponnachan, where we could see them frenziedly digging in. This called for an attack rather than a quiet stroll over to the road. Calling up "B" and "C" Companies, we laid on an attack over flat country covered with scrub and bushes. A most convenient line of pagodas gave us a start line. Covered by the fire of the machine gunners and with the prospect of some interesting identifications from the Jap convoy we had strafed, the companies went in. Tony Bridge, the Brigade Major, had suddenly appeared at the command post with a party of twenty-odd United States Army Air Force pilots all raring to see an infantry combat. Unfortunately we couldn't give them much. The artillery concentration on the wood, or rather banana groves, had been too much for the Nip and he pulled out as fast as he could, being chased by the fire of the machine gunners.

We soon got these two companies astride the road in an excellent road-block position. When we took a count of the damage done earlier in the morning we found that we had bagged nine staff cars and jeeps and the Worcesters had got seven. Furthermore, we discovered that this convoy had been the Japanese 15th Divisional Headquarters pulling out of Mandalay.

The Battalion were now deployed in a straight line, with "B" and "C" Companies blocking what we had discovered was the main Japanese escape route, "A" Company holding the pagoda and covering the railway exit, and "D" Company sitting astride the south-west (Ava Road) exit from the city. I accordingly shifted my Battalion Headquarters to an area at the north end of the fort midway between "A" and "D" Companies. I had reason to regret this move later.

The Brigade was having quite a lot of work to do mopping up various parties of Japanese and patrolling in all directions. Away on the right towards Kyaukse the 4th Brigade was involved in a bitter struggle with Japanese trying to break out to the south.

In the middle of the afternoon General Sir Oliver Leese, the

Commander-in-Chief of the Allied Land Forces, South-East Asia (previously 11th Army Group), arrived in the Brigade area and paid the Battalion a visit. He visited "D" Company and insisted on being taken over to "A" Company, where, from the pagoda, I was able to point out the situation in our area. We assembled as many of the men as possible, and, standing on my jeep, he gave us a most interesting talk on the over-all picture, pointing out the necessity of making the next four hundred miles to Rangoon even faster than we had come already, in order to get there before the monsoon broke. He did promise that we would not have to walk all the way!

Just as he was leaving us, word came through from the 19th Division that, after ten days' intense siege, Fort Dufferin had fallen and that Mandalay was ours. We were all very excited and the men gave the Commander-in-Chief a great send-off, as he insisted on getting back to his light plane with all speed and flying over to General Rees to congratulate him.

What a strange day the 20th of March was! Quite enough had already happened. My final orders just after the departure of General Leese had been to instruct Paget Fretts to deploy his company a bit more and to alter some of the lay-out of Battalion Headquarters. I considered that altogether too many people must have been seen congregated on the exposed terraces of the pagoda during the day. The Nip may have lost Fort Dufferin, but South Mandalay was by no means clear and I could not help but feel that some Japanese gunner must have got us taped for an evening blitz.

Apart from that we were in a holiday mood and for the first time since crossing the Chindwin a number of the men were a bit idle about digging in. We were to receive a rude awakening. At about 0200 hrs. the enemy opened up with about eight guns, apparently into "the blue". Unfortunately, "the blue" happened to be Hmandan Fort in general and my Battalion Headquarters in particular. It was especially galling, as the number of rounds mounted up, to think that I had so carefully located Battalion Headquarters away from some recognizable feature. About two hundred rounds fell in about an hour and a half and we lost two men killed and three more wounded. Private Burden, another of our real Dorset men and a very old and trusted member of "A" Company, was killed while carrying out his duties as a stretcher-bearer. What had happened, we guessed, was that the Japs were just emptying their guns and shooting off their ammunition before pulling out. This assumption was further strengthened later the same night when two 75-mm. guns were picked up by "C" Company at their road block. The next morning the 19th Division reported having found eight Japanese guns in the area of the Government Dairy Farm. It was from this area that our gunners had considered that the firing was coming and had made a suitable reply. It was two years later that I heard the sequel to this. A patrol of the 19th Division, prowling around the dairy farm area, had found these guns lined up and had heard the Japanese officer giving out his fire orders. The patrol leader hurried back to his headquarters and got his gunners on to the target. The result, judging by the number of dead bodies around the guns the next morning, so the commanding officer of the field regiment concerned claims, was most satisfactory. We would have all, however, had a quieter night if that patrol had had a forward observation officer with them.

Throughout the night "C" and "B" Companies on the Kyaukse Road had an exciting time in their road block and, apart from the two 75-mms., quite a number of the rats walked into the ambush. But for the impetuosity of an over-enthusiastic machine gunner, a far larger bag would have been scored.

The next morning I was ordered to link up with the 19th Division at a certain cross-roads in Mandalay. I sent out Highett with the carriers, who reported back that all was clear. This was to be a tactical link-up, and one of the objects was for Brigadier West to meet his opposite number in the 19th Division. On receiving Highett's signal the Brigadier decided to go up himself, taking me with him. Accordingly, mounted on Grants and led by the carriers, we stormed into Mandalay. There was no one at our rendezvous except a military policeman, who directed this imposing patrol into Fort Dufferin. On arrival there we passed King Thebaw's Palace (or the ruins, as the Japs had burnt it to the ground as a last gesture before pulling out) and burst suddenly on to a ceremonial parade! Elements of all units of the 19th Division were paraded on the site of Government House for the ceremonial raising of the Union Flag by the Army Commander, attended by the Corps Commander and all three divisional commanders.

In this way, though uninvited, the Fifty-Fourth managed to arrive in at the kill. It was perhaps most fitting that the Dorsets gate-crashed this party to represent the 2nd Division, as we and the troop of the 3rd Dragoon Guards with us were the only troops of the Division to fight in Mandalay itself.

The ceremony over, Lieutenant-Colonel Sam Symes took us to his battalion headquarters and showed us something of the fierce fighting which the 19th Division had gone through to capture Mandalay in such quick time.

The capture of Fort Dufferin does not belong to this story, but it was an epic in the account of the Burma War. Ancient though its defences were, its ramparts had stood up for many days against the full weight of modern explosives. Medium guns had been brought up to point-blank range in an attempt to breach the walls before an entrance could be effected. It was a magnificent conclusion to the great advance that the 19th Indian Infantry Division had made through Burma.

We spent forty-eight hours in our same position in the suburbs of Mandalay, carrying out patrols and making up deficiencies on "Tojo" and "Tokyo", our two long-suffering Jap trucks. We captured more Japanese, and the Intelligence Section, under Tiger Havers, had a great time. I sent as many men as possible on sightseeing tours of the Golden City. Their disappointment was keen. The Japanese had done practically nothing to restore the city during the three years they had been in charge. At last the Battalion had come to a city where there were trams, but not a tram had run for three years. The once-beautiful gardens and parks were a shambles, which is strange considering how fond the Nip is of horticulture in his own islands. Clubs and places of amusement seemed to have been completely neglected. Obviously the Allied air forces had done nothing in the past few months to encourage the Nip to repair the ravages of war, but the whole city had that air of desolation which seemed to prove that he had made no effort during his long tenancy even to maintain the most normal amenities, such as public services and shops.

So ended the fight for Mandalay, and it was good to be in at the kill. We were all very tired after this hectic fortnight, and I was beginning to get worried about the health of the Battalion. What we wanted was a good ten days' rest in a hill station like Maymyo. The weather was getting intensely hot and those of us unlucky enough to contract a septic sore found that it took quite a time to heal. The Division had been going flat out for a long time and the constant drain on numbers through battle casualties and sickness only increased the work for the survivors. At Mandalay my Adjutant, Graeme Gordon Wright, was very off colour. He refused to be evacuated, but he had to lie up in the pagoda, into which I had moved Battalion Headquarters, for a couple of days.

Except for the urgent necessity to reach Rangoon before the monsoon was due to break in about six weeks' time, the Higher Command must have been most pleased with the situation after the fall of Mandalay. The capture of the city itself was of great political importance. In point of fact, I suppose that the capture of the airfields at Meiktila and the disruption of the Japanese forces cut in two by the swift advance across Burma by the IV Corps had an even greater immediate bearing on the military situation than the annihilation of the Japanese northern force by the XXXIII Corps.

Both together ensured our subsequent speedy victory. The fall of Mandalay, a city so well known, was, however, a great morale raiser throughout the Allied nations, though at home the story of its fall must have been to a certain extent eclipsed by the great deeds in Europe at the time. However, none of us who fought in Burma can fail to agree with the Prime Minister, Mr. Winston Churchill, who, when announcing the capture of the old Burmese capital in the House of Commons, is said to have remarked, "Thank God they've at last got to a place I can pronounce!"

Dirty Pagoda Ridge

THE ADVANCE TO POPA

The Battalion sets out for Kyauktaga

The Medical Platoon on the road to Popa

The three Commanding Officers of 5th Infantry Brigade, Lieut.-Col A. J. Somerville McAlester (Camerons), the author, and Lieut.-Col T. A. Irvine (7th Worcesters)

THE FINAL ADVANCE

Dorsets and 208 Field Company, R.E.

Carabiniers held up by Jap road block

Mount Popa from Popa village. "A" Company's bivouac area in foreground.

CHAPTER FIFTEEN

"POPALONG TO POPA"

"Our troops are pursuing the enemy rapidly towards Rangoon."

[Tokyo Radio]

GENERAL SIR OLIVER LEESE, in his talk to the Battalion on the 20th of March, had compared the Battle of Mandalay, as far as the time period of six weeks that it had taken, with the Battles of Cassino and Kohima. That phase of the campaign was now over and it was necessary, as General Leese had also said, to press forward and reach Rangoon before the rains broke early in June. We all hoped that the monsoon would not arrive early as it had in the Naga hills the year before.

General Stopford's XXXIII Corps were first of all ordered to press south and link up with General Messervy in Meiktila, which the Corps Commander did with General Gracey's 20th Indian Infantry Division, and then be prepared to advance south towards Rangoon, astride the Irrawaddy, on the right of the Fourteenth Army. This meant fresh regrouping. The 7th Indian Infantry Division, our old friend of Kohima days, which had made the crossing of the Irrawaddy at Nyaungu, through which General Messervy had flung his armour to Meiktila, came under the XXXIII Corps, and the 19th Division, having taken over the 2nd Division's commitments south of Mandalay, were to revert to the IV Corps. Meanwhile, the 2nd Division had somehow to be lifted bodily from the Mandalay area to Myingan, eighty miles to the southwest, a most important road and riverhead on the Irrawaddy.

The enemy was completely confused. The loss of his main lines of communication, Rangoon to Mandalay, had foxed him and sandwiched between the XXXIII Corps in the north and the IV Corps in the south were the remnants of the Japanese Fifteenth, ThirtyThird and Twenty-Eighth Armies. He had lost most of his armour and was trying hard to rally and prevent any further penetration. Elements of the 54th and 55th Divisions escaping from the attentions of the XV Corps in the

Arakan were known to have escaped over the An Pass and were likely to become involved in future operations of the XXXIII Corps.

Whilst all this planning and regrouping at high level was being undertaken, the 5th Infantry Brigade Group pulled out of the Mandalay area for a rest and refit.

We were not sorry to set out from Mandalay at 0300 hrs. on the 24th of March. We crossed the Myitinge at first light by a Class 30 floating Bailey bridge in place of the Class 40 rafts which had ferried the Brigade across in the later stages of the advance to Mandalay, and found an excellent breakfast waiting for us at Ava.

The Dorsets were bivouacked in a quite attractive Paungyi Chaung area where there was plenty of shade. We settled down immediately to clean up and reorganize and take full advantage of the liquor ration which had been sent up to us. There seemed to be plenty of beer for once and a quite admirable spirit issue. Despite the presence of cholera, Ava really seemed to be a good place and we looked forward to our long-promised rest. I had hopes of being allowed to send a party of our worst "jungle-sore" cases up to the hill station at Maymyo to recuperate.

At Battalion and company headquarters there was a good deal of reorganization to be done. We had lost many junior leaders in the last fortnight and new company teams had to be formed.

Our most serious loss in these days was the departure of those two old veterans C.S.M. Osmond and Sergeant Seale. Both originally had been bandsmen and had many years' service to their credit. C.S.M. Bertie Osmond was one of the four survivors who had been in the Battalion in November, 1921, and had come abroad with us again in 1942. Both Osmond and Seale were one-time stars of the Battalion Rugby football side which some twelve years earlier had reached the semi-final of the Army Cup; these two stalwarts were still playing Rugby for the Battalion in the spring of 1942. Nothing had deterred C.S.M. Osmond throughout the long and arduous training in India and the extremely tough fighting and advance we had made in the past year. He was promoted Company Sergeant-Major of H.Q. Company at Kohima and had continued to serve the Battalion as faithfully and as energetically as the youngest and most toughened member of the Guerrilla Platoon. Sergeant Yorky Seale's exploits have been recounted again and again in these annals. His personal bravery and power of leadership made him a first-class platoon commander, and his enthusiasm as a company sergeant-major was a constant encouragement to "D" Company. Wounded at Dirty Pagoda, he insisted on fighting on, until he was wounded again at Kadozeik and had to be evacuated for good. He was awarded an immediate Distinguished Conduct Medal at Dirty Pagoda, having already earned a Commander-in-Chief's Certificate for Gallantry for his services at Kohima. C.S.M. Osmond's services were subsequently recognized by the award of a mention in despatches.

I was most fortunate in still having my "first eleven" company commanders with me, and that great stalwart Graeme Gordon Wright as Adjutant, with O.R.Q.M.S. Vaughan in the office. Paget Fretts had rejoined us at Schwebo after his "go" of scrub typhus, his energy apparently unimpaired, and he had taken over "A" Company in place of John Bowles. At Rear Headquarters I had David Harris, who took a great weight off all our shoulders by his most competent ability to deal with the abstrusest problems of administration. He and Bert Smith, the Quartermaster, as lively as ever, with the able assistance of R.Q.M.S. Hayward, made a very formidable "B" Echelon team.

At Ava I personally had to work hard to catch up on arrears of correspondence and regimental work. My clerks always used to fear these clerical blitzes of mine, and were much happier when I was busily employed in fighting the Battalion. However, it was labour well spent. For the first two years we were abroad there was practically no touch with the Depot, Infantry Training Centre or any Regimental connection with the United Kingdom. So bad was it that at Christmas, 1944, I received a very nice parcel from a hostess in Capetown who had gone out of her way to entertain a party of officers of the Battalion on our way through that most hospitable city in 1942. In her covering letter she wrote: "I have recently read in an English paper that a battalion of the Dorsets have been missing for over two years and no one knows where they are. Feeling that this must be you, I am sending this parcel of food, hoping that it will enliven your Christmas, if it ever reaches you." Bless her and all the good folk of Capetown who continued to correspond with members of the Battalion long after we had sailed from their hospitable shores.

With the arrival of Lieutenant-Colonel John Hewick to command the Infantry Training Centre the situation changed immediately and from then on we were not only in constant touch with home but also felt that we had not been forgotten. In token of the gratitude we felt for his efforts we had sent John Hewick and No. 2 Infantry Training Centre one of the first Japanese flags that we captured in this "second innings".

John Hewick's News-Letters became famous throughout the Regiment, and I can say that they were eagerly awaited by us. The compilation, however, of our own part and the subsequent distribution of copies of his letters to about thirty Dorset addressees known to me throughout India and South-East Asia Commands placed a great additional strain on our limited office facilities until I was able to get Lieutenant-Colonel "Flash" Seaton, at G.H.Q., New Delhi, to undertake the latter task.

Then there was the Cigarette Appeal. During the recent fighting prior to the crossing of the Irrawaddy, I had been amazed at the sudden cleanliness of the company areas. There seemed to be a total absence of my pet anathema—strewn tea leaves lying around the place. On making further inquiries I found that tea leaves were being carefully hoarded. When dried out and mixed with a portion of the rum ration they did not make an unpalatable smoke—at least, not too bad. We had sunk so low on smokes, at the time when ammunition and petrol came well ahead of tobacco and even food on the air-lift priorities, that the Battalion smoked anything they could find: Japani cigarettes, those comic Burmese cigars, tea leaves and, in fact, anything that would generate smoke. With no other form of relaxation we needed our smokes badly. I wrote home and put the case to Lieutenant-Colonel T. S. Rendall, O.B.E., a retired Dorset officer. Tommy Rendall worked wonders: he launched an appeal and, thanks to the good offices of such old friends of the Regiment as Mr. Alan Jefferies of Dorchester and numerous women's institutes throughout the county, cigarettes and pipe tobacco started pouring in at about this time. We tried to thank every donor individually, and by letters in the Western Press express our gratitude collectively, as so many of these kind people remained anonymous. It was a grand gesture from the county and deeply appreciated by all members of the Battalion.[17]

All this, as you will realize, took time. At my command post the usual drill of an evening would be for my Second-in-Command, the Adjutant and the Intelligence Officer, all keen bridge players, to take over the "G" Office jeep trailer which we had constructed, and with the help of another officer make up a bridge four. I am afraid that I was of no use to them, and it must have been a constant source of irritation to three such keen players that the fourth member of Battalion Headquarters was a non-player. Meanwhile, I shut myself up in my bivouac and got down to my correspondence and the compilation of records. These letters are, as you may guess, proving invaluable as I

---

17 As a result of this appeal, the Battalion had received 131,000 cigarettes and 83lb. of tobacco from the county of Dorset and friends of the Regiment by the end of May, 1945.

write these annals. On checking back I find that in the field I used to average seventy or eighty "D.O." letters a month.

A great feature of this short, only too short, stay at Ava was that we could all get around and visit each other.

For forty-eight hours, except for routine guards, we could relax our vigilance and companies were able to take full advantage of their "liquor ration" by organizing impromptu sing-songs.

Before marching out of Ava, after having explained the future operations to the Battalion, I took the opportunity, as we were quartered in the ancient capital of the kingdom of Burma, to relate to the Battalion the exploits of their predecessors in Burma a hundred and twenty years earlier. These notes had been supplied to me by Captain C. T. Atkinson, the historian of the Regiment, from whom I have always received the greatest interest and assistance.

On the 27th of March we had to hand in our empties and move off with the greatest speed by mechanical transport on an eightymile march to Myingyan away to the south-west on the east bank of the Irrawaddy nearly opposite to where the Chindwin joins it from the north.

The journey was one of the most unpleasant that we have ever made: the road was extremely dusty, it was very hot, and there were constant delays owing to the presence of roving parties of Nipponese. In the evening we arrived at the Brigade concentration area of Taungbe to the south of Myingyan. Oh, where was the shade of Ava? This part of the country, away from such towns as Myingyan, is bare, rocky and sparsely populated. A desert in an otherwise fertile land. From now on companies were going to look for two things when selecting their localities—shade and reasonably soft ground in which to dig. This was not always possible to find, and later as we became more and more tired I had to be most firm with company commanders, who on occasions were too easily tempted to sacrifice a tactical lay-out for these two considerations.

On the 28th the Brigade concentration was complete, and the same day the Dorsets returned through Myingyan, where a broken bridge over a wide, sandy chaung made mechanical-transport movement most difficult, and moved off through a battalion of the Madras Regiment to clear up some Nips on the east of the town.

The next day we carried out an attack on a suspected Japanese position on the high ground east of the village of Kyaukyan which turned out to be a T.E.W.J. The Japanese were now caught between the pincers formed by the 5th Brigade advancing from the west and the 4th Brigade bearing down on them from the east. On the 31st of March our carriers met a patrol from the 4th Brigade at Natyogyi and a column of the Madras Regiment advancing south from Myotha at the same place. The 2nd Division's task was virtually completed in this Myingyan area and we were ready to move farther on and take our part in the opening of the Kyaukpadaung Road to the south in conformity with the advance of the 7th Indan Division down the line of the River Irrawaddy on our right.

Meanwhile, at the highest levels great concern was felt over the problems of administration. Despite the opening of the river port of Monywa, which each day took a hundred and fifty tons of stores (floated down the Chindwin from Kalewa), the opening of Myingyan as a port by the 1st of April, and the fly-in of two thousand four hundred tons, the peak had been reached. Men and machines would not be able to maintain this astounding figure, and, furthermore, if we did not get to Rangoon before the monsoon, most of the airfields and all but the very few main roads would be put out of action. It was found necessary, in order to get the smallest possible force to Rangoon, to send another division back to India in addition to the 36th Indian Division, which, with its two white brigades, was being flown out anyway. The 2nd British Division, with its all-white cast, was the most difficult to maintain, and with great reluctance it was decided to return the Crossed Keys Division to India.

This decision did not at first affect the 4th and 5th Brigades, which were committed to road-clearing tasks, but on the 3rd of April the 6th Brigade and Divisional Headquarters started to fly out to the Calcutta area.

On the 2nd of April the Dorsets, once more in reserve, moved by mechanical transport from Kyaukyan through Myingyan and Taungtha to the Brigade concentration area at Wellaung, about thirty miles to the south. A few miles to the south the 2nd Reconnaissance Regiment made contact with the Japanese at Legyi.

We were now on the Myingyan—Kyaukpadaung Road, not a main axis, but owing to the reasonably good surface one that it was felt would stand up fairly well under monsoon conditions and would make a useful administrative axis for future operations; besides which the Japanese had decided to hold the Popa bastion about twenty-five miles farther to the south, with quite a formidable army. It was estimated that we had against us the remainder of the Twenty-Eighth Army Yamamoto Force which had been formed to push the IV Corps' bridgehead back into the Irrawaddy and had met with such signal ill-success. We reckoned to find in addition at least two battalions of the 112th Regiment of the 55th Division and elements of the 154th Regiment of the 54th Division, both from the Arakan. It was known that Headquarters of the 72nd Independent Motor Brigade (I.M.B.) were north of Kyaukpadaung, and their three motor battalions were milling around between us and the river. We also heard that at least one regiment (16th Regiment) of the Japanese 2nd Division had moved up from Rangoon and had become involved in the area. We had always wanted to have a smack at our opposite number. Later we encountered the 2nd Indian National Army Division, so altogether it was, we hoped, to be a battle of the "Twos". A year earlier the Saigon Radio had referred to the British 2nd Division at Kohima as "Churchill's Butchers", and we were very keen to test the mettle of the Japanese 2nd Division.

Wellaung was no place to stay in long. Our stomachs were quite loose enough already when, to our horror, we found that not only was water as scarce as hens' teeth, but what was available was permeated with a local variety of Epsom salts.

We were now on a road with milestones again. These were numbered in miles from Rangoon and so decreased as we advanced from MS429 at Wellaung and took over the next day from the Worcesters at MS417, which was one of the dreariest places we had yet encountered.

During the night large numbers of Indian National Army sepoys started coming over to us. These were a very different brand from the fanatics who had fought against us in the Tamu campaign a year before. To a large extent they were the Indian soldiers who had, despite the greatest pressure, remained loyal to the KingEmperor until advised by their officers to enlist in the Indian National Army in order to escape to the British and Indian forces at the first opportunity. They came over in large batches. It had not been easy to escape. The Japanese had an unpleasant habit of slashing with their swords the arms of those caught deserting. When we captured the 2nd Indian National Army Division headquarters at Popa and read their Part II orders (in English), the number of admissions to hospital with sword slashes showed clearly those who had been unfortunate enough to be discovered in the act of returning to their own side. These members of the Indian National Army seemed to be well fed and looked fit. They were dressed mainly in our own peace-time foreign-service kit of greyback shirts and khaki shorts and were well armed. The one thing my gunmen and certain of the company commanders yearned for was a tommy-gun. We had not been particularly fortunate with the old mark of Sten gun, with which we were armed. Here was a heaven-sent opportunity to equip ourselves, as we relieved these ex-sepoys of their weapons on their arrival at our outposts.

Five miles ahead of us the Camerons had bumped the Japanese at Legyi. An infantry attack supported by artillery, both field and medium, and an air strike had failed to dislodge the Nip, who was in a very strong rocky position astride the main road. Little or no support could be gained from the Grants of the 3rd Dragoon Guards owing to the nature of the ground. The Brigadier decided to try to work the Worcesters round the right flank and this was done when Tom Irvine moved right round the Japanese flank and took up an excellent position on his (the Nip's) left rear.

This "hook" having been successfully accomplished, Brigadier West then ordered me to lead my Battalion round through the Worcesters and try to get across the road at about MS414, one mile south of Legyi, and not only block the escape of the Japanese but also prevent him being relieved from the Popa area.

This all happened on the 4th of April, the anniversary of the crossing of the Brahmaputra, and by early in the afternoon we were in position. It never failed to amaze us that the Japanese allowed two battalions to pass in full view around his flanks. If there had been the slightest degree of co-operation or even communication between the Japanese main body and the Legyi garrison, I am sure we would have been counter-attacked. As it was, I was able to get the Battalion into an excellent position for a road block. "A" and "D" Companies were on either side of the road where it passed through a rocky defile, with "B" Company laid back on a rocky feature to the left on the east side of the road and "C" Company away to the right on a prominent feature about a thousand yards to the west.

Shortly after dark a Japanese convoy with lights on was seen coming down the road straight for our position. It drove right into the ambush and received a very rough reception. Unfortunately the tail vehicle escaped unscathed and its occupants broke away into the rough country on either side of the road. There followed one of the noisiest and most hectic nights we had yet had, reminiscent of the old Kohima days. This party of Japanese jittered us hard the whole night. We had learnt from experience to rely to a very great extent on grenades for night work, and we certainly got through a large number that night. To make the confusion even greater, the Japanese had some Indian National Army with them who were using British No. 36 grenades, and it was most difficult at times to discover who was throwing what and at whom.

At first light there was still a party of Japanese loose in the Battalion Headquarters area. These were driven into a culvert under the road. Their end was typical. We heard some orders being given, followed by a rustling of equipment. Obviously the commander, whom we subsequently found had been an officer, was giving orders for his party to commit hara-kiri by numbers, because even as we were closing on them five grenades went off and there were five fewer Japanese with whom to deal.

At dawn we were able to discover the success of our ambush. This had obviously been a convoy for Legyi with supplies and reinforcements, as the trucks were well loaded with food and clothing. Our bag was most satisfactory, and tired as we were after the night's fighting we felt greatly elated. Our elation was subsequently tempered that evening when the Japanese, having realized that we had got between them and Legyi, opened up with intensive artillery fire on the Battalion area. There was, after all, some method in the Japs' madness. They would let us arrive, move around, strip to bare buff, dig in, and congregate round the water truck and cookhouse area, and then open up suddenly from quickly alternative positions with their very mobile 75's and battalion guns. Happily our own casualties that night were light, though the sick rate was increasing.

The Japanese resistance in Legyi was most stubborn and it took the combined efforts of the Camerons and the Worcesters until the 9th of April before the position fell after an attack by the Camerons directed by their Second-in-Command, Major Allan Roy.

Meanwhile, we had been patrolling actively on the south and to the flanks, mopping up odd parties of Nipponese. One "C" Company patrol, under Lieutenant Gerry Overman, put up a particularly good show in the village of Gwedaukkon about three thousand yards to the south-west. Here they caught a Japanese company at breakfast in a pangyi kyaung and had a very gay five minutes with grenades and sub-machine guns, causing great execution with no loss to themselves.

It would repay us, whilst this long-drawn-out struggle at Legyi was taking place, to consider one or two special factors affecting this business of fighting in South-East Asia.

There are many schools of thought, from the "green hell" school of the British tabloid Press to the "at least the mud is warm" school of that famous Chindit leader Mike Calvert, the brother of our C.R.E.. In point of fact, our own war was run on very much the same lines as anyone else's. There were, however, some outstanding features.

The war against the Japanese in the East was run on a very much smaller scale as regards the actual combat than was the case in Europe.

With us it was essential for the section commander not only to lead his men but to possess that tactical knowledge necessary to enable him to operate on his own. General Nye, the ViceChief of the General Staff, when he visited us after the Irrawaddy crossing, emphasized this point. With us, he pointed out, it was necessary for all commanders down to the lance-corporal to be able to make an attack on his own, and not just follow the crowd, and in so doing they had a very much more interesting war.

The junior leader was not helped by the constant change in the terrain over which we were fighting. There were days in which we moved from jungle grass to bare rock and through thick trees and back to jungle grass all in one advance, and the junior leaders of the Battalion just had to keep their wits about them in order to cope with the possibilities of each situation as it arose, and further to try to anticipate just what their next move would be. It was not the sort of war in which the soldier and junior non-commissioned officer could, to quote General Festing, "wander along in a browned-off trance".

Climate and terrain did play a most enormous part in the campaigns in the East. To the British soldier bred and raised at home the wilder parts of Asia, in which we were fighting, must have appeared as one gross exaggeration after another. When he came to a hill it was a mountain; the sun was not just warm but extremely hot; and when the rains came they did not drizzle in the familiar fashion of a "storm" at home but poured down in torrents. As if this were not enough to wear down his morale, we were, through shortage of numbers, of necessity, made to spend very long periods "out of stable". In this theatre there was no rest area to which tired battalions could be sent: the Japanese were no respecters of reserve battalions in a brigade, and any unit, forward or back, usually the latter, was fair game to their jitter parties.

Reduced to the level of the private soldier, this meant that for months at a time he slept with his boots on and took his turn at "stag" nightly; turns which recurred only too frequently as one's strength decreased, with no prospect of reinforcements with which to step up numbers. One's commitments never decreased, I have remarked, only the number of bodies with which to fulfil them.

Finally, whilst on this subject of terrain, there was never any future in capturing a Burmese town. No bright lights, trams or even cinemas— just the never-ending tale of burnt-out bashas, wrecked cantonments and the inevitable coolie bibbies padding through the dust.

There was one saving grace: it was never really cold. We were often cold, especially at night, when, unable to carry extra clothing on our limited transport, and not always being able to bring up the blankets, we were faced with a drop of thirty degrees in temperature. But in consolation one always had the never-ending thrill of the Eastern dawn and the prospect of a warm, often too warm, day ahead.

By the time we reached the plains the hot weather was upon us and the days were really stoking up, especially in this plain around Legyi. For some weeks we had found that it was undesirable to fight after 1000 hrs., unless it was really necessary. We tried every possible way by which we could ferry the men's packs and save them the task of carrying them in the heat. This was not always possible, as during the long and hurried advance to Mandalay, but at this time we evolved a very sound drill by which we could dump our packs before an action, and collect them later. It was mainly owing to the heat that we disliked so much having to wait until the hottest part of the day for an air strike to be prepared in support of a ground attack.

The health of the Battalion was a factor which every commanding officer had to consider continually during this campaign. Whether fighting took place in the hills or in the plains, in the monsoon or through the hot weather, the slightest slackening of the Battalion's hygiene routine could result in the most disastrous consequences.

It was a serious problem and we (I write as a commander) were not helped in any way by what Kipling so adequately describes as the "innate perversity" of the British soldier. To Private Thomas Atkins the fly never meant a thing. If only the fly, Indian or Burman, had been equipped with a bullet which would inflict an immediate wound, I think that the soldier would have appreciated the danger. As it was, the fly was a delayed-action weapon, and what did it matter if tins were scattered around the area, or latrines were not filled in or, far worse, not used at all? It was so much easier to disappear behind a bush only a few yards short of the section latrine trench! One saw one's pals stricken with various tummy troubles and complaints, but that did not mean that oneself would meet the same fate.

No; this question of hygiene in the field, to which we pay a certain amount of lip service on training at home, was a most tremendous factor in the campaign in the East. We must have become fairly good at it, otherwise our casualties would have been very much greater. One would like to think that one's own battalion was entirely above reproach in this respect, but I would be the first to admit that it was not. The answer lies with the junior non-commissioned officer: he is the man living with his section; he, if no one else, is in a position to notice the man who slides off behind the nearest bush to perform his daily duty when an adequate ditch has been dug a few yards off. If a unit is new to war it won't have dug those ditches, as no one would have rubbed it in sufficiently that a latrine service for eight hundred men is something that requires a twenty-four-hour service, and that practically the very first hole to be dug must be the section latrine.

I will admit that in this Legyi area we were not helped by the natives. The lower class of Burman hereabouts was undoubtedly possessed of no moral scruples when it came to acquiring someone else's kit, be it British, Indian or Japanese. I had taken a pretty poor view of them when some native helped himself to my Bergen steelframed rucksack and my precious silver flask, laid temporarily aside whilst I was directing the final phase of the action at Ye-U. That was nothing to the natives of the Legyi area, who, after they had dug up our latrines and refuse pits, immediately on our departure, would pass on to our graves and disinter the bodies in order to steal the very blankets in which they were shrouded.

To rise to a higher plane, the one remaining outstanding factor of fighting in the East which the European-trained soldier would find strange was the shortage of mechanical transport and the variety of any other kinds of transport, coolie, bullock or mule, that one had to improvise in order to move at all. To North-West European ideas we must have seemed most primitive, with our nine jeeps and a handful of Dodges, backed up by "Tojo" and "Tokyo"—and our fighting echelon maintained on mules. But as far as I can see there is no system of roads in the East that would take transport on the European scale— we ought to know: we had a very good try at it in Assam, but had to give up—and I would only refer to a remark purported to have been made by a former officer of the Regiment, Major-General Dudley Ward, who, when commanding a division in the mountains of Italy, is supposed to have said, during a discussion on the possibilities of the latest mechanized and armoured units developed during the war: "The fastest thing between two points is still the infantryman on his feet."

One final point before I close this digression and return to the fortunes of the Fifty-Fourth. I cannot let this record pass without a mention of air supply. Although the planning and worries of supplying this huge army on this colossal front were conducted far from the infantryman in contact with the enemy, we all appreciated how completely reliant we were on air support.

General Browning, I have been told, for all his experience of airborne and air-transported operations in Europe, was amazed when he came out to South-East Asia, as Chief of Staff to the Supreme Commander, to realize to what great lengths air supply had been developed on the Fourteenth Army front.

This is not the time or place to quote masses of statistics. I have said enough to indicate how completely we relied on air supply during the three weeks we were cut off more or less from normal maintenance in the Kohima battle. Our advance through Burma, however fast we marched on our feet, could not have been achieved if those excellent Dakota and Commando pilots had not been right on our tails supplying us with our daily needs. The Air Transport Command had four hundred planes at their disposal. This figure was given to me in 1945 and varied considerably, but it is a good round number. They flew three or four sorties a day and could and did achieve a fly-in of over two thousand tons and eleven hundred personnel a day at peak periods.

To convert this to terms of sea lift, one has only to consider that the tonnage alone was a third of that achieved in the "Mulberry" harbour at Arromanches, as big as Dover Harbour, in its peak days. The figures for April, 1945, are worthy of record: during that month fifty-four thousand tons of stores were flown in, either dropped (six thousand) or air-landed (forty-eight thousand), and nearly twelve thousand personnel were flown in and ten thousand evacuated.

This does not begin to give an idea of the variety of stores and personnel and animals carried by this means. Mules, sick, reinforcements and even five-ton petrol locomotives to restart the Burma railway travelled by air. Perhaps the one thing that really brought home the value of air supply to the private soldier was that his mail arrived in his slit trench within five days from home. This was the best figure (eight to ten was the normal) and Monday's Daily Telegraph could be read in my command post on Friday evening, considerably ahead of the Calcutta Statesman and Times of India, and very often only a short time after the arrival of SEAC.

This quick turn-round of mail, because it worked both ways, had the most beneficial effect on the morale of the troops, and was, to their intense satisfaction, so out of all proportion to the enemy's mail services. The Japanese soldier, as we gathered from captured correspondence and notes in their diaries, had to wait for anything up to three years for a letter from home, and then was lucky to receive a postcard.

It took a few days to clear up in the area before we set off on the final stage of the advance to Mount Popa. Ahead of us in the glittering sunshine, rising sheer out of the plain, stood the immense Popa massif, which in turn ascended steeply in the east to the summit of Mount

Popa at five thousand feet above sea-level. Native reports claimed that the Japanese held the massif in strength and even had troops on the peak. We didn't mind about the peak, the home of the Hamadryad-worshipping natives and their repulsive reptiles, but if we were to open the road we must capture the massif.

Accordingly, on the 12th of April, after a couple of days' preliminary softening-up by the 498th Battery of the 134th Medium Regiment, R.A., we advanced on Kyauktaga. The three-mile advance deployed on either side of the road was tough going, but we reached this village, with its very prominent gilded pagoda, without incident. Having occupied the village, we started to climb the hill to the south, the first stage of the climb to the massif. As we left the village we could see, to our amazement, enemy positions. That the enemy were there was not unexpected; what did surprise us was that we could see the positions and we could also see enemy moving around. This looked altogether too unlike the Japanese, who seldom if ever moved around by day. There seemed to be something very familiar about the defences, and then we realized that they were Indian National Army positions dug in accordance with British teaching and by men trained under British ideas. All the mistakes which on training we so deplore from our own troops were obvious in these enemy positions, and for a moment it was difficult to realize that we were not on manoeuvres. Obvious as the defences were, the Indian National Army holding the forward positions did not give up without a fight. It was difficult for them, as a jemadar captured by "B" Company explained, to do so, as the Japanese before withdrawing to their main positions left enough Nips around to ensure that the Indian National Army did not come over to us without at least a show of resistance.

After a short but brisk fight we had occupied the positions and had reached the village of Gyaingwa at MS410½ when I called a halt for the day. The final advance and combat had been carried out in the pouring rain, a torrential storm having burst unexpectedly as we moved forward from Kyauktaga. We collected a most satisfactory number of Indian National Army and from them learnt a great deal of the intentions and plans of the Japanese.

We had now come up against the massif proper, which rose sheer eight hundred yards in front of us for about a thousand feet, and then flattened out into a plateau in the middle of which lay the villages of Popalong and Popa.

The next morning, the 13th, I was ordered to reconnoitre in force to find out whether the massif was occupied. Accordingly, "A" and

"C" Companies advanced and actually got elements to the top. The resistance, however, was strong, especially from the right. We tried to get a tank down the road with an infantry escort, but it was brewed-up on a mine and completely blocked the road. The Brigadier, realizing that we really had come up against a strong position, ordered me to withdraw my leading companies and the Worcesters moved forward across the main road under the massif.

We were now up against the toughest physical obstacle we had encountered since Kohima. The massif was the most wonderful natural position to defend, especially suited to the Nip, and we realized that we would have to call on every form of support that we could raise to break through at this point. A battalion of the Madras Regiment was placed under the command of the 5th Brigade, which stepped up our man power, whilst, unknown to the Nip, round his flanks and destined to advance up the road behind him from the south, was hurrying the 268th Indian Infantry Brigade.

There was a great deal of reconnoitring and patrolling required to fix the weak spots in the enemy's defences. With the men available to him, even allowing for the impregnability of the position, he could not hold everywhere. Local native reports were limited by the scarcity of the population and the doubtful value of the informers. We had a feeling that the very same natives who were carrying water for us were also slipping across the rocks and acting as bhistis to the Japanese. The 10th Field Regiment and the battery of mediums under command had a rare time plastering every likely and unlikely position. The mortars of the Brigade, grouped under Captain Potter of the Worcesters, also had some good shooting.

The Japs themselves were also far too active for our peace of mind. Never before had they been so active around our rear at nights. I feel that these parties which jittered the Brigade tail, even as far north as Brigade "B" Echelon in a nullah at MS418, were really lost bodies trying to find a way out. But in the forward positions parties of Japanese would descend from their rocks at night and raid us until they found that they were losing too many men. Their artillery continued to worry us. Night after night we would be strafed by 105's and 155's. Major "Legs" Lyon, who was commanding the 10th Field Regiment, acted as Brigade C.R.A., and his counter-battery shoots against the Jap gun positions were most accurate. Mere spotting, however, was not entirely successful, as we saw when we had opened the road. The Nips had got these huge guns away off the road up a steep and very narrow defile through the hills, and they were practically unassailable except from the air.

About the 18th of April I flew over the massif in an Auster observation-post plane, and was not much comforted by the prospect of having to attack over that ground.

It was about the night of the 18th or 19th that the enemy really gave us a pasting with their artillery, and Brigade Headquarters in Kyauktaga, along with "A" Company, were situated right in the beaten zone, but the casualties were surprisingly small.

Our preparations were nearing completion and we were due to make our attack on the 22nd of April, with the Dorsets leading, on the right, and the Camerons, echeloned back slightly, on the left.

The Brigadier went down with some form of fever on the 18th, but refused to be evacuated. That evening a strong air strike went in on all known and suspected enemy concentration areas. We had heard from a staff officer of the 7th Division who had flown over to us that the 268th Brigade were making good progress, and we hoped to meet them in Popa.

On the morning of the 20th our leading troops saw a Burman make his way down the main road from Popa. Could it be that the Japanese had "bargoed"? It was too good to be true.

This friendly Burman was brought to my headquarters and produced the following document, which I have treasured ever since. Written in pencil on a piece of rough paper was the following message (the spelling is his):

> To The Commonder in Chief
> Camp Kyauktaga side.
> Sir, I most respectfully report to you, all the japanese soldiers have ran away to Ywathit village and Letpanaing village side. They will run up to Yenangyaung no soldier at Popa hill your troops can come easily but all the roads have with explosive please take carre.
> yours faithfully
> HEADMAN AUNGH
>   Members U Khin Maung Yee
> We are wondering your troops to come.

The bearer of this note turned out, on questioning, to be the Headman of Popa, the Mayor of Popa as we called him, himself, all dressed up in his best shirt and lungyi for the occasion. I rushed him along to the Brigadier, who was on his bed of sickness, and requested permission to advance at once. Brigadier Michael West agreed as heartily as his temperature of a hundred and two degrees would allow, and I prepared to move immediately.

The Mayor of Popa's prognostications that we could come easily turned out to be a bit optimistic. The Japs had been pretty thorough in their preparation of road blocks and cratering, as well as the abundant use of "explosive", but I could get the foot soldiers along, and the 208th Field Company, assisted by my pioneers, in no time at all built some form of temporary bridges over the craters for the Carabiniers' tanks.

By that evening we had passed through the village of Popalong and were occupying the late 2nd Indian National Army Divisional Headquarters at Popa. A few minutes after our arrival at Popa a patrol of the Mahindra Dal Regiment from the 268th Brigade appeared from the south and the road was open. A most satisfactory ending to a battle in which the Brigade had accounted for two hundred counted enemy dead.

Popa lay in the middle of this very fertile plateau and it was like a scene from one of Ganpat's books to arrive suddenly on this strange plateau after the heat and dreariness of the plain below. Stretching above us rose the peak of Mount Popa where, it was said, the most strange rites were practised in the worship of the King Cobras.

The village itself was a shambles, as the last air strike had caused a great many casualties and dead bodies, mostly Indian National Army, lay everywhere.

We collected a great deal of material from the 2nd Indian National Army Division headquarters which we hoped was of value to the Intelligence boys and subsequent inquiries into the conduct of the Indian National Army.

Most of us remember Popa, not only for its strange name but because, our task completed, it was now our turn to fly out of Burma for a refit and temporary rest in India. The 4th Brigade had, after a final and successful ambush, started to fly out on about the 8th of April, and that the 6th Brigade and Divisional Headquarters were firm in the Calcutta area was shown by the receipt of an invitation from "C" Mess at Divisional Headquarters to a party at "The Green Shutters" in Calcutta, timed for the very day on which the Brigade attack on the massif should have been made.

We spent the 21st of April clearing up the village, patrolling and doing some good honest-to-God rubbernecking.

Before one could say "Popa" the "vultures" were upon us; everyone from the rear wanted to make up their spares in mechanical transport parts and tools. Brigadier Dyer, who quite justifiably reckoned that he had a lien on everything south of Popa and had less transport than anyone else, guarded his hoard most jealously, and the 268th Brigade had quite a job beating off unwelcome visitors. As for us, we could not care less, as in order to fly out we had to jettison all our transport, including our old friends "Tojo" and "Tokyo", which had lasted us out right to the end. What we did not want we bequeathed to the Madras battalion, who were very under strength in cars and vehicles of all kinds.

It was interesting to drive forward and try to find the Nip guns which had given us so much worry. Sure enough, there they were, up an incredible defile in positions which must have taxed the ingenuity and resources of their teams to the utmost to get them there at all, let alone fire them.

We climbed a pagoda set on one of those extraordinary pinnacle hill features which seem to abound in this area. My driver, right at the end of the tour through Burma, at last found, at Popa, a bucket seat for my jeep. Joe Turner was so pleased to find that for which he had spent a year searching that when I had to abandon my faithful jeep at Myingyan a few days later he carried this seat to the plane on his head and installed it in my new vehicle in Calcutta. That seat was still in my jeep when I left the Battalion in Japan eighteen months later, and very grateful I was for it during the many miles I covered in that time.

Our last act at Popa was to hold a memorial service in the banana grove to all those who had given their lives in this last campaign. It was a sad moment when I read the list of the thirtynine officers and men who would not return with us; but we left the battle at a time when we knew that our task was well on the way to completion, and we knew that their sacrifice had not been in vain. We were especially pleased to have the Brigadier read the lesson at this service. Though not fully recovered, he was his cheerful self again.

On the 23rd of April we set out on our long journey back to India. No one knew our destination and the most popular rumour held it to be Ranchi, the thought of which depressed us. We moved by mechanical transport to Myingyan and went into a staging camp near the airfield.

The next morning the Corps Commander came down to our bivouac to bid the Battalion farewell. We had had a long innings under General Stopford, from January, 1944, until now, and not a man in the Battalion but regretted passing from the command of such a great leader as "Sir Monty". The General complimented the Battalion on its performance in the past thirteen months, and we all climbed into our planes the next day feeling more than ever that we had achieved something worth while.

General Stopford's farewell visit and our fly-out the next day terminated thirteen months' campaigning in Assam and Burma. For over a year the Battalion had been fighting hard in what was one of the toughest quarters of the world. They had fought a long and continuous infantry battle against a very formidable enemy— and against him had advanced nearly seven hundred miles, mostly on foot, under all degrees of climate, weather, vegetation and ground.

The 5th Infantry Brigade had been the first brigade of the 2nd Infantry Division to arrive in the Dimapur area, the first to meet and inflict a defeat on the Japanese, and the last brigade of the Division to leave the theatre of operations.

If ever anyone sits down to write the story of the 5th Infantry Brigade, with its long and continuous career since the Napoleonic Wars, the deeds performed by the Worcesters, the Camerons and the Dorsets in those thirteen months must take a very honoured place in these annals. Kohima, Viswema, Maram, Tamu, the Mu, the Irrawaddy, Dirty Pagoda, Ava, Mandalay and Mount Popa will never be forgotten by those who made this long march and fought these battles.

The Brigade generally was by now very tired. We, in company with numerous other regiments, had proved conclusively that the white man could not only fight through the monsoon but also, as had our predecessors for two centuries, through the hot weather in the plains—but we also had learnt how exhausting this could be.

Despite the efforts of everyone to preserve our health, we were very run down; scratches developed, despite constant care, into septic sores which spread over our bodies, and the slightest malady was apt to raise a fever, and there is no doubt that we were ready for a rest, fattening-up and rehabilitation after the prolonged exertions of the past year.

The emplaning went off smoothly enough, except for a little trouble over the guns. The American pilots at that time were repatriated after six hundred flying hours, and if they could only achieve two or even three sorties a day in good weather they could very soon aggregate enough hours to get them back to the States. The prospect of a delay on the ground whilst our cannon were being loaded did not please them at all. Our men with three and a half years to serve abroad before "Python" would claim them took a poor view of this attitude. However, the gunners' professional pride overcame their prejudices and by showing the Americans that they could load their own guns in something under twenty minutes the pilots agreed to wait that long and honour was satisfied.

This was a 2nd Division move and therefore we could expect it to go smoothly however complicated the journey might be. This time we employed every means of travel: mechanical transport, rail, river boat,

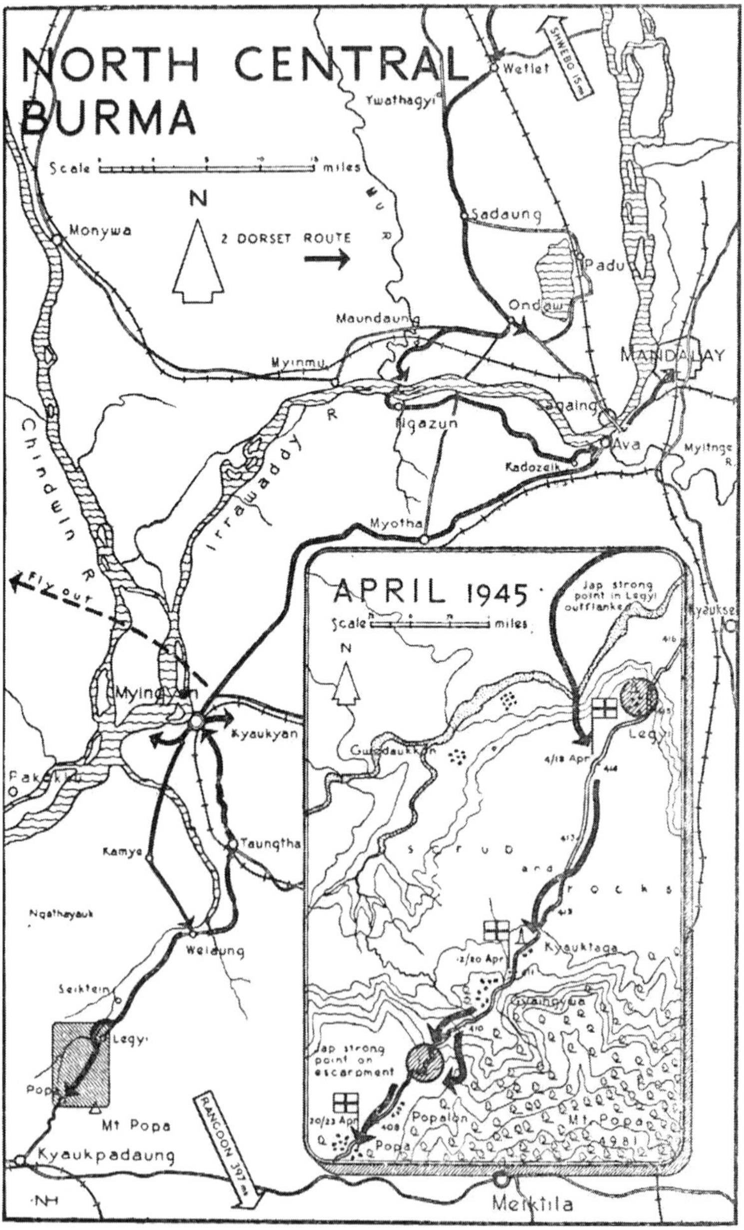

NORTH CENTRAL BURMA
Scale miles
N
2 DORSET ROUTE
Wetlet
SHWEBO 15 mls
Ywathagyi
Sadaung
Monywa
Padu
Ondaw
Maundaung
Myinmu
MANDALAY
Sagaing
Ngazun
Ava
Myitnge R
Kadozeik
Irrawaddy R
Chindwin R
Myotha
Fly out
APRIL 1945
Jap strong point in Legyi outflanked
Kyaukse
Myingyan
Kyaukyan
Legyi
4/18 Apr
Pakokku
Taungtha
Kamye
Ngathayauk
Welaung
Seiktein
Legyi
Popa
Mt Popa
Kyaukpadaung
RANGOON 397 mls
Kyauktaga
12/20 Apr
Jap strong point on escarpment
20/23 Apr
Popalon
Mt Popa
4981
Popa
Meiktila
NH

more rail and ending up on our feet. The whole way was made smooth for us. At Chittagong, in Bengal, where we deplaned, Colonel Mitford Slade, the late Second-in-Command of the 5th Brigade, had an efficient staging organization laid on and gave us a good welcome. Here we found Captain Teddy Edwards, our old Quartermaster, who was on his way home on "Python" and had delayed for a couple of days to travel out with his old battalion. Here also was Major Molyneux, who had been posted from the Battalion to a training job just before we went into action and who had had a number of adventures since. His sudden death a few weeks later came as a great shock to his many friends in the Regiment.

We were ordered to detrain on arrival at a place called Bandel just north of Calcutta. The 6th Infantry Brigade had completed their period of fattening-up and were off to join in the Rangoon operation. We were to go into their camp among the banana trees at Bandel for a similar period of rehabilitation before following up this brigade.

Bandel itself was a bit of a shock. Extremely hot and mosquitoridden, we all agreed that our predecessors of the 1st Battalion had the right ideas about the place. To quote Cannon in his Historical Records of the Thirty-Ninth, when writing about Clive's expedition to Bengal in 1757: "On the 12th January Captain Coote with fifty of the Thirty-Ninth and twice that number of Sepoys marched to Bandel, a large village three miles off, where they destroyed several granaries of rice..." We couldn't have agreed more, and on comparing distances, the Thirty-Ninth must have camped very near to the grove in which we found ourselves.

However, the warmth of our reception in every other respect more than made up for the discomfort and heat of Bandel. As we were to be fattened up for further use, no hindrance was put in our way in re-equipping ourselves. Commanders at all levels were insistent that we should relax and take full advantage of civilization. "Passion" trains were run to Calcutta, and liberal rations of beer and spirits were made available. We scored even further, because the 6th Infantry Brigade had had to move off without drinking all their share, a slowness of swallow for which the 5th Infantry Brigade very soon made amends.

General Leese laid on receptions for officers, warrant officers and sergeants and for the junior ranks. Our old friends of the West of England Society of India, finding that we were in the neighbourhood, laid on a special "char and wad" party for the West Countrymen of the Battalion, whilst the various members of the Society went to great trouble to entertain the officers and a number of other ranks. Limited leave of four to five days was opened for all, and we soon had parties in Calcutta and Darjeeling as well as at Puri by the sea.

With the fall of Rangoon at the end of May it became obvious that the 4th and 5th Brigades would not be immediately employed. In fact, until a very big reorganization had been carried out, we would not be employed at all. The Division had by now been abroad for over three years and well over half the men would be due for repatriation in October, and it seemed hardly feasible to launch them on another expedition which could not be ready for some months. Calcutta was altogether too hot, and by the end of May we were all satiated with the delights of civilization.

At the beginning of June the Division moved to the new allweather camp at Kamareddi, sixty miles north of Secunderabad, and settled down. As originally constructed in 1943, the camp may have been all-weather, but, having been unoccupied for two monsoons, it did not stand up very well to a third.

There followed a period of two or three months in which the men had the time of their lives, if playing games and doing little work can be so described, whilst the officers and non-commissioned officers were "milked" to find the masses of extra staff and extraregimentally employed personnel required to assist in the launching of the huge expedition against Malaya.

During this time I was at home,[18] having, in company with a number of other commanding officers and seconds-in-command of the Fourteenth Army, been flown to the United Kingdom on a lecture tour. Whilst at home I was able to visit the Infantry Training Centre and the 2nd Holding Battalion, which we shared throughout the war with the Royal Norfolk Regiment, and was able to give a first-hand account of what we had been doing during our wanderings abroad. It was a great opportunity to meet and thank personally all the people who had done so much in the past six months to help us. By good fortune I was able to be present at the presentation of the Freedom of Lyme Regis to the Regiment, when Captain Jock Wilson led the representative 2nd Battalion party. For the first time for over three years the crossed keys of the 2nd Division were seen on parade in England as these veterans of Burma marched through the streets of Lyme Regis and Dorchester in company with representatives of their brother battalions bearing the distinguished badges of the 43rd and 50th Divisions.

The news of the Japanese surrender came through whilst we were celebrating in Dorchester, and, anticipating a change of role for the Battalion, I hurriedly flew back to India.

---

18 Major Tony Bridge had rejoined the Battalion as Second-in-Command in May after serving for a year as Brigade Major of the 5th Infantry Brigade. He commanded the Battalion during my absence.

ADVANCE TO POPA
208 Field Company, R.E., clear the road for tanks of the Carabiniers

CHAPTER SIXTEEN

"THE KING IS DEAD. LONG LIVE THE KING!"

The Colonel an' the regiment an' all who've got to stay,
Gawd's mercy strike 'em gentle—Whoop! we're goin' 'ome today.
We're goin' 'ome, we're goin' 'ome,
Our ship is at the shore,
An' you must pack your 'aversack,
For we won't come back no more.

[RUDYARD KIPLING]

IT WAS GOOD TO SEE once again the familiar green sign and the white "61" with its crossed keys and Marabout Sphinx as I drove into Marabout Lines at Kamareddi exactly seventy hours after having left Dorset in a B.O.A.C. Sunderland flying-boat. There was Sergeant Fincham, as ever on duty, and Cripps sounding a routine call. Graeme Gordon Wright greeted me, and over a couple of pegs in the mess basha explained that I must not be surprised if a great number of familiar faces were missing. Owing to its very high proportion of personnel due for repatriation it had been found impossible to employ the 2nd Infantry Division on the projected invasion of Malaya. Obviously, however, the experience of those due for home was of great value in the launching of this the greatest of all armadas ever to sail from India. For this reason the Division had been milked of all its key personnel, leaving a bare sufficiency of officers and non-commissioned officers to administer the Divisional Cadre and train such reinforcements as had not been taken away to make up gaps in the operational battalions. How thorough this milking had been was immediately brought home to me when I discovered that even those three stalwarts my Quartermaster, Bert Smith, Joe Chamberlin (the doctor) and Gus Claxton (the Padre), who had been with us long enough to have become Battalion institutions, had been called away.

The Battalion, or what remained of them, were waxing fat on their enforced rest and were showing every sign of breaking out into that dread disease "scrubberitis", a disease then prevalent throughout the Army and most infectious among men just due for release or, if abroad, repatriation. Most battalions had their own names for those about to be discharged; our name, chosen by the men themselves at Kamareddi, was "scrubbers".

I find that I continue to employ a series of symbols, code names and abbreviations, though I have tried hard to overcome this. These must be confusing to the civilian reader, and if he loses himself in a maze of "Pythons", "Liaps" and "Lilops" I would ask him to consult the glossary at the end of this book.

The one never-ceasing topic of conversation in the Division since it had become obvious that we would not be operationally employed again was what were they going to do with us, and would those due for release and repatriation be home for Christmas, the first at home since 1941?

These questions were answered shortly after my return from the United Kingdom when, on the 10th of September, General Nicholson arrived back from Delhi with important news. That evening I was called to Brigade Headquarters and Brigadier Michael West gave me the most brief but exciting orders. The Brigade had been chosen to be the British brigade in the force being formed for the occupation of Japan. In order to make the Brigade as representative as possible of the United Kingdom, the 2nd Royal Welch Fusiliers from the 36th Division were to take the place of the 7th Worcesters, who, as a Territorial battalion, were expected to be sent home fairly soon. We were to wear Union Jacks on our arms, but keep the crossed keys up as well. We were to get a complete replacement of kit. I was to cast off all men due for "Python" and release up to and including Age and Service Group 26 (27 for officers), absorb a hundred and fifty reinforcements from the 7th Worcesters and another four hundred from the 10th Glosters in the 36th Division, move to a concentration area at Nasik, near Bombay, and be prepared to sail for Dai Nippon on the 20th of September—that is to say, in ten days' time. Any questions?

The following week was one of the most hectic and saddest I can recall—hectic because of all the sudden recruiting, casting off, reorganization and movement involved, and sad because of the imminent break-up of such a magnificent team. Perhaps after all it was better this way—prolonged farewells, especially with a large body of men, are never very satisfactory. Units of the 2nd Division could throw a pretty good party under any circumstances, and there was no end to the possibilities if the farewells became too protracted.

The next day the General explained what a great fight had been waged in Delhi to keep the 2nd Division alive at all, and how a compromise had been reached by the merger of the 2nd British and the 36th Indian Infantry Divisions. The latter, already well known to the reader of these lines, was, despite its name, as nearly all-white as the 2nd Division. The new Division, less the 5th Brigade, was to be employed, explained the General, in Malaya, with one brigade in Hong Kong, but meanwhile top priority in requirements for personnel, clothing and stores went to the Camerons and ourselves, as we had to be ready to sail from the country in ten days' time. No one at that conference could foresee that eventually both the 4th and 6th Brigades would be in Malaya four clear months before we even began to leave India!

The Divisional Commander explained that the actual selection of battalions to compose the new 2nd Infantry Division had depended to a great extent on the current reinforcement situation. However, I was given the hint, and this was subsequently confirmed later by General Slim himself, that the selection of the Fifty-Fourth for occupational duties in Japan was not entirely a question of record groups and reinforcements. The late Commander-in-Chief of the Fourteenth Army had especially asked that the Fifty-Fourth be included in the force to be sent to Japan on account of its record in the Burma campaign. With such a compliment to encourage us, those of the "new" Battalion set to with a will to rebuild the unit with a dire shortage of experienced officers and non-commissioned officers.

In the short time at our disposal we tried very hard to encourage as many as possible of the old Battalion to take advantage of the proffered opportunity of "taking on" for a limited period. However, we had been abroad too long and the calls of domesticity were too strong. If only we had been allowed, or it had been possible, to transport the Brigade to the United Kingdom, give them their "Python" leave and a chance to look around "Civvy Street" I have no doubt that a large number of key men of all ranks would have re-engaged on some short tour of duty in order not to miss this chance of a visit to Japan. I cannot speak too highly of those three hundred-odd officers and men of the Dorsets and the one hundred and fifty reinforcements of the Worcesters sent over by John Brierley, once more in command of his old battalion, in the manner in which they set about immediately to re-form the new Battalion from the old. A large proportion of the men were young reinforcements who had joined the Brigade after we had come out of battle and had already been pushed around quite a lot from one unit to another.

I was helped to a very great extent also by the determined efforts of the young officer reinforcements who, at a moment's notice, undertook tasks and responsibilities far above their ranks. It was obvious that we had a lot to learn from the moment that I had completed the unpleasant task of separating the old from the new. The clock had gone back three and a half years, and this new Battalion had to set about learning, just as their predecessors had, the art of living in an Indian camp. Fortunately, for a short time, we had a wealth of experience on which to draw, and these reinforcements had already had a month or two to accustom themselves to living in the East.

My office rapidly took on the form of an employment bureau for officers seeking jobs. I had been given carte blanche to make up any deficiencies I could from local resources and therein I was helped by Lieutenant-Colonel Tim Wilkins of the Norfolks, who unhesitatingly offered me the services of his reinforcement officers who had volunteered to come with me. In this manner John Archer, yet another Adjutant-to-be of the Fifty-Fourth, arrived in the Battalion just as we were falling in the new Battalion to have a look at ourselves before we marched away.

Saturday, the 15th of September, 1945,[19] the official date of the formation of Force 152 (Japanese Force) and the re-formation of , the 2nd Battalion The Dorsetshire Regiment, was for all of us one of the saddest experiences of our lives. It was the end of an epoch. Those of us who had come abroad together, had seen a lot and done great things, were at the parting of the ways and "The Colonel and the Regiment and those who've got to stay" had a busy time ahead of them if they were to build up the new Battalion to the high standards of the old.

That night I published the following Special Order of the Day:

---

19 On the 15th of September, 1945, the following officers who had embarked on the Reina del Pacifico in April, 1942, were still on the Battalion books, though only Captain Jones and myself continued the journey to Japan: Lieutenant-Colonel O. G. W. White, Majors A. V. N. Bridge, H. P. K. Fretts and C. Chettle, M.C., Captains R. D. Castle, N. Havers, J. G. Hodder, L. T. Highett, D. E. B. Harris and H. L. K. Jones, and the Medical Officer, Captain J. A. Chamberlin. The Padre, Major L. E. M. Claxton, was now at Divisional Headquarters, but we still considered him to be very much one of the family.

> *After six years of war and campaigning in Europe and Asia the 2nd Bn. The Dorsetshire Regiment has been reformed for special duties.*
> *Those who now leave the Battalion depart home with the best wishes and thanks of us all.*
> *From the initial actions in France, through Dunkirk, Kohima, Assam and Burma you have not only maintained but have enhanced the great name this Regiment holds in the British Army. It has been my great privilege to lead you in the field for over a year.*
> *No commander could have been more faithfully or enthusiastically served. I have had at times to call on you to undergo great trials and hardships—together we have undertaken the most formidable of tasks—but your indomitable spirit, unending energy and cheerfulness have always carried us to victory.*
> *You return home now with the feeling of a great job well accomplished and in going you take my earnest thanks and the very best wishes for the future from all who remain.*
> *If you tackle the future with the same energy and zeal and spirit and co-operation you have shown throughout the war, you will play an equally successful part in winning the peace.*
> *To those who remain and to all our reinforcements I would say that we have a very great task to perform.*
> *We have got to re-form and maintain in peace the very high standard handed on to us by those now going home.*
> *To those departing 'Good luck and God-speed.' "To those remaining, 'On, on, 2 Dorset.'*

On reading this order through as I write these lines I notice that no mention is made of our future role. Of course we were much too near to the end of the war for any movement of troops to be other than "Secret," and even the force which we were joining was disguised as Force 152 and the code word to cover our movements (though we were never quite certain from whom) was "Ribbon".

I did not accompany the Battalion on their railway journey on the Nizam's "Emmetlike" small-gauge train, but drove by jeep nearly four hundred and fifty miles in one day to visit the 10th Glosters at our old original camp at Pashan, near Poona, now developed out of all recognition. The Glosters, I found, not unnaturally, to be very sad at their imminent disbandment. In their short life, this war-time battalion had had a varied and distinguished career. I was, however, most cheered by the impressive selection of officers, warrant officers and non-commissioned officers who Lieutenant-Colonel Britten told me were available for transfer. By the nature of things mostly young, and mainly lacking in experience, they all seemed most keen. The Glosters had had the opportunity of grooming their junior ranks for stardom by running various courses, and how well these reinforcements from the 10th Glosters did in their new home will be related in future chapters. The officers were an especially strong team, all of whom were to distinguish themselves in one way or another in the course of the next eighteen months.

I eventually arrived at Satpur to find the Battalion just moving in, and any elation I may have carried away with me from Poona if not already dissipated by an eight-hour journey in the pouring rain was completely swept away by the first impressions of Satpur Camp. Erected earlier in the war, on the inevitable cotton soil, some miles from the nearest cantonment of Deolali, this camp had been used as a transit camp for over three years. No one unit had ever remained long enough to implement really vital repairs, and it was virtually worn out. Arriving as we did in the monsoon, we found the domestic services to be quite literally flooded out.

We were now at Nasik and it was only two days before our scheduled time to leave the country. The 5th Brigade were complete—that is to say, they had a headquarters and three very reinforced and under-staffed battalions, but precious little G1098 equipment and clothing. It took us all the next forty-eight hours to locate Force Headquarters, which had not yet formed. General D. Tennant Cowan, C.B., C.B.E., D.S.O., M.C., our G.O.C., was, we gathered, still in New Delhi struggling to get us organized and equipped. The battalions of the 268th Indian Infantry Brigade (our old companion formation from Burma, with once again a complete change of complement) were arriving from the North-West Frontier, Burma and Italy.

As the rain poured down, this latest edition of the 2nd Battalion The Dorsetshire Regiment, feeling suddenly very new and inexperienced, set to with an energy and a will, inherited from its predecessor, to master the art of living in a war-time camp in India, and to prepare itself for further adventures.

Dorset Memorial, St. John's Church, Calcutta

The end of the road.

CHAPTER SEVENTEEN

"TIME MEANS NOTHING IN THE ORIENT"

He had forty-two boxes, all carefully packed,
With his name painted clearly on each:
But, since he omitted to mention the fact,
They were all left behind on the beach.

[LEWIS CARROLL]

THROUGHOUT THE REMAINDER of September and well into October, 1945, we continued to work at ever-increasing pressure. "Latrineograms," the name peculiar to the 5th Infantry Brigade for the "bush telegraph", or, in other words, the constant and unvarying rumours always circulating among the men, assured us that "there was a boat in Bombay" ready to take us away. I well remember, even as late as the first week in October, shopping for the Battalion in Bombay and insisting that Messrs. Thackers complete our order for visiting cards, note-paper and Christmas cards by the 10th of the month. At the same time, I had to decide whether or not to have the word "Japan" printed on the Christmas cards, so optimistic were we that we would be in residence in Nippon at that season of the year.

However, we were soon to lose our priority: the shipping claims at the time were tremendous—repatriation of prisoners of war and internees who had been in Japanese hands, dispatch of the soldiers due for "Python" and release, the outbreak of Oriental awfulness in Indonesia all claimed far more attention than the dispatch of a purely token force to represent the British and Indian Forces in conquered Japan. The very international composition of the British Commonwealth Occupational Force (hence to be referred to as B.C.O.F.) itself, with its unusual set-up of one brigade each from the British, Indian, Australian and New Zealand Forces, its Royal Navy and Royal and Dominion Air Force elements, its British and Indian divisional headquarters, two independent Dominion brigade headquarters and an unwieldy Force Headquarters balanced precariously at the head, all required a great deal more mounting than had originally been anticipated.

Meanwhile, at Satpur Camp we had our hands full re-forming the 2nd Battalion The Dorsetshire Regiment. Within a very short time the dreaded cry of "Release" and "Repatriation" was once more to be heard ringing through the Battalion and company offices. So great was the turn-over in personnel at this time that during the seven months we were to remain in Satpur my Quartermaster equipped over eighteen hundred men—that is, well over two hundred per cent.—and, mark you, we were a picked force with a high priority.[20] This, however, was a state of affairs common throughout the Services at the time, and I will make no further reference to it, but before going on I must pay tribute to the great help and interest devoted to the personnel affairs of the 5th Infantry Brigade by Lieutenant-Colonel Sam Key and his staff at New Delhi. We must have been only one of their many headaches, but we can never be too grateful for the great help and personal interest they gave to our many problems.

By the middle of October it became pretty obvious that we would be celebrating the first peace-time Sarah Sands Day on the 11th of November in India. I therefore determined that the new Battalion would appear on show for the first time on that occasion. We had already begun drilling hard. Once again we were able to prove the efficacy of ceremonial drill as a first-class welding material. In working the Battalion up to a very ambitious ceremonial parade standard I was assisted to a very great degree by Captain Tony Cross, an ex-Guardsman who assumed the duties of Drill Adjutant and Officer in charge of the Drums. Twice a week I held a Commanding Officer's parade and in a very short time it became obvious that the Battalion would be able to take its place on the plaza of the Imperial Palace in Tokyo and give a good account of itself.

---

20 To give a further idea of the run-down at this time:
    a. The hundred-odd Regular soldiers who had fought throughout the Burma War with us had dwindled to a mere handful.
    b. On a check in December, 1945, I found that I could muster four officers and one hundred and thirty-eight other ranks who had fought with the Battalion in Burma. The total number of all ranks with any campaign experience at all was three hundred and sixteen.
    c. By the time we trooped the Colour in Tokyo in June, 1946, the Kohima veterans had dwindled to a mere twenty and all ranks with war medals were getting equally scarce.
    d. When the last of the Burma Star men left with me in November, 1946, the average age of the officers I left behind, including those on long home leave and extra-regimentally employed, was down to 22½ years.

The re-formation of the Corps of Drums was a miracle in itself. On the 15th of September, when we left Kamareddi, we could muster but one so-called "drummer", who could just sound "Defaulters" on a dance-band trumpet with the music attached. By the 10th of November we had a complete Corps of Drums, who even if they not mastered the "twiddly bits" in the Regimental March, "The Maid of Glenconnel," at least played throughout the parade and marched us past nobly to "The Farmer's Boy".

The Drum-Major was discovered in "A" Company's cookhouse, where Private Stanley was doing the duties of permanent mess orderly. He had, it was discovered, been in a Boys' Brigade band for many a long year. Throughout the Battalion musicians came forward: Pope, a first-class bugler and a versatile instrumentalist, Westlake, who was later to take over Drum-Major, and Knight, the leading "tipper" deserve mention. I am afraid that the Corps of Drums became a very special body of men with privileges far above their rights, but my generosity in this respect, irritating as it must have been to a succession of Company Sergeant-Majors of H.Q. Company, paid a great dividend in the ensuing months. As I had hoped, the Drums flourished and waxed strong on encouragement and by the time we reached Japan they and their by-product the Dance Band were our great show pieces.

Leaving the Battalion for a moment drilling on the square, and the officers being put through their paces in an attempt to reduce to some uniformity the thirty-odd variations of the military salute then current among them, we will take a quick look round this force assembling for duty in Japan.

Here in the Nasik area Force 152 was gathered together in rather an "Alice in Wonderland" manner. We were never to be entirely divorced from this Lewis Carroll atmosphere, which tended to increase rather than decrease the farther east we moved.

The 5th Infantry Brigade was the only formation which had any real background as such. With the exception of the Royal Welch Fusiliers the Brigade Group had fought together since 1940 and we had been from time to time associated with this battalion of the Royal Welch in our combined-operation days. This family feeling continued even after the departure of Brigadier West, as his successor was Brigadier Jock McNaught, already familiar to the reader as a one-time Commanding Officer of the Fifty-Fourth.

The Indian Brigade, however, had no such background. They bore the number of that famous formation, which under Brigadier (now Major-General) Dyer had fought throughout the Burma campaign with us from Kohima to Popa. Their new commander, however, Brigadier K. S. Thimayya, D.S.O., elected to cut loose from any such association as the number of the Brigade implied, and started afresh with the 5th/1st Punjab Regiment from the Arakan, the 2nd/5th Royal Gurkha Rifles from Central Burma, and the 1st/5th Mahratta Light Infantry from Italy.

At this time the Indian Brigade had no worries about release and repatriation, and with their great wealth of old soldiers settled down far quicker than the British Brigade to the business of peace-time soldiering. They were, of course, greatly assisted in this task by having their Colours, drums, a certain amount of full dress, and their mess silver laid up in store within the country.

"Brindjap", as Force 152 was beginning to call itself, was scattered in three widely dispersed camps. At Wadholi, General Cowan was collecting together his headquarters and special units and services which we were to take with us. General Cowan himself was a famous commander of the Burma War. He had not only fought his division (17th Indian Infantry) out of Burma in 1942 but had spent the next three years fighting the Japanese inside Burma, and, finally, in 1945, had led the "Black Cats" back in triumph to the very place from which they had set out on their withdrawal, over three years before.

Most of the Divisional Headquarters staff came from other theatres—Europe, Italy and India—but one or two, like Dennis Calvert, the C.R.E., had been with the 2nd Infantry Division, and Dicky Willans, the C.R.I.A.S.C., had served in that capacity with General Festing's 36th Indian Infantry Division, now amalgamated with the 2nd Infantry Division.

A special feature of this Force was the large number of women's services that were to accompany us to distant Nippon. These ladies were assembled from all over the world. Many of them had seen active service: W.A.S.B.) from Burma, F.A.N.Y. from India and the United Kingdom, and a small but energetic team of W.V.S. (United Kingdom) from home; to be joined later by, confusingly enough, a team of W.V.S.(I.) recruited from India. In addition there were the nursing sisters of the Q.A.I.M.N.S. and a strong representative party of Y.W.C.A. and S.S.A.F.A. We will meet these gallant and hard-working ladies throughout our story, but I mention them here to give the reader some idea of the complex nature of the Force being assembled to move to Japan.

The departure, at sudden notice, of Brigadier Michael West, just as we were beginning to stand on our very much re-formed feet, was a serious blow to the 5th Infantry Brigade. From the day that he had taken over command of the Brigade during the Kohima battle, his energy, enthusiasm and cheerful spirit had permeated all ranks. For nearly eighteen months he had been our constant inspiration, and his tenure of command must rank very high in that list of distinguished officers who have, during the past century or so, led the 5th Infantry Brigade of the British Army against the enemy.

Our feeling of loss was to a great extent tempered by the return of Brigadier Jock McNaught to command the Brigade. He had with this appointment made the complete round of the Division, having commanded the 4th Infantry Brigade in action and subsequently the 6th Infantry Brigade in the occupation of Burma after the cessation of hostilities.

General Cowan was most insistent that as full as possible a programme of sports be inaugurated, and by the end of November the Battalion had won the Force football competition by defeating the Camerons after what surely must have been one of the best and most exciting matches in this eight-year-long series of "local Derbies". It was only a fortunate goal in the last minute which saved both Commanding Officers from biting their nails down to the quicks. In the sporting and social world we were greatly helped by the enthusiasm for equitation of the local Indian Mountain Artillery Regiment. Major Colin Kennedy, one of the battery commanders, not only organized weekly drag meets and point-to-point meetings but also undertook the instruction of my officers in equitation. Those of us who took advantage of this excellent offer of horses had a very pleasant winter's riding.

At the end of October the "Relpats" went home: we had all expected that the new Battalion would be the first to move, but as it turned out the old hands were celebrating Christmas at home whilst we were still in Nasik.

The Fifty-Fourth took the lead from the beginning in the social whirl of Brindjap. We opened the season with a cocktail party on the morning of Sunday, the 3rd of November, to which we invited the ladies of the First Aid Nursing Yeomanry and the Women's Voluntary Service (United Kingdom).

This was followed the next Saturday by Sarah Sands Day. At 0900 hrs. we led off with a full-blown ceremonial parade. The setting was good. Our indefatigable Pioneer Officer, Lieutenant Quantrill, had erected a "shamiana" on the football pitch covered with the flags of all nations, and before representatives of the whole Division and a very strong concourse of local commanders and their wives we welcomed General Cowan to the eighty-eighth anniversary of the conflagration on board the troopship Sarah Sands.[21] The ceremonial parade went off extremely well: we fired a feu de joie and advanced in review order as to the manner born; this was followed by a march past in column and a return in close column. Later in the day the soldiers laid on an excellent "paghal" gymkhana, followed by the first post-war Sergeants' Mess dance, held by kind permission of the committee in the clubhouse of the Royal West of India Golf Club at Nasik.

Shortly after Sarah Sands Day the Mahrattas, who had attended the parade in force, invited us to take part in a reunion in their lines. For most of the two hundred-odd officers and other ranks who made the trip to Mashrul this was the first occasion on which they had witnessed a display on the Malkamb pole and had seen a Legim dance. Altogether, Derek Leeming and his officers ensured, by their hospitality, the continuance of the very strong feeling of fellowship between the Mahrattas and ourselves.

During the remainder of November the Brigade practised for the Brigade ceremonial parade at which we were to receive the Commander-in-Chief of India prior to our departure. Towards the end of the month I considered that it was high time to take the Battalion out on some training, and as a result we had a very enjoyable five days up in the ghats near Lake Arthur Hill, a most healthy and invigorating spot about fifty miles from the camp.

At Christmas General Cowan decided to go flat out to produce a whole week or more of entertainment for all ranks, and this festive season was more than adequately sealed by the Camerons' Hogmanay dance.

Everyone at the turn of the year, despite the current activities and our taking full advantage of vacancies in leave centres at Juhu, near Bombay, was getting rather fed up with Nasik. About the middle of January the Commander-in-Chief, General Sir Claude Auchinleck, arrived and after inspecting the Brigade on a ceremonial parade presented us with a flag to take to Japan, and we all felt that it was time we left.

Originally we had been ordered to be part of the first flight to land in Japan. However, the number of the various ships detailed for this task diminished daily, and in the end we had to give best to the

---

21 1857. En route to India in November, 1857, the troopship Sarah Sands caught fire. Mainly owing to the discipline and courage of all ranks of the 54th Regiment on board, the ship was kept afloat and after a perilous voyage of eight hundred miles brought safely to Mauritius. The traditional feature of Sarah Sands Day celebrations in the Fifty-Fourth is the Sergeants' Ball.

Camerons, who, being fully equipped with bagpipes, were in a better position to make the most appropriate martial noises on landing and we were destined to travel by two ships.

The first flight left at the end of March, travelling in the *Arundel Castle*. The second flight followed at the beginning of April in the *Cheshire*.

Before we left India, however, we sent a strong team of Burma veterans to Calcutta to attend the dedication by Archdeacon Tucker of our War Memorial in St. John's Church (see Appendix "D"). I was personally most sorry to miss this ceremony, as I was laid low in hospital at the time.

After the departure of the first sea echelon we found ourselves high and dry in Satpur, and I appealed immediately to the kindness of Brigadier Mould to allow us to move into the comparative comfort of an empty wing of the Homeward Bound Trooping Depot at Deolali. I very nearly, in my anxiety to reach Japan, fell into the trap of accepting passage on the Rajula. Luckily I was warned in time against such a move. However short of shipping we may be, it seems criminal that boats in as poor condition as the Rajula are allowed to roam the high seas carrying soldiers of any nationality. I was horrified to hear that a year later she was still in commission as a trooper and had turned up at Kure to evacuate the 5th Infantry Brigade from Japan.

On the 4th of April, 1946, the Battalion slid down the ghats from Deolali and on one of the hottest afternoons I can remember embarked in Bombay harbour on the Cheshire (Master, Captain Brooks). We sailed the next day, with the Corps of Drums playing us out of Bombay harbour, past the Gateway of India, and saw for ourselves what for many people is the best sight in the world— Bombay from the stern of a steamer moving out to sea! This, however, was no homeward-bound trooper, and within a very short time we had looked in at Colombo and were on our way to Singapore. At Singapore the 2nd Infantry Division had made a great "bundobast" for our reception. For various reasons, however, we were not allowed ashore and so General Arkwright, who had succeeded General Nicholson, came to visit us as we lay in the roads. From Singapore onwards we were making Regimental history, as no battalion of the Dorsets had ever yet penetrated these seas and to us was given the opportunity, with the Camerons and the Royal Welch Fusiliers, of being the first and so far only British battalions to sail to Japan.

Our first view of Dai Nippon was one of great relief and thanks —thanks for the atom bomb. This may sound a very narrowminded view, and those of us on board who had fought the Japanese in Burma may at some future date have cause to eat our words. However, at the time, I say, our feelings were one of immense relief. Remember, it would probably have fallen to the lot of many of us on that ship to have made an assault landing somewhere on the Japanese coast. We had trained hard over the coastline of India in an assault role, and I have in the past few months visited and studied the assault landings in Normandy, and nowhere have I seen such a naturally impregnable defence line as that presented by the island-studded, rocky coast of Japan. Every island was a potential bunker, and the Creator, in an outburst of tactical enthusiasm, must have designed each island to be mutually supporting, standing out as sentry posts before the even more formidable coastlines of the larger islands. No; whatever else one may feel about the atom bomb and its potential horrors, we all felt, as we approached Nippon, that the timely destruction of two Japanese cities saved at least a million Allied casualties.

We halted, or whatever a ship does, for the night half-way up the Inland Sea and took on a Nip pilot. There he was again, the old familiar buck-toothed, scruffily dressed, sawn-off, little runt, wearing the same old rubber-soled canvas shoes with one large split for his splayed big toe. So familiar were we to find the appearance of Japanese in the cast-off form of military dress which passed for plain clothes in their own land, that it took quite some time for us to overcome the immediate reaction to shoot them on sight. The Inland Sea was still pretty heavily mined, and, although Captain Brooks had already made the trip once, when taking out the advanced party, he was not yet prepared to make the trip in the dark.

Early on the morning of St. George's Day, the 23rd of April, the Cheshire crept forward through the Inland Sea, passing on the way many signs of the destruction of the Japanese Navy, and at 0930 hrs. we came to anchor off the very battered harbour of Kure. Kure is the Japanese equivalent of our Portsmouth, their greatest naval centre and as such had been most effectively flattened by the United States air forces.

The Battalion disembarked the next afternoon, in the pouring rain, which deprived us of our chance of marching ashore with drums beating and colours flying—a ceremonial to which we had given much time and effort in the way of drills and rehearsals during the voyage. Commander John Hamilton, of H.M.S. Glenairn, was one of the first callers. A brother of Lieutenant-Colonel "Lucius" Hamilton of the Regiment, he took an active interest in helping us on our way through Kure. Unfortunately, we ourselves were to see but little of this cheerful and hospitable ship's company and their ever-helpful Captain, Captain John Grindle, R.N., to whom all units in B.C.O.F. were in some way or another to become indebted.

The long wait was over and here at last the Fifty-Fourth had arrived in this far-off land, whose inhabitants, with their strange customs and manners, were to be our main interest for the next twelve months.

A "Basha" camp.

"TIME MEANS NOTHING IN THE ORIENT"

BRINDJAP FORMS—NASIK, 1945

Major-General D. Tennant Cowan, C.B., C.B.E., D.S.O., M.C., Commander, British and Indian Division

5th Infantry Brigade, October, 1945. Commander, Brigadier R. S. McNaught, Lieut.-Colonel M. H. ap Rhys Pryce, Commanding 2nd R.W.F., Lieut.-Colonel O. G. W. White and Lieut.Colonel A. J. J. Somerville McAlester.

Two Divisional Commanders: Major-General D. Tennant Cowan discusses with Major-General J. M. L. Grover, Director of A.W.S., Nasik, October, 1945.

TWO GENERAL INSPECTIONS

Return of the Colours. Flown out from England, the Colours marched past Lieut.-General J. Northcott, G.O.C.-in-C., B.C.O.F., Nasik, January, 1946.

Farewell visit of the Commander-in-Chief. General Sir Claude Auchinleck presents M.C. to Capt. H. F. Wetherbee, earned with 5th Dorset in Normandy.

CHAPTER EIGHTEEN

"ARRIVAL AMONG THE NIPS"

"It'll be all right, old boy, when our stores are deployed"

["Brindiv" cry]

WE NONE OF US had been frightfully clear, up to the time of embarkation in India, as to our exact destination in Japan. Even that usually most sound of all authorities, the Commanding Officer's batman, was at a loss to be able to anticipate with his usual accuracy the future home of the Battalion. Betting had swung away from Tokyo but was in favour of the atom-bombed port of Hiroshima. This rumour had gained even greater credence when it transpired that the various sea and air advance parties had fetched up at somewhere called Hiro, actually quite a different place but similarly enough named to cause confusion.

The truth was that we had, as we were soon to find out, as yet no permanent home. The arrival of the British Commonwealth Force in bits and pieces had caused a great deal of regrouping of the American forces, but the whole question of accommodation was causing such a terrific headache to the authorities that no firm arrangement could be made for some time after our arrival. It would be a month or two at least before the British Commonwealth forces could take over entirely their allotted portion of the country which covered the western end of Honshu (the largest of the Japanese islands) and the island of Shikoku to the south, across the Inland Sea. Meanwhile, my leading echelon had been dispatched to the north coast of Honshu and thither we followed them. The game I found the Brigadier playing hard was to fulfil all his commitments and moves without causing his battalions to make any change of station more than was absolutely necessary. Not an easy game at any time, but harder still with Brindiv stretched out between Honshu in Japan and the Bombay Presidency in India. Furthermore, it was imperative, for reasons I shall explain later, that the Division should settle into its permanent quarters just as soon as possible.

Meanwhile, the position as I found it on arrival in Kure was this. Brigade Headquarters and the Camerons were in Hiro, a suburb of Kure, just over the hill, not very far on the map but owing to the state of the road nearly thirty minutes by jeep. With them were Divisional Headquarters and most of those Divisional troops which had arrived already. The Royal Welch were on Eta Jima Island, just off Kure harbour. We were to be deployed a hundred miles away on the north coast of Honshu on an eighty-mile front (four hours by train) between Matsue and Hamada. This lay-out, so the Brigadier explained to me, was a purely temporary arrangement, dependent on the future deployment of the American occupation forces and the estimated time of concentration of the remainder of Brindiv. Eventually the 5th Infantry Brigade would take themselves off to Shikoku Island, the 268th Brigade would take over the colder north coast of Honshu, the Australians would assume responsibility for the Kure—Hiro—Hiroshima area, and Divisional Headquarters and the remainder of Brindiv would take one pace (of a hundred miles or so) right close and set up shop in the Okayama area. To complete the rather "Alice in Wonderland" picture, British Commonwealth Headquarters would take themselves to Eta Jima Island in the middle of the Inland Sea. The only people who didn't appear to be joining in this game of general post to any large extent were the New Zealanders, who had found themselves a corner of Honshu and were settling down very nicely.

Unfortunately, decisions as to moves and future deployment of the Force were subject to constant revision, and our leading echelon had already started off with great energy to settle themselves in to Matsue before they were told, a couple of days before the arrival of the main body, that this was not going to be their permanent home at all. Inevitable as this was, it didn't please them much to realize that we were once more playing the old Indian game of preparing a camp for someone else.

I had no sooner stepped ashore for a conference at Brigade Headquarters, whilst the Cheshire was still in mid-stream, than I heard various new cries such as "S.C.A.P. Directives" and "Pre-emption" for the first time, and so before moving off to join the advanced echelon at Matsue it would be well to give the reader a quick run through the general set-up in Japan as it affected the Battalion newly arrived to take part in the occupation of Nippon and the regeneration of the Japanese.

S.C.A.P., or the Supreme Commander, Allied Powers, was none other than General of the Army Douglas MacArthur, who ruled Japan from Tokyo. By the terms of the Potsdam Treaty, the Americans were allocated Japan as their sphere of influence. They controlled the whole country, and, as we were to discover later, the British Commonwealth did not even have a zone in Tokyo, such as was the case in Berlin. There is no comparison between the two occupations, and probably if that fact had been more firmly fixed in our heads at the outset there would have been far less heart-burning and cause for dissatisfaction between the British Commonwealth and the American forces. The decision to allow the Americans a free run in Japan had been made at the very highest level on the Churchill-Truman-Stalin "net" at Potsdam, and there was nothing that the mere soldier could do about it.

General MacArthur ruled the country through a series of directives—directed for the control and reorganization not only of the Japanese themselves but also of the Allied forces. That we had arrived six or seven months too late was unfortunate; but again that decision must have been made at the highest level. In those first six months the United States Eighth Army, which had fought its way right through the Pacific islands to Japan, had had the run of the country and from all accounts a very nice run too. It was not until the spring of 1946 that the American G.H.Q. (S.C.A.P.) in Tokyo really got around to tidying up and regularizing the practices of their army of occupation. To us their idea appeared to be: "Now, boys, you've had time to get settled in comfortably and have grabbed all the swords you want, let's get settled down. In order to see how much the Japanese will be allowed to deduct from their reparations, all requisitions must be regularized and in future there will be no 'pre-emption'." "Pre-emption" is an awful word and one which I confess I had never previously come across. Pre-emption, I soon learnt, was the act of grabbing something which you wanted, such as a building for a cookhouse, a horse for parade or an electriclight bulb—in fact, anything which one's own army had failed to provide and which during a campaign one would have taken as a matter of course. The theory of "pre-empting", I gathered, was to demand what one required, and after submitting masses of forms the article was duly requisitioned and the whole deal thereby regularized. All very fair and understandable—unfortunately, there is something about filling in a form which imposes instant delay—and the immediate effect of the S.C.A.P. directive regarding pre-emption was that there was a delay of at least eight weeks on anything one required for use at once.

Another S.C.A.P. directive which was published on the day we landed was that all timber would be "frozen" from the 1st of June. The idea was that the occupational forces should by now have completed all their building requirements, and it was necessary to "freeze" the timber in order to discover just how much was left to allow the natives to start their own reconstruction.

It was most unfortunate that the publication of these two directives so closely coincided with the arrival of the British forces. The Americans may have been well settled in, but we certainly were not, and it did nothing to enhance the relationships between our men and our allies to see the Americans well set up and materials going to the Japanese whilst we lived in the greatest discomfort.

None of us had ever served with the Americans before and were as yet unadapted to the feeling of "poor relation" when the obvious differences in social amenities were encountered by our soldiers for the first time.

That our subsequent relations with the soldiers of the United States in Tokyo were so good was entirely due to the excellent spirit of co-operation between all officers at battalion-brigade-divisional level and the common sense of the British other rank and American enlisted man. There was little else in the initial set-up, we found on landing, to encourage a feeling of amity and comradeship between the two armies.

It would be best to draw a veil over the first day ashore in Japan. The torrential rain increased to monsoon force as the Battalion moved to the blitzed station some two miles from the quayside. The hollowness in our stomachs increased as the hours went by, and the prospects of the cooks making any form of hot meal became dimmer and dimmer as the rain flooded the station platform. It was, it will be admitted, very early days for an integrated headquarters to be functioning well at all levels, but the Movement Control officials appeared to be notable only by their absence at the more critical stages of the proceedings. Finally the Japanese hereabouts appeared to be not only lazy but insolent until the older warrant officers and non-commissioned officers started to work on them.

Finally, there was the Japanese train! Fundamentally, of course, there was simply nothing one could do about it, because the Nip train, like their houses and latrines, is built for this race of midgets. Obviously a six-foot-odd Englishman can never achieve the slightest degree of comfort over a long period on a hard seat designed for a five-foot Japanese.

Further, the United States Army had taken over, through the agency of No. 3 Military Railway Services (3 M.R.S.) the entire running of the Japanese railway system as far as military movement was concerned. All available first-class coaches were being used on the main lines through, to and in the American zone. I was horrified—here was a British battalion arriving to occupy the country and being invited to accept conditions of rail transport very much less comfortable than those imposed on troop movements in wartime India and most ill-according with the dignity of the British soldier.

The men were better off than the officers, comparatively speaking, and once they had adjusted themselves to the size of the seats they were able to settle down to sleep and feed and relax into that "browned-off trance" into which every British soldier retires as a sort of protection against the horrors of military movement.

The conditions for the officers were thoroughly bad. They were herded together into a second-class carriage, differing in no obvious way from a third-class carriage, unless the stench of the Japanese "benjo" or lavatory was slightly less pronounced.

I was furious and the memory of that initial trip across Honshu is one of continual anger. The lack of arrangements at Kure, despite the fact that the ship had already been in thirty-six hours, and the bad accommodation were in no way helped by the continuance of the rain and the fact that we were held up by land-slides throughout the night.

We arrived in glorious sunshine at 1000 hrs. at Matsue three and a half hours late, still soaking wet from our drenching the night before. The water supply on the train had long given out, depriving us thereby of an opportunity of a shave or a cup of tea for breakfast on the way. This was one of the very few occasions I can remember of a Japanese train arriving late. Punctuality was one thing their rail services did guarantee. Immediately our spirits rose and they were stepped up even farther by the sight of Captain Phil Roberts and C.S.M. Maule faultlessly attired in comparison with our filthy and unshaven condition, and accompanied by a working party from the leading echelon. We really appreciated that we had arrived among our own folk again.

Owing to the fact that our mechanical transport had been and was still lost somewhere in the maze of mountains in Central Honshu, it was necessary for the Battalion to march to Koshibara Barracks, which as usual we had renamed "Marabout Lines". I had hoped to avoid this initial march in our scruffy condition, but soon realized that the Nips, accustomed as they were to a shockingly low standard of turn-out from their own soldiers, would notice very little out of the ordinary in this respect about the arrival of the latest but travel-stained garrison of Matsue.

There was one astounding character gathered with the various police and other local authorities to greet us, and that was the Japanese manager of one of the beer gardens in the town. He was dressed in the military-cut jacket affected by the Nip as plain clothes, but about his person were already sewn the Brindiv Union Jack flash and the 2nd Divisional crossed keys, and supported in a leather cross-belt was a huge Union Jack!

The barracks themselves were another pleasant surprise. Tucked away in the side of a hill about a mile out of the town, these onetime infantry barracks of the Japanese consisted of large doubledecker barrack blocks. By keeping one company on detachment, there was just room to house the Battalion according to our scales of accommodation.

The officers' accommodation was bad—a feature of Japanese garrison life with which we were to become horribly familiar as we moved round the country. There were an adequate messroom and ante-room in a separate building, but for sleeping accommodation the officers had to be doubled or in some cases put into dormitories above the Battalion Headquarters offices, all mixed up with the clerks and batmen and various odd bodies of H.Q. Company.

Our difficulties in this respect lay in the inherent differences between the American ideas on officer accommodation and ours. It was apparently enough for an American officer to be allotted a corner, sometimes curtained off, sometimes not, of the men's dining-hall in which to eat, a modicum of space in which to sleep and for the rest he relaxed in his "club". When it is considered that an American field officer rated less cubic—or is it square?—footage of sleeping accommodation than the Indian sepoy on our scale, the reader will appreciate the difficulties we had in this respect on our wanderings when taking over barracks designed originally for the Jap and already once modified to American standards.

The Nips must have herded their men in like sardines. At our final station of Gomen we counted hammock hooks for over two hundred and fifty men in barrack rooms that we thought over-full with sixty British other ranks.

There was obviously an immense amount of work to do to these barracks at Matsue. Again the Americans, with their much more luxurious scale of G1098 equipment, were able far easier to settle down in a more confined space than we were. A simple example: in order to produce meals for a company we required a cookhouse in which to mount our most inefficient Indian pattern cooker and build our ovens. The Americans, with their far more satisfactory streamlined kit, merely set down their efficient "all in one" cookers on a barrack-room floor and there was their cookhouse.

The advanced party had set to with a will, once the initial delay imposed on them by the uncertainty of the Dorsets' destination, even up to the time of the arrival of the leading echelons on the Arundel Castle, had been settled. That they had done a great deal of heavy work to get the place fit for the arrival of the main body was obvious. However, a few days before our arrival news had come through that this was not to be our permanent station after all and enthusiasm for making Matsue the "No. 1" infantry barracks in the B.C.O.F. area had waned a great deal.

A few days before the arrival of the main body the ladies of the Women's Services had been detailed to units, and on General Cowan's instructions we had been "issued" with our old friends of Burma days, a detachment of W.A.S.(B.) under the command of Lieutenant Miss Elaine Cheverton, a one-time member of the 2nd Infantry Division W.A.S.(B.) team at Maram.

They had already moved into a very comfortable "Wasberry" in the town and were hard at work, when we arrived, trying to get the canteen and institutes working. As in Burma, I have nothing but praise for the enthusiasm and enterprise of our team of W.A.S.(B.), who, whilst they were with us, cheerfully accepted our hardships, tribulations and disappointments and shared with us the pride in whatever successes we scored. For various reasons it was considered inadvisable at that time to suggest that they adopted our crossed keys sign, which some of them had already worn on active service. The family feeling, however, was so strong that in order to cement the alliance, I invited Miss Cheverton to accept for each of her girls a Dorset collar-badge, which they wore after the fashion of the A.T.S., at home, above their left breast pockets. The girls accepted this distinction with great pride. Scattered as we were in isolated communities, I found it most important that the girls of the W.A.S.(B.) be considered members of the Officers' Mess, and take part as far as was possible in every form of Regimental activity. They entered into our life with great zest and it was not long before they had acquired a dog, named "Chinx" to celebrate the union of the Dorset Sphinx and the Chinthe of the W.A.S.(B.).[22]

"B" Company, under the command of Major Roy Turner, had been leading a very restless life since their arrival in Japan. They had been called out on internal security duties to ensure that the elections at the neighbouring town of Imaichi went off without undue disturbance.

---

22   This original W.A.S.(B.) team consisted of Lieutenant Miss Cheverton, Miss Rutherford from Australia, the sergeant of the team, and the Misses Margaret Sothers, Joan Rossiter, Yvonne Thompson and Anne Cowan. The last-named, the daughter of the Divisional Commander, was later awarded a mention in despatches for her work in the field during the previous year.

The Japs were being initiated into this strange business of a democratic election, and it was considered advisable to have Allied bayonets available in case the object of the exercise was not fully understood by the rowdier elements.

They had no sooner settled down into the very crowded barracks at Imaichi than Roy was dispatched farther down the coast to the port of Hamada, where there was a certain amount of black marketing, smuggling of Koreans and other subversive activities to be controlled.

"B" Company flourished on detachment and I was most impressed when, a few days after our arrival, I went down to visit them. I had a feeling that, having been away from Battalion control for so long, their drill and other activities may not have been up to the standard we were setting ourselves for our prospective tour in Tokyo. I need not have worried. From the moment I put them through their paces that afternoon at Hamada I never had a moment's doubt as to which company had earned the right to act as escort to the Colour when we should come to troop the Colour in Tokyo a few weeks later.

We found this corner of Northern Honshu to be most attractive. The population were for the most part the descendants of the original inhabitants of Japan who, during the course of centuries, had gradually been pushed into this corner of the main island by the more formidable feudal lords from the north. (I think north is correct; the main island of Honshu, with its dog-leg bend in the middle, is always a most confusing place in which to orientate oneself.) This area had, generally speaking, been untouched by the war apart from having to find its quota of men for the forces, and the natives, traditionally opposed to the late rulers of Japan, greeted us with extreme courtesy and even friendliness. We soon discovered the overwhelming power of the Japanese police, and the Chief of Police of Matsue himself never failed to give me, in my capacity of garrison commander, the greatest possible assistance. We certainly kept him busy, as I soon discovered that the only really satisfactory way of getting anything done was to send for the Chief of Police, and, lo and behold! it was done immediately—that is to say, as immediately as anyone quite so orientally minded as the Nip can perform a task.

The men were thrilled with Matsue. For the first time for many years we were quartered in a real town, with all its attendant amenities. Granted there were many embargoes on fraternization extant within the British Commonwealth Force, which had by no means come into line with current American policy on this point, and other restrictions which hindered the soldier's capacity for amusing himself and must have been a great irritant. However, on the credit side there were excellent beer gardens in the town, run exclusively for the men. Here beer was served in those ridiculous pony glasses, which are the largest form of tumbler available in Japan, by not unattractive Nipponese girls in gay kimonos. Then there were shops, where the British soldier could indulge to his heart's delight in his favourite game of bargaining. There was a cinema or two, but these, despite the American captions and the priority accorded to British troops, were not very popular.

Taken by and large, our first acquaintance with Japan, if you exclude the frightfulness of the railway system, the appallingness of the roads and the ever-present smell of the "honey pots"[23] was good, and if we had been allowed to stay there is no doubt that we could have developed Matsue into a really first-class one-battalion station.

One of the first things I discovered about garrison life in Japan was that even before one had hatched, or taken over, a purely tactical internal security scheme, one had two immediate priorities. The danger of fire was so great in these huge wooden double-decker barrack blocks that we soon laid on an invariable drill of practising a fire alarm immediately on arrival, both by day and by night. After the fashion of standing-to on service, fire drill became an automatic drill. The second priority was the disaster plan. One had continually to be prepared for a typhoon, earthquake or some other act of God. In the short time we were in Japan we managed to have not only a typhoon but a real honest-to-God earthquake, and so it will be realized that these precautions were necessary. We soon discovered that Matsue was a sort of nodal point for all and every kind of "visiting fireman". With the development of an entire brigade area on the north coast of Honshu there was of necessity a continual stream of visiting staff officers and unit advanced parties of all kinds, and so life was certainly never dull and we did not suffer from that cut-off feeling so often found in isolated garrisons far removed from formation headquarters.

One of our very first visitors was the Divisional Commander himself, who arrived, as he had warned me in Kure, in his special train within two and a half days of our arrival.

A very great deal seems to have happened during these first twenty-four days in Japan. After the departure of the General on his continued tour of the area, I sat down in earnest to interviewing

---

23 The Japanese rely on the collection of human excreta to manure their fields. Every day carts make the rounds of the houses to collect their evil-smelling loads in their so-called "honey pots", creating a never-to-be-forgotten odour for those unlucky enough to encounter these "benjo" carts.

the local potentates—the Mayor of the town, the Deputy Prefect of the Prefecture, the late Japanese area commander and his naval equivalent. Both of these ex-senior officers were now in charge of the demobilization of the Japanese forces. Part of their task was the completion of the records of the Japanese killed in action or missing. Every day those little paper bags of bones, familiar to those of us who had taken over positions and villages recently occupied by the Nip on service, used to arrive at the railway station, to be met by the next-of-kin and carried off to some burial ground.

It might have been expected that upon our arrival at our destination we would have been spared, for some time at any rate, the worries of release and repatriation. We had been made to jettison, as we stepped on the boat in Bombay, yet another couple of age and service groups, just in case they could not be shipped home from far-off Japan in time for their release at the appointed day in the United Kingdom. Among these had been our very popular and useful President of the Regimental Institutes, Captain Gerry Parton, M.C., late of the 7th Worcesters. Not the officer a battalion commander would wish to drop from the side, without any warning, just as he was embarking for some foreign shore. However, even during these first three weeks in Japan, with nary a reinforcement in sight, we had to dispatch our first draft for the United Kingdom. The Japanese must have thought us quite mad. Here were we, less than three weeks in the country, all rushing down to the station to dispatch soldiers to the Mother Country, with the Drums playing their hastily learnt rendering of "Auld Lang Syne"—a melody with which they were to become only too familiar during the course of the next few months, when the exodus swelled so greatly out of proportion to the intake.

Before we left Matsue the sergeants celebrated the opening of the first Sergeants' Mess of the Battalion in Japan by inviting the officers to dinner. I personally cannot remember a former occasion on which all the officers and members of the Sergeants' Mess sat down to dinner together.

Our final show in Matsue was the celebration of the second anniversary of the Battle of Kohima. I was determined to take the opportunity of celebrating this great battle not only whilst we still had a handful of survivors but also to make a flag march through the town. I sent for the Chief of Police and gave him my orders, which must have been pretty forceful, because he hurried away and produced the following instructions which were circulated round the town, issued down to many addressees, published in the Press and displayed in prominent places:

CIRCULAR

May 9th, 1946.
MAYOR, Ei KUMANO,
CHIEF OF POLICE, KOKICHI KUYA.

To Every Chief of Street Association.
Every Chief of Neighbourhood Association.
Every Schoolmaster.
Every Manager of Factory.

Salutation to the British Regimental Flag and the Commanding Officer

On the morning of May 13th (hours undetermined) British Occupational Forces at Koshibara are going to parade through this city under the command of Commanding Officer Lt.-Col. White, taking the below mentioned route. City people should show their hearty welcome and be careful not to fail to salute the Regimental Flag and Commanding Officer.

Hereafter, people who see the Regimental Flag and Commanding Officer anywhere should salute them without fail.

Parade route will be as follows. [*Here follows a list of quite unpronounceable names.*]

On this occasion I decided that we would put all our ceremonial irons in the fire. The colours, the drums and at the head the carriers, all freshly smartened up, under Tony Cross. The Chief of Police fell over himself trying to find three suitable horses for the Second-inCommand, Adjutant and myself. From the very "jungli" collection of ex-Japanese cavalry chargers (New Forest ponies to us), which seem to have long been relegated to the more mundane duties of the "honey pot" carts, we selected the three most presentable. They turned out to be old friends and were not only inseparable but seemed to have a remarkable number of horse acquaintances in the town, all of which they never failed to greet with a loud neigh so ill-according with the dignity of the procession.

The population certainly did answer the call of the Chief of Police and turned out in force, though it was hard to discover who was stealing whose thunder. I know that the Drum-Major got most of the salutes, but I am told that Desmond Wakely in the rear of the column, in between his efforts to restrain his horse from rushing up the ranks to join the Adjutant's horse, was kept just as busy acknowledging salutations.

We formed up in the square below the old Castle of Matsue outside the American post. Major Osbourne, commanding the detachment of the American Military Government, not only acquiesced to my request that I should be allowed to fly the Union Jack from his flagstaff during the ceremony but also turned out with a representative detachment for the parade.

Arrived below the Castle, the Battalion formed hollow square with the carriers on the flank, and on the open side of the square were formed up the two dozen Kohima veterans still serving, the W.A.S.(B.) under the command of Sergeant Miss Rutherford, and the Americans. In the centre of the square were the colours. This square looked most impressive with the men "at ease" whilst I told them the story of Kohima and the subsequent annihilation of the Japanese 31st Infantry Division. The large number of Japanese present listened attentively, but, from their polite applause at the conclusion of this description of their first heavy defeat at the hands of the British, I gathered that not much of what I had been saying had sunk in. After the Union Jack had been lowered and raised and Lance-Corporal Pope had sounded the "Last Post" and "Reveille" in memory of those of us who still lie in the compound of the District Commissioner's bungalow, we marched back by a different route.

Later that morning we held a reunion of the Kohima veterans, had our photograph taken and dealt very smartly with a quantity of Japanese ale. During this latter session it transpired that one of the Nip washers-up in the company lines, with an ugly neck wound, was a survivor of the District Commissioner's bungalow and claimed not only to have been very lucky to have escaped but when he heard that the Dorsets were in Matsue he immediately sought employment with us, as he claimed that he was already well acquainted with the Regiment.

These ceremonial parades and other martial occasions were a constant, though by no means unfriendly, source of controversy between us and the Americans owing to their diametrically opposed views on matters imperial, democratic and ceremonial, and I will therefore ask the reader to submit to yet another translation, this time from the Japanese vernacular Press. The Shimane Shimbun, the local "Daily Echo" of that part of the world, did us the honour of making the Kohima Day parade not only front-page news (back page to them) but also included two photographs, one of the drums and another of the carriers, in their issue of the 14th of May. Under the rather unusual headlines of "British Troops Marching Through Matsue With Traditional Beauty", we find the following write-up of the parade which must have puzzled them, though they were too polite to say so:

The British Occupational Forces at Matsue made a splendid parade with smart and orderly footsteps to the bright melody of the band on May 13th.

In celebration of the peace and victory they started from Koshibara Barracks, under the command of the Commanding Officer, Lt.-Col. White. With six tanks ahead they marched through the city. Both sides of the streets were lined with spectators, who gathered to show their hearty welcome.

Figures of five hundred soldiers coloured with formal and traditional beauty, especially a beautiful figure of a drummer wearing white gaiters and gloves and a splendid fur, attracted all spectators' attention.

On the evening of Kohima Day we entertained the officers of the American Military Government to dinner. When thanking Major Osbourne for his courtesy in allowing us to fly the Union Jack from an American military post, I could not refrain from pointing out that this was not the first time that the Fifty-Fourth had achieved the feat of hoisting the British flag on an American staff. "However", I added, "the last time we assaulted you with bayonets; tonight our attack is confined entirely to the liquor you will find in this mess."

Before leaving Matsue I find I have left the reader with little if any idea of the Japanese countryside, over which our patrols roamed in search of warlike stores and various odd people who had not toed the Allied line and were up to no good.

I do not think I can do better than to quote from a News-Letter I wrote home shortly after our arrival:

No wonder the little devil was so good at jungle fighting! The whole hinterland of this west end of Honshu is very reminiscent of theNaga hills on a smaller scale.

To appreciate the country one has only to land as we did at Kure (after spending twenty-four hours threading our way through a maze of islands, each one of which would have made an ideal defended locality) and make one's way north to Matsue.

To give some idea: take a Naga hill; wind round it the worst imaginable just jeepable khud track; cover the whole with thick

> *bamboo jungle, except for every square inch of flat or terraced land, which is wet paddy, add a density of population rather more than the Andheri suburbs of Bombay; intersperse various odd vehicles as disreputable-looking as the late lamented 'Tojo' and 'Tokyo'; shake on millions of grinning buck teeth; mix in a large number of amiable sawn-off but not unbeautiful pink-faced women in gaily coloured kimonos; wrap the whole up in a thick monsoon mist and rain and you have Dai Nippon.*

A few weeks later, when the country became hotter than Calcutta in the hot weather, we had cause to amend our ideas about the rain, but in those early weeks it seemed more prevalent than at Old Trafford in Test Match week.

When, after three weeks' sojourn in this very pleasant station, we were ordered to move, we left behind two exceptional institutions. The one was "Pop", that ever-cheerful and willing Japanese interpreter who had spent most of his life in the States and culd not do enough for us. An oldish man, he had the energy of a youth of twenty-four and a way of getting things done acquired after years of making his own way around the world.

The second institution was the magnificent Hot Springs resort a few miles from the town. Pleasantly set in a picturesque valley in the hills, this resort was the Japanese equivalent of, say, the old Rhine Kurort of Schlangenbad, where this Battalion spent so many happy hours during the first occupation of the Rhine. The varieties of baths were infinite and we were able to send quite a number of men as well as many of the officers to bathe and refresh themselves in these thermal springs, where the Japanese appeared not to worry about such odd Western customs as bathing-dresses or the segregation of the sexes.

We were all genuinely sorry to leave Matsue, with its co-operative Chief of Police, "Pop" and the funny little buck-toothed stationmaster, who was always so surprised at our demands but who overcame all sorts of rules and red tape to meet our wishes.

The journey to Gomen, destined to be our permanent station on the south coast of Shikoku (suddenly made free for us by the departure of the Americans ahead of schedule), reached depths of discomfort which even the journey to Matsue had not plumbed. At Uno we embarked on the first of many trips across the Inland Sea by that comic old paddle ferry steamer to Takamatsu, an hour away in a calm sea. This involved trans-shipment and memories of the crossing of the Brahmaputra ferry at midnight came vividly to mind as we detrained, embarked, disembarked and re-entrained all during the small hours of the morning.

There is one great consolation in travelling with the British soldier: he will always conjure up a cup of tea in the most inconceivable places, and the number of individual "brewings-up" on that ferry would have caused consternation to a less imperturbable man than the Japanese skipper.

The unluckiest party were the Mechanical Transport Platoon, who, through lack of forethought in higher circles, or, more probably, through complete inability to conjure up sufficient stock from the 3rd Military Rail Services, had to travel the hundred and eightyodd miles with nigh on two hundred tunnels, on open flat cars, with their vehicles. It took them days to get the soot out of their hair and the dust out of their eyes, let alone clean the accumulated dirt off their faces. It was quite inconceivable with what cheerfulness the British soldier would accept conditions like this and by the same token how completely wrong the appropriate authorities were to inflict such unnecessary hardship on troops who were already submitting cheerfully to no inconsiderable amount of being mucked about. I am afraid that my letters to higher command throughout the Japanese odyssey on the subject of rail travel always had to be reread carefully the next day before my Adjutant would allow them to be passed to Brigade.

BRITISH FORMATION SIGNS IN JAPAN

B.C.O.F   BRINDIV

CHAPTER NINETEEN

OPERATION *PRIMUS*

"PRIMUS IN TOKYO"

And to the drummers he did give commande,
Again to change the taptue,[24]
And every day they were learning to playe,
A deal of new beatings for shows.

[JOHN SCOTT]

THROUGHOUT THE LONG WAIT IN INDIA we had discussed over and over again what form the assault of the 2nd Dorsets on the Japanese capital would take. The first intimation I had that we really were bound for Tokyo was from my General as I reported to him on stepping off the Cheshire in Kure harbour. General Cowan, greeting me, said: "Geoffrey, the Dorsets have had a pretty raw deal on the way out from India, and so I am going to send you to Tokyo first. Be prepared to relieve the New Zealanders there on the 15th of July."

More urgent matters occupied our attention at the time, and, in April, July seemed a long way off, but we were all thrilled at being the first British Regular battalion to visit the capital and so add "Primus in Tokyo" to the list of Regimental honours.

Towards the end of May I had to find an officer to help organize the Empire Day parade in Tokyo and in addition, together with a party of ten British other ranks, I left to take part in the celebrations.

I was fortunate to have on this reconnaissance of the big city no less a person than Lieutenant-Colonel F. J. C. Piggott, D.S.O.. Francis Piggott had, as a subaltern, studied the language and actually served with a Jap battalion in Tokyo, and his father had been Military Attaché there up to the entry of the Japanese into the war.

The parade itself was disappointing. Since General MacArthur

---

24 Taptue : seventeenth-century spelling of "Tattoo."

had decreed that for the whole of the 24th of May Tokyo was to be considered a British city, we had hoped that the British Commonwealth ceremonies would have accorded with the prestige of the Empire. It was not, however, until the evening reception at the British Embassy, held by General Sir Charles Gairdner, the Prime Minister's personal representative and head of the United Kingdom Liaison Mission, and Mr. MacMahon Ball, of Australia, the Commonwealth representative on the Allied Council, that we felt that our national morale was really restored. There may be a tendency these days to allow the Empire to dissipate into thin air, but surely the time has not yet arrived when not only on one but on two parades on the same day the Union Flag of the United Kingdom is set on the left of the line to those of Australia, New Zealand and India.

The British reception in the old Ambassador's house in the undamaged British Embassy was a function long to be remembered, even if only for the abundancy of its refreshment and hospitality, and not merely for the galaxy of senior officials of the Commonwealth and the Allies who were gathered together.

Immediately on my return I produced my proposed plans for putting Operation "Primus", as we had decided to call the occupation of the enemy capital by the Fifty-Fourth, into force. I expected to have six weeks' grace, but no sooner had my "O" Group left my office on the evening of the 28th of May than a signal arrived inviting us to take over in Tokyo from the 1st of June, owing to the last-minute defalcation of the New Zealanders.

My visit to Tokyo had confirmed my views that Operation "Primus" was best conducted as an entirely social affair, a campaign of visiting cards, entertainments, drums beating and colours flying rather than a strictly military occupation of the defeated enemy's capital, which was being more than adequately carried out by the large American forces in the area.

In the short time we had left, we settled down to intensive ceremonial and cleaning, polishing and painting; there is another uglier word in favour among the soldiery. In a corner behind the Orderly Room, I personally, for lack of other instructors with experience, had to teach the subalterns the art of carrying the colours, and under my personal instruction R.S.M. Elbro, dragged from his newly cemented sentry beats and projected pigsties, had to gird on my own sword and learn to drill with it. Away in a remote corner of H.Q. Company Lance-Corporal Maddison could be heard polishing up the Dance Band for their forthcoming audition on Radio Tokyo. The Drum-Major and his

Corps of Drums worked frantically at maintaining the silver drums and knocking the final shape into the fifers, who hadn't really yet mastered the twiddly bits of "The Maid of Glenconnel". In the Mess Desmond Wakely, the President of the Mess Committee, and Sergeant Thomas made calculations about the liquor stocks and searched frantically for the Mess invitation cards we had had specially printed by Thackers in Bombay before leaving India.

Over all hung a pall of white dust as the Battalion, in the intervals of "Slope—order—present—slope—order" on the square, blancoed themselves up.

In the Adjutants' office John Archer's face took on an even more worried look as the full purport of the notes I had brought back from Tokyo sank in. "What! Only accommodation for seven hundred and twenty all ranks and we have to find two hundred men a day for guard? Someone's going to do an awful lot of sentry-go." At his side O.R.Q.M.S. Vaughan, who had seen me and many other Commanding Officers, as well as nigh on a dozen Adjutants, through far worse crises, merely assured him that it would be all right, because if we really did start running out of men for guard he would go on "stag" himself.

In the "Wasberry", as we called the shack where our W.A.S.(B.) s lived, long-concealed evening dresses appeared out to air. Some enterprising Japanese made a raid whilst the W.A.S.(B.)s were in mess one night. We never did understand what future a flat-chested Nipponese girl would find in some of the more intimate garments constructed for our outstandingly well-developed team of British girls, which disappeared that evening.

In the officers' quarters behind the Orderly Room house-girls were set to work by the batman stitching on B.C.O.F. signs. This question of signs was becoming quite a traditional game. In India the 5th Brigade had fiercely resented any attempt to remove the crossed keys of the 2nd Infantry Division which we had carried from France through Yorkshire and India to Burma. General Cowan had agreed to a compromise by which we wore the Union Flag of Brindiv on our right shoulders and retained our crossed keys on the left. On being selected for Tokyo we became B.C.O.F. troops, and both the old and new Commanders-in-Chief of the British Commonwealth Occupation Force were most insistent that everyone in the Force should wear what was in point of fact the Corps sign. Hence the frantic sewing by the house-girls; down came the Brindiv sign on the right arm, up went the B.C.O.F. crown, whilst the Union Flag moved to the top of the left arm and the crossed keys dropped a couple of inches but still stayed on the arm.

Finally, to complete the picture of the rapid preparations for Tokyo, we find the guard room suddenly filling to an alarming extent owing mainly to the potency of the local indigenous beer which suddenly appeared in the canteen. Over-indulgence, especially around the time that the bar was due to close, invariably filled certain soldiers with a desire to up and smite someone, preferably someone senior. Perhaps it was this beer that the Japs used to give their troops before committing them to a "banzai" attack.

On arrival in Tokyo we settled down to serve a number of masters. As the B.C.O.F. guard battalion we came directly under the Commander, British Commonwealth Sub-Area, Tokyo (BRICOSAT), who dealt direct with B.C.O.F. Headquarters in Kure, three hundred miles away. Operationally we were under the command of the 2nd United States Cavalry Brigade in the 1st United States Cavalry Division, which was responsible for the Tokyo area.[25] Apart from the fact that the BRICOSAT Commander had no power to convene a court-martial, I still had my allegiance to my own parent Brigadier at Kochi, three hundred and twenty miles to the south across the Inland Sea, and to my own Divisional Commander, who I admit was closing up a bit by moving his headquarters during this time from Hiro (Kure) to Okayama, a mere two hundred miles away. As you can see, this gave me plenty of scope, and the Dorsets, after years of training in what was probably one of the most independently minded brigades of any Regular formation, were well able to hold their own.

Ebizu Barracks were the bottom. How often in the past few years has that apt description been applied to some temporary home of the Fifty-Fourth! This time it really was true. Located in a blitzed suburban area six miles from the city centre, the "barracks" consisted of some very damaged buildings which were once a great Japanese marine engineering factory. As such they must have been good, but the combined efforts of the United States Army Air Force at some stage of the war and the hasty demolitions of the Nips before the arrival of the Americans had done nothing to make them even remotely suitable as the home of the B.C.O.F. guard battalion.

Our predecessors, Colonel Jackson and his Australian Battalion, must have done wonders. I know that they removed one thousand one

---

25 It is of interest to note that when the Fifty-Fourth, in their first campaign, encountered the American Army at the Battle of Brooklyn in 1776, they had been in General Howe's 5th Brigade, and now, a hundred and seventy years later, under far happier circumstances, they were in the 5th Infantry Brigade when they came under operational command of the United States Forces in Tokyo.

hundred three-ton loads of rubble from the barracks area during their tour. We, and presumably our successors, continued the work and I suppose by about 1950, if there is still a Commonwealth Force in Japan, Ebizu Barracks may represent something worthy of the Empire whose representative battalion they accommodate.

Just over two hundred men were required for guard every day. These guards varied from the "No. 1" "Buck House" guard on the Imperial Palace to small posts of "one and three" on such places as the Meiji shrine. For the whole of our stay we had very nearly the equivalent of a company permanently under the command of the United States Army Air Force (A.F.P.A.C. Headquarters). The guards were very scattered throughout the Tokyo area, with, in addition, a Consulate guard at Yokohama.

This necessitated a radical change in Battalion organization. To deal with A.F.P.A.C. I dispatched a much-reduced "D" Company to the Americans under the command of Lieutenant Haynes. This was a most popular assignment, as it meant American food, PX cards and an American way of life which in most cases provided not only indoor sentry posts in their huge office blocks but seats for the sentries. I made H.Q., "A" and "B" Companies up into three "watches", temporarily disbanding "C" Company to do this. Each watch in turn mounted at 1030 hrs. and stayed on guard for fortyeight hours. During this time they found all public duties. On their four days off I tried to give every man at least twenty-four hours absolutely free, and in many cases we were able to get the men away for forty-eight hours to the various leave centres in the hills and by the sea. The remainder of the time was occupied in drill, duty companies for all calls other than guards, and the old Army game of cleaning up for guard, which came round again on the fourth day after they had dismounted.

The Imperial Palace guard was the most interesting and the hardest, as there was no relaxation, and even by using mechanical transport it took so long to relieve the posts that the men lost a great deal of rest time. Out of the eleven posts around the Imperial Palace five were shared with an American sentry. Each sentry did his own drill and went his own way. In general it worked remarkably well, though it could be quite disconcerting during our impressive guard-mounting parade to have an American ten-tonner come roaring up and deposit a sentry who took over the post by the simple process of girding himself with the painted white belt and taking over the charged magazine of the outgoing number and assuming his position.

I cannot speak too highly of our sentries, who, throughout those seven long weeks, maintained the high standard of drill and alertness on sentry that we expected of them. It is not easy to remain smart and soldierlike by our standards when your companion on the post allows himself a rather more relaxed form of stand-at-ease, and it is most disconcerting to have a doughnut offered you on the end of a bayonet.

So we settled down to the routine of Tokyo. Every second day was livened by the ceremonial guard mounting on the Plaza, which, under Captain Cross's expert supervision, rapidly turned into a most popular spectacle, if one can judge by the mass of Service men and women of all nations who used to watch it.

The men were reasonably well off. The forty-eight hours on guard were a grind, but there was plenty of time off and somewhere to go. With as yet no B.C.O.F. Club established in Tokyo, we had to rely practically entirely on the hospitality of our hosts. However, Brian Robbins, the Battalion Entertainment Officer, assisted by others, managed to obtain a large number of vacancies on the various functions run by the American Red Cross, an organization to whom we will always be grateful.

The more junior officers had a great time. They were taken for guard along with their watches, but when off duty their time was virtually their own. Company commanders and their headquarters seldom got a break. With an ad hoc company on the move every six days and apt to be very split up, they had to work hard. But it was at Battalion Headquarters that the real strain was felt in those early days. Apart from routine work, the dealing with so many masters, and the aggravations of slow communications, we had before us two immense tasks. First, the job of making social and official Tokyo conscious of the presence of the first British battalion in their city. Secondly, the planning and execution of Plassey Day, with its ceremony of the trooping of the colour and the officers' reception in the evening.

To help out John Archer I brought back Tony Cross to his old job of Drill Adjutant, and Danny Lee, the Mechanical Transport Officer, practically motorless for the time being, I made Assistant Adjutant with an almost whole-time job finding men for guard.

For my part I had to rewrite, reproduce and give instruction in the entire ceremonial of the troop. The Manual of Ceremonial had not been rewritten since the days when we used to drill in fours, and a ceremonial designed for the Horse Guards Parade in London was not too easy to fit on to the Plaza of the Imperial Palace in Tokyo.

In addition, my Second-in-Command or Executive Officer (as he came to be called, after close association with the Americans) and I had to make necessary outside contacts in a sphere of operations where "commander to commander" was the customary way to get things done.

Meanwhile, preparations for the great day went on. Invitations were sent out, the paraphernalia attendant on a martial display gradually collected and the leading actors rehearsed. There were three main difficulties. First, after arrival in the capital I could get the Battalion on parade only twice before the big day, with a week between rehearsals. Secondly, more perhaps than in any other form of ceremonial, the officers and warrant officers had to play a very prominent and individual part, including an ability to march in slow time across the square to their guards. Thirdly, all ranks had to be put very clearly into the picture and be thoroughly acquainted with the very complicated manoeuvres which are an essential part of this ceremonial. The Battalion I was not worried about: I knew they could drill and was prepared to rely to a great extent on that extra one hundred per cent that a battalion of Dorsets can always produce "on the day". The officers and the warrant officers were a problem, and many a long and weary hour we spent on the flat roof of Ebizu Barracks acquiring the art of slow marching. Then there was the Regimental Sergeant-Major's sword drill and the Ensign's colour drill—but enough of this: let us get on with our story.

My original plan was to run a show for our own General, General Cowan, and we hoped that he would bring with him our own Brigadier, Jock McNaught. As guests we would have the British colony of Tokyo, and Americans up to and including General Chase, Commanding General, 1st U.S. Cavalry Division, under whose command we came operationally.

Before we knew where we were the outgoing Commander-inChief of B.C.O.F. had notified his intention of passing through Tokyo on his way back to Australia, and the new Commander-inChief had decided that this was a good time to come up and see the big city. Added to this, we were delighted, and greatly honoured, when General Eichelberger, the Commanding General, Eighth U.S. Army, the Land Forces Commander in Japan, indicated his desire to witness the parade as a spectator, together with MajorGeneral Byers, his Chief of Staif. Three lieutenant-generals, three major-generals and a number of "one-star" generals of both Armies! I could see our own Brigadier being crowded off the dais if we were not careful.

General Cowan raised a further complication when he arrived on Plassey Day minus one. A question had arisen as to whether it was politic or not, in this year of grace, for a battalion of the Dorsetshire

Regiment to celebrate the Battle of Plassey at all. An effort by the Australian Canteen Services to refer to it as the "Battle of Cressey" did not cool the wrath of one Indian Army officer, who appeared to be rather touchy about certain incidents which had occurred in a dungeon in Calcutta nearly two hundred years earlier. I had, to a certain extent, anticipated a question or two and had prepared the address which I was going to make during the parade. Unlike the babus in India, I could not expunge all reference to the Black Hole from the very fine parade programme which had been printed, but instead I essayed to prove conclusively that General Cowan's British and Indian Division, in which we were now serving, was a direct descendant of Colonel Clive's British and Indian Division, which had defeated Dupleix's French and Indian Division under the command of the Nabob of Bengal at the Battle of Plassey. That went off well except for a crack from the French Ambassador when I next met him after the parade.

None of us at Battalion Headquarters are likely to forget the three days culminating on Friday, the 28th of June, 1946. Three British generals to welcome and furnish with appropriate guards of honour, fix programmes, arrange visits and answer questions. In addition, there were two rehearsals to fit in, one skeleton with officers, warrant officers and markers on the Plaza, and a full-blown rehearsal with the whole Battalion on the 8th U.S. Cavalry square.

The last general to arrive was the new Commander-in-Chief, General Robertson, who had to be met with a full guard of honour two hours before the parade. Poor old "B" Company, how they must have cursed me and rued the day when they put up such a magnificent display at Hamada in April that I had no choice but to select them for escort company for the troop!

The Great Day. Out on the Plaza Tony Lewis, the Second-in-Command, and his Japanese labour team were putting the finishing touches to the ground. The Battalion were debussing out of sight four hundred yards away, and around the dais O.R.Q.M.S. Vaughan and Sergeant Jesty, in their scarlet sashes, were marshalling their collection of "moles", as the inner line of sentries. To raise this line, every available man had been dragged from his office stool or batman's kitchen. After all, there must be no little urgency when one finds not only the Orderly Room Quartermaster-Sergeant and the Battalion Medical Sergeant but also the Commanding Officer's batman on parade.

At 0945 hrs. we were all set, and the Divisional Band of the Royal Welch Fusiliers marched on parade to play their "overture", designed to show that there was some martial display afoot.

Thirteen years earlier, as a very young officer, I had been privileged to carry the Regimental Colour on the last occasion on which the Fifty-Fourth had trooped their Colour. That parade was held in a howling gale on top of Portland Rock, and my arm ached for days afterwards. The standard of drill had been really first class, and should have been after the weeks of preparation that we had put in. The troop of 1946, I am convinced, lost nothing by comparison with its predecessor. Granted we had a lot in our favour this time: the weather, the galaxy of spectators and the thrill of performing our ceremony on the Imperial Plaza. There was something about that Plaza. Probably the designers, well versed in the art of showmanship, had contrived the effect, but suffice it to say that every man in the Battalion had this feeling of being on the stage. Young soldiers as they were, inexperienced in the art of ceremonial by comparison with their forebears, they produced that day a display of drill of the highest order.

Many times in the past three years had I had ample cause to feel proud of the Fifty-Fourth, but as I stood in front of them that morning on the Plaza of the Imperial Palace in Tokyo I felt prouder than ever. This latest generation of Dorset soldiers were more than upholding the tradition of the Regiment. There were a mere handful of us left, twenty, including Jock McNaught, who had crossed the Brahmaputra River and had completed the march to Tokyo, but this young battalion were more than holding their own in perpetuating the deeds of their predecessors at Festubert, Kohima, Ye-U, the Irrawaddy, Dirty Pagoda and Popa.

The first to congratulate the Battalion after the parade was General Eichelberger. I will quote him: "Not only was the ceremony beautiful", said the Eighth Army Commander, "but its execution was the most exact I have ever seen, and you know I have seen troops all over the world. It was very impressive indeed and I congratulate the Dorsets."

Prior to Plassey Day I had sent Plassey Day greetings, as was our former custom, not only to our present commanders, from General MacArthur to Brigadier McNaught, but also to our old commanders Lord Louis Mountbatten of Burma, and Generals Stopford, Grover and Nicholson, from all of whom we received most gracious replies. General MacArthur signalled: "It is peculiarly appropriate that your Battalion should spend the anniversary of the historic Battle of Plassey in Tokyo after having contributed so much to the campaigns which brought victory to the Allied Army in the present war. I send to all ranks my cordial greetings."

Lieutenant-General Sir Montagu Stopford, our old Corps Commander in Burma, and now Commander-in-Chief, A.L.F.S.E.A., in Singapore, replied: "I greatly appreciate your most kind signal on Plassey Day. I well remember the gallantry which the Fifty-Fourth Foot displayed in all actions during our great days together. It is good that you can complete your motto, 'Primus in Tokyo'. I hope we may meet again one day, but in the meantime best wishes to you and all ranks."

Owing to the strain of finding duties it was impossible to lay on a party for the other ranks on Plassey Day, other than to make a free issue of beer: the other ranks' dance was to come later. That night, however, the officers held a reception on the top floor of Empire House, kindly lent to us for the occasion by the Sub-Area Commander. To this party we welcomed again the distinguished gathering who had witnessed the parade in the morning, and we all enjoyed meeting the United States Eighth Army Commander and his charming lady under less formal circumstances. Desmond Wakely and Sergeant Thomas had worked wonders in their preparations and the party was a great success. We have many acts of kindness to remember in Tokyo, but the assistance provided by the 8th U.S. Cavalry in providing some special delicacies and ice-cream on this occasion was most memorable. It was not until well after first light that the party looked like finishing and the last of the enthusiasts had been collected in from the roof garden.

For the remainder of the tour our life continued with its routine of guards, but for everyone in the Battalion there was a change. The Dorsets had arrived and the hospitable American and Commonwealth residents threw endless sources of amusement open to us. By the time that we marched out at the end of July, I reckoned that, except for the men actually standing on sentry (and exciting things even happened to them at times), the whole Battalion were out in the town on some party or other. For me and my "executive" it became rather a strain. Return invitations were always couched in most specific terms, which precluded, unlike the British Army custom, the Commanding Officer from being able to delegate who should represent the Battalion at certain official functions. We all made our "contacts" and towards the end, as a sentry came off guard, he would arrange to meet his American opposite number in the 7th Cavalry Squadron Club in half an hour. Throughout Tokyo Dorsets would be found earning that enjoyment and relaxation which they would not find on their return to Shikoku. We had, it must be stated, our setbacks, such as the night when C.S.M. Maule was stabbed by a couple of Nipponese "terrorists", and the evening when some of our younger soldiers rashly took it into their heads to take on a party of enormous American troops with razor blades.

The President of the Regimental Institutes, Captain Len Futter, with his usual thoroughness, ensured the success of the all ranks' dance in our last week. On the 4th of July Tony Lewis and I were invited to be guests of the 1st Cavalry Division at their celebrations connected with Independence Day, and this was followed on the 14th of July, by General Petchkoff, the French Ambassador, inviting a very strong team of officers to the French Embassy to celebrate the anniversary of the Fall of the Bastille. This for most of the officers was their first glimpse of the Supreme Commander, General MacArthur, and his most charming lady.

The dance band certainly worked overtime. Invariably our hosts would ask for our band, and in the end I had to leave them behind for another fortnight in order to fulfil all their engagements. These not only included private and official functions but also "going on the air" at Radio Tokyo. The Drums beat "Retreat" at the British Embassy when the newly arrived Ambassador, Mr. Gascoigne, entertained the officers of the Battalion. The next day we went to Yokohama, where the Drums beat "Retreat" before Admiral Survees. That day a very powerful team from the Battalion had spent the day on board H.M.S. *Bermuda*, when our host was Lieutenant-Commander Morris Greig, who had known the 1st Battalion well during the siege of Malta.

I have as yet said little of our American allies with whom we were integrated during this tour. Limitations of space preclude me from listing all those officers and ladies of the American Forces to whom we were indebted and who went out of their way to ensure that our visit was made as enjoyable as possible. If this book should ever reach the hands of any of our friends of the 1st Cavalry Division, the 2nd Cavalry Brigade, the 7th and 8th Cavalry Regiments, the American Red Cross and our many friends in the Tokyo garrison, I hope they will understand how much we all appreciated the warmth of their welcome and how happy we were to serve in partnership with them. The 1st Cavalry Division of the United States was a fine formation with an outstanding active service record in the Pacific War—they really had been "first in Tokyo" and to us had every justification to be, as they claimed, in their own army, "The First Team".

As we were handing over to Lieutenant-Colonel Philip Townsend and the 2nd/5th Royal Gurkha Rifles I received two letters, extracts from which I am sure should be recorded in these annals. General Eichelberger, the Eighth U.S. Army Commander, wrote:

Your splendid unit is one which I will always remember in pleasant retrospect. I have no doubt that every officer and man of my command who had the pleasure of meeting the Dorsets will agree with me that not only is your Battalion a fine group of soldiers but also the spirit you display is much to be admired.

Brigadier-General Hugh Hoffman, Commanding General of the 2nd Cavalry Brigade, under whom we served operationally, wrote:

... I wish to express my appreciation of your co-operation and assistance in performing the occupational duties assigned to this Command. The conduct, appearance and efficiency of the troops of the 2nd Dorsets have been exemplary during their stay in Tokyo. ...

Two such reports from our Allied commanders, together with an equally congratulatory signal from General Cowan, gave us cause for great satisfaction. We departed for the paddy fields of Gomen with the feeling that we had adequately completed our allotted task and had not only upheld but enhanced the reputation of British arms.

CHAPTER TWENTY

"OVER THE HILLS AND FAR AWAY"

Gomenasai—Excuse please.

DORSETS HAVE BEEN SENT TO many queer places during the past two hundred and fifty years, but never before, I believe, to a place called "Excuse," which is apparently what the word "Gomen" means in Japanese.

At first sight there was little to recommend Gomen as a station. Gomen itself, the nearest village, was a good three miles from barracks, and the town of Kochi, where Brigade Headquarters and the Camerons had come to rest, was a further ten or a dozen miles to the west. The barracks themselves were set down among the paddy fields in the narrow coastal belt between the Pacific Ocean and the steep hills of the island, which in places rose up to seven and eight thousand feet.

This latest site for "Marabout Lines" had formerly been a kamakase (suicide) pilot training centre and, fortunately for us, had an airfield, over which we could train and play without becoming bogged down in the inevitable paddy field. A mile to our south lay the Pacific Ocean and one of the few possible "landing" beaches on Shikoku Island. The Pacific Ocean, we found, was unsuitably named; it was seldom as smooth as its name implies, and except on very few beaches the ground swell was so strong that it was impossible to allow any but the strongest swimmers to bathe.

The main road to Brigade was so bad that it took half an hour in a jeep to get into Kochi, and we were eight or nine hours by rail from Divisional Headquarters at Okayama on Honshu Island.

Owing to the tenuous nature of the road-rail communications on the island, both the line and the main road were easily put out of action by landslides for some days after even the smallest amount of rain.

There were a number of advantages, however, in Gomen. We never felt shut in: a feeling of freedom of movement attained from living on an airstrip, denied to the Camerons, who led a very enclosed life in Asakura Barracks, Kochi. Our accommodation, except for that of the officers, was pretty good. The battalion of the 19th U.S. Infantry had certainly made many improvements during their stay in Gomen and bequeathed us an excellent gymnasium and a first-class theatre and canteen building.

The airstrip tended to take a very important place in our order of things: we developed its wide expanses to make hockey pitches and games areas and obviously its possibilities as a drill square were not overlooked. Being the only airstrip in Southern Shikoku, we became a reception unit for the numerous "visiting firemen" and wandering staff officers who came to visit the Brigade. An SOS to Iwakuni, for a plane to evacuate an urgent case from the 5th Field Ambulance (the medical facilities for troops on the island were impossibly inadequate) would bring a Dakota roaring over our heads. The stream of visitors, which we had thought had reached its peak during our stay in Tokyo, continued unabated. Staff officers from the Joint Chiefs of Staff Committee in Melbourne, Australian concert parties, and Members of Parliament from the United Kingdom all in their turn dropped out of the sky. It certainly helped to make us feel that we were not quite as isolated as we thought, though no doubt the various guard commanders would have appreciated a little less activity from such high-powered guests.

Our initial efforts at settling in were rudely shattered by the arrival of a typhoon a few days after our return from Tokyo. We received the "warning yellow" in the early hours of a Monday morning on such a brilliantly fine day that it seemed quite out of the question that such a calamity could be rushing at us at three hundred miles an hour. However, we started to carry out the drill prescribed by the latest "Instructions in Case of a Typhoon". Fortunately, before the "red" was given, the typhoon had altered course and its centre hit Kyushu Island, a hundred and fifty-odd miles to our west. By the time the "red" warning had arrived we were so soaked through and wind-swept that we could not have cared less. The rain, with a hurricane force behind it, poured down with an amazing intensity. None of the barrack-room windows fitted and this rain certainly found every conceivable crack and crevice. I was worried that the river flowing a quarter of a mile to the east of the barracks would overflow and swamp us out. Fortunately, though it rose to the top of its high-built-up banks, the wind and rain abated before this disaster occurred. Towards evening I had to call the W.A.S.(B.)s in from their wooden shack, and put them to sleep in the field officers' quarters above the command post, those officers doubling up elsewhere for the occasion. The great problem, which we never finally decided, was whether to let the troops remain in upstairs barrack rooms and get blown over with the buildings or order them downstairs and wait for the buildings to fall on them. At Gomen we had no convenient hill nearer than nine or ten miles to which we could evacuate the Battalion, in accordance with the drill prescribed by the authorities.

However, the worst nights come to an end some time, and after about twenty-four hours the wind and sea and rain abated, and, soaked through though we were, we were able to set about clearing up in watery sunshine. Why the Pacific did not break over the beach and across the low-lying airfield to flood the barracks I do not know; there was absolutely nothing to stop it and the immense line of drift-wood and wreckage cast to the top of the beach, which we saw the next day, testified to how close this danger had been. The breakers, even a day later, presented one of the most magnificent sights of angry seascape I have seen—those huge waves, not content with having swollen to gigantic proportions, were hurrying inshore so fast that they were mounting up four on top of each other.

Communications with B.C.O.F. Headquarters, which by now had been established on the island of Eta Jima in the Inland Sea, much to the despair of those who had to visit them and had very little time to spare, became so chaotic after this episode as to give rise to the popular belief that the typhoon had blown itself out in the Central Registry of this Headquarters.

Like many other acts of God and phenomenal visitations in Japan, typhoons play to very rigid seasons, and with its departure we were told by the local inhabitants that the season was over and, following the lead of the Japanese fishermen, we bent our energies seawards. We refused to believe that there was simply nowhere on this long coastline that we could bathe in this glorious warm water. After long reconnaissances certain beaches were discovered. Bathing, however, had always to be very strictly controlled, life-saving parties carefully detailed and the men called in on the slightest change of wind, which was usually sufficient to cause a ground swell, dangerous to the inexperienced swimmer.

The greatest factor in our enjoyment of life at this time of year was the weather. It was glorious and the summer weather, comparable to the heat of India, lasted at Gomen until right to the end of October. After the sticky, Calcutta-like heat of Tokyo, we found the climate at our seaside resort most invigorating and we took full advantage of the sun. At night, certainly, we had our troubles. This was the season of the mosquito-borne "B-Encephalitis" bug or mite or what have you, which produced some most unpleasant form of disease. Consequently it was necessary to take very full and elaborate anti-mosquito precautions. These involved the continued wearing of boots and anklets, or puttees, with the usual rolled-down-sleeve precautions after dusk. This was not the first time during the past few years that we had suffered similar restrictions, but never before had we tried to lead a peace-time existence with socials and dances and other forms of entertainment with all ranks of both sexes booted and gaitered throughout the evening's proceedings.

We came to envy the Japanese their communal mosquito-nets. The reader will remember how in Tamu we had acquired a number of these large, green nets, under which a number of Japanese soldiers must have sheltered, and how useful we found them when applied to our cookhouses and places for preparing food in our everlasting efforts to defeat the Burmese fly. Now we could see for ourselves how the Nip used these nets in his own home.

Japanese domestic life is essentially simple. Their floors are covered with strips of matted straw called "tatami" and every function is carried out on the floor. They live, eat, cook and sleep on the floor. Chairs seem to be unknown to them, and even the Japanese "benjo" or lavatory is designed more after the tastes of the squatting Oriental than the seat-trained Westerner. The drill at night seems to be for the family to slide back the doors (doors of any kind are made to slide in Nippon, and seldom open and shut) of one of the innumerable built-in cupboards and bring out their bedrolls. At the same time, the tallest member of the family gets out a huge mosquito-net and slings it from hooks at each corner of the room and the whole family crawl inside and settle down to a night's sleep. They are early risers and first light, around five-thirty, usually found a peasant making a loud splashing noise with one or other of his weird paddy-field implements immediately under my window.

We will not continue this digression on the domestic habits of the Nip just now, though I shall return to him later.

On return from Tokyo I considered that we had a number of things to do—none of them as exciting or as interesting as the seven weeks in the capital, but all important and familiar to anyone who served in the Army during this time, so I will only bear on the situation as it especially affected us in far-off Japan. First and foremost we had to settle down and try to turn this wilderness into a barracks worthy of the Regiment who occupied it. R.S.M. Elbro forsook his (or rather my) sword for a ploughshare which he had discovered somewhere and took over the portfolio of "Minister of Agriculture and Fisheries", or Officer in charge of Gardens. Fishing being his favourite hobby, he engendered enthusiasm in that direction as well.

Secondly, we had to train not only those of the higher age groups who had had no training for nearly six months but also the longpromised reinforcements when they should arrive.

Thirdly, we had various operational roles, about which I will have more to say.

Cutting across every activity in the Battalion was a very ambitious scheme of education, which, like the oft-quoted birth of a child, had been far easier to conceive at a higher headquarters than to deliver at unit level. Brian Robbins and his staff worked very hard and enthusiastically under the most unpromising circumstances to pump some degree of education into the masses. His most successful efforts were with his evening classes of bright boys who were studying for some definite examinations.

Finally, there was the all-absorbing task of keeping the Battalion reasonably amused and occupied in this far-flung garrison. Everyone joined in this task of alleviating the off-duty hours by providing some alternative to the dreariness of "walking out" in the local village or through the blitzed town of Kochi, with its uncomfortable three-quarter-of-an-hour journey each way by three-tonner or Nip tram or a combination of both. Our most outstanding success in this line was due to the enthusiasm of Major Phil Roberts, commanding H.Q. Company, who produced a concert party from his company alone. That this party was ever produced, or trained to such a high pitch, that I found that I could send it on a tour through Shikoku and to Brindiv and B.C.O.F. units on the mainland, was entirely due to the magnificent work put in by that prince of regimental comedians Lance-Corporal Maddison. He was ably supported by Drum-Major Westlake and the dance band, of which Maddison was himself a leading light.

Meanwhile, in another part of the same building Miss Cecilia Buckland (who had taken over from Miss Elaine Cheverton) and her team of W.A.S.(B.)s, now sadly denuded of our original Wasbies and made up to strength by members of the W.V.S. recently arrived in the country, continued in her cheery way to run the canteen and to make it the off-duty centre of the Battalion. We tried very hard, but unfortunately with no real success, to open up an additional canteen in the nearest village.

Shikoku is a large island, shaped like a dumb-bell, about a hundred and sixty miles long and eighty miles wide at its two wide ends, narrowing to about forty miles in the centre. That is to say, it is considerably larger than Wales, and about as long as Ireland without Ulster.

The Brigade were at this time fairly scattered. In the south, as I have said, Brigade Headquarters and the Camerons were at Kochi, and we were at Gomen, only fifteen miles away. The Royal Welch, however, were at Tokushima on the north-east coast, a good five to six hours away by rail and eleven by road, with the R.A.S.C. Company at Wadashima, about ten miles from the Royal Welch. Here also came the Indian field battery, the only unit not of the 5th Brigade on the island.

About two hours from Takamatsu, farther west and still on the peaceful Inland Sea, was the old Japanase naval air station of Takuma, which General Cowan decided to develop as a holiday camp, and a remarkably fine leave centre this became, with its equal facilities for both British and Indian troops.

Farther west still, about four or five hours by road from Kochi, at the extreme north-west of the island, was the holiday resort of Matsuyama, famous for its thermal baths. Here the Camerons were fortunate enough to have a company quartered and Major Maitland-Makgill-Crichton opened his Divisional battle school.

Shikoku Island was virtually one large range of mountains rising to heights of seven and eight thousand feet in the centre and running straight down to the sea, leaving only a very narrow coastal strip of cultivation nearly the whole way round the coast.

Communications were not only primitive but practically nonexistent. The main roads, few as they were, were very "jungli". Not only extremely narrow and ill-constructed, they were perilous in the extreme, especially the north-to-south axis, as it wound its way perched, literally supported by baulks of timber in many places, over deep chasms and gorges. A road did stretch from Kochi to Matsuyama, but this was so often blocked by landfalls that its use was always problematical. The railways followed the two main roads, with a branch line to Tokushima. Virtually the only way to move a large party, as most of these roads were impassable to threetonners, was by rail, and I have said enough about Nip railways.

There were no other motorable tracks across the mountain in the centre of the island, and the native telephone communications or "mushi-mushi" telephone services were most primitive. The railway itself was a feat of engineering worthy of a very high place in the annals of world's railway history. For most of the way the line followed a river and in places was perched as precariously over steep precipices as the road itself.

Like Julius Caesar, Brigadier McNaught divided his territory into three more or less equal parts, corresponding roughly to existing Japanese prefectures. To the Royal Welch Fusiliers fell the north-east territories. To us fell the wide area in the middle of the dumb-bell, but including the southern end of the eastern "bell", and the northern end of the western "bell". To the Camerons fell the "bandit territory" of the south-west, with even fewer communications than we had by land, but very much more accessible from the sea than was our province.

Each commanding officer had in his own "gau" a formidable list of operational targets still to be cleared up. Many of these targets, when finally discovered, after a long trek through the thick jungle which covered the entire hinterland of the island, turned out on examination to be no more than a slit trench or two, but sometimes we came across something of interest.

Besides demilitarization we were also responsible for ferreting out and suppressing the black market activities of the natives in our areas. There was also the constant checking up on the various activities of local societies and running to earth of known bad characters who weren't answering too well to the call of democracy. I am sure that the average Nip, to quote an American colonel in Tokyo, "hadn't the faintest idea of whether democracy was something you eat or something you put on your hair", but our commitments in this direction, light as they were compared with the wholetime job of the American Military Government, were quite enough to keep our S.E.A.T.I.C.[26] Officer more than fully employed.

In an effort to combine training with our operational commitments, I decided during August and September to send the rifle companies, with occasionally a platoon of H.Q. Company, off on a week's detachment to various parts of our territory. Setting up their headquarters in some centre, be it a mountain village or a seaside town, the company commanders would organize their patrol programme and at the same time carry out some much-needed training. The mere fact that there was an object, however nebulous, to this weary foot-slogging through the hills, gave the training a fillip and interest which produced most satisfactory results. There was also a thrill in penetrating the villages which had hardly ever seen a Japanese soldier, let alone an Allied one. We found the mountain folk, as they are the world over, to be simple-living and courteous and every ready to help our patrols in any

---

26 South-East Asia Translation and Interpretation Corps. Attached to the Dorsets was Captain R. D. Farthing, of the Intelligence Corps, who with his knowledge of the language was a most useful member of my headquarters staff.

manner they could. Companies who visited the larger towns invariably received the greatest attention from the chief of police, and it was not uncommon for an official reception and a "saki-aki" party to be laid on for the officers and non-commissioned officers.

The coastline in our south-eastern area was not at all unlike the wilder parts of the Cornish coast with its small fishing villages, each with its minute harbour protected by a small mole from the fury of the Pacific. The Japanese man who lives on the coast seems to spend an incredible amount of his time in the water, swimming around with a pair of goggles over his eyes and, in his hand, a spear with which to catch fish.

Accommodation was our chief difficulty on these expeditions. Owing to the heavily over-cultivated nature of the country (the Nip does not waste a square inch of land on which he might grow something) it was practically impossible to find camping places except on the sea-shore—the problem was solved during August at the time of the school holidays, but became acute again in September when the schools returned and we were not allowed by S.C.A.P. rules to billet in these buildings.

I find I have written remarkably little of the customs and habits of the Japanese—and to overcome this deficiency I will recount briefly a trip I made with the Brigadier when we went on a fourday tour of my "gau". I had already had companies out in the centre of the island and down in the south-east corner in the Muroto Point area, which was the local Land's End, and we had come to know these areas fairly well. The trip planned by the Brigadier was to explore the north coast, where Shikoku Island basked lazily on the southern shores of the Inland Sea and north-west corner, where we hoped to find a hill station to where we could evacuate those of the Brigade who, like the Brigadier himself, were suffering from a particularly unpleasant form of prickly heat.

Brigadier Jock McNaught was also planning to move Brigade Headquarters and the Camerons to Zentsuji, near the north coast. I, most keen not to be left isolated and stranded at the end of this very attenuated line of communication during the winter, was eager to examine the possibilities of some old Japanese barracks farther to the west on the north coast, which might more suitably be developed as the Regimental Headquarters of the Fifty-Fourth. Having had to accept the south coast in the first place, we were all trying hard to get to the northern end of the island, where the communications were better, the climate more propitious and the chances of our being cut off for perhaps weeks at a time not quite so definite.

349

During this four-day trip we covered over four hundred miles, explored areas that had never previously seen a foreign soldier, let alone a brigadier's reconnaissance party, and encountered many of the problems which make travel in Japan such an adventurous undertaking, and had still at the end of it not nearly covered the whole compass of the Dorsets' "gau".

On our way we visited Zentzuji, which appeared to be an ideal place for a British garrison. It was the nearest approach to an Indian cantonment we had met in Japan and we had not realized that the Nip soldiers had it in them to organize such a comfortablelooking garrison. The next morning we visited Takuma. Certainly Brindiv had poured a great deal of money into this divisional holiday centre, but from what we could see of it the results were excellent. It was early days to judge, as we visited it just before the official opening. Every art and device of the W.V.S. had been put into this one-time Japanese naval air station to turn it into the No. 1 holiday centre of Japan in an effort to provide something better for B.C.O.F. than the facilities afforded for the G.I. by the "Eichelberger string of luxury hotels" in the American zone.

That day we pushed on west in an effort to find a reported hotel site on the lower slopes of the highest peak in Shikoku, Ishizuchiyama, which rose to nine thousand six hundred feet and promised to answer our problems. We made an unsuccessful visit to Imabari in search of a new barracks for the Battalion, and, acting on poor – or shall we say poorly understood? – information from the chief of police in this town, we tried to reach this mountain from the north. As dusk was falling we found ourselves in the very remote village of Kawagachi-bashi. For all the world we might have been back in a mountain hamlet of the Austrian Tyrol—exchange the inevitable print of some past local potentates, hanging in the dining-room, for some nineteenth-century Austrian princeling, leave the inevitable engraving of a "Stag at Bay", the same in any country, and there was very little difference. The same pedlar came in to tout his wares whilst we were eating our evening meal, and the landlord might well have been taken for the proprietor of a mountain pub in far-off Austria before the Anschluss. I suppose that the villages must have felt the war, but, if so, there was little indication of it. As everywhere in Japan, we found that even the remotest mountain chalet had its own electric light, with those most inadequately powered bulbs on their long flexes reaching almost to the floor, to cater for these people who, as I have indicated, live on the floor. If there was anything in Japan to cause me to revise the very firm ideas I had formed on the Japanese from fighting them it was the simple kindness and hospitality of these remote mountain folk in Northern Shikoku. The night before, we had stayed at a popular hotel in Kotahari, a town of shrines and much sought after by Japanese pilgrims. Furthermore, it had been developed by the Americans as a playground for enlisted men—and, compared with the vulgar display and lack of attention we received in that so-called first-class hotel, the simple hospitality, frugal as it was, of mine host of this wee mountain inn was overpowering. The Allied Forces on their wanderings had to be self-supporting, as there was no question of living on the country. All we could do was to hand in our pack rations and hope that, under the batman's supervision, the Japanese would not make too much of a nonsense of preparing a meal for Western palates. It cannot be denied that occasionally an egg or a head of corn appeared miraculously in place of a tin of bully beef, but by the rules of the game we were never allowed to sit down to a Japanese meal in a Japanese hotel.

A prominent feature of Japanese life on which I have not yet touched is the "pot, boiling, missionary", or the Japanese bath. It does not take one long to realize that handwriting is not the only thing that is done backwards in Japan. For example, saws are designed to pull and not to push, but probably one of their most upside-down habits is the bath. In the Japanese bathroom there stands a large cauldron which is heated by a fire lit underneath. That is the bath, but it is only there for the bather to soak in. First of all, he or she must wash and be scrubbed squatting on the cold tiles outside the bath (in the old days, I understand, the custom was that the house girl performed this operation). The bather is then rinsed out and every trace of soap removed before he or she is allowed to step gingerly into this cauldron. I say "gingerly" not only because of my length, which I found hard to curl up in this pot, but also because, having penetrated the top layer of recently added cool water, one suddenly strikes the boiling-hot water at about two feet, and as one stretches one's leg in agony one's foot encounters the red-hot bottom of the pot which has been in contact with a raging fire for some hours. As one finally acclimatizes oneself to the heat and prepares, Japanese fashion, for a long soak, or, British fashion, a mild sing-song, the fire decides to smoke and before long one is driven out into the cold exterior by overwhelming fumes of wood smoke. That is the worst case. I personally always enjoyed my "pot, boiling, missionary", though there were degrees of enjoyment dependent chiefly on the shape and capacity of the bath. The Jap method is certainly economic in water, if slightly messy according to European ideas. After all, we are not used to using the bathroom floor as a means of soaping down, scrubbing and finally rinsing ourselves with buckets of water before soaking in the bath, but, on the other hand, we insist on one bath full of hot water per person, gross extravagance to the Japanese, who, in their specially constructed bathrooms, can clean off their entire family with all their friends and relations at one brew-up.

This mountain hotel went to great trouble to ensure that their military guests were bathed, and before we sat down to our Japanese cooked Pacific "pack" ration we had all sampled yet another version of the Japanese bath.

The Japanese do not treat nakedness with the same seriousness as Western people. They have certain definite codes, all rather confusing to us, but it seems quite in order for the odd man to wander about his house with nothing on at all, and for the women to carry out her household chores in what we are pleased to call bare buff. I would add that this rule seems to apply mainly to aged men and women over sixty! However, the basic Japanese man's garment of the "fundoshi", or a pair of triangular-shaped pants, leaves little to the imagination.

Whilst on the subject of Japanese clothes or the lack of them in the summer, I must refer to their footwear. The normal Japanese shoe for both sexes is the "geta" or plain wooden sole with two bars two to three inches deep nailed laterally under them, on which the entire nation seems to clatter around the place. A most useful form of footwear for these apelike people, who all, from highest to lowest in the land, obey the invariable rule that no form of footwear shall be worn in the house—an excellent rule for a nation that lives off the floor. Those of us who lived in Japanese houses very soon learnt to do likewise, troublesome as it was at times to remove boots and puttees, and strange as it felt to move around in bare or stockinged feet. Some of the idler members of the British community had a special form of canvas covering made for their own and their guests' boots, and on arrival one would be invited to don a pair of "Mickey Mouses", as these contraptions came, rather obviously, to be called.

I find that I have said very little about the Japanese people as we found them. What, for example, had happened to that energetic jungle soldier who had fought us so stubbornly and at times most skilfully? Where was the brutal sub-human who had inflicted such appalling atrocities on his prisoners, not only in the internment camps in the rear areas, but right up in the front line? What had happened to the fanatic who could turn himself into a human antitank mine by crouching in a ditch with a two-hundred-and-fiftypound aircraft bomb between his knees and a stone in his hand waiting to detonate the charge immediately one of our tanks should overrun his trap? It was difficult to reconcile the Jap against whom we had fought with these peaceful and courteous peasants tilling their fields, the hard-working fisherman on the coast or the cheerful highlander up-country.

To the Americans it was all a case of fraternization and getting to know the Nip. Their attitude was explained to me by a senior officer of the 2nd U.S. Cavalry Brigade in Tokyo. He summed up by explaining that they had arrived, nine months earlier, straight from the Pacific War, like us raring to have a go at the Nip in his own country, since when they had got down to this business of teaching the Japanese democracy and educating him to a better way of life. They considered that the Nip had not the faintest idea of the meaning of democracy, and unless the Americans encouraged their soldiers to get around and talk to the Japanese they never would. That may be so and there is a wealth of sense in their attitude, irreconcilable as it was with the then current B.C.O.F. ruling of NO repeat NO fraternization.

However, it is my own view that the Nip we knew in war was fundamentally the same person as the demobilized service man we came across pursuing more peaceful activities in Japan. Whenever I felt that I was beginning to trust a Jap too much, or my sense of judgment was being affected by the courteous and prompt compliance with my instructions or if I were beginning to feel overlenient in any particular decision I had to make concerning them, I thought back to a small room in Yokohama. It was a room in the Allied Mausoleum, and I went there to try to trace the whereabouts of the remains of the son of an old regimental quartermastersergeant of the Regiment. I was taken into a room, by no means small, and was staggered to find that all four walls, from floor to ceiling, were covered with shelves, each shelf loaded with little black boxes containing the ashes of the three thousand-odd Commonwealth prisoners of war and internees who had died in captivity in Japan alone.

In this mood I did not have to think back very far to remember the British soldier bayoneted and buried alive at Ondaw or the Burman mutilated and burnt to death at Ye-U, to quote only two of thousands of cases, and to hope and pray that whilst this business of democratization and re-education of the Japanese proceeds, the Allies maintain a very firm grip on this beautiful land which breeds a race, the habits of whose males are as unpleasant as those of the women are charming.

Whilst the companies had been going out in rotation on their various patrols and had been opening up other parts of the "gau", we were busy planning and trying, despite the continued "freezing" of building materials, to develop the barracks in Gomen itself.

Gradually we were breaking the huge Japanese barrack rooms into cubicles and the living quarters and playing fields were improving out of all knowledge. The school and the church continued to function in the "ruined" block about half a mile away, which building had been badly blitzed and subsequently stripped by our predecessors to provide timber for repairs to the main buildings. There was little that we could do about this, despite the constant pleas of Brian Robbins and the Padre.

Later the Brigadier decided that the visit to the Royal Welch Fusiliers for the Brigade swimming meeting was an excellent opportunity to try out the seaworthiness of his boat, a harbour motorlaunch called the Ring o' Bells, and accordingly one morning a party which was virtually his "R" Group set out to reach Takushima by sea, journeying around the south-east point of the island and forging northwards on the most adventurous trip that boat had yet made. The swimming was a great success and it did us all good to visit the Royal Welch, so long removed from the remainder of the Brigade, and discuss afresh our worries and problems.

The Brigadier and I had to hurry back to Kochi by land to welcome the Divisional Commander, who was due to visit us. The General was in great form—he dined in the mess and we gave him an anniversary party to celebrate the first birthday of Brindiv. The next day, after inspecting the barracks, the General attended a Brigade boxing meeting and that night the Cameron officers were "at home" to him.

To our great joy some reinforcements had arrived out at last. Not for the first time in our recent history did we find our longpromised reinforcements to be redundant gunners. These young soldiers, released by the disbandment in India of the old 2nd Division Field Artillery Regiment, the 99th (Royal Bucks Yeomanry), set to with the same spirit to master the art of foot-soldiering as had our anti-aircraft gunners in Burma in 1944.

Lieutenant Gerry Overman had also returned from "Liap", bringing with him the mess silver, or certain selected items, which was a great joy to us. Another cause for satisfaction was the arrival of the photographs of the King and the Queen, both of which had been signed especially by Their Majesties. These were promptly placed in a position of honour in the dining-room alongside the Colours of the Battalion.

The Officers' Mess and Sergeants' Mess (whose silver had also arrived out) were now really beginning to look homely and attractive, and it was quite like old times to walk into the front door of the mess and be greeted once again by Peter Dowling's elephantfoot postbox.

Suddenly, out of the blue, I was detailed to find, at very short notice, a company to take on guards at Divisional Headquarters for a fortnight.

Our main worry in having to accede to such a request at short notice was that we had reluctantly been forced, owing to the shortage of men and especially non-commissioned officers, to disband "D" Company for a month or two, and so we were functioning on only three companies. Like the soldier showing socks at kit inspection we had "one on", that was the company out on patrol; "one in the wash", a company at training and doing extra-regimental duties, Brigade fatigue parties, guards for Koreans and the like, and "one here, sir", which was the duty company fully employed in making Marabout Lines function at all.

I appreciated that this sudden call to court was an excellent opportunity to show the flag, and I determined that the General must have the best possible material to guard him. Accordingly, I instructed the company commanders to find a platoon each of their known best drillers and "medal" men, stepped up with a very ample reinforcement from H.Q. Company, and pushed them off under the command of Major Phil Roberts of H.Q. Company, my only other field officer left apart from Tommy Thomas, who was at the time away up in the hills on the north coast.

With the guard company I sent the Drums and the concert party and dance band, which as I have said was in effect the Drums "off parade". We were determined to put on a show, and when I reached Okayama some days later to attend the guard company's "At Home" I found that they had all done their utmost to repeat a minor Operation "Primus".

It was most unfortunate that the first rain for weeks should have arrived on the very day that we were billed to beat "Retreat" for the General and Divisional Headquarters and Divisional troops, but the officers and British other rank parties went off as planned. It was the season of Dusera, the Hindu "Christmas", and the General was kept more than busy attending all the various functions. In view of this I cannot say how much we appreciated his taking time off on a night when he had at least three other engagements to attend the guard company officers' cocktail party in the Gunner mess, the non-commissioned officers' sing-song in their Club, and finally to drop in at the all ranks' dance given by the W.V.S. for the Dorsets in the really first-class British Other Ranks' Club that had been started in Okayama. The concert party had meanwhile performed twice and with such success that they were overwhelmed with bookings to such an extent that I had seriously to curb their ambitious projects before they were lost to the Battalion and their normal duties for the remainder of the winter.

As September turned gradually into October so the activities of the Brigade increased. Companies continued to disappear in rotation on Mondays and by the end of the week Dorset patrols would have penetrated far up into the hills. Meanwhile, for the remainder back in barracks, there was plenty to do. The Brigade Commander insisted on the Brigade taking an active interest in every kind of sport, and various competitions kept us very busy indeed. At about this time there was a resurgence of athletics in preparation for the challenge we had thrown out to the 34th Australian Brigade to come and spend the week-end and compete with us at track and field events.

At the beginning of October the 34th Australian Brigade athletics team with about a hundred supporters crossed from Honshu and visited the 5th Infantry Brigade at Kochi. At first the whole show looked like falling through owing to rain. Not just rain which flooded the very improvised track on the Camerons' square, but really torrential rain which caused one of the worst-yet landslides on the railway and cut off part of the Australian team, most of their spectators and the majority of the ladies of the Women's Services, invited down for the occasion to help out the limited number of hostesses available on Shikoku for the two dances we hoped to hold that week-end.

The track meeting postponed from the Saturday to the Monday was a great success. The Australians had been in training for the whole summer, whereas the units of the 5th Brigade, not having led quite such a settled existence, had started very much later in the season. We had had great difficulty in raising a team at all, mainly due to the modern soldier's preference for the role of spectator, or, if he must play something, his complete indifference to any sport other than Association football.

However, mainly owing to the enthusiasm and fine performance of Captain "Digger" Irvine, one of the Camerons' "lend-lease" Australian officers, the two Brigades were all square at the last event, the one-mile relay, and the 5th Brigade, although taking over in the lead for the last leg, were beaten by a truly match-winning sprint by the final Australian runner.

The meeting concluded with a display by the massed drums of the Royal Welch Fusiliers and the Dorsets, the pipers of the Camerons and the Australian band. The whole week-end, despite the efforts of the clerk of the weather to upset it, was a great success and did a very great deal to bring the two Brigades to a better understanding of each other's ways of life.

I must now strike a purely personal note, for at the end of October I was ordered home to attend a course at the Staff College. I had to leave the Fifty-Fourth in which regiment I had been born and which for nearly three years, some of the most exciting of its long life, I had had the great privilege to command. There can be no greater honour for an officer than to command a battalion of his own regiment in action, and when he has been faithfully served and has been able to see a successful campaign through to its logical conclusion by leading that battalion to the very heart of the enemy's empire, then indeed have the fates been kind.

At the risk of being egotistical, I would say that this is also the most suitable point at which to close the war records of the FiftyFourth. When at the beginning of November the *Empress of Australia* pulled out of Kure harbour she carried on board the last of the "Burma Stars", all due home on "Python" or release. Only three staunch veterans, O.R.Q.M.S. Jack Vaughan, C.S.M. Johnson and Sergeant Jesty, M.M., all three of whom had seen the Odyssey through from the beginning, remained.

WITH BRINDIV IN JAPAN, KOHIMA DAY, 1946

Battalion parade outside U.S. Army post, Matsue

Kohima veterans still serving with the Battalion on the second anniversary at Matsue, 13th May, 1946.

"OVER THE HILLS AND FAR AWAY"

TOKYO, JUNE 1946

Dorset guard takes over from Australian Battalion at Imperial Palace. Note American sentry with whom these posts were shared

Main entrance to Imperial Palace

Dorset sentry on Empire House

PLASSEY DAY 1946

The Corps of Drums

The Ensign (Lieut. J.Q. Terry) takes over the Colours

The Troop

PLASSEY DAY, 1946

General Eichelberger greets the Company Commanders

Allied Commanders on the Saluting Base

Tokyo as we found it

SHIKOKU

General view

A Japanese village

The Kochi Road after the earthquake

The main North-South axis across the island

EPILOGUE
6th January, 1948. Farewell parade of the 54th, Depot Barracks, Dorchester

Lieut.-Colonel D. B. Gaye hands over the Regimental Colour to Lord Shaftesbury

The Colours taken into the Officers' Mess, Regimental Depot, for safe keeping.

EPILOGUE

Take my drum to England, hang et by the shore,
Strike et when your powder's runnin' low.

[SIR HENRY NEWBOLT]

LITTLE DID I THINK, when our train pulled out of Gomen to the strains of "Auld Lang Syne", that just over a year later I would again hear the same sad tune played on the Depot square at Dorchester, as the Colours of the Fifty-Fourth were marched off parade for the last time. But that is how it was to be, and why I have come to add this final chapter to the war-time exploits of the 2nd Battalion The Dorsetshire Regiment.

The rapidly declining age rate of the officers of the Battalion took a sharp upward trend in December, 1947, with the arrival of Lieutenant-Colonel Douglas Gaye to command, accompanied by a new Second-in-Command, Major L. J. Wood, and the evergreen Teddy Edwards, returning to reoccupy his old stool in the Quartermaster's Stores. Both the new Commanding Officer and Second-inCommand had formerly served for a number of years in the Fifty-Fourth and had been with the Battalion during the occupation of the Rhine nearly twenty years earlier. As for Teddy, eighteen months' service at home had been more than enough for this old warrior, who now, in his thirtieth year of service, had gone abroad again to add yet one more Christmas to the already formidable number he had already spent overseas with the Regiment.

The Battalion, however, were not destined to spend a peaceful or prolonged existence in Japan. Douglas Gaye had hardly arrived before Shikoku was shattered by an earthquake which quite literally shook the Battalion out of bed into the cold darkness of a winter's morning. Happily the Pacific did not overflow into the low ground of the airstrip, but great havoc was caused by the tidal wave which forced its way up the long, narrow creek and flooded the countryside between Gomen and Kochi. For many days everyone was busily employed on all manner of rescue work. Communications ceased to exist and what had been a mere fourteen-mile run to Brigade became a forty-mile struggle over an abominable track along the foothills. The Dorsets earned special commendation for the part they played in alleviating the distress of the native population.

No sooner had the elements quietened and order been more or less restored than instructions were received that the British Brigade was to be withdrawn from Japan. There is no doubt that the grave manpower situation at home in 1946 made imperative the reduction of the Services and the withdrawal of British garrisons from the remoter parts of the world. The removal of the 25th British Independent Infantry Brigade[27] from Japan was one of the first of those evacuations of British troops with which we were to become all too familiar as the year rolled by. Whatever the reasons for the withdrawal of the British Brigade from Japan, this decision could not but be a great disappointment to those of us who had served in the occupation. That British, Dominion and United States forces were in a position mutually to tackle the problems of restoring Japan provided in itself an opportunity to study in peace the problems of integration so essential for the smooth conduct of operations. This was, however, little compared to the unique opportunity, the first and probably the only one, of studying the Japanese in their own country; a good chance, the value of which could not but be greatly reduced with the withdrawal of the British element from B.C.O.F..

At about the middle of February the Union Flag of Great Britain was lowered at Gomen for the last time as the Fifty-Fourth set out on their long journey towards home. On this occasion, following the example set by the Battalion when marching out of Bad Schwalbach in 1929, the flag was lowered by the oldest soldier, Captain Edwards, the Quartermaster.

A few days later the Battalion sailed from Kure in a snowstorm and by the beginning of March had arrived at their new station, an unfinished jungle camp at Kluang in Malaya. To the men there were few if any redeeming features in this move from Japan to South-East Asia. Barren in many ways as had been their existence on Shikoku Island, they had at least been occupational troops, a corps d'élite in a

---

27 At the end of 1945 a nine-year-long association with the 2nd Infantry Division was concluded. On the reorganization of the British Army the 2nd Infantry Division, a Regular formation, was re-formed in B.A.O.R. The units of the old 2nd Division remained in the Far East, and the brigades became independent formations, putting a figure "2" before their numbers. To perpetuate the association with the 2nd Division and to commemorate their tour with B.C.O.F. in Japan, Brigadier McNaught adopted as a formation sign for the 25th Brigade a Japanese Torii with the crossed keys inset.

picked force on a special role. They found but a poor substitute in the comparative dreariness of a peace-time garrison life under war-time living conditions in a basha camp in Malaya.

It was not long before it became apparent that the Fifty-Fourth were not to escape the greatest of all "axes" in the history of the British Infantry. Invariably in the past, the cessation of hostilities has brought about the reduction of junior regiments, but normally this process of "standing down" has been confined to what we now know as war service battalions. Never before in its long history has the British Army been faced with the disbandment, attempt, as you will, to anaesthetize the pain with any high-faluting term, of half of its premier war-winning arm, its Infantry. At one fell swoop one battalion of every regiment of the line ceased to exist!

By the autumn, or whatever goes for that season in Malaya, the Battalion knew their fate, and sadly the Fifty-Fourth packed their baggage for the last time. What a wealth of experience was stowed away with those precious heirlooms into that miscellany of crates and boxes which go to make up a regiment's impedimenta!

For one hundred and ninety-three years the Fifty-Fourth have campaigned and moved throughout the world. For nigh on two centuries the Regiment, raised by Colonel Campbell, have pursued the King's enemies and helped to maintain the British way of law and order throughout the globe. Their wanderings have carried them far and wide. From their initial experiences of service on the Rock of Gibraltar, through the forests of North America to their last station in the jungles of Malaya, what countless countries have heard the roll of their drums and the whistle of their fifes! The Battalion has penetrated during its lifetime west to Canada and Monte Video, south to the Cape of Good Hope, north to Pomerania, and east to Japan. It has encountered death from disease in the West Indies and the jungles of the Arakan and has endured the scorching heat of the deserts of North Africa and the plains of Central India. Finally, to wind up their record of service they made the great march from the Brahmaputra to Tokyo, and now they were returning home to be placed in honourable retirement.

The Battalion arrived home during the first week of January, 1948, having made the long voyage from Singapore in H.T. *Dilwara*. On Twelfth Night they marched through the town of Dorchester to receive an official but none the less enthusiastic welcome from the Mayor and Corporation. This was the first occasion on which any battalion of the Regiment had availed itself of the privilege of marching through the ancient Royal Borough with bayonets fixed and colours flying: an honour bestowed on the Regiment with the grant of the Honorary Freedom of the Borough in 1946.

Less than two hours later, witnessed by scores of old soldiers and friends of the Regiment, the Fifty-Fourth of Foot paraded for the last time in the pouring rain. On the Depot square, the home of the Regiment, the Colours were handed to the Lord-Lieutenant of the County, Lord Shaftesbury, who, in turn, surrendered them to the Depot for safe custody. As those Colours were trooped in slow time past the Battalion and marched off parade to the strains of "Auld Lang Syne", one could not but feel how appropriate were the words of Sir Henry Newbolt, at the head of this chapter, when applied to this sad occasion.

There, in our own county, we handed over our Colours, those emblems which we of the Infantry hold more sacred than Sir Francis Drake's followers ever held his "drum". The Battalion on their return home paid a final tribute to their Colours, knowing as they did so that should ever the call to arms ring out again then successors would be found to those generations of officers and men who have served His Majesty's one-time Fifty-Fourth Foot and 2nd Battalion The Dorsetshire Regiment, successors who would muster in force not only to maintain, but to add to, the proud traditions of the Battalion and the Regiment.

APPENDIX A

2ND BATTALION THE DORSETSHIRE REGIMENT

ROLL OF HONOUR 1939–1946

This roll is intended to cover only those who lost their lives whilst serving with the 2nd Battalion, or as a result of becoming a casualty whilst serving with the Battalion.

Intentional omissions include those officers and men who may have at one time served with the 2nd Battalion but who died or were killed whilst employed elsewhere.

It is realized with regret that this list may not be complete. Despite carefully kept records within the Battalion, a number of deaths occurred either among the prisoners of war in Germany during their long confinement or in the base hospitals of India.

OFFICERS

112802	2/Lt	Asser, J. J.	B.E.F.	27/5/40
129404	Lt.	Mayer, H. H.	Kohima	27/4/44
124852	Lt.	Deane, A. D.	Kohima	12/5/44
197212	Capt.	Morice, M. A.	Manipur Road	28/5/44
193782	Capt.	Davies, E. A.	Manipur Road	4/6/44
74659	Capt.	Purser, R. L. M.	Manipur Road	19/6/44
156959	Capt.	Smith, R. J. C. (R.A.)	Maram	4/11/44
147177	Major	Bowles, H. D.	Mu River	4/1/45
170157	Lt.	Cuthbertson, R. M.	Advance to Mandalay	10/3/45

OTHER RANKS

Dates marked with an asterisk are approximate

5723371	Pte.	Foot, G. E.	B.E.F.	15/10/39
5726236	Pte.	Hughes, E. W.	B.E.F.	10/5/40*
5723904	Pte.	Chapman, W.H.	B.E.F.	22/5/40
5726037	Pte.	Toseland, B. A.	B.E.F.	22/5/40*
5724236	Pte.	Bryant, C.	B.E.F.	24/5/40*
5727552	Pte.	Butler, W.	B.E.F.	25/5/40

576297	Pte.	Gray, P.	B.E.F.	25/5/40
5727369	Pte.	Palmer, D. A.	B.E.F.	25/5/40
5724091	Pte.	Cronin, T. P.	B.E.F.	26/5/40
5725802	Pte.	Cotton, J.	B.E.F.	26/5/40
5727720	Pte.	Danon, F. J.	B.E.F.	26/5/40
5722307	Pte.	Guy, S.	B.E.F.	26/5/40
5723434	Pte.	Goodman, W. H.	B.E.F.	26/5/40
5727513	Pte.	Hall, F.	B.E.F.	26/5/40
5722108	P.S.M.	Meakin, H.	B.E.F.	26/5/40
5726246	Pte.	Newman, G. H.	B.E.F.	26/5/40
2567373	Pte.	Needham, J. T.	B.E.F.	26/5/40
5727704	Pte.	Price, R.	B.E.F.	26/5/40
5724468	Pte.	Preece, F. A.	B.E.F.	26/5/40
5722469	Pte.	Pook, C. E.	B.E.F.	26/5/40
5723354	Pte.	Riggs, W. L. G.	B.E.F.	26/5/40
5726146	Pte.	Sinnott, J. J.	B.E.F.	26/5/40
5721920	Cpl.	Shanks, J. C.	B.E.F.	26/5/40
5727670	Pte.	Smith, R.	B.E.F.	26/5/40
5727536	Pte.	Smith, C. G.	B.E.F.	26/5/40
5726271	A./Cpl.	Benton, H.	B.E.F.	27/5/40*
5103520	L./Cpl.	Hill, W. A.	B.E.F.	27/5/40
5726412	Pte.	Nolan, J.	B.E.F.	27/5/40
5725540	Pte.	Orpwood, J. W.	B.E.F.	27/5/40
5726231	Pte.	Swinchatt, L. D.	B.E.F.	27/5/40
5723250	Pte.	Harris, R.	B.E.F.	28/5/40*
68021	Pte.	Pigott, W. A.	B.E.F.	30/5/40
5725974	Pte.	Crowter, D. B.	B.E.F.	31/5/40
5727283	Pte.	Hare, J. H.	B.E.F.	31/5/40*
5723184	Pte.	Humphries, C. W.	B.E.F.	31/5/40
5723009	Pte.	Gloyn, E. C.	B.E.F.	1/6/40
5726050	Pte.	Gooch, W.F.[28]	B.E.F.	9/7/40
5726047	Pte	Provett, S.R.	B.E.F.	29/8/40
5726212	Pte.	Clarke, D. H.	B.E.F.	3/3/41*
5728773	Pte.	Lewis, W. J.	South Africa	21/5/42
5729361	Pte.	Kellaway, L.	South Africa	17/6/42
5724350	Pte.	Hayes, S. J.	India	7/8/42
5733826	L./Cpl.	Nursaw, G.	Kohima	12/4/44
3907267	Pte.	Taylor, W.	Kohima	14/4/44
5728409	Pte.	Bash, F.	Kohima	14/4/44

---

28 Served as F. J. Smith.

5729025	Pte.	Atkins, S.	Kohima	14/4/44
5729649	Pte.	Callcott, P.	Kohima	14/4/44
5727682	Pte.	Gaze, T.	Kohima	26/4/44
5727928	Pte.	Colyer, A.	Kohima	26/4/44
5727888	Pte.	Gould, D.	Kohima	26/4/44
14353081	Pte.	Collins, C.	Kohima	26/4/44
5723694	Sgt.	Adams, G.	Kohima	27/4/44
5722833	Cpl.	Softley, H.	Kohima	27/4/44
5774246	Pte.	Mathews, D.	Kohima	27/4/44
5727034	Pte.	Maidment, R.	Kohima	27/4/44
5727535	L./Cpl.	Smart, W.	Kohima	27/4/44
5733780	Pte.	Rogers, W.	Kohima	27/4/44
14548603	Pte.	Fenn, W.	Kohima	27/4/44
5731790	Pte.	Maxwell, D.	Kohima	27/4/44
5729638	L./Cpl.	Khan, H.	Kohima	27/4/44
5729108	L./Cpl.	Haytree, A.	Kohima	27/4/44
5729533	Pte.	Harris, J.	Kohima	27/4/44
2562757	L./Sgt.	Perrett, W.	Kohima	27/4/44
14541716	Pte.	Reynolds, W.	Kohima	27/4/44
5728489	L./Cpl.	Hunt, H.	Kohima	27/4/44
5729251	Pte.	Gray, B.	Kohima	27/4/44
5728229	Cpl.	Berry, D.	Kohima	27/4/44
5628765	Cpl.	Hooppell, E.	Kohima	27/4/44
14557254	Pte.	Bird, C.	Kohima	27/4/44
5728260	Pte.	Backey, K.	Kohima	27/4/44
5730899	Pte.	Dudman, P.	Kohima	27/4/44
5730983	Pte.	Davies, E.	Kohima	27/4/44
5728831	Pte.	Holder, E.	Kohima	27/4/44
5731921	Pte.	Grandfield, H.	Kohima	27/4/44
5727297	Pte.	Hoadley, H.	Kohima	27/4/44
5728954	Pte.	Wright, F.	Kohima	27/4/44
5726968	Pte.	Clark, F.	Kohima	27/4/44
5733097	Pte.	Zeitman, J.	Kohima	27/4/44
5727223	Pte.	Carvell, H.	Kohima	29/4/44
5729597	Pte.	Osborne, E.	Kohima	30/4/44
14334541	Pte.	Bone, F.	Kohima	30/4/44
14353147	Pte.	Jones, H.	Kohima	30/4/44
14353068	Pte.	Upson, C.	Kohima	30/4/44
5727262	Pte.	Fossey, F. L.	India	30/4/44
5722158	C.S.M.	Downton, H.	Kohima	1/5/44
5725039	Sgt.	Varley, C.	Kohima	1/5/44

5730381	Pte.	Blake, E.	Kohima	1/5/44
5725462	L./Cpl.	Toms, R.	Kohima	1/5/44
5732510	Pte.	Nixon, A.	Kohima	1/5/44
5729528	L./Cpl.	Culverwell, C.	Kohima	1/5/44
5724673	C.S.M.	Draper, G.	Kohima	2/5/44
811100	L./Sgt.	Cobb, H.	Kohima	2/5/44
5728810	Cpl.	Plantard, J.	Kohima	2/5/44
5726010	Pte.	Fraser, A.	Kohima	2/5/44
5727100	Pte.	Lawrence, E.	Kohima	2/5/44
5727273	Pte.	Godsell, G.	Kohima	2/5/44
5730889	Pte.	Andrews, L.	Kohima	2/5/44
5725709	Sgt.	Clarkson, R.	Kohima	3/5/44
5734100	Pte.	O'Reilly, M.	Kohima	3/5/44
5729693	Pte.	Gregory, W.	Kohima	4/5/44
5628181	Cpl.	Murphy, W.	Kohima	4/5/44
14408212	Pte.	Evans, G. M.	Kohima	4/5/44
3908172	Pte.	Evans, L.	Kohima	4/5/44
14410527	Pte.	Baxter, D.	Kohima	4/5/44
5728217	Pte.	Handell, D.	Kohima	4/5/44
14377902	Pte.	Billing, S.	Kohima	4/5/44
14207969	Pte.	Bates, J.	Kohima	4/5/44
5730903	Pte.	Harwood, R.	Kohima	4/5/44
5725719	Cpl.	Bottrill, F.	Kohima	4/5/44
5723882	Sgt.	Messenger, G.	Kohima	4/5/44
5728369	Pte.	Pitt, A.	Kohima	5/5/44
5630333	Pte.	Wignall, J.	Kohima	5/5/44
5732861	Pte.	Marshall, R.	Kohima	6/5/44
5734180	Pte.	Turner, G.	Kohima	6/5/44
5728951	Cpl.	Woolford, D.	Kohima	6/5/44
5733090	Pte.	Welsh, E.	Kohima	6/5/44
5732153	Pte.	Gregory, J.	Kohima	7/5/44
5729127	L./Sgt.	Manning, E.	Kohima	8/5/44
5728066	Pte.	Wicks, C.	Kohima	10/5/44
5722674	Pte.	Smith, S.	Kohima	11/5/44
5729116	L./Cpl.	Hinton, S.	Kohima	12/5/44
5723613	Cpl.	Siggins, A.	Kohima	13/5/44
14386913	Pte.	Laythorne, T.	Kohima	14/5/44
3907267	Pte.	Taylor, W.	Kohima	14/5/44
5724586	L./Cpl.	Taylor, W.	Kohima	14/5/44
5729464	Pte.	Hobby, L.	Manipur Road	4/6/44
5727568	Cpl.	Green, N.	Manipur Road	4/6/44

5728872	Pte.	Collis, J.	Manipur Road	4/6/44
5731158	L./Cpl.	Theed, F.	Manipur Road	5/6/44
14356734	Pte.	Willimott, L.	Manipur Road	12/6/44
5730535	Cpl.	Robinson, F.	Manipur Road	20/6/44
14398292	Pte.	Grant, I.	Manipur Road	21/6/44
5729157	Pte.	Pearce, A.	Manipur Road	21/6/44
5577620	Pte.	Dalton, T.	India	23/6/44
5733597	Cpl.	Taylor, J.	Manipur Road	8/7/44
5726605	Pte.	Park, F.	India	17/7/44
5735312	Pte.	Weaver, A.	India	13/8/44
5730846	Pte.	Lucas, G.	India	20/8/44
5731805	Pte.	Neal, A.	India	20/10/44
11426102	Gnr.	Heywood, L.	India	10/11/44
155368	Gnr.	Sexton, T.	India	14/11/44
5679680	Pte.	Mears, A.	Yazagyo	17/12/44
14300828	Gnr.	Edmunds, R.	Ye-U	2/1/45
5726058	Pte.	Fish, M.	Ye-U	3/1/45
1635755	Gnr.	Park, W.	Ye-U	3/1/45
5187911	Bdr.	Crawford, A.	Mu River	4/1/45
5189898	Gnr.	Warner, R.	Mu River	4/1/45
11271165	Gnr.	Hopkins, T.	Mu River	4/1/45
11051862	Pte.	Page, W.	Mu River	4/1/45
11420960	Gnr.	Jones, A.	Mu River	4/1/45
1829541	Gnr.	Roberts, F.	Mu River	5/1/45
5728598	Pte.	Roche, P.	Schwebo	9/1/45
1769951	Gnr.	Hindes, W.	Burma	9/2/45
5624783	Pte.	Guest, F. (1st Glos)	Irrawaddy	25/2/45
4203299	Pte.	Walsh, E. (1st Glos)	Irrawaddy	25/2/45
1825227	Gnr.	Hall, J.	Irrawaddy	25/2/45
5726295	Cpl.	Reynel, A.	Irrawaddy	26/2/45
5570574	Pte.	Pinnegar, A.	Irrawaddy	26/2/45
3451166	Pte.	Wrigley, E.	Advance to Mandalay	10/3/45
5727765	Pte.	Merchant, A.	Advance to Mandalay	10/3/45
5728873	Pte.	Casey, W.	Advance to Mandalay	10/3/45
1520022	Gnr.	Stark, R.	Advance to Mandalay	10/3/45
5731698	Pte.	Painter, F.	Advance to Mandalay	10/3/45
859272	Pte.	Easter, R.	Advance to Mandalay	10/3/45
5568771	Cpl.	Hughes, W. (1st Glos)	Advance to Mandalay	10/3/45
5727764	L./Cpl.	Hicks, H.	Advance to Mandalay	10/3/45
5629163	Pte.	Collins, C.	Advance to Mandalay	10/3/45
14412975	Pte.	Peavoy, J.	Advance to Mandalay	10/3/45

5728932	Pte.	Silkman, H.	Advance to Mandalay	10/3/45
1829210	Gnr.	Cole, V.	Advance to Mandalay	10/3/45
968981	Bdr.	Harris, A.	Advance to Mandalay	10/3/45
5728157	Pte.	Hett, H.	Advance to Mandalay	10/3/45
2081982	Gnr.	Hemming, A.	Advance to Mandalay	5/3/45
11051786	Pte.	Cromer, R.	Advance to Mandalay	15/3/45
14398207	Pte.	Hampton, C.	Advance to Mandalay	15/3/45
1601985	L./Bdr.	Steggles, W.	Advance to Mandalay	15/3/45
1565091	Gnr.	Kidner, L.	Advance to Mandalay	15/3/45
5190966	Gnr	Cullimore, B.	Advance to Mandalay	15/3/45
1493913	Gnr.	Bailey, A.	Advance to Mandalay	15/3/45
1708505	Gnr.	Skues, H.	Mandalay	15/3/45
5731222	Pte.	Acourt, R.	Mandalay	20/3/45
5730893	Pte.	Burden, G.	Mandalay	21/3/45
1829561	Gnr.	Howe, J.	Mandalay	21/3/45
5989996	Cpl.	Crane, P.	Advance to Popa	29/3/45
3911731	L./Cpl.	McCrudden, J.	Advance to Popa	5/4/45
1829527	Pte.	Oscroft, P.	Advance to Popa	7/4/45
5728186	Pte.	Elford, H.	Advance to Popa	8/4/45
5575665	Pte.	Ball, H.	India	17/4/45
5728090	L./Sgt.	Kennedy, E.	Burma	6/6/45
5734313	Pte.	Rudman, J.	India	15/11/45
5577620	L./Cpl.	Beckett, R. E.	India	25/2/46
14843083	L./CpI.	Kinman, J.	Japan	22/9/46
14847018	Pte.	Box, G. A.	Japan	19/11/46
14986513	L./Cpl.	Hewison, K.	Japan	29/12/46

APPENDIX B

HONOURS AND AWARDS RECEIVED BY MEMBERS OF THE 2ND BATTALION THE DORSETSHIRE REGIMENT 1939—1946

"France" includes Flanders, 1940.
"Burma" includes Assam and Manipur State, 1944-45.

OFFICERS

DISTINGUISHED SERVICE ORDER

Lieutenant-Colonel E. L. Stephenson, M.C.	France
Lieutenant-Colonel R. S. McNaught	Burma
Lieutenant-Colonel O. G. W. White	Burma

OFFICER OF THE ORDER OF THE BRITISH EMPIRE

Major R. E. C. Goff, M.C.	France
Major B. G. Symes	France

MILITARY CROSS

Captain J. G. Heron	France
Captain H. A. A. Bray	France
Captain J. A. L. Peebles	France
Captain C. Chettle	Burma
Major T. G. Tucker	Burma
Captain L. T. Highett	Burma
Captain J. A. Chamberlin (R.A.M.C.)	Burma
Captain L. E. M. Claxton (R.A.Ch.D.)	Burma
Captain J. F. Thom (R.A.)	Burma

MEMBER OF THE ORDER OF THE BRITISH EMPIRE

Lieutenant F. J. Edwards	India
Captain N. Havers	Burma

MENTIONED IN DESPATCHES

Lieutenant F. J. Edwards	France

Major H. D. Bowles	Burma
Major T. G. Tucker, M.C. (Hampshire Regt., attached)	Burma
Lieutenant L. T. Highett, M.C.	Burma
Lieutenant V. C. Pullin (1st Glosters, attached)	Burma
Captain R. L. M. Purser	Burma
Lieutenant-Colonel O. G. W. White, D.S.O.	Burma
Major H. P. K. Fretts	Burma
Major G. C. Gordon Wright	Burma
Captain J. R. Main	Burma
Lieutenant G. G. Overman	Burma
Captain A. C. Mackenzie (Somerset L.I., attached)	Burma
Captain J. A. Chamberlin M.C. (R.A.M.C.)	Burma
Major A. V. N. Bridge	Burma
Major D. McL. Baynes	Burma

OTHER RANKS

MEMBER OF THE ORDER OF THE BRITISH EMPIRE

5721400	R.S.M. H. Smith	India
5723313	R.Q.M.S. R. G. Hayward	Burma

DISTINGUISHED CONDUCT MEDAL

5721994	P.S.M. E. Giles	France
5724708	Sergeant W. J. Cooper	France
5720440	P.S.M. S. Brown	France
5718503	P.S.M. R. A. Brown	France
5722194	Sergeant W. F. Seale	Burma

MILITARY MEDAL

5724467	Sergeant R. F. James	France
5726158	Private T. Tabb	France
5725357	Private H. West	France
5728400	Sergeant R. Given	Burma
5723975	Corporal W. Mansfield	Burma
14417029	Private F. J. Clarke	Burma
5730366	Corporal F. H. Warren	Burma
5723746	Lance-Corporal H. C. Jesty	Burma

MENTIONED IN DESPATCHES

5724455	P.S.M. H. D. Bowles	France
5720640	Sergeant D. S. Mullins	France

5724674	Sergeant H. J. Pearcey	France
5721482	Sergeant F. J. Smith	France
5722597	Corporal J. W. Adams	France
5726027	Private M. Dunne	France
5723346	Private J. G. S. Morton	France
5726146	Private J. J. Sinnott (posthumous)	France
5726306	Private J. Graham (escaped as POW)	France
5723742	Private C. G. Knight (escaped as POW)	France
5728882	Corporal M. J. Evans	Burma
5725275	Corporal D. E. Shearer	Burma
5723313	R.Q.M.S. R.G. Hayward	Burma
5728760	Sergeant A. T. Critchley	Burma
5723356	Sergeant F. A. Curtis	Burma
5722194	Sergeant W. F. Seale	Burma
5728879	Lance-Corporal W. T. Davies	Burma
5728027	Sergeant T. L. C. Knowles	Burma
5723746	Lance-Corporal H. C. Jesty	Burma
5723746	Private H. H. Bishop	Burma
5727589	Private R. Taylor	Burma
5724973	Corporal G. H. M. Cripps	Burma
5718457	C.S.M. A. Osmond	Burma
5727586	Sergeant J. D. Watling	Burma
5724356	Lance-Corporal A. E. Woodford	Burma

COMMANDER-IN-CHIEFS CERTIFICATE FOR GALLANTRY

5722194	C.S.M. W. F. Seale	Burma
5728760	Sergeant A. T. Critchley	Burma

COMMANDER-IN-CHIEF'S CERTIFICATE (HOME FORCES)

5721400	R.S.M. H. Smith
5722158	C.Q.M.S. Downton

The following officers and men, whilst serving away from the Battalion, received the undermentioned awards for the campaign in Burma. All these officers and men served with the 2nd Battalion at some time during the war and occupation of Japan from 1939 to 1947.

COMPANION OF THE BATH

Major-General G. N. Wood, D.S.O., O.B.E., M.C. — OC 2nd Dorset 1941-42

COMPANION OF THE ORDER OF THE BRITISH EMPIRE

Major-General G. N. Wood, C.B., D.S.O., O.B.E., M.C. — O.C. 2nd Dorset, 1941-42

DISTINGUISHED SERVICE ORDER

Major-General G. N. Wood, O.B.E., M.C. — O.C. 2nd Dorset, 1941-42
Lieutenant-Colonel B. G. Symes, O.B.E. — Coy. Cmdr., 1939-41
Lieutenant-Colonel J. M. K. Bradford — H.Q. Company, 1939-40

MENTIONED IN DESPATCHES

Major-General G. N. Wood, C.B., C.B.E., D.S.O., M.C. — O.C. 2nd Dorset, 1941-42
Lieutenant-Colonel B. G. Symes, D.S.O. — Coy. Cmdr., 1939-41
Lieutenant-Colonel J. M. K. Bradford, D.S.O. — H.Q. Company, 1939-40
Major G. N. Crowther — Coy. Officer, 1941-43
Lieutenant-Colonel L. J. Wood — Second-in-Comd., 1946-47
Major C. S. H. Doran — Adjutant, 1944
Major E. K. Govett (twice) — Signal Officer, 1942-44
Captain S. H. Prebble — I.O., 1941-43
5724367 Sergeant E. H. Burnett — Duty N.C.O., 1939-40
5721199 Sergeant F. Bagnall — Ration N.C.O., 1941-44
5721464 Lance-Corporal J. H. Singleton — C.O.'s Batman, 1941-42

APPENDIX C

THE DORSETS CERTAINLY GET AROUND.

TABLE OF MOVES OF THE 2ND BATTALION THE DORSETSHIRE REGIMENT, 1939-47

General Northcott, when bidding farewell to the officers of the Battalion in Tokyo, made the remark quoted at the head of this appendix. Between 1939 and 1948 the Battalion travelled from England to Tokyo and back. It is of interest to tabulate their wanderings in this appendix.

Actual campaign moves, towards or in contact with the enemy, as opposed to purely operational moves (which most war-time moves were anyway) and "peace" moves are shown in block capitals.

The dates are as nearly accurate as can be ascertained, but may be a day or two out in some places. In some cases there is no firm indication on record of the exact date of a move and the month only is given.

The moves, unless otherwise indicated, are of Battalion Headquarters.

Date dep	From	To	Date arr'd.	Remarks
1939				
23 Sept.	Aldershot	Cherbourg	24 Sept.	To join B.E.F.
24 Sept.	Cherbourg	Boussay	25 Sept.	
30 Sept.	Boussay	Achiet le Grand	3 Oct.	
5 Oct.	Achiet	Rumegics	5 Oct.	Battle positions.
2 Dec.	Rumegies	Agny	2 Dec.	Rest area.
23 Dec.	Agny	SAAR	23 Dec.	"D" Company only.
24 Dec.	Agny	Lecelles	24 Dec.	
1940				
14 Jan.	Lecellcs	Rumegies	14 Jan.	Action Stations.
Jan.	SAAR	Rumegies	Jan.	"D" Company only.
4 Apr.	Rumegies	Louvencourt	4 Apr.	Training.
9 Apr.	Louvencourt	Rumegies	9 Apr.	
11 May	Rumegies	MARAIS DE WIRIE (Nr. TOURNAI)	11 May	Start of Campaign. Move into Belgium.

Date dep	From	To	Date arr'd.	Remarks
12 May	MARAIS	GENVAL	12 May	Divisional concentration area on River DYLE.
16 May	GENVAL (area)	GHOY	17 May	Withdrawal begins.
19 May	GHOY	ORCQ (TOURNAI)	19 May	
20 May	ORCQ	TAINTIGNIES	20 May	
21 May	TAINTIGNIES	ST. MAUR	21 May	
21 May	ST. MAUR	MERLIN	21 May	
22 May	MERLIN	MOUCHIN	23 May	Recrossed frontier into France.
24 May	MOUCHIN	FESTUBERT	24 May	
27 May	FESTUBERT	ESTAIRES	28 May	
28 May	ESTAIRES	WATOU	28 May	
28 May	WATO	BERGUES	29 May	
29 May	BERGUES	DUNKIRK (area)	29 May	
31 May	DUNKIRK	Margate	31 May	
31 May	Margate	Pudsey	1 June	
22 June	Pudsey	Hornsea	22 June	
1941				
Mar.	Hornsea	Selby	Mar.	
18 May	Selby	Hornsea	18 May	
15 June	Hornsea	Selby	15 June	
19 Aug.	Selby	Boroughbridge	19 Aug.	
9 Dec.	Boroughbridge	Banbury	10 Dec.	
1942				
10 Apr.	Banbury	Liverpool	10 Apr.	Embarked H.T. *Reina del Pacifico*.
12 Apr.	Liverpool	The Clyde	13 Apr.	
15 Apr.	The Clyde	Freetown	29 Apr.	
3 May	Freetown	Capetown	15 May	
19 May	Capetown	Bombay	2 June	
5 June	Bombay	Poona (Kirkee)	5 June	Pashan Camp.
13 July	Poona	Secunderabad	15 July	Gough Barracks, Trimulgherry.
17 Sept.	Secunderabad	Kharakvasla (Poona)	19 Sept.	C.T.C. (I)
1 Oct.	Kharakvasla	Secunderabad	3 Oct.	Gun Rock Camp.
3 Oct.	Secunderabad	Ahmednagar	11 Oct.	Ex TREK.

Date dep	From	To	Date arr'd.	Remarks
30 Nov.	Ahmednagar	Anand	2 Dec.	Internal Security Duties.
27 Dec.	Anand	Ahmednagar	29 Dec.	
1943				
16 Jan.	Ahmednagar	Juhu	17 Jan.	
1 Feb.	Juhu	Aksa	1 Feb.	
15 Feb.	Aksa	Juhu	15 Feb.	
18 Mar.	Juhu	Bhiwandi	19 Mar.	
1 Apr.	Bhiwandi	Bombay	1 Apr.	Training aboard H.T. *El Hind*.
6 Apr.	Bombay	Bhiwandi	6 Apr.	
30 Apr.	Bhiwandi	Mahableshwar	4 May	Staging Poona (Pashan), Wai.
31 May	Mahableshwar	Nira-Gulunchi	31 May	
31 Oct.	Gulunchi	Bombay	1 Nov.	Ex *Swordfish* H.T. (*Winchester Castle*).
11 Nov.	Bombay	Visapur	12 Nov.	
27 Nov.	Visapur	Astoli (Belgaum area)	29 Nov.	Staging Satara, Belgaum.
23 Dec.	Astoli	Belgaum	23 Dec.	
31 Dec.	Belgaum	Visapur	1 Jan.	Staging Satara.
1944				
2 Feb.	Visapur	Jagalpet (Belgaum area)	4 Feb.	Staging Satara, Belgaum.
19 Mar.	Jagalpet	Dandeli	19 Mar.	
21 Mar.	Dandeli	Ahmednagar	23 Mar.	Staging Belgaum, Satara.
28 Mar.	Ahmednagar	BOKAJAN, ASSAM	4 Apr.	5th Brigade concentration area.
10 Apr.	BOKAJAN	DIMAPUR	10 Apr.	
11 Apr.	DIMAPUR	MANIPUR ROAD MS31	11 Apr.	Into action.
26 Apr.	Battalion enters perimeter at GARRISON HILL, KOHIMA			Under command 6th Infantry Brigade/
15 May	KOHIMA	Dimapur	15 May	Rest and refit.
23 May	Dimapur	KOHIMA (area)	23 May	The Battle of KOHIMA continues, reverted to 5th Infantry Brigade.
3 June	KOHIMA	PFUCHAMA	5 June	Break out begins.

Date dep	From	To	Date arr'd	Remarks
7 June	PFUCHAMA	KIGWEMA MS54	7 June	
9 June	KIGWEMA	VISWEMA (area) MS59¼	9 June	Battle of VISWEMA.
17 June	VISWEMA	KHUZAMA MS64	17 June	
18 June	KHUZAMA	MS77½	18 June	"Primus ex Indis."
19 June	MS77½	MS82	20 June	Night advance. Battle of Maram.
22 June	MS82	MS 100	22 June	Manipur Road opened.
27 June	MS100	IMPHAL	27 June	Rest and reorganize.
19 July	IMPHAL	PALEL MS29	19 July	Tamu Road.
23 July	PALEL	SHENAM RIDGE RECCE. HILL (MS39¼)	23 July	With 23rd Indian Division.
29 July	RECCE. HILL	MS46	29 July	
3 Aug.	MS46	BULLDOZER RIDGE	3 Aug.	
4 Aug.	BULLDOZER RIDGE	"ORANGE" MS62	4 Aug.	
10 Aug.	"ORANGE"	MS46	11 Aug.	
11 Aug.	MS46	PALEL	11 Aug.	
12 Aug.	PALEL	Maram MS82 (Manipur Road)	12 Aug.	Reorganize and refit.
29 Nov.	Maram	YAZAGYO	1 Dec.	Divisional concentration area. Staged Palel, Tamu.
20 Dec.	YAZAGYO	CHAUNGZUN	21 Dec.	Crossed CHINDWIN, 1st light, 21 December.
24 Dec.	CHAUNGZUN	THETGYGIN	25 Dec.	The advance begins.
25 Dec.	THETGYGIN	OKHAN	25 Dec.	
26 Dec.	OKHAN	PYINGAIN	27 Dec.	
29 Dec.	PYINGAIN	SAUKHAN	30 Dec.	
31 Dec.	SAUKHAN	LETLAW	31 Dec.	
1945				
1 Jan.	LETLAW	WETPO	1 Jan.	Advance to contact.
2 Jan.	WETPO	YE-U	2 Jan.	Skirmish and occupation of town.
3-4 Jan.	THE PASSAGE OF THE R. MU			
5 Jan.	Battalion concentrates at THAYETPINZU in the bridgehead.			
7 Jan.	THAYETPINZU	KANTHIT	7 Jan.	

Date dep	From	To	Date arr'd	Remarks
8 Jan.	KANTHIT	Pt. 346 Road YE-U—SCHWEBO	8 Jan.	
9 Jan.	Pt. 346	SCHWEBO		
11 Jan.	SCHWEBO	MOKSOGYON	11 Jan.	
12 Jan.	MOKSOGYON	HALLIN TWINMA	12 Jan.	"Hot Springs"
18 Jan.	HALLIN TWINMA	WETLET	18 Jan.	
29 Jan.	WETLET	ONDAW	29 Jan.	Under Command 4th Infantry Brigade.
4 Feb.	ONDAW	MAUNGDAUNG	4 Feb.	Reverted 5th Infantry Brigade.
8 Feb.	MAUNGDAUNG	area DAWETE-TADAING	8 Feb.	
25 Feb.	Battalion crosses the IRRAWADDY RIVER.			
26 Feb.	Advance to and capture NGAZUN Extension of bridgehead.			
7 Mar.	NGAZUN	To area 1,000 yds. EAST of NGAZUN	7 Mar.	
9 Mar.	EAST of NGAZUN	PAUK-AINGGON	9 Mar.	
9 Mar.	PAUK-AINGGON	DIRTY PAGODA HILL	10 Mar.	Night infiltration.
11 Mar.	DIRTY PAGODA	KYAUKTALON	11 Mar.	
13 Mar.	KYAUKTALON	LETPANZIN	13 Mar.	
14 Mar.	LETPANZIN	SINDE	14 Mar.	Skirmish: Right "Hook" across country.
15 Mar.	SINDE	KADOZEIK	15 Mar.	Action: Right "Hook" across country.
16 Mar.	KADOZEIK	NGAYAGA	16 Mar.	
17 Mar.	NGAYAGA	AVA	17 Mar.	
18 Mar.	AVA	AVA BRIDGE	18 Mar.	Crossed MYITINGE at first light.
19 Mar.	AVA BRIDGE	MANDALAY	19 Mar.	In contact 19-20 Mar.
24 Mar.	MANDALAY	AVA	14 Mar.	
27 Mar.	AVA	TAUNGBE	27 Mar.	

Date dep	From	To	Date arr'd	Remarks
29 Mar.	TAUNGBE	Area East of Myingyan	29 Mar.	
30 Mar.	Advanced Eastwards to clear area - Bivouacked EAST of KYAUKYAN.		30 Mar.	
2 Apr.	KYAUKYAN	WELLAUNG MS429	2 Apr.	Road MYINGYAN-KYAUK-PADAUNG
3 Apr.	WELLAUNG	MS417	3 Apr.	
4 Apr.	MS417	MS414	4 Apr.	Battle of LEGYI (Right "Hook")
12 Apr.	MS414	MS410½	12 Apr.	Advance to contact. Skirmish at GYAINGYWA
12-20 Apr.	Operations before MOUNT POPA.		20 Apr.	Road opened.
20 Apr.	MS410½	POPA		
23 Apr.	POPA	Myingyan	23 Apr.	
25 Apr.	Myingyan	Chittagong	25 Apr.	By air.
25 Apr.	Chittagong	Bandel	27 Apr.	By rail — water transport. 30 miles north of Calcutta.
3 June	Bandel	Kamareddi	5 June	60 miles north of Secunderabad.
16 Sept.	Kamareddi	Nazik	18 Sept.	Satpur Camp.
1946				
16 Mar.	Nazik	Bombay	16 Mar.	1st Sea Echelon embarked H.T. J *Arundel Castle*.
17 Mar.	Bombay	Kure	4 Apr.	
25 Mar.	Nazik (Satpur)	Deolali (Nazik Road)	25 Mar.	Billeted with H.B.T.D.
4 Apr.	Deolali	Bombay	4 Apr.	Embarked H.T. *Cheshire*.
5 Apr.	Bombay	Kure, Japan	23 Apr.	Called Colombo and Singapore.
24 Apr.	Kure	Matsue (Honshu)	25 Apr.	
18 May	Matsue	Gomen (Shikoku)	19 May.	
8 June	Gomen	Tokyo	12 June	Leading echelon took over Public Duties on 11 June
22 July	Tokyo	Gomen	26 July	

Date dep	From	To	Date arr'd.	Remarks
1947				
14 Feb.	Gomen	Kure	15 Feb.	Embarked H.T. *Rajula*.
17 Feb.	Kure	Kluang (Malaya)	2 Mar.	Calling Hong-kong, Singapore.
2 Dec.	Kluang	Singapore	2 Dec.	Embarked H.T. *Dilwara*.
2 Dec.	Singapore	Southampton		
1948			3 Jan.	
3 Jan.	Southampton	Dorchester	3 Jan.	

APPENDIX D

MEMORIALS

The following memorials were erected by the 2nd Battalion during their foreign tour, 1942-47.

1. KOHIMA MEMORIAL

A small stone plinth has been set up on the District Commissioner's Bungalow Spur at Kohima. The memorial overlooks the Manipur Road down which we advanced to succour the besieged garrison of Imphal.

It stands, not far removed from the graves of our soldiers in the Imperial War Graves Commission's cemetery, on the very site where the majority of our deaths were sustained in the fierce fighting in April and May, 1944.

The memorial bears two bronze plates. On one is engraved the Regimental Sphinx, with the Battalion number, LIV, and the motto "Primus in Indis." On the other plate is inscribed:

> *In memory of All Ranks*
> *The 2nd Battalion*
> *the DORSETSHIRE REGIMENT*
> *who fell in action*
> *in these hills between*
> *April—June, 1944*
> *"Who's Afear'd?'*

This memorial was constructed, through the kind offices of Colonel (now Major-General) J. F. E. Steedman, C.B.E., M.C., Chief Engineer, XXXIII Indian Corps, by the Corps Engineers. Another instance of the ever-willing help and assistance provided in this campaign by the Royal Engineers.

I am not permitted to reveal those responsible for the really first-class engraving of the bronzes, but can assure those who are interested that the result is as excellent as anything ever produced by this particular department.

2. SOUTH-EAST ASIA CAMPAIGN MEMORIAL

This campaign memorial took the form of a presentation of a cross, candlesticks and vases for the Lady Chapel of St. John's Church in Calcutta. Conceived whilst we were still in action, the idea of this memorial was brought to fruition with the help of the Archdeacon of Calcutta and the West of England Society of India, who acted as trustees on our behalf. It was made possible only by the generosity of the many friends and relatives and past and present members of the Regiment who answered our appeal, and whose help is recorded on a silver plaque in the Lady Chapel.

St. John's Church is not only one of the oldest in Calcutta but was at one time the Cathedral Church of the Diocese of India, Burma, Ceylon, Africa, the Far East and Australia. The suitability of Calcutta as the site for our memorial needs little explanation. I need only remind the reader that the 1st Battalion, or the Thirty-Ninth Foot, as they were in 1757, helped to liberate Calcutta from the oppression of Surajah Dowlah and played their part in establishing the British Raj in India—a period of rule which historians of the future will surely reckon as one of the greatest examples of beneficent rule the world has ever seen.

This memorial to our comrades who fell in the campaign in South-East Asia was dedicated by Archdeacon Tucker on Sunday, the 3rd of February, 1946, and attended by a party of all ranks who had fought in the campaign.

3. MEMORIAL TABLET, FORT ST. GEORGE, MADRAS

In June, 1943, the officers of the 2nd Battalion filled a long-felt want when they presented to the guard room at Fort St. George, Madras, a bronze tablet on which were inscribed the various occasions on which battalions of the Regiment have been quartered in the fort.

Though there were already a number of other brasses, ours had hitherto been conspicuous by its absence. As we were the first King's regiment ever to be quartered there, and on two occasions, both the Thirty-Ninth and Fifty-Fourth in turn had set out for a campaign from this station, it was felt it was high time that this situation was remedied.

The Commandant of the Madras Guards (A.F.I.), Colonel D. M. Reid, O.B.E., M.C., E.D., A.D.C., whose battalion was at that time quartered in the fort, was most enthusiastic about this project. Through his assistance the memorial was constructed locally and his regiment provided a guard of honour on the occasion of the unveiling of the tablet in June, 1943, by Major D. McLeod Baynes, representing the Dorsetshire Regiment.

When you go home
Tell them of us and say,
For your tomorrow
We gave our today.

(Inscribed on 2nd Division Memorial, Kohima.)

APPENDIX E

CLOTHING, EQUIPMENT, ARMS AND ACCOUTREMENTS

In 1939 the 2nd battalion mobilized and marched off to war in the new Army battle dress. Gone were the white-metal Sphinx collar-badges and brass shoulder-titles of peace and in their place the men wore a slip-on black worsted title on their shoulder-straps and the officers had nothing to distinguish them from another corps except the cap-badge, which remained bronze for officers and white metal and brass for the other ranks.

The head-dress was confined, officially, to the "fore and aft" pattern khaki field service cap and the steel helmet. In those days gas-masks and capes with their eye-shields accompanied the soldier everywhere he went, both on and off duty.

As far as one can gather from the few photographs extant and occasional references in personal diaries, the officers were as much a law to themselves in that first year of the war as ever they were later. Custom dies hard, and many of them retained their service dress, or at least parts of it, right through the campaign to Dunkirk.

The uniform remained essentially the same after the return from Dunkirk right up until that day in 1942 when, two days out of Freetown, we changed into tropical dress. Not unnaturally, steps were taken to smarten up the battle dress as much as possible, and I remember when I rejoined the Battalion in October, 1941, being much impressed by the appearance of the men with their Divisional signs and two scarlet infantry strips (for the 2nd Brigade in the Division). The non-commissioned officers had blancoed their chevrons and the officers had whitened their badges of rank, which showed up well against the scarlet backings. The officers, too, taking the lead from Lieutenant-Colonel George Wood, had universally adopted battle dress even for church parade. This confused me a bit, coming straight from the 4th Battalion, where Lieutenant-Colonel Harold Matthews had always encouraged his field officers not only to wear service dress but breeches and field-boots as well.

By the time the Battalion had reached Banbury the officers' ceremonial dress was even further smartened up, and we went to church wearing khaki-blancoed web belts, two shoulder-braces and a revolver and ammunition pouches. On our heads those officers who had them, and the Corps of Drums, wore the undress green-and-blue field service caps.

For the journey to India the Battalion were issued with those twin abominations inflicted on troops moving to the East the Wolseley helmet and the turned-up shorts. In an effort to smarten up the corps of officers, visits were paid to a firm of outfitters in Harrogate, who equipped them with a modified peace-time scale of khaki-drill uniform with brass titles and buttons.

To distinguish ourselves, the Commanding Officer decided to adopt a green, two-inch-square patch on the right side of our topees. This decision to wear the patch on the right was determined upon after reference to the Regimental dress records. I was able to produce a picture of the Thirty-Ninth (1st Battalion) officers taken in the eighteen-seventies, showing them wearing a most elaborate patch on the right. As this must have been one of the very first instances of a topee patch being worn at all, we decided to perpetuate the custom.

On arrival in India we took the opportunity to smarten ourselves up considerably. The Battalion were given a more up-to-date issue of khaki drill, which was sufficient not only for training but also to ensure that the men presented a clean appearance when "walking out". Gradually, more speedily after the first monsoon, the Wolseley helmets were replaced by the smarter-looking and very much lighter pith helmet.

Gone were the days when the soldier received a clothing allowance and was expected to titivate himself up to Regimental standard out of his own pocket. Now the Battalion had to bear the expense of the smartening up, and for this reason, and also because of the uncertainty of our immediate future, it was not possible to do more than to ensure that the officers and sergeants "put up" the two green stripes of the 2nd Dorsets (as opposed to the single strip of the 1st Battalion) in their pagris. Hose-tops were dyed green for everyone, and during this process the officers took the opportunity of dipping their revolver lanyards in the dye baths. By now the green shoulder-lanyards had, for some time, been worn correctly and as originally intended—that is, fully looped and not with the loose end concealed in the pocket.

In India we found bush shirts to be the fashion, and soon they were worn by all ranks when off parade, though we remained faithful to the ordinary pattern shirt for training. At first there was a tendency to embellish the bush shirts with the brass buttons and titles brought out from the United Kingdom, but very soon leather buttons and cloth titles with worsted badges of rank were adopted by the officers for general wear. The khaki-drill tunic, with its hot and uncomfortable collar and tie, had, fortunately, become a thing of the past, and the bush shirt, except for Government House and similar occasions, was the recognized dress for the evening. On our first arrival Lieutenant-Colonel Wood had insisted on our wearing ties in mess in the evening.

In those early days in the Deccan, the other ranks, when "walking out", had a great deal to do to cope with local battalions, which, having been stationed in India since before the war, still had access to their white walking-out dress. It was most satisfactory to see the pains, involving a certain expense, to which the soldier would go voluntarily to turn himself out well for an evening in the nearest cantonment.

Finally, on our arrival in India we embellished the green pagri patch with the Roman figures "LIV" in yellow (rudely referred to by one company as standing for "Labour In Vain").

At the beginning of 1943 the G.R. Platoon were issued with the new "hat, felt, Gurkha", or the bush hat, which was to become the universal head-dress for the Fourteenth Army. By the time of our ceremonial parade on Plassey Day in June, 1943, the whole Battalion had been issued with this the most comfortable and practical head-dress the Army had ever worn. I can't help feeling that it would be an excellent head-dress both for home and abroad - it is smart and practical, and can serve equally as well on service as for ceremonial. For the latter occasions it can easily be embellished with the addition of badges, flashes and plumes of every possible size and shape.

At first I insisted that we wore these hats with the left side cocked up in the Australian fashion, and chin-straps were the rule. Later we found that it was more comfortable, and in a tropical climate certainly more sensible, to wear it Gurkha fashion with the brim down, and by the end of 1943 we had formally adopted this method.

We continued the custom, started with the topee in the year before, of wearing the Divisional sign on the left side of the hat, and originally I insisted that we perpetuated the peace-time custom of wearing cap-badges for ceremonial. However, by the time the bush hats had been issued there were so few badges left in the Battalion that this custom was restricted to Battalion and company guards, and very shortly was dropped altogether.

Throughout 1943, as I have indicated elsewhere, we were issued with and experimented upon with every conceivable form of kit and equipment for use in the jungle and as protection against the mosquito and other menaces.

However much we were made to muff ourselves up for work in the jungle, the great tendency, during the day at any rate, was towards nudity. It is always difficult to say who really starts fashions that in a very short time are general practice, but I do know that the 5th Infantry Brigade, acting on Brigadier Hawkins's instructions at Juhu in January, 1943, was definitely a prime mover in this business of wearing "bare buff". Unless actually out of barracks on training, our normal working dress consisted solely of boots, socks, puttees, shorts, belt and head-dress—a most practical and satisfactory form of dress. This sensible attitude towards the sun in Eastern climates was one of the triumphs of the war, and in a very short time many of the old medical shibboleths were overthrown.

New Year 1944, just prior to our second visit to the Belgaum jungle, our olive-green battle dress appeared, an order of uniform that remained with us to the end. This dress, with certain slight modifications, such as the substitution of the angola shirt for the cellular blouse (cut on the European battle-dress blouse model and never very satisfactory) became our universal dress for the remainder of our tour abroad. I remember being most impressed with the Battalion on their first parade ih this kit, prior to a night exercise. I had the same feeling as the hero of Kenneth Roberts's book "Northwest Passage" must have had on his first sight of Rogers Rangers. There was something most serviceable and practical in this dress, topped off by a bush hat. Unfortunately, however, this kit did not lend itself to ceremonial, and we regretted the lack of a tropical shade khaki uniform when, two and a half years later, we came to troop the Colour in Tokyo, in what (despite our smartening up and introduction of such aids as sergeants' sashes) the Americans, in confusion with their own orders of dress, referred to as our "fatigue" uniforms.

Incidentally, when we went into action in this jungle battle dress, we surprised the 161st Brigade, who, although they had been fighting for some months in the Arakan, were still wearing the outmoded khaki drill uniform. There was no longer any question of fighting in shorts and hose-tops, the traditional dress of the armies of the East, and the one in which the earlier campaigns had been fought. In order the better to guard against disease we wore short puttees in place of gaiters and impregnated both puttees and socks with a preparation called "Skat". At first we wore our steel helmets continually, but subsequently only when in contact. Our gas-masks, thank heavens, moved with us in bulk and as far as I know are still in store at Gauhati. Having carried them continually on training in India, I can't say how relieved we were that we did not have to fight with them (or in them) under tropical conditions. Slung from our equipment we carried a messtin (in a spare water-bottle carrier), water-bottle, and, in addition to the bayonet, some form of bush-knife, be it matchet or kukri. The Indian-made matchet was an indifferent article and happy was the soldier who had acquired one of the American models. Every man carried some form of entrenching tool, on which subject I have already discoursed at some length. We had discarded the small battle haversack in favour of the large pack, as the latter, filled with the official contents of the former, still allowed room for a mosquito net or extra rations for long-range patrols.

In an effort to disguise the leaders from the Japanese snipers, it was at first the practice for officers to go into action without badges of rank. All most confusing, and this lack of distinction was subsequently overcome by the officers wearing badges of a colour which blended more with the shoulder-strap material and, in the 2nd Division, the non-commissioned officers moved their badges of rank to their shoulders, the stripes, crowns and other emblems being painted on to small slip-on straps, such as were worn by the officers. This was a 2nd Division idea, first ordered at Maram in the autumn of 1944, and though subsequently adopted by other formations remained to the end the hallmark of the 2nd British Infantry Division.

During the 1945 campaign the farther we got from our base the more our head-dress tended to become varied. Luxuries like bush hats took a very low place on the list of priorities, and if a soldier lost his head-dress, as he so often did, he was left with only his steel helmet. Owing to these losses the men contrived to make berets out of the end of their American blankets, and very smart some of them were, with their "LIV" patches sewn on instead of badges. At this time a new form of sun hat began to make its appearance - known by us as the hat "I.W.T." (I Was There) - a product of a Calcutta firm. Perhaps the most sensible, if not the most military-looking, of all our various forms of head-dress, this hat became most popular among those who were prepared to pay the exorbitant price demanded by the manufacturers.

Altogether, our fighting kit was most practical and comfortable, and had the virtue of being easy to exchange when it had become too impossibly dirty. Most of the time the men did their own "dhobie," but periodically some form of bath unit would catch up with us and B.O.W.O. would issue a fresh set of kit on the "one for one" basis.

As regards our weapons, there was very little change throughout the war. We all ended the war and took to Japan with us that most serviceable of all rifles the S.M.L.E.. At some time during our training we had to turn in our T.S.M.G.s and received in exchange a very obsolete pattern of Sten gun, a "mark" which caused a great many casualties in the 5th Brigade. No wonder that at every possible opportunity we tried to equip ourselves with T.S.M.G.s. Another weapon we found to be most useful was the U.S. Army carbine. We eventually acquired enough for the company commanders and myself - a really excellent, accurate and handy weapon.

For Operation "Ribbon" (the occupation of Japan) the lavishness of the scale of clothing issued more than made up for the poor quality of the material supplied. We had hoped that this was a suitable opportunity for the authorities to equip us with the very practical jungle clothing and equipment that had been on issue at home in the summer of 1945. This was not to be, and the General was unable to obtain for us anything better than the products of the Indian mills, with many variations of shade. For web equipment we received what appeared at first sight to be the cast-offs from the arsenals of India. However, some skilful tailoring by the ever-attendant Ramswammy Rao dealt with the clothing, and lavish expenditure of blanco covered the blemishes of the equipment.

Each man had two sets of equipment, or rather two belts, anklets, bayonet frogs and rifle slings. The one set he kept whitened for ceremonial and the other blancoed a drab shade. We kept our S.M.L.E. rifles, which stood us in good stead when it came to public duties in Tokyo. With the help of the I.T.C. at home we soon had enough scarlet titles to issue to every man for his serge battle dress. I have already explained our multiplicity of Divisional signs; the reader will remember that by the time we reached Tokyo we carried no fewer than three. One, the B.C.O.F. badge on the right arm, and two, the Union Rag of Brindiv and the crossed keys of the 5th Brigade on the left.

The Brigade parades at Satpur Camp prior to sailing provided opportunities for sartorial experiment scarcely afforded to commanding officers since the days of King George IV, though, I venture to say, far less extravagant. Each battalion vied with the other, and remember the Dorsets started off with a severe handicap. We had no goat at the head of the Battalion, and no kilts in which to swing past the saluting base. We had to depend entirely on smartening up the issued kit, embellishing it with pipe-clayed equipment, and relied for making our name entirely on the manner in which we drilled.

General Cowan had, on questions of dress, to adjudicate between the demands of commanding officers who had served in at least five different divisions, and on the advice of senior staff officers from quite the same number of formations again. It was obvious, therefore, that certain much-prized customs would have to cease in order to fall into line. In this way we lost our 2nd Divisional privilege of carrying the non-commissioned officers' stripes on their shoulders.

Again with the help of the I.T.C. we were able to dress our sergeants in red sashes. There is an interesting story attached to these traditional sashes of the Infantry. Our predecessors in Tokyo, the Australian Guard Battalion, were called out very suddenly one day to cope with possible Communist riots. So sudden was the call that the scattered guards had no time to change into fighting order and the sergeants were still wearing their sashes. This had a most happy effect on the Communists, who hailed the Australian non-commissioned officers as "comrades" and behaved throughout the proceedings in the most orderly fashion.

By the time we were forming up for Japan, shorts had ceased to be an issued order of dress in India. This was sad, because with the withdrawal of shorts, hose-tops also disappeared. However, to perpetuate as long as possible the Dorset custom of wearing full green hose-tops, we raised sufficient to fit out the officers, warrant officers, sergeants and normal routine guards.

Finally, with the re-formation of the Battalion, I received enough cap-badges from home for us to adopt the correct green patch and replace the cap-badge in our head-dress, and the old familiar "LIV" patch under which we had fought through the Burma campaign fell into disuse.

APPENDIX F

B.B.C. BROADCAST IN THE NINE O'CLOCK NEWS TALK ON WEDNESDAY, 17TH MAY, 1944

Mr. Richard Sharp, of the B.B.C., who shared so many of the adventures described in this book, recorded the final assault on the District Commissioner's Bungalow at Kohima on the 13th of May, 1944, and sent home a recording which was included in the B.B.C. News a few nights later.

With the kind co-operation of Mr. Sharp and the British broadcasting Corporation, it is possible to reprint the actual text of this recording:

THE TENNIS COURT

Announcer : There are now no Japanese on the six hills which form the dominating ridge round Kohima. The only interference is Jap gun fire on the southernmost side of the village. We hold the whole of the ridge running westwards from this point, and the whole of the District Commissioner's garden, including the famous tennis court. It was captured in heavy hand-to-hand fighting, described in this cable from Richard Sharp.

Sharp: We are still on the six hills in the centre of Kohima. We've mopped up nearly all the Japs on them, and we've taken the famous tennis court. A half-smashed bunker on one of the hills was giving us a good deal of trouble, but we took it at one to-day, and I've seen the hill myself. It's covered with dead Japs. I counted up to forty of them and then stopped. Our men have been sprinkling them with quicklime—a necessary precaution in this weather.

It's difficult to make sure of facts in this catch-as-catch-can type of war-fare, but I know we've taken the tennis court, too, because I've been on it this afternoon. The men who took it came from a battalion of a West Country regiment. They've been plugging away at that tennis court for sixteen days, and when I got there at noon they were on it at last. In these sixteen days they'd become personal enemies of the Japs there, who used to taunt them at dusk, calling across the tennis court:

"Have you stood-to yet?" Today they're on top and they walked on their toes, laughing, among the bulges in the earth of dug-out roofs, their muscles limber, ready to swivel this way or that in an instant. There was a company commander[29] - a robust man with a square, black jaw covered with stubble. The skin between his battle-dress trousers and his tunic was bloody, and he swayed as he stood with his legs straddled But his brain was working at full speed, and he laughed and shouted to his men as they went eagerly from fox-hole to fox-hole with hand grenades and pole charges - that's twenty-five pounds of explosive at the end of a six-foot bamboo.

In the excitement of this hand-to-hand fighting some strange things happened. Three of our men and a major were in a shallow trench and three yards beyond was the bulge of a fox-hole roof. There were two Japs in the fox-hole - live, fighting Japs. One of our men thrust the pole charge in the hole and then squatted back, looking at his empty hands in astonishment. He said: "They've pulled it out of my hand!" and rolled backwards into the trench. So the major got another pole charge and stuck it in while every-one lay close. He was giggling with excitement. "May I get in your trench, please?" he said politely, as he rolled in beside his men.

Well, there were lots of incidents like this and now all that's left is the litter of war - piles of biscuits, dead Japs black with flies, heaps of Jap ammunition, broken rifles, silver from the District Commissioner's Bungalow. And among it, most incongruous of all, there's a man cleaning a pair of boots, another boiling tea, and an official photographer,[30] who used to photograph Mayfair lovelies, saying: "Move a little to the left, please." And there's another chap reading a story headed "Edgar Wallace Thriller" in a Sunday newspaper. Yes, today's been a great day for this battalion. Here's hoping that they hold the tennis court through the night.

---

29 Captain Clive Chettle.
30 Mr. Antony Beauchamp.

GLOSSARY

THE SOLDIER'S JARGON and expressions in vogue in the European War must have been confusing enough to the civilian. The vocabulary acquired by the Fifty-Fourth in its Odyssey round the world, enriched as it was by constant touch with many oriental races, must be even more unintelligible. Slips into the lingua franca of the soldier are inevitable, and in order to assist the reader I have compiled this glossary rather than inflict on him or her the constant irritation of a series of footnotes.

Adm Area	Area in which is laid out the unit or formation administrative echelon.
AFPAC	Air Force Pacific Air Command (U.S. Army).
ALFSEA	Allied Land Forces, South-East Asia.
AOR	African other rank.
ATC	Air Transport Command (U.S. Army).
Bandobast	(India) Arrangement, plan—more often abbreviated to "Bando."
"Banzai" attack	Form of massed attack practised by the Japanese—so called from the Nipponese habit of signalling their presence by advancing to the accompaniment of cries of "Banzai!"
Bargo(ed)	Corruption of Indian verb, used by British soldiers to imply departure or absence.
Basha	A jungle hut of bamboo and straw matting.
"B" Echelon	The administrative echelon of a unit.
BGS	Brigadier, General Staff.
Bhisti	Water carrier.
Bibbi	A woman (Indian).
BIC	Burma Intelligence Corps. Officers and men of this Corps, raised originally in Burma, were subsequently allocated right down to brigades and battalions and proved themselves of undoubted value throughout the campaign.

Bobbery	Obstreperous, lively.
BOR	British other rank.
BOWO	Brigade Ordnance Warrant Officer. Responsible for supply of ordnance stores in an infantry brigade.
BRASCO	Brigade Royal Army Service Corps Officer. The supply officer of an infantry brigade.
BRICOSAT	British Commonwealth Sub-Area, Tokyo.
Canjee	Starch
C.G.	Commanding General (U.S. Army). Equivalent of our G.O.C..
Chae (Char)	Tea. (Urdu)
Chaung	Stream or river-bed (Burmese)
CRA	Commander, Royal Artillery. The senior Artillery officer in a division.
CRASC	Commander, Royal Army Service Corps. The senior R.A.S.C. officer in a division. Also CRIASC in formations whose supply and transport element was found by the Roayl Indian Army Service Corps.
Cushi	Happy, comfortable, easy. (Urdu)
Dekho	A look-see.
Dherzi	Tailor.
Dhobi	Washerman
Dhurri	Indian bed mat issued to soldiers in India.
Dhurri bundle	Soldier's bed roll.
Dhurri line	Length of cord to secure a dhurri bundle
DO	Demi-official (form of military correspondence).
Do	Two (Indian) – often used in connection with a unit number: 2 Dorsets.
EBZ	Effective beaten zone – area in which bullets from an automatic are expected to fall.
"F" Echelon	The fighting echelon of a unit, normally used in relation to vehicles.
FOO	Forward Observation Officer – Artillery officer controlling support for infantry and usually up with the infantry.
Fundoshi	Japanese pants – triangular undergarment.
G1098	Vocabulary Number of an infantry battalion's war equipment.

Ghat	Mountain – eg Western Ghats.
GPT Coy.	General Purpose Transport Company, R.I.A.S.C., for moving troops by M.T..
Grenadier Coy.	Formerly the right-flank company of a battalion, composed of the tallest men. The C.O. in 1942 decided to commemorate the past outstanding service of the grenadier companies of the 54th by permitting 'A' Company to carry the grenade as a badge and adopt the unofficial title of Grenadier Company.
HBTD	Homeward Bound Trooping Depot.
"Ichi for the Nichi"	Appalling "dog" Japanese for "One for the road"—a familiar Tokyo cry.
In	Lake (Burmese).
IOR	Indian other rank.
Kamakase	Suicide (Japanese), used in reference to the suicide pilots employed at the end of the war.
Khana	Urdu for a meal. Used by British troops in reference to any form of food.
Khud	Hill, also khudside, khud track, etc.
Koihai	Literally "Who's there?" Used for calling servants in the East. This term has come to be used to describe Europeans who have spent many years in India.
L5	A type of light aircraft.
Leave Schemes	
(a) LIAP	"Leave in Addition to Python"--—twenty-eight days' leave in the United Kingdom, which entailed returning and completing foreign tour.
(b) LILOP	"Leave in Lieu of Python"—sixty-one days in the United Kingdom, followed by a further tour of two years abroad.
(c) LOLLIPOP	"Lots of Local Leave in place of Python"—an entirely unofficial form of "leave" much in demand by those whose interests lay in hill stations.
(d) LIDAD	"Leave Incorrectly Described as Duty"—another entirely unofficial form of leave

	which never appeared in the books. Ascribed to those officers who had a claim on a vehicle and an excuse for paying visits. A main rendezvous of real "Lidad" experts was the Harbour Bar of the Taj Mahal Hotel, Bombay.
Legim dance	Traditional Mahratta dance.
Light Coy.	Designed originally as a company lightly equipped for skirmishing purposes, the Light Company formerly took post on the left of the battalion line. When, in 1942, "A" Company was accorded permission to adopt the style of Grenadier Company, "D" Company assumed the bugle badge, traditions and title of Light Company in memory of the outstanding services of the Light Company throughout the Regiment's history.
LMG	Light machine gun.
LOB	Left out of battle. Military term used to refer to personnel not actually required in an engagement.
Lungyi	Burmese garment.
Ml 91A	An American rifle grenade with high penetration properties against Japanese bunker positions.
Maidan	Open space—often used as a parade ground. Indian equivalent of a village green.
Malkamb pole	Traditional sport of the Mahrattas. A survival from the days when the Mahrattas were a great seafaring race and every village had its malkamb pole set up, on which the boys and young men of the village were trained.
MS	Milestone.
MTO	Motor Transport Officer.
"M & V"	Meat and Vegetables—a standard tinned meat ration (stew).
"Mucker"	British soldier's term for his special comrade who invariably shares his slit trench and makes a team of two to carry out the multitude of chores required of a soldier

	both in and out of action.
Muggah, Magar	Alligator (Indian).
"Mulberry"	Artificial harbour used in Normandy landings.
Mushi mushi	Hullo, hullo (Japanese).
Nullah (Nala)	Stream or river bed (usually dry) (Indian).
"O" Group	A Commander's Order Group—i.e., the gathering of the next junior commanders, to whom orders are given.
"One for one" basis	Basis of exchange of clothing and equipment by which the soldier hands in his soiled clothes and receives fresh garments in return.
OP	Observation post.
Orcha	Tea (Japanese).
PAD	Passive air defence.
"Peg"	A measure of liquor, normally whisky.
Put on a charge	Military method of reporting a soldier for a misdemeanour.
"Python"	Code name for foreign tour. Python service—i.e., service abroad on one tour—varied according to the state of the war and the reinforcement situation. In 1945 it was three years four months.
Rasta kiwasti	Anglicized Indian for "One for the road."
2 Recce	Official abbreviation for the 2nd Reconnaissance Regiment, Royal Armoured Corps.
Recce	Reconnaissance. Also Recce party, Recce group.
Relpats	Unofficial abbreviation coined by the 2nd Infantry Division to signify those who were due for release or repatriation in September, 1945, and would therefore not be available to proceed to the Far East with the Division.
"R" Group	The Reconnaissance Group—i.e., those whom a commander takes on a reconnaissance.
SACSEA	Supreme Allied Commander, South-East Asia (Admiral Lord Louis Mountbatten).
Saki-aki	Ceremonial Japanese meal.

SCAP	Supreme Commander, Allied Powers (General MacArthur).
SEAC	South-East Asia Command. Also name of Service newspaper for troops in that theatre.
SEWLROM	Short End of War Leave, Regular Officers and Men. A leave scheme granting personnel of the Regular Forces twenty-eight days' leave on the conclusion of hostilities.
"Shabash"	Indian cry of congratulation.
Shamiana	An awning, usually highly decorated or beflagged, covering a dais or grandstand.
Shivaji	Famous Mahratta warrior of the seventeenth century and founder of the Mahratta nation.
Sigri	Indian pattern charcoalbrazier.
SP	(i) Start Point. (ii) Self-propelled (Artillery).
Swing, To	(*verb*)Specialised military slang used in reference to someone not actually carrying out his normal duties. Usually such a person has been relieved on such duties to undertake some specific task or to be rested.
Taisho	Japanese light machine gun.
Tamashi	Party or show (Urdu).
Tatami	The form of matted straw flooring used in Japanese houses. Tatami makes a not uncomfortable bed, the object for which it is designed. It is made up into standard strips and the rental for a Japanese house is determined by the number of these tatami strips used.
Tiffin	Lunch (Urdu).
Torii	Japanese memorial arch of peculiar design, normally erected at the entrance to their shrines.
Zareba	A hedged or palisaded enclosure

INDEX

Page numbers shown in bold indicate photographs.

PEOPLE

Adams, Cpl J W 376
Adams, Sgt G 111
Affleck-Graves, Capt D A 6, 9, 13
Aldous, Brig 55
Archer, Capt A J 299, 335
Arkwright, Gen 310
Asser, 2/Lt J J 25, 28
Atkins, Pte S 84
Auchinleck, Gen Sir Claude 309, **314**
Bagnall, WOII D 119, 377
Baker, Lt-Col Pooh 247
Baldwin, Lt 111
Barclay, Capt P 10
Bartrum, Capt 195
Bash, Pte F 84
Baynes, Lt D M 3, 6, 14, 49, **67**, **68**, 167-8, 375
Beal, Lt C 183, 210
Beasley, Sgt 258
Bedlow, CSM 209
Bell, CSM A 5
Bell-Syer, 2/Lt R L 3, 6
Belson, WOII 50
Berry, Cpl D 111
Bickford, Lt-Col W 85
Bishop, Pte H H 210, 376
Bolingbroke, Maj J R H 4, 114
Bond, CSM 156
Bonsor, Maj B 208
Boon, Lt-Col P G 43-4
Bottrill, Cpl F 110-11

Bowles, Maj H D xvi, xix, 30, 62, **67**, 97, 99-100, 106-7, 110, 133, 165, 167-8, 172, 195, 199-200, 202, 204-5, 209, 212, 275, 375
Boyle, Lt R **67**, 179, 202, 206
Boyt, Maj J 265
Bradford, Capt J M K 3, 199, 226, 377
Bray, Lt H A A xviii, 6, 19, 25, 34, 42, 374
Breely, L/Cpl J 106
Brewster, Lt C V H 3, 6, 10
Bridge, Maj A V N 6, 43, 49, 54, **67**, 133, 194, 217, 266, 294, 299, 375
Brierley, Lt-Col J 142, 150-2, 154, 159, 298
Brind, Capt P H W 6, 12, 14, 20, 25, 43
Britten, Lt-Col 301
Brooke-Fox, Maj B 255
Brown, PSM R A S 375
Brown, PSM S 375
Browning, Lt-Gen Boy 284
Bruce, Col J 247
Buckland, Miss Cecilia 346
Burden, Pte G 267
Burnett, Capt 97
Burnett, Sgt E H 377
Byers, Maj-Gen 336
Calcott, Pte P 84
Calvert, Brig M 281
Calvert, Col D 197, 247, 307
Carroll, Lt-Col J 142, 147-8
Castle, Capt Dick 80, 97-8, 110, 299
Cattle, Sgt Tom xvii, xix

403

Cavendish, Lt-Col Ronny 55
Chamberlin, Capt Dr J A xviii-xix, 49, **67**, 87, 103, 155, 211, 296, 299, 374
Chettle, Maj C xvi, xix, 49, **67**, **93**, 101, 111, 116-17, 121, 138, 141, 144, 152, 156, 165, 168, 172, 196, 203-5, 228, 229, 254, 264, 299, 374, 375
Cheverton, Lt E **129**, 321
Chichester-Constable, Lt B 256
Churchill, Cpl 220, 230
Churchill, Pte 180
Clarke, Pte F J 375
Clarkson, Sgt R 111
Claxton, Capt The Rev L E M xviii, 10, 19, 49, **67**, 81, 87, **94**, 296, 299, 274
Cleeves, Col E 197, 247
Cobb, L/Sgt H 111
Collis, Pte J F 139
Collister, Lt P 241
Cook, Sgt 117, 155
Cooper, Sgt W J H xviii, 27, 30, 48, 57, 375
Cotton, Capt J T 3, 6
Cowan, Maj-Gen D T 167, 301, 307-9, **313**, 321, 330, 332, 336-7, 341, 347
Cowan, Miss A 321
Cowie, Capt H E 3, 6, 12
Cranham, L/Cpl 119
Cripps, Cpl G H M 60, 102, 182, 246, 296, 376
Critchley, Sgt A T 84, 121, 376
Cross, Capt A 305, 325, 335
Crowther, Maj G N **67**, 377
Curtis, Sgt F A 376
Cuthbertson, Lt R xix, 257-8
Davies, Capt E A 67, 104, 118, 135, 138-9
Davies, L/Cpl W T 376
Day, Lt 98, 111
Day, Miss Frances 249
Deane, Lt A D **67**, 106, 111
Delara, RSM G 61
Dickinson, Pte 174

Doran, Capt C S H 30, 105, 140, 148, 154, 165, 175, 195, 377
Doughty, WOII J 49, 57, 107
Douglas, Maj A 140
Dowling, Maj P 355
Downton, CSM H 107, 111, 376
Draper, CSM G 107, 111
Dunne, Pte M 376
Dupont, Lt R J M
Dutot, RQMS Duey 5
Dyer, Brig 188, 264-5, 289, 306
Easter, Pte R 258
Edwards, Capt F J 4-6, 36, 49, 57, 61, 66, **67**, 111-12, 237, 293, 364-5, 374
Eichelberger, Gen 336, 338, 340, 350, **361**
Elbro, RSM 331, 345
Evans, Cpl M J 376
Farthing, Capt R D 348
Fawcett, Lt 213
Feeney, Capt P 146-7, 165, 168, 195, 222, 228
Fellowes, Pte 220
Festing, Gen F 59, 282, 307
Fincham, Sgt 190, 296
Fooks, Pte 182, 194
Foot, Pte G 246, 258
Fox, Sgt 213
Fretts, Maj Paget King 10, 15, **67**, 83-4, 110, **130**, 179, 182, 215, 228-9, 231, 245, 254, 267, 275, 299, 375
Futter, Capt L 340
Gairdner, Gen Sir Charles 331
Gartland, Brig G I 36
Garwood, Lt-Col J 100
Gascoigne, HE Ambassador 340
Gaye, Lt-Col D B **363**, 364
Giffard, Gen 142
Giffard, Lt **67**
Giles, Capt E H 19, 49, **67**, 375
Gill-Davies, Maj D 62
Given, Lt R xix, 117, 121, 142, 208, 246, 375

Goff, Lt-Col R E C xvi-xvii, xxvi, 3, 6-7, 10, 18, 24, 27, 29, 31, 43, 374
Goldson, RSM 165
Gordon Wright, Maj C G 54, 80, 111, 134, 141, 165, 179, 195, 269, 275, 296, 375
Govett, Maj E V **67**, 377
Gracey, Maj-Gen D 167, 273
Graham, Pte J xviii, 376
Green, Capt G G 3, 6
Greig, Lt-Cdr M 340
Griffin, Lt R W D 3, 6
Grindle, Capt (RN) 310
Grover, Maj-Gen J 50, 48, 81, **89**, 95, 143, 151, 159-60, 166, 173, 243, **313**, 338
Guest, CSM F **40**
Haddon, Sgt 114
Halahan, Lt J L **67**, 113, 132
Hamilton, Cdr J 311
Hamilton, Lt-Col L 311
Harris, Capt D 179, 275, 299
Harvey, Pte 103
Havers, Maj N xix, xxvi, 49, 114, **130**, 175, 205, 246, 269, 299, 374
Hawkins, Brig V F S 55-6, 63-4, 81, **90**, 95, 133
Hawkins, Capt M 55
Haycock, Lt **67**
Hayne, Brig 132
Haynes, Lt 334
Hayward, Lt 111
Hayward, RQMS R G 119, 142, 275, 375, 376
Heath, Maj J 183, 194, 213, 215
Heathman, Sgt A 57
Hector, Sgt 213
Heron, Capt J G xviii, 27, 43, 374
Hewick, Lt-Col J S 275
Hickling, Capt, H J 3, 6
Highett, Capt L T xix, **67**, 101, 114, 117, 135, 137, 139, 144, 156, 179, 185, 196, 198-200, 259, 268, 299, 374-5
Hill, Pte 172

Hodder, Lt J G **67**, 299
Hoffman, Brig-Gen H 341
Hoopell, Cpl E 111
Hopkins, Sgt A xviii
Hounsome, Pte 181
Howard, Capt **67**
Hughes, Capt T 49, 54, 67, 134
Hunt, WOII 49
Ingham-Clark, Maj F 55
Irvine, Capt Digger 356
Irvine, Lt-Col T A 236, 242-5, 265, **271**, 280
Isaacs, Lt-Col 65
James, Sgt R F xviii, 26, 375
Jefferies, Alan 276
Jesty, L/Cpl H C xviii, 210, 337, 357, 375-6
John, L/Cpl 49
Johnson, CSM 357
Johnson, Lt R 179, 210, 213, 254, 258
Johnson, Pte 81, 101
Jones, Lt H 57, 65, **67**, 179, 213, 262, 299
Jones, Maj M 178, 194-5, 202, 206, 211
Joslin, Capt J 179, 262
Keegan, WOII 49, 98, 135
Kennedy, Maj C 308
Key, Lt-Col Sam 305
King, Brig R 171
King, Pte 144
King-Clark, Lt-Col R 86
Knight, Dmr 306
Knight, Pte C G xviii, 376
Knowles, Sgt T L C 376
Laugher, Capt F F 42
Laverty, Lt-Col 85
Lee, Lt D 335
Lee, Sgt 258
Leeming, Lt-Col D 309
Leese, Gen Sir Oliver 267, 273, 293
Lewis, Maj A D 337, 340
Linklater, Capt R H 3, 6, 7, 13, 42, 62, 65
Lloyd, Gen Sir Charles 5
Lowe, Lt-Col 182

405

Loxton, Capt Dr S D 3, 6, 13
Lyon, Maj 287
Macarthur, Gen D 316, 330, 338, 340
Mackenzie, Capt A C xix, 142, 147-8, 155, 196, 375
Mackenzie-Kennedy, Lt-Col 157
MacLaren, Mrs Alison 181
Maddison, L/Cpl 331, 346
Main, Capt J R 179-80, 221, 230, 375
Maitland-Makgill-Crichton, Maj 347
Manning, L/Sgt E 111
Mansfield, Cpl W 106, 140-1, 375
Marrs, Lt **67**
Maule, L/Sgt 105, 139, 182, 319, 339
Mayer, Lt H H 83, 98, 111
McAlester, Lt-Col A 150, 228, 236, 239, 241, **271**, **313**
McArthur, Maj 221
McNaught, Lt-Col R S xxvi, 65, **70**, 82, 84-5, 87, 95, 102, 113, 121, 137, 143, 146, 161, 220, 306, 308, **313**, 336, 338, 348-9, 365, 374
Meakin, PSM Joe 30
Merchant, Pte 258
Messenger, Sgt G 111
Messervy, Maj-Gen F 134, 250, 273
Mitford-Slade, Col C 227, 293
Molloy, Col T P L 3, 5-6, 12, 14, 16-17, 32, 42-3, 47, 49, 54, 57, 59, **67**
Molyneux, Capt K E A 42, **67**, 293
Morgan, Pte 106
Morice, Capt M A **67**, 98, 104, 135
Morris, Sgt 119
Morton, Pte J G S 376
Mould, Brig 310
Mountbatten, Adm Lord Louis **129**, 163, 338
Mullins, Sgt D S 375
Murrills, Capt Jock xix, xxvi, 99, 108-9
Nicholson, Maj-Gen C G C **89**, **129**, 173, 188, 197, 213, 226, 239, 256, 297, 338

Northcott, Lt-Gen J **314**
Nott, Sgt A 213
Nursaw, L/Cpl G 83
Nye, Gen Sir Archie 282
O'Callaghan, Father J 165
O'Donnell, Lt J 179, 210
O'Driscoll, Lt J P xix, **67**, 100, 105, 111
O'Reilly, Pte 48, 109
Oakey, Maj J 62
Osbourne, Maj 326-7
Osmond, CSM A 57, 111, 274, 376
Overman, Capt G G 183, 281, 354, 375
Packham, Cpl 230
Palmer, Pte 112
Pank, Maj G 208
Park, L/Cpl 180, 193, 221, 230
Parton, Capt G 324
Patterson, Capt N 3, 6-7
Peach, Maj E N 42
Pearcey, CSM H J 111, 376
Peatey, Pte 9
Peebles, Capt J A L xviii, 14, 34, 43, 374
Penn, CQMS O 57
Petchkoff, Gen 340
Piggott, Lt-Col F J C 330
Plantard, Cpl J 111
Pope, Bugler 306, 326
Potter, Capt 287
Pratt, WOII **40**, 49
Prebble, Capt S H 49, **67**, 148, 377
Pryke Howard, Lt A D 82, 101, 104, 111, 159
Pullin, Lt V C 210, 375
Purser, Capt R L M xix, 49, 65, **67**, 109-10, 136, 138-9, 375
Quantrill, Lt 308
Radcliffe, Lt-Col Tommy 4
Ramsay, Lt I F R 6
Randall, Lt
Rees, Maj-Gen Pete 218, 251, 267
Rendall, Lt-Col T S 276
Reynel, Cpl 241

406

Rhodes, Maj E 62, 108
Rhys Price, Lt-Col M H ap **313**
Richards, Capt Dr 13
Robbins, Lt B 335, 346, 354
Roberts, Maj-Gen 167, 170-1
Roberts, Capt P 319, 346, 355
Robertson, Gen 337
Robertson, Maj 265
Rolfe, Lt **67**
Roper, Capt K T 36
Rossiter, Miss J 321
Roy, Maj A 238, 281
Rutherford, Miss 321, 326
Saunders, 2/Lt C H S 6
Saunders, Brig 143
Schuster, Lt P 169
Scott, Lt-Col R 85
Seale, CSM W F xix, 84, 108, 111, 121, 163, 196, 257-8, 274, 375-6
Seaton, Lt Col Flash 276
Selby, L/Cpl **130**
Seward, CSM 111
Shaftesbury, Lord **363**, 367
Shapland, Brig J 82, 85, 120, 169
Sharp, Richard 112, 120, 395-6
Shearer, Cpl D E 376
Shearman, L/Sgt 117
Siggins, Cpl 117
Singleton, L/Cpl J H 377
Sinnott, Pte J J xviii, 26, 376
Slim, Gen Sir Bill xv, xvii, 180-1, 188, 219, 298
Smith, Capt 213
Smith, Capt H 45, 57, 112, 119, 149, 161, 275, 296, 375-6
Smith, Capt W L 6, 10
Smith, Sgt F J 190, 222, 229, 376
Softley, Cpl H xviii, 99, 111
Sothers, Miss M 321
Stanford, Sgt 143
Stanley, Pte 306

Stark, WOII 49
Stayner, Lt-Col D J P P xvii-xviii, 3, 5-6, 13-14, 16, 28
Stephenson, 2/Lt C T P 37
Stephenson, Lt-Col E L xvi-xvii, xxvi, 2, 5-6, 9, 16, 20, 29, 38, **40**, 43, 374
Stocker, Lt-Col J 152, 236, 238
Stopford, Lt-Gen Sir Monty xxi, xxvii, 53, 75-6, **91**, 120, 132, 145, 153, 156, 158-60, 182, 186-8, 225, 250, 273, 290, 338
Street, Lt-Col C 57-8, 222, 227-8
Strong, Col C 57-8
Stroud, Pte 181
Sturmey, Sgt 180
Swallow, Capt Dr N 119
Symes, Lt-Col B G xvi, xviii, xxvi, 3, 6-7, 14, 18, 21, 24, 26-30, 38, 218, 268, 374, 377
Tabb, Pte T xviii, 26, 375
Tayleur, Miss P **129**
Taylor, Pte R 376
Taylor, Pte W 84
Terry, Lt J Q **360**
Theobalds, Col J 103
Thom, Capt J xix, 209, 374
Thomas, Lt H V xxvi, 6, 13
Thomas, Maj T 355
Thomas, Sgt 332, 339
Thorburn, Maj I 113
Thompson, Miss Y 321
Todd, Lt-Col 230
Towills, WOII 49
Townsend, Lt-Col P 340
Tucker, Archdeacon 310
Tucker, Maj T G xix, 167-8, 195, 199, 206-8, 210, 245-6, 255-8, 374-5
Turner, L/Cpl **130**, 220, 290
Turner, Maj R **67**, 152, 321
Turner, Pte 80, 144
Tyrell, Pte L xxiii
Valler, Pte 57
Varley, Sgt C 111

Vaughan, CSM Jackie xxvi, 165, 275, 332, 337, 357
Vine, Sgt 165
Wakely, Maj D V W 326, 332, 339
Walch, Pte 57
Ward, Lt **67**
Ward, Maj-Gen A D 284
Ware, Capt A 202, 204
Wareham, Pte 143
Warman, RQMS 49
Warren, Brig 84
Warren, Cpl F H 257, 375
Warren, WOII 49, 57
Waterhouse, Sgt G xvi, xix, 62, 116
Watling, Sgt J D 376
Watts, Lt Alan G 6, 49, **67**, 83, 107, 109-10
Wavell, Field Marshal Lord 166, 177, 187
Wells, Maj P 152
Wells, Sgt 258
West, Cpl 30, 57
West, Brig M M A R xxvi, 61, **90**, 133, 137, 145, 153-4, 158, 172-3, 182, 201, 217, 235, 265, 268, 280, 290, 297, 306-7
West, Pte H 375
Westlake, Drum-Major 306, 346
Wetherbee, Capt H F **314**
Wheatley, Capt R H 6
Wheeler, Maj S 56
White, Lt-Col O G W passim, **67**, **123**, 271, 313
Wilkins, Lt-Col T 299
Willans, Lt-Col R 307
Willcox, Lt Willco 179
Williams, Sgt 258
Wilson, Capt J 65, **67**, 101, 294
Wilson, CSM 48
Wiltshire, Pte 182
Winter, Lt-Col G 57
Wood, Cpl 265
Wood, Maj L J 364, 377
Wood, Maj-Gen G N xvii, xxi, xxvi, **41**, 44, 49, 51-3, **67**, **70**, 112, 119, 121, 153, 155, 159-60, 377
Woodford, L/Cpl A E 48, 111, 376
Woodward, Pte 153,
Woolford, Cpl D 111
Wyllie, Lt J H 31

BRITISH AND INDIAN ARMY UNITS

Argyll & Sutherland Highlanders 27, 28, 32
Black Watch 10
Border Regt 11
Cameron Highlanders, 1st 7, 8, 17, 20, 21, 22, 28, 37, 55, 56, 65, 80, 81, 95, 140, 149, 151, 154, 158, 174, 177, 182, 201, 206, 211, 213, 222, 226, 236, 239, 246, 252, 257, 264, 280, 281, 288, 298, 308, 309, 310, 316, 342, 347, 348, 349, 354, 356
Commando, No 5 43
Devon Regt, 1st 229
Durham Light Infantry 85, 86, 87, 118
Essex Regt, 2nd 81
Gloucestershire Regt, 10th 297, 300, 301
King's Own Yorkshire Light Infantry 18
Lancashire Fusiliers, 8th 16, 19, 24, 27, 28, 32, 240
Mahratta Infantry, 4th 57, 58, 64, 65, 66, 169, 309
Manchester Regt, 2nd 0, 86, 111, 154, 157, 199, 200, 242
Norfolk Regt, 2nd 10, 57, 85, 142, 146, 148, 223, 294
Oxfordshire & Buckinghamshire Light Infantry 133
Queen's Own Royal West Kent Regt, 4th 76, 80, 85, 96, 103
Queen's Royal West Surrey Regt 134

Rajput Infantry, 4th 112-13

Royal Armoured Corps

    3rd Dragoon Guards Carabiniers 201, 202, 218, 225, 240, 242, 259, 268, 280, 289

    7th (Indian) Light Cavalry 101, 104

    2nd Reconnaissance Regt 56, 151, 226, 278

    149th Regt 62, 86, 101, 108, 116, 150, 157

    150th Regt 62

Royal Artillery

    10th Field Regt 6, 50, 152, 201, 202, 208, 255, 287

    18th Field Regt 201, 202

    16th Field Regt 149

    99th Field Regt 149, 201, 202, 208, 209

    134th Medium Regt 286

    141st Field Regt 152

    100th Anti-Tank Regt 105, 259

Royal Engineers

    208th Field Coy 56, 173, 289

Royal Berkshire Regt xvi, 84, 85, 97, 98, 99, 101, 103, 213, 218

Royal Gurkha Rifles, 5th 170

Royal Irish Fusiliers 24, 31, 32

Royal Scots 11, 15, 48, 95, 133, 142, 149, 157, 223

Royal Warwickshire Regt, 2nd 7, 8, 13, 31, 32

Royal Welch Fusiliers 22, 85, 103, 152, 177, 181, 182, 199, 235, 236, 238, 241, 242, 297, 306, 310, 316, 337, 347, 348, 354, 356

Worcestershire Regt, 7th 3, 16, 17, 19, 29, 32, 42, 47, 50, 55, 56, 80, 81, 83, 142, 149, 151, 152, 153, 154, 158, 172, 173, 174, 177, 201, 206, 211, 212, 213, 218, 222, 226, 228, 235, 236, 237, 246, 252, 255, 264, 279, 280, 281, 287, 297

I have tried for to explain
Both your pleasure and your pain,
And, Dorsets, here's my best respects to you!

(With apologies to Kipling.)

JAPAN 1946

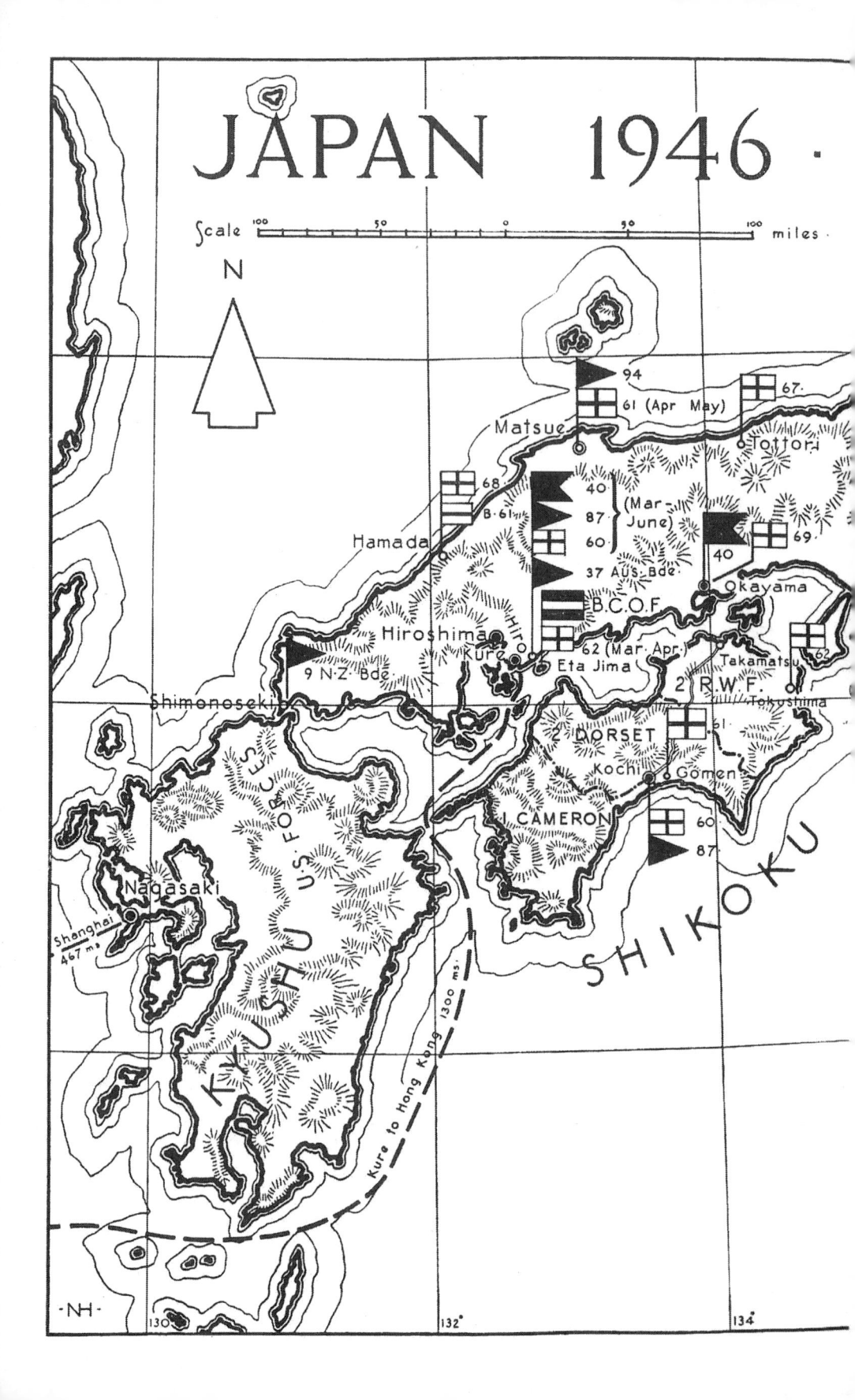